The Initial Psychotherapy Interview

To "Scott"
Whose kindness made this book possible
and to his brother "David"

To dear friends
Terrance Flynn and Bill Bartelt

The Initial Psychotherapy Interview
A Gay Man Seeks Treatment

Edited by

Charles Silverstein

ELSEVIER

AMSTERDAM • BOSTON • HEIDELBERG • LONDON • NEW YORK • OXFORD
PARIS • SAN DIEGO • SAN FRANCISCO • SINGAPORE • SYDNEY • TOKYO

Elsevier

32 Jamestown Road London NW1 7BY

30 Corporate Drive, Suite 400, Burlington, MA 01803, USA

First published 2011

Notices

Knowledge and best practice in this field are constantly changing. As new research and experience broaden our understanding, changes in research methods, professional practices, or medical treatment may become necessary.

Practitioners and researchers must always rely on their own experience and knowledge in evaluating and using any information, methods, compounds, or experiments described herein. In using such information or methods they should be mindful of their own safety and the safety of others, including parties for whom they have a professional responsibility.

To the fullest extent of the law, neither the Publisher nor the authors, contributors, or editors, assume any liability for any injury and/or damage to persons or property as a matter of products liability, negligence or otherwise, or from any use or operation of any methods, products, instructions, or ideas contained in the material herein.

British Library Cataloguing-in-Publication Data

A catalogue record for this book is available from the British Library

Library of Congress Cataloging-in-Publication Data

A catalog record for this book is available from the Library of Congress

ISBN: 978-0-12-385146-8

For information on all Elsevier publications
visit our website at www.elsevierdirect.com

This book has been manufactured using Print On Demand technology. Each copy is produced to order and is limited to black ink. The online version of this book will show color figures where appropriate.

Working together to grow
libraries in developing countries

www.elsevier.com | www.bookaid.org | www.sabre.org

ELSEVIER   BOOK AID International   Sabre Foundation

Cover Illustration by G. Lynas, NYC

Contents

List of Contributors

Donald Bux
Montefiore Medical Center,
Bronx, NY, USA

Armand R. Cerbone
Private Practice, Chicago,
and Board of Directors,
The American Psychological
Association

Corinne Datchi-Phillips
Center for Adolescent and
Family Studies,
Indiana University-Bloomington,
Bloomington, IN, USA

Jacob Gershoni
Psychodrama Training Institute,
New York City, NY, USA

John C. Gonsiorek
Argosy University/Twin Cities,
Eagan, Minnesota, USA

DeMond M. Grant
Department of Psychology,
Oklahoma State University,
Stillwater, OK, USA

Ronald E. Hellman
South Beach Psychiatric Center,
Brooklyn, NY, USA

Margaret Nichols
Institute for Personal Growth,
Highland Park, NJ, USA

Ralph Roughton
Psychoanalytic Institute,
Emory University,
Atlanta, GA, USA

Charles Silverstein
Institute for Human Identity,
New York, NY, USA

Michael C. Singer
Private Practice,
New York City

Peter S. Theodore
California School of
Professional Psychology,
Los Angeles, at Alliant
International University,
Alhambra, CA, USA

Gil Tunnell
Department of Counseling and
Clinical Psychology,
Teachers College,
Columbia University,
Accelerated Experiential Dynamic
Psychotherapy (AEDP) Institute,
New York City, NY, USA

LaRicka R. Wingate
Department of Psychology,
Oklahoma State University,
Stillwater, OK, USA

Foreword

Some half century ago, Harry Stack Sullivan's book *The Psychiatric Interview* was published. Evolving from psychoanalytic theory, it became a classic in the field and a standard text for programs in the professional training of psychiatrists, psychologists, social workers, and others in the mental health field. Other books on interviewing, including attention to the most important initial interview, have been published, but this one is different from them and unique in many respects. It brings us up to date on contemporary theories and therapeutic procedures.

This book is like a psychological autopsy in order to examine client–therapist interactions. Responses of both the client and the interviewer affect each other. Charles Silverstein interviews "Scott," a 30-year-old gay man. Scott seeks therapy after the death of a much loved and admired older brother, also gay. The interview, however, fleshes out a much more complete story of Scott and his personal issues. A transcript of the interview is included with responses to it from a multitude of authors who comment on the process, sometimes praising the conduct of the interview, while at other times chastising the interviewer for errors of technique. The book is different from previous books on the initial interview, most of which have only one theoretical perspective, in that it includes responses to the interview from a wide variety of therapeutic approaches.

It is also different in that Silverstein himself gives special attention to the errors he makes in the interview. Unlike in most books on interviewing, Silverstein lets the reader see his failures in technique and redefines aspects of counter-transference in the interview as "gremlins." These include over-identification with the client, punishing the client (such as ignoring what he or she says), rescue fantasies, and inappropriate self-disclosure.

As well as building on traditional theory, this book draws on different approaches to elucidate the intricacies of interviewing and the insight that one initial interview can provide. These range from traditional psychoanalytic theory to contemporary therapies such as cognitive-behavior therapy, from reflective stances to more directive treatments. Silverstein also includes responses ranging from family systems to psychodrama. Other authors, from diverse settings, comment on Scott's behavioral problems as elucidated by the interview and how treatment might progress. These include an interesting chapter as to how the interview might have progressed if Scott were female rather than male, and how the interview is influenced by the sexual orientation of the client. I know of no other book that discusses how gender and sexual orientation influence the interviewing process. It is hoped that other books will follow this theme. One is struck that Scott's "gayness" is treated as a normal variant of sexual behavior and the responders are much more focused on Scott's problems of bereavement, family disorder, and searching for love, components in the lives of all of us.

The wealth of reactions to the interview is a special feature of this book. Not only do the responses give us some idea of how an individual practitioner might use the material, but they also include interviewing and treatment options within diverse settings. Scott would be treated differently according to whatever practitioner he might see but also with respect to the setting in which he finds himself. Regardless of the practitioner or setting, this initial interview, conducted with care and compassion, provides a wealth of information that will impact treatment.

This is the first ebook written on this subject and, as such, launches us into the twenty-first century of instantly available and widely disseminated published works. The book is written for students in training to be psychotherapists. The author asks that the reader go through the transcript noting her or his responses both to the interviewer and to Scott. As such, the reader is included in the process of the interview and can match her or his impressions with those of the experts that respond. Although written for students and early career practitioners, the book is useful for the experienced clinician as well. It is remarkable and surprising that an initial interview in the hands of a skilled professional can provide so much insight and information.

Bonnie R. Strickland, Ph.D., ABPP

Dr. Strickland has served as president of the American Psychological Association and on numerous APA Boards and Committees. She received her Ph.D. in clinical psychology from The Ohio State University in 1962. She has been on the faculties of Emory University and the University of Massachusetts in Amherst as administrator, clinician, consultant, researcher, and teacher. A diplomate in clinical psychology, her primary research interests have been in expectancies and behavior with a special focus on women's health. She has published more than a hundred scientific and scholarly works, including two *Citation Classics* in psychology.

About the Editor

Charles Silverstein, Ph.D., is known for his 1973 presentation before the Nomenclature Committee of the American Psychiatric Association on the deletion of homosexuality as a mental disorder. It was deleted in December 1973. In 1971, he founded Identity House, the first peer-counseling center in New York City for gay people, and in 1973 founded the Institute for Human Identity, a full-time psychotherapy center for gay people in New York City. He founded the *Journal of Homosexuality* in 1974, and served as its first editor. It is now in its 57th volume. He received his Ph.D. in Psychology from Rutgers University in 1974. Silverstein has published six books on homosexuality, and many chapters in anthologies and professional papers. He formerly served as an instructor in the Department of Psychiatry, New York University School of Medicine, and is now chair of the board of directors of the Institute for Human Identity, where he is also a supervisor. Silverstein received a Presidential Citation from the American Psychological Association in 2009, a Distinguished Professional Contribution from Division 44 of the American Psychological Association in 2005, and an award from the Gay and Lesbian Psychiatrists of New York in 2002. He is a Diplomate of the American Board of Sexology, a member of the Ethics Committee of the New York State Psychological Association, and is in private practice in New York City.
Email: csilverstein2@nyc.rr.com;
Website: www.drcsilverstein.com

About the Authors

Donald Bux, Ph.D., is an attending psychologist at Montefiore Medical Center in Bronx, New York, and the clinical program director for Next Steps, a welfare-to-work program for substance abusers. He has worked previously as a research scientist for the Research Foundation for Mental Hygiene and the National Center for Addiction and Substance Abuse, both in New York City, conducting research on the efficacy of motivational and cognitive-behavioral interventions for substance abuse. He has authored or coauthored over 70 research articles, book chapters, and conference presentations on substance abuse, motivational interviewing, and related topics in clinical psychology.
Email: donald.bux@me.com

Armand R. Cerbone, Ph.D., ABPP., has been in independent practice in Chicago where he has been counseling LGBT individuals and couples since 1978. He is a fellow of five divisions of the American Psychological Association (APA) and holds a diplomate in clinical psychology. He coauthored the APA's *Guidelines on Psychotherapy with LGB Clients* and chaired the working group that developed the APA's *Resolution on Sexual Orientation and Marriage* and *Resolution on Sexual Orientation, Parents and Children*. Dr. Cerbone is a past-president of the Illinois Psychological Association and currently serves on the APA Board of Directors. His is a former director of behavioral health at the Howard Brown Memorial Health Center, the Midwest's largest LGBT health center. In 2001 he cochaired the first international conference on LGB psychology. He has received many awards for his contributions to psychology, including the Stanley Sue Award for Distinguished Contributions to Diversity in Clinical Psychology. He is also a member of the City of Chicago Gay and Lesbian Hall of Fame.
Email: arcerbone@aol.com

Corinne Datchi-Phillips, Ph.D., is a native of France. Prior to coming to the United States in 2000, she taught in the English department at the University of Paris-Saint Denis and published on topics related to sexuality and gender issues. In the United States she earned a master's degree in counseling and guidance at New Mexico State University and a doctorate in counseling psychology at Indiana University-Bloomington. While in graduate school, she volunteered at the office of the GLBT Student Support Services and coled a support group for individuals that identify as queer, transsexual, transgendered, or intersex. She is now working as research associate at the Center for Adolescent and Family Studies, Indiana University-Bloomington, where she conducts research, provides family and couple therapy services, and supervises the Indiana Family Project, a collaborative partnership between Monroe County Probation Department and the Center for Adolescent and Family Studies. She also is a certified national Functional Family Therapy consultant. As such, she trains and supervises therapists in local mental health and community corrections agencies. Since 2009, Corinne has been actively involved in the Society for Family Psychology as hospitality suite chair and convention program chair. She also has served as the newsletter editor of Division 17's Section for the Advancement of Women (SAW) and will soon assume her new role as chair of the section. Corinne's interests include evidence-based practice, couples work, transgendered relationships, qualitative research methodology, performativity, and gender.
Email: cdatchip@indiana.edu

Jacob Gershoni, L.C.S.W., is a psychotherapist in private practice, specializing in experiential, expressive, and interactive group therapy. He is a Licensed Clinical Social Worker, Certified Group Psychotherapist (CGP) as a Trainer, Practitioner and Educator (TEP) by the American Board of Examiners in psychodrama, sociometry, and group psychotherapy. He is a staff member at Columbia Presbyterian Medical Center and a codirector of the Psychodrama Training Institute in New York City. Previously, he was a Senior Psychiatric Social Worker at Queens Child Guidance Center. Jacob has been a staff therapist at Identity House, a peer-counseling center for the LGBT community since 1980. He has led workshops and presentations in many local and international conferences and has ongoing therapy and training groups. Jacob is the editor of *Psychodrama in the 21st Century: Clinical and Educational Applications* (Springer, 2003) and articles about psychodrama published in professional journals.
Email: jacobg12@gmail.com

John C. Gonsiorek received his Ph.D. from the University of Minnesota in clinical psychology in 1978, and holds a diplomate in clinical psychology from the American Board of Professional Psychology. He is a past-president of American Psychological Association Division 44, and has published widely in the areas of professional misconduct and impaired professionals, sexual orientation and identity, professional ethics, and other areas. He is a fellow of APA Divisions 9, 12, 29, and 44. He is currently professor in the Psy.D. program at Argosy University/Twin Cities and has taught at a number of other institutions in the Twin Cities area. For many years, he provided expert witness evaluation and testimony regarding impaired clergy and professionals, standards of care, and psychological damages and has provided training and consultation to a variety of religious denominations and organizations. He is a consulting editor for *Professional Psychology: Research & Practice*. His major publications include: *Breach of Trust: Sexual Exploitation by Health Care Professionals and Clergy*; *Homosexuality: Research Implications for Public Policy* (with Weinrich); *Male Sexual Abuse: A Trilogy of Intervention Strategies* (with Bera and Letourneau); *and Homosexuality and Psychotherapy: A Practitioner's Handbook of Affirmative Models*. For 25 years, he had an independent practice of clinical and forensic psychology in Minneapolis and now primarily works as a consultant, aside from his faculty duties. Email: jgonsiorek@comcast.net

DeMond M. Grant received his Ph.D. from the University at Buffalo—SUNY in 2008, and currently is an assistant professor at Oklahoma State University. He is primarily interested in factors that influence the development of comorbidity among anxiety and mood disorders. His past research has been published in *The Journal of Abnormal Psychology*, *The Journal of Anxiety Disorders*, and *Behaviour Research and Therapy*. Current research focuses on anxiety-related thought processes such as worry and rumination. Email: demond.grant@okstate.edu

Ronald E. Hellman, M.D., M.S., F.A.P.A., is the director of the LGBT Affirmative Program of South Beach Psychiatric Center that he established in New York City in 1996. He has published numerous research papers in the area of sexual identity development, gay health care, and LGBT program development. He is the coeditor of the *Handbook of LGBT Issues in Community Mental Health*. He is the recipient of numerous awards including the Mental Health Achievement Award of the Gay and Lesbian Psychiatrists of NY, the Moffic Award for Ethical Practice in

Community Psychiatry, and the Babbott Award for Distinguished Service to the Medical Profession. He is a fellow of the American Psychiatric Association.
Email: sbopreh@omh.stateny.us

Margaret Nichols, Ph.D., is the founder/director of the Institute for Personal Growth, 8 South Third Avenue, Highland Park, New Jersey, 08904, USA and since 1983 the founding member and first director of the Hyacinth AIDS Foundation in New Jersey. She is a certified sex therapist, American Association of Sexuality Educators, Counselors, and Therapists (AASECT), and a diplomate of the American Board of Sexology. She is an author and presenter on LGBT clinical issues and psychotherapy with clients from the BDSM and polyamory communities, a feminist therapist, bisexual lesbian mother, sex radical, and mother of Cory, Alejandra, Diana, and Jesse (6/6/1994–6/2/2004).
Email: shrnklady@aol.com; Phone: 800-379-9220;
Website: www.ipgcounseling.com

Ralph Roughton, M.D., is a clinical professor emeritus of psychiatry and the director of the Psychoanalytic Institute at Emory University. He is a supervising analyst and training analyst emeritus in the Emory University Psychoanalytic Institute. He was the founding chair of the Committee on Gay and Lesbian Issues of the American Psychoanalytic Association and, in that capacity, oversaw its rapid evolution from de facto exclusion of gay men and lesbians from analytic training to a proactive, gay-friendly organization that takes public advocacy positions on gay marriage, gay parenting, military service, etc. Dr. Roughton has been on the editorial boards of the *Journal of the American Psychoanalytic Association*, the *International Journal of Psychoanalysis*, and the *Journal of Gay and Lesbian Psychotherapy*. He has written extensively on the analytic process and about working with gay men in treatment, one example being, "Four men in treatment: An evolving perspective on homosexuality and bisexuality, 1965–2000, *Journal of the American Psychoanalytic Association* (2001), *49*, 1187–1217."
Email: rroughton@bellsouth.net

Michael C. Singer, Ph.D., is a clinical psychologist trained at the Gordon F. Derner Institute for Advanced Psychological Studies, Adelphi University. He has taught at Hunter College, Adelphi University, and The Glass Institute for Basic Psychoanalytic Research, and now serves as a psychotherapy supervisor in the Clinical Psychology doctoral program at City College of New York (CCNY). As chief family therapist at The Center for Urban Community Services, Dr. Singer works with individuals and families to repair the emotional damage that results from early trauma and abuse. As a consultant to the Hetrick-Martin Institute and St. Christopher's School, he helps develop effective programs to address the specific psychological needs of at-risk adolescents. His articles on LGBT treatment issues and the training of LGBT therapists have appeared in *Psychoanalytic Psychology, Journal of Gay & Lesbian Mental Health,* and *The Handbook of LGBT Issues in Community Mental Health.* Dr. Singer's private practice in New York City includes both children and adults, and also specializes in creative artists. His monograph *The mind of the musical artist* is awaiting publication as part of The Psychological Issues Monograph Series of Yale University Press.
Email: drmichaelsinger@aol.com

Peter S. Theodore, Ph.D., is a licensed and practicing psychologist in the state of California whose expertise traverses the fields of HIV-prevention, substance abuse treatment, and clinical health psychology. He is currently an assistant professor in the Clinical Psychology Ph.D. Program of the California School of Professional Psychology at Alliant International University, Los Angeles, and a faculty affiliate of the university's Rockway Institute (a center for LGBT psychological research and public policy). He earned his Ph.D. from the University of Miami in clinical psychology in 2005 during which time he completed an NIMH predoctoral fellowship in HIV/AIDS research and was the recipient of an APA Dissertation Research Award for a community-based project investigating recreational drug use and sexual risk behaviors among gay and bisexual men. He formerly directed a methamphetamine-abuse treatment program designed specifically for gay and bisexual men, and served numerous roles on various federally funded projects addressing the intersection of substance abuse and HIV-prevention. His current research addresses health disparities among LGBT persons and reducing LGBT-related prejudice, discrimination, and violence. He has presented at numerous conferences and published in journals including *Sexuality Research and Social Policy: Journal of NSRC, AIDS and Behavior,* and *Journal of Homosexuality.*
Email: ptheodore@alliant.edu

Gil Tunnell, Ph.D., received his doctorate in social/personality psychology from the University of Nebraska in 1976 and completed a postdoctoral clinical respecialization program at the University of Massachusetts in 1984. He was the director of family therapy training at Beth Israel Medical Center and senior psychologist at NYU Medical Center. He was a founding member and chair of the Task Force on AIDS of the New York State Psychological Association and has published on working with AIDS patients in group psychotherapy. He currently serves as adjunct assistant professor of psychology and education, Teachers College, Columbia University, and senior faculty of the Accelerated Experiential Dynamic Psychotherapy Institute in New York City. He has published extensively on working with gay male couples and is coauthor with David Greenan of *Couple Therapy with Gay Men* (Guilford, 2003). He is also in private practice in New York City.
Email: giltunnell@verizon.net

LaRicka R. Wingate, Ph.D., received her doctoral degree from Florida State University in 2006. Her research investigates the interpersonal causes, correlates, and consequences of suicidal behavior. Specifically, she is interested in resilience, strengths, protective factors, suicide risk assessment, treatment, and suicidality in ethnic minority groups. Dr. Wingate has published over 20 peer-reviewed papers, several of which are on suicidal behavior and depression. She is currently an assistant professor of psychology at Oklahoma State University.
Email: laricka.wingate@okstate.edu

Part One

The Initial Interview

1 Introduction

Charles Silverstein

Institute for Human Identity, New York, NY, USA

The following incident took place many years ago, long before the *American Psychiatric Association* removed homosexuality from its list of mental disorders (American Psychiatric Association, 1973). A 16-year-old boy, ashamed of his homosexual feelings, sought the counsel of his family physician. The doctor, as much a victim of his generation's attitude about homosexuality as the boy was of his, wrote the name of a nearby hospital and told the 16-year-old to go there and ask for the psychiatric clinic. Nothing more was said, and the teenager left with only a piece of paper to show for his courage. He made the appointment at the hospital. Of course, his parents knew nothing of his dilemma.

Arriving at the clinic, the 16-year-old was shown into a large office. A man who was smoking a cigar conducted the interview, and he seemed far more interested in blowing smoke rings with it then listening to the boy. In a far corner were two other men, each of them writing upon a pad. No one introduced them and the young 16-year-old was far too frightened to ask who they were and what they were doing there. He thought that his interview was going to be private and confidential; how could he divulge his secret when there were two anonymous men in the room? He immediately felt as if he was on trial, the building a prison, and the three men his jailers. No one asked how he felt or acknowledged the fear increasing with volcanic force in the teenager.

After about 30 minutes, the man with the cigar announced that they (meaning the four of them) were required to move into another room in order to meet a different person for a further interview. More from terror than obedience, the teenager followed, but he was even more confused. The small party walked into a second office. There were three more people there (making a total of seven), who once again were not introduced and whose presence was not explained. The teenager felt as if he was in the midst of the Inquisition, and its leader a modern Torquemada. He simply fled, ran out of the room and out of the hospital, never to return. It would be years before he would make another attempt at psychotherapy.

I was that teenager and I remember the experience with pristine clarity.

Only weeks before while bored with some high school class, I had looked out the window of my schoolroom to a clock above a storefront church across the street. Above it was a sign that read, "It Is Time to Seek the Lord." I knew which sinner they had in mind! For the rest of the school year, I spent every lunch hour in

The Initial Psychotherapy Interview. DOI: 10.1016/B978-0-12-385146-8.00001-8

the small library down the street from my high school and read everything on the shelves about homosexuality. What I read filled me with dread. The 1950s were the heyday of the "phobic theory" of homosexuality. Psychoanalysts such as Socarides (1968), Bieber et al. (1962), and Hatterer (1971) were prolific members of the adaptation school of psychoanalysis, who believed that homosexuality in both men and women was the result of faulty parenting. Bieber's work, in particular, led to the well-advertised theory that homosexuality in men resulted from a distant father and an overprotective mother. A proper psychoanalysis, they all claimed, would lead the man or woman to normal sexual behavior, by which they meant heterosexuality. These three men had been students of Sandor Rado (1949) who challenged Freud's theory of bisexuality (Freud, 1905/1938). Rado said that it was not true that an infant was born with both homosexual and heterosexual components. He argued that only heterosexuality was biologically given, and that homosexual desire in a man was motivated by a phobic fear of the vagina, a displaced representation of the man's mother. He avoids vaginal intercourse for fear that his penis will be cut off, a slight transformation of Freud's castration anxiety. This theory was the origin of subsequent *vagina dentata* jokes.

Even more strident were the writings of Bergler (1956), another psychoanalyst of the 1950s. After more than a half-century, one can still feel his anger against gay people. He calls them megalomaniacs, hypernarcissistic, and people who are convinced of their superiority over others. He is (at least I believe him to be) extremely angry about gay male sex, and argues that it is a re-enactment of the baby—mother interaction. "In fellatio, the hungry 'baby' sucks at the mother's 'breast,'" (1956, p. 64). Bergler didn't ignore lesbians who, he believed, suffered from a similar unresolved masochistic conflict with the mother during infancy. He also makes some strange statements about the correlations between lesbian desire and frigidity in women!

Rereading the works of these old psychoanalysts from the 1950s made me wonder why they were so condemning of gay people. I suspect that sex per se was not the primary issue. It was the violation of gender roles that bothered them the most; lesbian for being "too masculine," and gay men for being "too feminine." MacDonald and Games' (1974) study on power is informative on this issue. They found that homosexual men were devalued because they voluntarily gave up their masculine prerogatives, but lesbians, perceived by heterosexuals as aspiring to masculinity, were judged as more powerful than gay men. I would like to suggest that gay peoples' violation of stereotypical gender roles was the driving force of the psychoanalytic movement before and after World War II.

There were no other theories about the origin of homosexuality on the shelves of the small library near my high school in those days, or in any other library. The powerful heterosexist bias in American society prevented any contrary message (Herek, 1991). Sodomy, usually defined as any orgasmic behavior that did not lead to conception, was against the law everywhere, and the legal penalties were severe (Leonard, 1997; Rivera, 1991). There was no mainstream church that accepted homosexuality, although there were occasional (if seldom read) publications calling for liberalization (Kosnik, Carroll, Cunningham, Modras, & Schulte, 1977). Mainstream churches called the practitioner a sinner, and extolled her or him to confess the transgressions and to cleanse their souls through prayer. "Moral turpitude" laws denied the licensing of any homosexual health-care professional, or from practicing the law, or any state license for that matter. The system of repression was complete.

The gay woman or man was a sinner, a lawbreaker, and a shame to her or his family, and the psychiatric and psychological professions of the decades up to the 1970s provided the rationale for a series of dreadful (some might say sadistic) treatments against gay people. Among them were aversion therapy, both electrical (Bancroft, 1974; Feldman & MacCullough, 1971) and chemical (MacConaghy, 1969; Tennent, Bancroft, & Cass, 1974) in which the man was either electrically shocked or forced to vomit through drug administration when aroused by a picture of an attractive nude man. And since gay men were thought to suffer from a deficiency of masculinity, some clinicians "butched" them up with injections of testosterone, hoping that the infusion would turn them toward women (Rosenzweig & Hoskins, 1941).

Oddly (and no one has adequately explained this), probably 99 percent of the homosexual subjects in these sexual convention studies were men. Lesbians did not volunteer for sexual reorientation. Were they smarter than the men? One wonders how that came about. Perhaps men's proclivity to concentrate upon frequent sexual contact made them more visible than women (Peterson & Hyde, 2010).[1]

Some treatments were even more damaging. In one bizarre study a researcher went so far as to surgically insert electrodes into the brain of a gay man and stimulate the "pleasure center" of the brain when a naked woman was introduced into the room in the hope that "pleasure" and a naked woman would be associated, leading to the man's "cure" (Heath, 1972). The experiment was a failure.

There were even earlier attempts to change homosexuals into heterosexuals through surgical techniques. Steinach was probably the first. He operated on at least eleven men from 1916 to 1921 (Schmidt, 1984). The operation consisted of performing a unilateral castration on a gay man, followed by transplanting testicular tissue from a heterosexual into the castrated man in the hope of "curing" him. He did not succeed. His assumption was that homosexuality in men was the result of deficient masculinity, and regretfully some uninformed people still believe this mistaken notion.

More brutal still was the use of cerebral ablation in Europe as a "treatment" for homosexuality or for masturbation (Rieber & Sigusch, 1979; Schmidt & Schorsch, 1981). "Informed consent" was not yet a requirement for surgery or for psychological experimentation, and the morality of these surgeries was finally questioned and the procedures terminated (Sigusch, Schorsch, Dannecker, & Schmidt, 1982). In the United States, castration was a legal penalty for deviant sexual behavior as early as 1917, and the medical establishment carried it out until it was outlawed in 1950 (Hughes, 1914; Schmidt, 1984). (For reviews of other damaging medical treatments against women such as cliterodectomies, and lobotomies for both women and men, see Baker-Benfield, 1976, and Braslow, 1997. For a review of the use of psychosurgery on sexual "deviants" and its effects, see Schmidt & Schorsch, 1981.)

The greater number of gay men and lesbian entered either psychoanalysis or psychotherapy as the preferred form of treatment to cure their same-sex attraction. The insularity of the process of psychotherapy kept gay people from one another

---

[1] For that reason, many feminists considered men to be phallocentric.

and reinforced the power of "the closet." But no matter. None of the treatments worked anyway, not psychoanalysis, not aversion therapy, not even cerebral ablation. There were hundreds of studies conducted in sexual reorientation, but no sexual preference changed. Some of the proponents, particularly Bergler (1956), Socarides (1968), Bieber et al. (1962), and Hatterer (1971) claimed success, which was never proven. Gay people who entered these forms of treatment did so because they failed to control their sexual desire; after the unsuccessful treatment, they felt doubly a failure. To counter the anti-gay bias in the professional community, the American Psychological Association passed a set of guidelines for the psychological treatment of gay people (American Psychological Association, 2000, 2009).

There were a few dissenting voices in the psychiatric community. Halleck (1971) argued against the illness theory of homosexuality and claimed that it was an example of a political, not a medical, diagnosis. He wrote: "Oppression of the homosexual today is primarily maintained by the irrational fear that homosexuality threatens the stability of the society and by the irrational belief that tolerating homosexuality implies weakness" (p. 107). Szasz (1977) argued that homosexuals were the scapegoat of society and did not suffer from a mental illness.

There were two other important contrary voices in the professional establishment. Freund, who pioneered some of the aversion therapy literature, displayed his integrity when he wrote that of his previously published cure rate of 20 percent, "Virtually not one 'cure' remained a cure" (Freund, 1977, p. 238). Davison, a leading behaviorist, argued against the use of any treatment to change sexual orientation on moral and ethical grounds (Davison, 1974). They were the advance guard of a movement against the discrimination of gay people that would shortly become a tidal wave. This tidal wave culminated in the elimination of homosexuality as a mental disorder by the American Psychiatric Association in 1973 (Silverstein, 1976–1977). For information about that tidal wave, see Bayer (1981) on the deletion of homosexuality as a mental disorder, and Silverstein (1991, 1996, 1997) for the rise of gay-affirmative psychotherapy (Malyon, 1982). For information about how heterosexist attitudes have been the foundation of anti-LGBT discrimination, see the excellent work by Herek (1984, 1986, 1991). (For information on using gay-affirmative psychotherapy, see Cerbone (Chapter 15) and Cornett, 1993; Stein & Cohen, 1986; Cabaj & Stein, 1996; Gonsiorek, 1982; and Ross, 1988. For information about treating gay couples, see Tunnell (Chapter 7) and Greenan & Tunnell, 2003.)

It was in that social and professional milieu that I grew up. Most gay men and women felt a sense of guilt after indulging in sex, but underneath that was shame, as if a toxin infected the person so that one was bad even if she or he didn't "act out," as the psychiatrists of the day called engaging in homosexual sex.

My interview at age 16 illustrated two problems with the treatment of gay people in the post–World War II world. It was, first of all, based only on the "cause and cure" theory. Because homosexuality was diagnosed as deviant and abnormal, the professional establishment searched only for its cause and its resolution—meaning how to make the person heterosexual. They were unconcerned about the lives of lesbian and gay people and their work shows how little they knew about the day-to-day lives of this sexual minority.

The second problem was the cold, Teutonic atmosphere of the consulting room. The doctor sat behind his desk and interviewed the patient, who answered whatever questions were asked. The doctor, usually a psychoanalyst, maintained the pre-scribed "blank screen" aloofness and believed it served the patient's needs. It did not; it drove the patient away as it did me so many years ago. The power structure between doctor and patient was set in stone, leading to what I believe was a sado-masochistic relationship between them, the doctor perpetually dismayed with the gay or lesbian patients' inability to stop "acting out," and the patients' feelings that they had once again disappointed a parent substitute. While the doctor who inter-viewed me when I was 16 asked whether I had participated in gay sex, he never asked me how I felt being in his office and I never felt that he cared.

I needed to feel cared for. I still do. Don't you? A woman or man, grown or still an adolescent or child, also needs to feel cared for. The person who enters the con-sulting room feels vulnerable, and while a sterile environment may be necessary for an operating room, it is deadly for human interactions. I think it inconceivable that another 16-year-old today would be treated as coldly as I was so many years ago. Still, therapists in training need to be taught that compassion and an inviting environ-ment are crucial in the consulting room, not only for the patient but for the therapist as well. The consulting room should be an island of safety in a hostile world, the place to say things rarely expressed verbally. Make the person feel safe. Everyone says that, so why is it so difficult to accomplish it? The complication is the therapist who is also a person, perhaps with his or her own secrets or feelings of ambivalence. Part of this book is about the interaction of patient and therapist because it is a crucial factor in a successful therapy. That's my bias but not all of my colleagues share it.

This is a book I have wanted to publish for many years. I have had many super-visees throughout my career and I have listened to their personal struggles entering upon our profession. "What should I say?" or "Is it wrong if I . . . ?" or "Am I good enough?" Even more challenging to them were their feelings while inquiring about a client's sexual life, fearful that they will either be aroused (bad therapist) or repelled (also bad therapist) by what they hear. They had all come from fine gradu-ate schools, but they were taught to follow a limited model of psychotherapy. It was focused solely on the patient and on her or his conflicts and needs. It was the medical model of diagnosis as the fulcrum between etiology and treatment (Gonsiorek, 1991). It ignored the other person in the room, the therapist, who had grown up in the same society as the patient, and who had her or his own set of par-ents. The therapist, therefore, brings emotions and biases to the consulting room almost as often as the patient does. Almost? Always.

The students' teachers were usually regarded as wise, almost always correct in their judgments and deserving of respect, perhaps even awe. What was left out of training was therapeutic fallibility. This book is meant to make some adjustment to that model and to argue for a more humane interaction in psychotherapy. That begins with the initial interview.

Students and early career therapists are usually and rightly told that they need to establish "rapport" with their patients and that without it a "therapeutic alliance" will be impossible. True enough, but how do students or young counselors do that, and how can they unintentionally block it? "Show me, help me, what does it feel like, look like?" they plead. The concept of a therapeutic alliance has become a cliché, a lecture or reading, anything but what the idea conveys. It is an emotional bridge between two people, the self-confessed patient and the all-knowing therapist conducting the initial interview. Students in the classroom do not know what it is because they do not *feel it* coming from their instructors. They hear the words, but miss the emotional connection.

The literature on the initial interview is scant. The first book was Sullivan's *The Psychiatric Interview* (1970), based upon a series of lectures dating back to 1944. Coming from a strict, but not Freudian, psychiatric background, he tells the reader to ask one pertinent question about her or his patient: "Who is this person and how does he come to be here?" (p. 132). In this early text, Sullivan tells us nothing about interviewing a gay person, even though he was himself gay (Blechner, 2005). He is the originator of the term "parataxic distortion," meant to combine both transference and counter-transference in the consulting room. Sullivan's parataxic distortion is a point of view with which I agree; it is discussed further in Chapter 3. Argelander (1976), a German psychoanalyst, wrote a short treatise on the initial interview and managed not to mention sex at all.

Shea (1998) wrote an excellent book on interviewing and contained the first complete transcript of an initial interview with the author's annotation. He clearly spells out the importance of empathy in the interview process and how "why" questions interfere with it. His discussion of counter-transference is limited, but he had the good sense to write, "... a direct correlation can be drawn between clinician confusion and the amount of time that the clinician spends with his or her mouth open" (p. 66). His attitude toward sexuality, including homosexuality, is very positive. This book should be in every clinician's library.

Marquis (2008) proposes a rather complicated system called "The Integral Intake" that is highly systematic. It is the first book I have come across on interviewing that includes a CD to accompany the book, and in three languages! The author's attitude toward homosexuality is extremely positive, and he even uses a gay-positive homosexual man as one of his examples of the intake process in action. Whether his more complicated and systematic theory becomes popular remains to be seen.

Morrison's book (2008) is the most cookbookish and comprehensive of the lot. It proceeds in logical order from meeting the patient to writing the final report. He demonstrates a very sex-positive attitude throughout, including the normality of homosexuality, and includes an annotated interview. Finally, while briefly listing and explaining a comprehensive list of therapist errors, the book fails to relate these errors to the personality and internal conflicts of the therapist or how they affect the interview. Still, it's a good first book on interviewing techniques.

None of the books noted above do the job well enough, and perhaps no single book ever will. The fact is that people today, regardless of gender or sexual orientation, speak more openly about themselves than ever before. More important, these books do not do justice to the counter-transferential problems of the interviewer. They represent a crucial factor in psychotherapy. It is inconceivable to me, for instance, that an interviewer hearing about a client's rape, would not be flooded with feelings of her or his own regardless of whether or not the therapist had a similar experience. So many of us fumble when overcome by our own feelings if they become entangled with those of our clients.

What is maddeningly difficult to do in a book is to teach students that they—not a required intake form—are the instrument during the initial interview. That is what my colleagues and I try to convey in this book: how we gain information and possibly become a source of help to our clients through the emotional bridge we build, not only by asking the right questions at the right time. Any damn fool can learn which questions to ask. Not all my colleagues in this book agree with me on the importance of the therapists' feelings and their effect upon the interview. Much depends upon their theoretical orientation, the specific clinical setting, and the degree of pathology of the patient. The reader will have to make up his or her own mind about the validity of this approach.

Seasoned therapists need to make a contribution by illustrating what we do in the consulting room. This book gives our students and younger colleagues a window through which they can see our work. We seek to make it safe for them to question us. We supervisors are always ready to gently criticize them, but we seldom allow them to see our own blind spots and liabilities. Perhaps we fear our students seeing past our armor of infallibility. Whatever is the reason, we have to do better; we have to let them stand on our shoulders and to see further than we ever have ourselves.

The subject of this book is "Scott," a young gay man who enters therapy because of the death of a much-loved brother. But Scott is only half the story; the other half is the psychologist who interviewed him. In Chapter 2 you'll find a complete and unedited transcript of the initial interview. I believe that this is the first time a complete transcript of a gay therapist interviewing a gay patient has been published. The full transcript brings them to life, ranging over a ground that moves from insights to blind spots, to significant therapist errors.

But why a book on only a gay man? It is not a book about a gay man; it is about the human interaction between two people, both of whom are gay. Can you see the difference? It is not their sexual orientation that is the issue; it is their interaction. It is about whether these two people, who had never met before, can form that emotional bridge that says, "I understand, and I care about you," without ever having to say the words. From a therapeutic point of view, Scott's initial interview is just as relevant to lesbians and to heterosexuals. The process remains the same. In Chapter 4, Nichols discusses this question in more detail.[2]

What is different is the subject, Scott. His experiences in the world as a gay man are different from those of heterosexuals and of lesbians; not better or worse, but different. He asked to see a gay male therapist because he did not want to spend time explaining himself to someone who is not intimately knowledgeable about gay life.

[2] One looks forward to the day when sexual orientation is perceived as a natural characteristic of a human being, not a special class to be either condemned or admired. That is already the case in large American metropolitan centers, but the cascading tidal wave slows down to a ripple in conservative, rural areas of the country. I remain optimistic that in time the whole country will stand up for the civil rights of all sexual minorities.

The man is part of the "Post-Stonewall" generation, women and men born after the rebellion at the Stonewall Inn in 1969 New York City that gave birth to the modern gay rights movement (Carter, 2004). He and his generational cohorts, unlike mine, did not grow up feeling that their homosexual feelings were a toxin infecting their bodies. He was not motivated by shame. While earlier generations were called "fag," and responded by wearing "Gay is Good" buttons, Scott's generation says, "Yea, so what?" They feel quite pleased to be gay, thank you. Scott must deal with the basic human problems of living and not with the additional burden of prejudice over his sexual orientation. (See Cerbone, Chapter 15.) I know this is not the case with every gay person in America, not even for some who live in the gay Meccas of America. It is still "The love that dare not speak its name" in many parts of the United States.

   With Scott's permission to tell his story, I looked for colleagues who are experts in particular fields. There are three sets of chapters that follow the transcript. In Part One we discuss the conduct of the initial interview (Chapter 3), the question of gender and sexual orientation (Nichols, Chapter 4), and intake procedures in an institutional setting (Hellman, Chapter 5). In Part Two colleagues write about topical issues of importance to Scott, such as bereavement (Singer, Chapter 6), attachment theory (Tunnell, Chapter 7), sexual abuse (Gonsiorek, Chapter 8), and the relationship between sex, drug use, and AIDS (Theodore, Chapter 9). Part Three discusses Scott from the point of view of a spectrum of therapeutic techniques, including motivational interviewing (Bux, Chapter 10), cognitive behavioral therapy (CBT) (Grant and Wingate, Chapter 11), family systems (Datchi-Phillips, Chapter 12), psychoanalysis (Roughton, Chapter 13), psychodrama (Gershoni, Chapter 14), and gay-affirmative psychotherapy (Cerbone, Chapter 15). I have been diligent in searching for different approaches to psychotherapy so that readers can decide for themselves what works best, and make decisions about future advanced training.

   In organizing the book, I used the following procedure. Scott and I discussed his participation in the book, and he signed a letter of consent to have the transcript of his initial interview published. All identifying information was changed in the transcript. Scott received a copy of the transcript demonstrating how identifying information had been changed and gave his approval. Each chapter author received the transcript and a CD recording of the initial interview. The CD was returned after the chapter was completed. The chapter writers were told that they would not be given any further information about Scott or my contact with him.

   In order to integrate the chapters, the authors were asked to follow the same format.

1. Give a brief history of their field of expertise, particularly as it relates to Scott and his presentation as a candidate for psychotherapy.
2. Identify the salient personality characteristics and emotional conflicts that underlie his difficulties.
3. Identify in what ways their approach differs from those of their colleagues in the book.
4. Discuss how they would have conducted the interview from their frame of reference.
5. Critique the interview, noting what the interviewer did to establish rapport with the patient, as well as errors of judgment or technique, and when appropriate, identify how counter-transference influences the interaction between patient and therapist.

6. Where possible, use the transcript for planning the patient's future psychotherapy.

7. End the chapter with a section, "If You Want to Learn More About This Approach," listing further readings.

The contributors were particularly encouraged to be specific and to state how they would have phrased alternative questions.

In reviewing the first drafts, I consistently asked the authors to demonstrate their reasoning, and when appropriate, their feelings about a particular section of the transcript. These chapters were not easy to write. A review article is a cinch; we all know how to summarize research. But laying out one's clinical skills (or the fear of being clinically deficient) for our colleagues to see is another story. We all knew that there would be occasional differences of opinion. If we professionals disagree about something, let the differences be clear. Readers can listen to the argument and make up their own minds about the issue. Our profession is simply not advanced enough to say that one approach is the golden road to successful treatment. I was also pleased that some of our authors disclosed personal information about themselves when they felt it relevant to their chapters. It helps to illuminate the debate about personal disclosure in psychotherapy, a question that repeatedly comes up in supervision (Gartrell, 1994; Isay, 1993, 1996).

We should talk about bias. Some of the authors in this text (including myself) work in a private practice setting. What a luxury that is. We can construct our own initial interview form, or not use one at all. We can spend as much time as we wish for the intake interview. We can choose not to collect some information about the patient in our first meeting, saving it for later. Compared to mental health clinics, there are few legal requirements in private practice beyond reasonable note-taking, filling out insurance forms, and respecting ethical regulations and state laws.

It is quite different in mental health centers and hospitals or any clinic that is fully or partially funded by public money. Their record keeping is considerable, and both federal and state governments conduct site visits and financial audits. It is likely that they have a very formal procedure and supervision for the initial interview with accountability at every step. Because federal and state-funded programs are so different from private practice, I am pleased that Hellman (Chapter 5) has joined us and described his program in community psychiatry working with the LGBT community at the South Beach Psychiatric Center. He has more experience in this work than any other psychiatrist I know, and his model of service will be helpful to institutionally based clinicians.

There is another potential difference between community mental health centers and private practice. Our patients in private practice are usually employed, have a decent income, and have medical insurance to cover most of the therapy bill. Some community mental health centers, such as Hellman's that deal with the severely disturbed, are populated with the unemployed and public assistance patients, often with debilitating physical illnesses and serious mental pathologies including dual diagnoses. The goals of treatment at these centers are often quite different from those of private practice. Other mental health centers in the country differ from Hellman's and compete quite successfully for privately insured patients. Still, even with these differences, the lessons to be learned in this book are of value whenever there is an interaction between a patient and a therapist. My own experience working in a mental hospital is that a word of kindness and understanding is returned with a greater payoff than in private practice.

As you read through the chapters, you will find that the authors disagree in the following significant ways.

1. *Structure of the Interview*

A structured interview contains an almost invariable set of questions, predetermined, and listed in an ordinal series, from the first to the last. It may contain a large number of closed-ended questions that can be answered by "yes" or "no," although a request for explanation, such as, "Please tell me more about that," may follow. Institutional settings and clinics use structured interviews most often because they ensure that legally required information will be noted and that the assessment of both serious mental and physical health questions are not ignored. Structure, however, does not mean robotic behavior, and every institution has procedures for immediately dealing with emergency situations, such as suicidal ideation, or the potential for violence. Because every clinician, regardless of discipline, is required by state laws to train in licensed clinics or hospitals, the therapist-in-training probably has experience using these forms. The fully structured interview is least likely to create anxiety in both the interviewer and the interviewee. Because the choice of questions is predetermined, it is least likely to lead to significant therapist errors such as ignoring significant psychological pathology. Finally, the more highly structured the interview, the fewer the opportunities for counter-transference to contaminate the evaluation. CBT (Grant and Wingate, Chapter 11) is an example of a structured interview.

In contrast is the completely unstructured interview, such as those one finds in psychodynamic psychotherapy and psychoanalysis (Roughton, Chapter 13). It generally begins with, "What brings you here today?" or something similar, with the interviewer sitting back and allowing the client to take the lead and discuss life's troubles. The interviewer follows the path charted by the client, rather than a preset list of questions. This lack of structure, in contrast to the structured interview, is likely to engender the greatest amount of anxiety in both the patient and the therapist, and, depending upon the patient, may lead to moments (sometimes minutes) of deafening silence in the room. The open structure also creates a fertile ground for significant transferential feelings from the client to the therapist. Counter-transferential feelings and errors of judgment on the part of the interviewer are also more common here.

Most clinics and hospital settings use a combination of the structured and unstructured interview, based upon the needs of the institution, the population served, and state licensing requirements.

2. *Information*

Another important disagreement centers on the relevance of information acquired during an initial interview. Some colleagues maintain that information gathering is crucial in order to assess the patient's medical, psychiatric, and drug history, or to plan the future psychotherapy (Gonsiorek, Chapter 8). The patient may have to be evaluated for medication, or referred to another agency for treatment. Others believe that information is secondary to establishing rapport, without which any therapy will be futile (Tunnell, Chapter 7; Datchi-Phillips, Chapter 12).

3. *Directiveness*

A third difference concerns how directive the counselor should be while conducting the interview. Some forms of therapy, such as CBT (Grant and Wingate, Chapter 11) or psychodrama (Gershoni, Chapter 14) are very directive, while psychoanalysis (Roughton, Chapter 13) argues against therapeutic intrusion, preferring to wait for personality dynamics to emerge.

4. *Interpretation and Intervention*

Should the intake counselor feel free to interpret or intervene in some way during the interview? If, for instance, the initial interview is perceived as information gathering only, then an intervention occurs in only the most extreme cases, such as major depression, over-the-top drug addiction, or the potential for violence. If, on the other hand, the initial interview is perceived as the first psychotherapy session, then the therapist may consider an intervention acceptable, such as in attachment theory (Tunnell, Chapter 7), family therapy (Datchi-Phillips, Chapter 12), and psychoanalysis (Roughton, Chapter 13).

5. *The Goals of Psychotherapy*

According to their particular schools of psychotherapy, the authors will differ on whether symptom resolution (Grant and Wingate, Chapter 11) or personality change (Roughton, Chapter 13) is the goal of psychotherapy.

6. *Personal Values*

Finally there is the question of personal values. There are times when a patient's behavior offends the moral beliefs of the therapist. An example might be when a practitioner of gay-affirmative psychotherapy is asked to "cure" someone of her or his homosexuality (Cerbone, Chapter 15). Other examples might be offensive sexual behaviors, such as unsafe sex or abusing recreational drugs (Theodore, Chapter 9). The authors will agree that therapists have a right to their own values, but differ about the wisdom of expressing them.

How to Read This Book

I suggest that you not sit down and read this book from cover to cover. Not yet. Start by doing what the chapter authors did—read the transcript. Then take a highlighter and a pen and paper and read the transcript again, this time highlighting all the passages you find meaningful. Take notes about Scott and about the interview.

Write down your thoughts about Scott's reasons for seeking therapy and how you would have conducted the initial interview. Are there other questions you would have asked, or something you would have wanted to say or do? See if you can identify places in the transcript in which the psychologist made errors of technique and where his own counter-transferential feelings contaminated the interview.

After you've taken your notes, read the transcript for the third time. Please be assured that all the chapter writers read it at least three times. Try to imagine what Scott looks like, and sounds like, as well as the feelings he expresses. Try to sense your own emotions as you "listen" to him.

Consider Scott's motivation to seek therapy. Someone he loved very deeply passed away, and he feels as if part of him has died as well (Chapter 6). He also came from a dysfunctional family (Chapter 12) and he feels lonely because he has not found another man to love (Chapter 7). Bereavement, family conflict, and loneliness; is he so different than from you or me? That is the main reason I chose Scott as the subject of this book. So many of his conflicts live in us all. We understand him because most of us have experienced in our lives the pain he feels in his. That should lead to a sense of compassion and empathy toward Scott. Unfortunately it can also create a landmine of counter-transferential problems (Chapter 3).

Then read the rest of the book.

A Final Note

This book represents a comprehensive examination of the initial interview, but it is not the final word for training mental health practitioners. No single book could be. One would need to write an encyclopedia for psychotherapy applicants that cross the boundaries of multicultural populations, gender, diagnostic categories, and more. Each of these categories of patient identifications is worthy of further study and publication. We have every reason to believe, for instance, that a Latino man or Latina woman seeking therapy would behave differently during the initial interview if interviewed by a Hispanic therapist, rather than by a native-born American, and that the same is true for a transgender client who might feel suspicious toward a non-transgendered therapist because of past discrimination by the professional community.

Fortunately, the contributing authors in this book have identified the salient characteristics of the initial interview from their unique perspectives. They have pointed to a universal way to examine the client—therapist interactions that are common to all people. It is hoped that the book will be judged on whether we have accomplished that goal. Other colleagues will have to expand our boundaries by writing about specific populations, and I wish them well in their task of adding to this literature.

References

American Psychiatric Association. (1973). Press release. December 15.
American Psychological Association. (2000). Guidelines for psychotherapy with lesbian, gay, and bisexual clients. *American Psychologist*, 55(12), 1440–1451.

American Psychological Association. (2009). Resolution on appropriate affirmative responses to sexual orientation distress and change effects. Policy adopted by the APA Council of Representatives, August, 2009.

Argelander, H. (1976). *The initial interview in psychotherapy* (H. F. Bernays, Trans.). New York: Human Sciences Press.

Baker-Benfield, G. J. (1976). *The horrors of the half-known life: Male attitudes toward women and sexuality in nineteenth-century America.* New York: Harper Colophon Books.

Bancroft, J. (1974). *Deviant sexual behavior: Modifications and assessment.* London: Oxford University Press.

Bayer, R. (1981). *Homosexuality and American psychiatry: The politics of diagnosis.* New York: Basic Books.

Bergler, E. (1956). *Homosexuality: Disease or way of life?* New York: Collier Books.

Bieber, I., Dain, H., Dince, P., Drellich, M., Grand, H., & Gundlach, R., et al., (1962). *Homosexuality: A psychoanalytic study.* New York: Basic Books.

Blechner, M. (2005). The gay Harry Stack Sullivan: Interactions between his life, clinical work, and theory. *Contemporary Psychoanalysis, 41*, 1–19.

Braslow, J. (1997). *Mental ills and bodily cures: Psychiatric treatment in the first half of the twentieth century.* Berkeley, CA: University of California Press.

Cabaj, R. P., & Stein, T. S. (Eds.), (1996). *Textbook of homosexuality and mental health.* Washington, DC: American Psychiatric Association.

Carter, D. (2004). *Stonewall: The riots that sparked the gay revolution.* New York: St. Martin's Press.

Cornett, C. (Ed.), (1993). *Affirmative dynamic psychotherapy with gay men.* Northvale, NJ: Jason Aronson.

Davison, G. (1974). Presidential Address to the Eighth Annual Convention of the Association for the Advancement of Behavior Therapy. Chicago, IL. November 2.

Feldman, M. P., & MacCullough, M. (1971). *Homosexual behavior: Therapy and assessment.* Oxford: Pergamon Press.

Freud, S. (1905). Three contributions to a theory of sex. In A. A. Brill (Ed.), *The basic writings of Sigmund Freud.* New York: Random House.

Freund, K. (1977). Should homosexuality arouse therapeutic concern? *Journal of Homosexuality, 2*(3), 235–240.

Gartrell, N. K. (1994). Boundaries in lesbian therapist–client relationships. In B. Greene, & G. M. Herek (Eds.), *Lesbian and gay psychology: Theory, research, and clinical applications.* Thousand Oaks, CA: Sage Publications.

Gonsiorek, J. (Ed.), (1982). *Homosexuality & psychotherapy: A practitioner's handbook of affirmative models.* New York: Haworth Press (Previously published as a special issue of the *Journal of Homosexuality, 7*(2/3), 1981).

Gonsiorek, J. C. (1991). The empirical basis for the demise of the illness model of homosexuality. In J. C. Gonsiorek, & J. D. Weinrich (Eds.), *Homosexuality: Research implications for public policy* (pp. 115–136). Newbury Park, CA: Sage Publications.

Greenan, D. E., & Tunnell, G. (2003). *Couple therapy with gay men.* New York: The Guilford Press.

Halleck, S. L. (1971). *The politics of therapy.* New York: Science House Inc.

Hatterer, L. J. (1971). *Changing homosexuality in the male.* New York: Dell Publishing Co.

Heath, R. G. (1972). Pleasure and brain activity in man. *Journal of Nervous and Mental Diseases, 154*, 3–18.

Herek, G. M. (1984). Beyond homophobia: A social psychological perspective on the attitudes toward lesbians and gay men. *Journal of Homosexuality, 10*(1/2), 1–21.

Herek, G. M. (1986). On heterosexual masculinity: Some psychical consequences of the social construction of gender and sexuality. *American Behavioral Scientist, 29*(5), 563–577.

Herek, G. M. (1991). Stigma, prejudice, and violence against lesbians and gay men. In J. C. Gonsiorek, & J. D. Weinrich (Eds.), *Homosexuality: Research implications for public policy* (pp. 60–80). Newbury Park, CA: Sage Publications.

Hughes, C. H. (1914). An emasculated homo-sexual. His antecedent and post-operative life. *Alienist and Neurologist, 35,* 277–280.

Isay, R. (1993). The homosexual analyst: Clinical considerations. In C. Cornett (Ed.), *Affirmative dynamic psychotherapy with gay men.* Northdale, NJ: Jason Aronson.

Isay, R. (1996). *Becoming gay; The journey to self-acceptance.* New York: Pantheon Books.

Kosnik, A., Carroll, W., Cunningham, A., Modras, R., & Schulte, J. (1977). *Human sexuality: New directions in American Catholic thought. a study commissioned by the Catholic Theological Society of America.* New York: Paulist Press.

Leonard, A. (1997). Equal protection and lesbian and gay rights. In M. Duberman (Ed.), *A queer world: The center for lesbian and gay studies reader.* New York: New York University Press.

MacConaghy, N. (1969). Subjective and penile plethysmography responses following aversion-relief and apomorphine aversion therapy for homosexual impulses. *British Journal of Psychiatry, 11,* 723–730.

MacDonald, A. P., & Games, R. G. (1974). Some characteristics of those who hold positive and negative attitudes toward homosexuals. *Journal of Homosexuality, 1*(1), 9–28.

Malyon, A. K. (1982). Psychotherapeutic implications of internalized homophobia in gay men. *Journal of Homosexuality, 7*(2/3), 59–69.

Marquis, A. (2008). *The integral interview: A guide to comprehensive idiographic assessment in integral psychotherapy.* New York: Routledge.

Morrison, J. (2008). *The first interview* (3rd ed.). New York: The Guilford Press.

Peterson, J. L., & Hyde., J. S. (2010). A meta-analytic review of research on gender differences in sexuality, 1993–2007. *Psychological Bulletin, 136*(1), 21–38.

Rado, S. (1949). An adaptational view of sexual behavior. In P. Hoch & J. Zubin (Eds.), *Psychosexual development in health and disease* (pp. 159–189). New York: Grune & Stratton.

Rieber, I., & Sigusch, V. (1979). Guest editorial: Psychosurgery on sex offenders and sexual "deviants" in West Germany. *Archives of Sexual Behavior, 8,* 523–527.

Rivera, R. R. (1991). Sexual orientation and the law. In J. C. Gonsiorek & J. D Weinrich (Eds.), *Homosexuality: Research implications for public policy* (pp. 81–100). Newbury Park, CA: Sage Publications.

Rosenzweig, S., & Hoskins, R. G. (1941). A note on the ineffectiveness of sex-hormone medication in a case of pronounced homosexuality. *Psychosomatic Medicine, 3*(1), 87–89.

Ross, M. W. (Ed.), (1988). *The treatment of homosexuals with mental health disorders.* New York: Harrington Park Press (Originally published as *Journal of Homosexuality, 15*(1/2), 1988).

Schmidt, G. (1984). Allies and persecutors: Science and medicine in the homosexual issue. *Journal of Homosexuality, 10*(3/4), 127–140.

Schmidt, G., & Schorsch, E. (1981). Psychosurgery of sexually deviant patients: Review and analysis of new empirical findings. *Archives of Sexual Behavior, 10,* 301–323.

Shea, S. C. (1998). *Psychiatric interviewing: The art of understanding* (2nd ed.). Philadelphia, PA: Saunders.

Sigusch, V., Schorsch, E., Dannecker, M., & Schmidt, G. (1982). Guest editorial: Official statement by the German society for sex research (deutsche gesellscaft fur sexual-forschung e. V.) on the research of Prof. Dr. Guner Doerner on the subject of homosex-uality. *Archives of Sexual Behavior, 11*, 445−449.

Silverstein, C. (1976−1977). Even psychiatry can profit from its mistakes. *Journal of Homosexuality, 2*(2), 153−158.

Silverstein, C. (1991). *Gays, lesbians and their patients: Studies in psychotherapy.* New York: Norton.

Silverstein, C. (1996). The medical treatment of homosexuality. In R. Cabaj, & T. Stein (Eds.), *Textbook on homosexuality.* Washington, DC: American Psychiatric Association.

Silverstein, C. (1997). The origin of the gay psychotherapy movement. In M. Duberman (Ed.), *A queer world: The center for lesbian and gay studies reader.* New York: New York University Press.

Socarides, C. W. (1968). *The overt homosexual.* New York: Grune & Stratton.

Sullivan, H. S. (1954). *The psychiatric interview.* New York: W. W. Norton.

Stein, T. S. & Cohen, C. J. (Eds.), (1986). *Contemporary perspectives on psychotherapy with lesbians and ay men.* New York: Plenum Publishing Corporation.

Szasz, T. S. (1977). *The myth of mental illness.* New York: Harper & Row.

Tennent, G., Bancroft, J., & Cass, J. (1974). The control of deviant sexual behavior by drugs: A double-blind controlled study of penperidol, chlorpromazine and placebo. *Archives of Sexual Behavior, 3*, 261−271.

2 Scott's Interview (Transcript)

Charles Silverstein

Institute for Human Identity, New York, NY, USA

First contact: By phone saying that his HMO referred him. He was looking for a gay therapist and asked if I was gay. I told him that I was and he seemed satisfied by the answer. He said that he was dealing with the death of a gay brother who had died a few weeks before, and that he had never been in therapy before. His voice was strong and he spoke without hesitation. I asked if it would be all right if I recorded his session, and he quickly said that it was. He was very negotiable about setting a time for our initial interview even though he would be required to arrive at my office during the workday. When he arrived at my office door, he immediately extended his hand to shake mine, and smiled at me. I showed him to the waiting room and asked him to fill out my initial contact form.

The patient is a **30-year-old** gay man who is HIV negative. He is tall, thin, fashionably but casually dressed in jeans and a T-shirt. He works in a creative profession. He sat upright in his chair, seemed to be immediately comfortable even though this was his first serious attempt at psychotherapy. His voice was strong, his demeanor confident and assured. He looked at me when either of us talked and rarely needed to be prompted to explain something he said. He was unconcerned about the audio recorder in the room. His responses were bold, perhaps even brash at times, but never aggressive, and he made every attempt to form a therapeutic bond with me. At the end of the session, he once more initiated shaking my hand. He did not give the appearance of being depressed or defensive.

T = Therapist, P = Patient (**Bold** type represents identification changes)

T1: Have a seat here. I'm going to take a few notes while we talk. I know ??? you've never seen a therapist before.

P1: I did one time, back in like '95, '96. A long time ago. But it was just one shot.

T2: Say that again.

P2: I did once. 1995 or 1996, a one-time deal. And I never went back.

T3: Why didn't you go back?

P3: Ah, you know, I don't know. I didn't really like the guy I met with. I, um, just didn't bother.

T4: Why did you go?

The Initial Psychotherapy Interview. DOI: 10.1016/B978-0-12-385146-8.00002-X

P4: At that time, um, ——— I guess I was struggling with my sexuality, and there were some other things, my father, that were surfacing. Um. Just some kind of al, allegations, maybe. Of ah, molestation. **(1:16)**

T5: Of your being molested.

P5: Yea.

T6: By?

P6: By my father.

T7: By your father.

P7: But, ah, not molestation as in like, you know full-on, you know, ??? It wasn't like hard-core molestations. Sort of. Who knows? Whatever it was didn't feel comfortable. Like showering, bathing.

T8: That he would shower you?

P8: Yea. At an older age. Both my brother and I.

T9: When you say an older age, what do you mean?

P9: Oh! I mean I was, you know six, seven, eight probably by the time that it finally stopped. **(2:00)**

T10: And that's it.

P10: Why was that back then?

T11: Yea.

P11: That's why I went back then. It was, it was difficult because my brother was seeing a therapist at that time as well and said to him that maybe it was that my brother was gay as well and, um, the therapist had suggested that maybe it was us coming to terms with our own sexuality and that we were being put in an environment that made us feel uncomfortable, when it was actually very normal. But then the older I got I thought about that, I don't, I don't see that.

T12: (Interrupting) How much older is your brother?

P12: My brother was **two years older**. He passed away three weeks ago, which is why I'm here now.

T13: OK, we'll get back to this later. So tell me why you're here. Your brother is named ...? **(3:07)**

P13: My brother was **David**.

T14: **David.**

P14: Why am I here? Well you know there has been a lot of shit happened to me this year. It sucked and um, I've thought about going several times, and then most recently my, my brother died and so this is kind of like the last thing, OK. Because on top of grieving with my brother's loss, we were very, very close. Um, I had this fucked up, pardon my French, um but I curse a lot. Um.

T15: Curse away.

P15: On top of this, my brother's dying, I have this total screwed up relationship with my parents on top of it. Which makes the grieving process and the recovery process that much more difficult to deal with because it's just more complicated, when it shouldn't be. In my opinion it should be—I'm with my family. Maybe I lean on them more than they lean on me. I don't know, but it's not that way at all ??? **(4:10)**

T16: OK, let's take them one by one. Tell me about **David**.

P16: **David.**

T17: (Interrupting) Tell me how he died.

P17: **David** died from AIDS.

T18: AIDS.

P18: Yes. Ah, **David** was a sweetheart, my best friend in the world. And he was a **nurse**, very young, passionate about curing people, and working with people, and his partner of **eight** years, **Harry**, who I'm quite close to now, um is HIV positive. **David** is negative, or he thought he was negative, going into a relationship, and then when **David** told me that **Harry** was positive, and he was going to be in a relationship with him, I was kind of scared, not really behind him. **(5:05)**

T19: When did he tell you that?

P19: Right when he met **Harry**. It was, it was early in the relationship. It was like August of **2000**.

T20: So you've known for a number of years.

P20: I've known this throughout the whole relationship. And my parents didn't know until **David** tested false negative test, repeatedly. It's like 1 percent of the population that wasn't testing, wasn't showing the wasn't coming up positive. And then he got sick, got MRSA (*methicillin-resistant Staphylococcus aureus*). And something was not right here. And then he got over the MRSA, and then about a month, then we went to **Paris** together and then about two weeks after he got back from **Paris**, um, he got pneumonia, and he was misdiagnosed again at **St. Sebastian's Hospital**. He went home, he got progressively worse. And then one day he just passed out when he went to the bathroom. Rushed to the ER, to **Columbus Hospital**. And um ———— just a decline, a plateau for a while. He was kept stable, not really getting better, and about two weeks into being at the hospital, then one morning I was on my way to work, and I was going to stop at the hospital to see him before I went to work, and he had respiratory failure while I was with him. **(6:42)**

T21: And what?

P21: Respiratory failure while I was with him. And um, they brought him into ICU. Gave him a chemically induced coma ??? It seems like he was getting, they were doing desensitization of Bactrim to combat PCP. And um, then he got another infection from being on the ventilator for more than a week, another pneumonia and that was basically it. He died on **February 28**. **(7:15)**

T22: Were you there at the time?

P22: We were all there. My parents were there. I was there, my brother's partner was there.

T23: But what was that experience like for you?

P23: It was awful—I mean I lost my, my protector—he was my Number One. He wasn't just my brother. You know he was my ego. He was my Number One—he had so much love to give me. It was unconditional. It's been really difficult. Dealing with it or trying to deal with it as best I can and when I tend to grieve I tend to, I need alone time a lot—but there are times when I want to be with my parents to get that solace, comfort from them and they don't bring it. In fact they give the opposite. **(8:17)**

T24: In what way?

P24: They don't bring me comfort in the fact that—I have a lot of anger toward my father, especially because of, well the whole molestation thing which never sort of came to a head. Then in the hospital, my brother brought something else up that I never even knew about, which is so weird that in this time all of a sudden it comes out. And then there is this whole money side to it as well.

T25: Wait a minute. What did your brother say to you? **(8:55)**

P25: My brother said that when he was a young kid, my father took him to a gym and there was a basically a circle jerk. Do you know what a circle jerk is? Um, and he was in the middle of it. He said my father didn't participate in it. He wasn't there, he didn't think he was there.

T26: That your father? Who was in the middle?

P26: My brother.

T27: Your brother.

P27: And the guys were coming all over the place, and he was watching all of this, and I don't know where my father was, we didn't get fully into it because my brother's partner was out smoking a cigarette when he told me, and then he came back up and **David** didn't tell **Harry** that much about this whole thing because like I said, there is allegations, and we don't know what's right and what's wrong. It all came out about years ago. That's when I went to the shrink the first time. My brother brought up to my parents and it was just a nightmare reaction obviously—the denial— my mother denying it. That's a tangent. I forgot where I was going. Yes that's what kind of set things off for me for that. Anger toward that and then in and that never left throughout my teenage years and my twenties as well. And then, in **February**.

T28: Sorry, what lasted into your teenage years and your twenties? **(10:28)**

P28: My anger toward that and my not understanding it in its entirety and not knowing what it means and then having sort of anger toward my mother— her reaction when it all came out and not supporting her children and quickly going to his side, and not even hearing us out. So there's that and then there's, in **February**. My father's a shady person. Throughout his whole life . . . . **(11:05)**

T29: (Interrupting) I'm sorry, your father's what?

P29: A shady person.

T30: Shady.

P30: He got money issues. He's always had money issues. Can't keep his head afloat so he tends to get desperate and when he calls now. He's a gambler, he goes to Gamblers Anonymous is his most recent thing. But um, he'll open up credit cards in my name and sign away, and then I'll find out, you know when I come home from college, for example. I come home, I check the mail and then I'd find a **Euro Card** addressed to me. I don't own a **Euro Card**. That's weird. Open up and there's a credit card with a $6,000 balance on it. And that's happened my whole life, as long as I've been aware, as long as I've been able to have a credit card, he's had credit cards taken out in my name. And, you know, it's the same old process, I get angry, have a huge fight. He apologizes, I stay angry for two weeks, we get over it. I try and move on. But then this past June, it was the biggest one yet. I mean I'm **30 years old** and still the same crap. I have an apartment, I have a life here in **San Francisco** and I got—I got a phone call from a bill collector saying, "Is this **Scott**?" "Yes." "Are you aware of a **Diner's Club Card**, a corporate card, with a balance of $20,000 on it?" he said. "No." "Well I think your father has been presenting himself—or, or, um, acting like you. I've been speaking to someone who says that he was **Scott**, but I knew he didn't sound like a **30**-year-old man." Blah, Blah, blah, a long story, short. I did some more investigation and I find out there's a **Diner's Club**, the $20,000 balance that went to collection, obviously, and then there were two additional credit cards for a grand total of $30,000 that my father took out in my name. **(13:14)**

T31: He's swindling his children?

P31: Right. And I dealt with the pressure of what I wanted to say was, "Fuck you," and call the cops and send his ass off to jail which had happened one time before. Not on my part—(???) for something else he had done, signing **someone else's name** on checks, but I dealt with my brother who supported me with whatever, with whatever decision I wanted to do. But I had my mother and my mother I know she's not college educated. She, she'd be lost without him, financially. She'd be, she thinks she would be in shambles, while meanwhile she has friends that adore her that would take her in like that. It wouldn't be a problem. But I thought about it really long and hard, and it would have torn my family apart. It wasn't the right thing. I thought about the right thing to do. Thought, for the sake of my family. So, I hadn't seen my father for six months, that was in, right after Father's, actually a week after Father's Day I found out. And then I hadn't spoken to him. I was done, I was done. I was trying to work with my mother, see her off and on and I did see her twice—and then **David** got sick and then that was the first time I had seen my father, six months after he (David) was in the hospital. **(14:40)**

T32: (Interrupting) Where did they live?

P32: **San Francisco.**

T33: So how have you dealt with **David's** death?

P33: I mean it's one day at a time. I don't know how else to deal with it. I take it day by day and I have waves of—I got a tattoo with his name. (Patient shows me a tattoo with his brother's name on it.) That's strictly dealing with it. But it's just day by day. Some days I'm really emotional and then I have some days when I really put up a façade and I'm fine or I think I'm fine. But he never leaves, he's always here, he's always with me, thoughts always with me. I mean I miss him incredibly. How to deal with it, I don't know. I just feel like, you know it's a day by day thing. I'm here, I'm living, and I'm breathing. **(15:25)**

T34: What made your relationship with **David** so close?

P34: I mean beside the obvious is that we're both gay. Just kind of random. What are the odds that two kids in a family are gay? Very close in age and other similarities, taste in music and beliefs in this world and then, you know, just childhood. Struggles that we both dealt with, the molestation thing I think brought us closer. He dealt with money issues with my father as well. We always shared common friends. We just, we were lucky, we were really lucky. Be close, have so many similar interests. So much.

T35: When did you find out that you were gay? **(16:18)**

P35: I always knew, but um, **David**—I was just telling my friends last night. I was five years old and he was like seven or eight, and we would talk about having crushes on our counselors, our male counselors, but we knew to never talk about it beyond the two of us. So I always knew but I . . . .

T36: (Interrupting) Five?

P36: I was five and **David** was seven or eight.

T37: Seven or eight, and the two of you are talking about the crushes you have on camp counselors?

P37: Yea, at five years old. But I came out to **David** when I was 16 or 17, so I was a sophomore or junior in high school. And I came out to my parents when I was 17 and basically everyone else then.

T38: Are there any other children in the family? **(17:20)**

P38: No.

T39: What made you come out to **David**?

P39: You know, it was kind of we both knew without even our talking about it. Because we had spoken about it since we were little boys. We always knew. I think it happened because he had a friend visiting from **Los Angeles**. Who was staying with us, a gay guy, and I hooked up with him.

T40: You hooked up with him?

P40: I was kissing him in the back seat of the car while my brother was driving. So it was . . . .

T41: (Interrupting) Do you remember how old?

P41: I was 16 or 17.

T42: What a bold kid you were.

P42: Yea. Definitely. We were laughing about it, you know. Surprise, **David**, I'm gay, too, kind of thing. Oh! I knew it anyway. I knew you knew it, you know. It was very like sort of like whatever, casual, nonchalant. **(18:10)**

T43: Did you and **David** ever have sex?

P43: Never. I mean we played around, you know when we were prepubescent, you know, but never, never. Why did you ask this? People do ask that quite often actually.

T44: Pardon me?

P44: People ask that often when you find out that both **David** and I are gay, so that's a common question for straight people, at least—did you and your brother ever hook up? (Laughs)

T45: What made you come out to your parents at 17?

P45: I actually did not come out to my parents. **David** outed me to my parents. **David** was fighting with them, struggling with his sexuality. He'd been out for about a year, and it was his first year in college, and he's been struggling with his image of identity, with various things, and there was this big brawl. They're having ??? And somehow ??? I don't know how, how the conversation evolved and bringing me into the equation, but somehow I was brought into it and um! His explanation for telling them was that there was a rift in our relationship. You know, 17, angry teenager, hated my parents, alone and wanted my, you know be alone and not deal with them. I think as normal, any teenager at that point. But he felt like— his explanation was that he wanted to tell them because he wanted to bring us closer. I think the obvious explanation is more that it was just a deflection. He wanted to bring the spotlight off him. And say, I'm gay, but guess what? Well **Scott** is too, so deal with him now.

T46: Share the blame? **(20:00)**

P46: Exactly. And it's fine. I don't hold any anger or resentment toward that because I feel like had he not done it ???

T47: (Interrupting) So what was their reaction?

P47: Their reaction? They were fantastic.

T48: They what?

P48: Fantastic. They were very supportive. I mean they're Jewish so there was that Jewish guilt. You can see it in their eyes. They want to be supportive anyway, but they were really great. They fucked up with **David** and their reaction they had toward him when he came out. They made the corrections for me the younger child, so I have to say in that, in that respect, my parents have a lot of faults, but in that respect they've been really great. They really have. I had my ex-boyfriend they adored. They were very supportive then, whatever you want **Scott**, we love you, blah, blah, blah, kind of thing. It was, it was, really, really easy. I was so blessed to have such a good reaction. Easy reaction.

T49: By the way, what's your HIV status? **(21:05)**

P49: I'm negative. To my knowledge, although I am worried now because, you know, my brother . . . .

T50: Because of **David**?

P50: Right. Because he tested false negative for years. I mean I'm pretty safe but we all make mistakes. I had an HIV test recently. It came back negative, but at the same time I need to get, I guess a more thorough blood test to really investigate and my parents are saying the same thing to me as well, that I should, you know.

T51: Does your physician know the background about **David** and his testing negative?

P51: I don't really have a physician that ——— I trust him to some degree, but I went to him because I had a cough. ??? If I had an HIV test it was done at public ——— a clinic at **Fenway Clinic**. **(22:00)**

T52: So you're saying your physician who you cannot trust about your personal life.

P52: I mean I'm sure I could. I haven't yet. I haven't gone to him in that way yet. I've only seen him twice. I barely know the man. But I mean it wouldn't bother me. I know I need to do, I know I need to go, it's just flat out say what happened.

T53: It's interesting because when you called me on the telephone, you said to me very plainly and upfront that you wanted to see someone who's gay. I understand that. Now you tell me that you're not willing to see a physician who you can trust and tell anything you need to tell that would relate to your health.

P53: Well, there's a difference, because he's straight. The physician is straight and ??? it does make things more complicated. **(23:12)**

T54: OK.

P54: It's like, you know, everyone is human, doctors are human. It's not a judgment that I, that I know.

T55: Well you must be afraid that he'll look down on you in some way.

P55: Maybe, to a degree, but I'd get over that real quick. I mean, I'd talk to him, I will. I'm not opposed to talking to him. I just don't have a relationship to him. That's the thing.

T56: Um. Tell me about your coming out years. How did you come out sexually?

P56: What do you mean?

T57: Um. Well, you've already told me that by the age of around five you and your brother are talking about the cute counselors in camp. You told me that you started kissing another man when you were about 15 in the back seat of the car. Um. When was the first time you had sex with a man to orgasm?

P57: Um. Probably the same guy. He was the first guy. I wasn't 15. I was, oh .... **(24:22)**

T58: (Interrupting) Your brother's boyfriend?

P58: No. Not his boyfriend.

T59: His friend?

P59: Yea. Um. It was my junior year in high school so I was 16 or 17. The first guy I was with I did everything with, my first kiss with a guy, my first intercourse, my first everything was 17 years old. 16 or 17.

T60: How did that come about?

P60: He was aggressive. He was 22 and he was just persistent. And I was weak. (Laughs) I think. We were sitting next to him in the back of the car and one thing led to another—hand on the thighs, hand on the thigh and then leaning in—I'm sure he was stoned or drunk or both and I—we kissed and then kissed again and kissed again, and then that night—I knew it was going to happen. I went down to his room where he was staying. **(25:20)**

T61: Now where was this?

P61: It was my parents' house.

T62: At your parents' house.

P62: **David** was home on a break, a college break. It was summer I remember, and he had his friend from **Los Angeles** visiting, staying with us in the house. And that kind of stuff.

T63: And you went down to his room.

P63: I got to his room.

T64: Why?

P64: 'Cause I wanted, I wanted more with him. And I had more. A lot more.

T65: A lot more.

P65: Um hum.

T66: So what did you do that first night? You kissed?

P66: We had sex, we had oral sex, and anal sex.

T67: Both ways? **(26:00)**

P67: You mean did he fuck me?

T68: Yea.

P68: No.

T69: You fucked him. So that was the first time you ever did that?

P69: Yea.

T70: And when you went back to your room, did you feel good about it?

P70: Oh my God, yea, I'll never forget I had work the next day. I was just like glowing. My girlfriend who I worked with at the time like "You look really different." ??? Yea, I know like this was incredible. Because up to that point I had been hooking up with girls. Knowing that I was gay, just going through the motions of girls ??? feeling like I had to, when I knew I didn't want to. And I haven't turned back since.

T71: And did you continue to have sex with him?

P71: I think I slept with him maybe once or twice more. He was only in town for a couple of days.

T72: And then what about other experiences? **(27:00)**

P72: It was hard in high school because I wasn't fully out so it was in **San Francisco** so it wasn't like I had the city at times. I went out with **David** in gay clubs, gay bars, whatever. But it was probably awhile after that first one when I came on to a kid that was in my graduating class. And we were friends, and I always knew he was gay. And I came on to him and we had a little bit of a sexual romp in the car. Soon after that, the summer after that I had my first boyfriend, which I met through another.

T73: The summer after that would have been around 18 or so.

P73: It was the summer before my senior year.

T74: Tell me about that boyfriend.

P74: ??? He's super sweet.

T75: What was his name?

P75: **Terrance.**

T76: OK. When you say that he was your first boyfriend, what do you mean? **(28:00)**

P76: We were a monogamous relationship, seeing him several times a week. I cared for him, he cared for me. He even said I love you at one point. My first boyfriend. It was very brief, maybe two or three months before it was over. I was going to college, he was a couple of years younger than me. I didn't want to have a boyfriend, going into school. So, eh, I broke up with him. And he ended up going to the same university as me two years later. (Amused) ??? the chances of that one. He said, "Oh! I didn't know you were going to **San Francisco State**." I was like excuse me, you didn't know I was going to **San Francisco State**. I was with you the summer before I went to college and now you're at the same school. We're still pretty much friends at this point. **(29:00)**

T77: What are your other experiences with lovers?

P77: I've had two serious boyfriends. My first . . . .

T78: Two what?

P78: Two serious boyfriends. Monogamous relationships. My most recent was—I lived in **Paris** and met him working in **Paris**. I met him while I was working there. And I thought he was the one. And I was wrong. We were together for two years. I lived with him for about a year in **Paris**, and then we did long-distance—**Paris/San Francisco** for a year. I saw him pretty often 'cause he was quite romantic. It was great. And we talked about him moving to **San Francisco** or us moving some place together, to be together finally, and it ended up not working out. He had priorities, his career, he took a job in **Paris** instead of moving to **San Francisco**. I just—I work for **Modern Design Magazine.** **(30:00)**

T79: You work for what?

P79: **Modern Design Magazine.**

T80: **Modern Design Magazine**.

P80: So he knew the good jobs. "You really shouldn't quit that anyway. I have a good job in **Paris**. I want to take this job. You should stay where you are." He didn't even give me even the choice for me to make up my mind, and say what I want ???

T81: (Interrupting) He said stay where you are.

P81: Right. So I said look I'm not going to push myself. You don't want to give me the option, you give me the right to sacrifice my—I was only an assistant there. It wasn't that big a deal for me. But I wasn't going to push for it. So we broke up, but we're friends now. So it's okay.

T82: And you said another serious relationship.

P82: Prior to him was my, he's a good friend of mine now, as well—I love him to death, I love him more now than when I was with him. His name is **Howard**, and um, we met, I suppose it was my, my junior year at college. First semester. It was really sort of tricky for him because **his mother just had a heart attack**, so he was a little sort of emotionally unavailable. Um, but we love each other. Just a little bit awkward. And then I went to **Palermo** for a semester, and before I went, I broke up with him, because again I really, he started pushing, I didn't really want to have a boyfriend going—I didn't want to be obligated if I met someone to worry about things, so it was a mutual understanding.

T83: Where were you at the time? **(31:45)**

P83: **San Francisco State**.

T84: So there you were in **San Francisco**—there's a very big gay population down there, and you chose two guys who live in other continents.

P84: **Howard** I went to school with. He was there for a semester. And then, then he dropped out of school. He went back to New York and I went back to **Palermo**. So basically, yea, two different continents, and yea I know the trends. I see the pattern ??? I'm established. I know that I choose, I choose men, besides my relationship that are emotionally unavailable. They give themselves to a degree and then it stops, and that's what I'm attracted to. I've seen it time and time again. That's what I desire the most.

T85: You know what my next question is, don't you?

P85: What?

T86: If you seek guys that are unavailable, why do you do that? Why not some guy who is available? **(32:46)**

P86: I don't know. I don't know. I don't know. There's. I'm a big believer in passion. And having that attraction and having that desire, and I find often that when it's too easy when they're easy to obtain when they really go that extra mile to show they're there for me. Or they would be good for me. I don't like it. I like a struggle, I like ... Initially, I'm saying. Initially I like a struggle to get to that point where you get to know one another and you're with them and you love each other. And then it's a common understanding. I don't like that from the get-go when it's like, it's easy because it's boring. And I don't want to be bored. I want a good person, but I want a passionate person. I don't want just a passionate person, and I don't want just a good person. I want the two in one. **(33:48)**

T87: How long have you been in **San Francisco**?

P87: I've been living in the city now for about three years. I got back from **Paris** in **2005**. So I've been in **San Francisco** for three years.

T88: And what have you been doing here?

P88: I'm an **art director**.

T89: And what have you been doing sexually, slash romantically?

P89: Lately?

T90: Well in these three years.

P90: When I first moved to the city I had a lot of fun. I lived in **The Castro**. And I had a lot of fun. Very social and going out five nights a week, whatever it was. Hooking up with guys, but not. I've had a lot of sex (Laughs) I have to say. I had. I mean since my ex, he was really the first person with whom I had consistent anal sex with, so I think ever since him I enjoy it and I'm aware of it now.

T91: You're talking about fucking him?

P91: No, fucking me. **(35:00)**

T92: Uh, huh.

P92: So ever since him I really enjoy it and I kind of experimenting if you may, and having more fun and meeting with guys . . ..

T93: (Interrupting) What do you mean by I've had a lot of sex?

P93: It's all relative.

T94: Exactly, that's why I'm asking.

P94: I mean, prior to him I guess I had slept with maybe three or four guys, and since him the numbers tripled so probably somewhere in the teens. But it's the accessibility, I mean it's so much easier here. **San Francisco** is obviously one of the gayest cities in . . ..

T95: (Interrupting) Well when was the last time you had sex?

P95: I had sex last weekend. Last Friday night, which was the first time in about three months since the whole with my brother . . . I met this guy before, right before this shit happened with my brother. We had one good date which was sweet and I was as horny as hell, so I called him up and I went over his place ??? **(36:16)**

T96: (Interrupting) But you said that before last week you hadn't had sex for about three months.

P96: Three months.

T97: But your brother only died three weeks ago.

P97: Uh, huh.

T98: So you're saying that you had a lot of sex. This doesn't sound like a lot of sex.

P98: Well, prior to. My brother was in the hospital for a while. He was sick for a while, so, it was, maybe it wasn't about three months, maybe about two months, yea. I know I wasn't in a frame of mind to be you know, physical with anybody. I couldn't get this off my mind.

T99: I can understand that.

P99: I'm a very physical person, sexually speaking, so the release was something that I needed, I thought I needed to do last weekend. Sort of, get back in the way I am in my routine. **(37:06)**

T100: (Interrupting) How did you meet him?

P100: This guy?

T101: Yea.

P101: Um. In **Club Cafe**. Um. Valentine's Day. I was with two friends. After a concert, and he tapped me on the shoulder, started talking. And we went on a date, maybe two weeks after that. And the next time. And then the stuff happened with my brother and we were texting back and forth and keeping in touch, but I'd hadn't seen him. But I thought about him. And then I saw him last Friday. That's right ???

T102: (Long pause) Do you have any medical problems?

P102: Medical? Not that I know of. I have a bit of anxiety lately.

T103: I beg your pardon?

P103: Anxiety. ??? I'm having anxiety now.

T104: You're not?

P104: I do.

T105: Is that because of our interview?

P105: Maybe.

T106: Well you said this is the first time you've ever done this.

P106: Um.

T107: You understand something about anxiety. Um, what about your history of alcohol and recreational drugs?

P107: I'm a pot head. I smoke pot. Way too much. Almost every day. Um, I'm a drinker but I'm not an uncontrolled drinker, I don't love alcohol as much as I love marijuana. I drink often, ah, at least twice a week. But it's not, uh, I'm never, I'm very controlled, I'm never ....

T108: What do you like to drink?

P108: Whiskey, wine.

T109: You do that at home, you do that just going out?   **(40:00)**

P109: Both. I don't think anything wrong with having a drink or two by myself before I go out or if I'm going to stay home alone. Yea.

T110: Was **David** a drinker?

P110: Yea, yea. Definitely.

T111: And did he smoke pot?

P111: He did when we were teenagers. He stopped when he got into **nursing**. He was having anxiety issues, I think ??? he stopped. But he did other drugs.

T112: What other drugs did he do?

P112: Coke and ecstasy.

T113: Ex. And did you do any coke and ex?

P113: No. I mean I did in college, I did a lot in high school. I'm over it.

T114: Why do you think you smoke so much pot?

P114: I don't know. I love it, I mean I've been doing it since I was 13 years old. And, uh, there's something about it that numbs me, where I get dumb and I'm just able to mellow out, stop thinking, I, I, the thoughts, always have a lot of thoughts running through my head. I find it very, very difficult to quiet myself, to relax, and my mind's always racing. And marijuana is like the one thing that just stops everything.

T115: Well, what thoughts are racing through your mind if you're not smoking pot?   **(40:30)**

P115: I mean it's work-related of course. I have a stressful job. Or it's men. That fucking loser that I've been seeing. What their reactions mean. What does that mean? What does that movement mean? You know. Or it was mostly something about my brother. Or it was the drama with my parents. Money, and as a whole the molestation thing. ??? thoughts that kind of flood my mind and I smoke weed and then I'll put on the idiot box and watch some television and not, you know, think about it as much. **(41:18)**

T116: The drugs push the thoughts to the back of your mind.

P116: It can. It can. Sometimes it has the adverse effect where it's even worse, where my thoughts are even more stress. Where I'm lying in bed, stoned, trying to go to bed, and I can't pass out because I'm crazy thoughts, you know, even worse.

T117: Are either of your parents like that?

P117: Like?

T118: So anxious they . . . .

P118: (Interrupting) My mother probably is more similar to me.

T119: Tell me about your mother. You haven't said very much about her.

P119: I mean I love her to death, I do. I love my mother with all my heart. I mean, I, I'm going home tonight, strictly for her. Uh, I didn't call the cops because of my mother. I love her. But I have a lot of issues with her because she doesn't know her own self-worth. She has a very traditional 1950s frame of mind about a man and happiness, and him providing financially for her and what that means. And I don't understand that mentality. I don't get it. As contemporary as, as a gay male, I, I just don't understand a lot about that, and most recently my biggest issue with her now is her grieving process is so alien to me. I am visibly upset sometimes where I cry openly, or I'm just visibly upset. Which I guess if there is a more normal, normal whatever way of, of responding, she's not. And theirs . . ..

T120: (Interrupting) How does she act, **Scott**? **(43:20)**

P120: My father keeps, my father, my father's attitude toward her is stoic. And that's what he says. She carries on—it's a little bit of denial mixed with anger. She's angry toward **David** because of her, her not understanding why he would involve himself with someone who's HIV positive. Why he wouldn't be safe with someone who is HIV positive. Why he wasn't tested. Why, why, why, why, why. She asked, she asked me a thousand different questions. And for me, my issue now is, you know, I'm back, I'm back in the midst. I'm back in the family and seeing them, I saw them for a month straight in the hospital when I hadn't seen them for six months. After that $20,000 **Diner's Club** thing. And there's almost—she said to me that she . . . very open relationship. I tell her everything. I said, "I don't understand how you're reacting." She said, "**Scott**, neither do I. I said when, when, when the drama happened with your father in June, I was hysterical. I was thinking about killing myself. I was thinking about getting on medication. I couldn't stop crying." And now **David** dies and it's not that late, and, and I know what it is, I know it. It's, I'm back in the equation and I feel like I've always been the slight favorite of the two kids, and now that they have me back, its, maybe it's a distraction or, I don't know, but it's like they, they lost one son before, but now I'm back. They lost their other son in obviously a more profound way, but because they have me back, for her, she's—I don't know, I think she's fixated on my happiness, and my, happy that I'm back with them, when the reality is I'm

only there because I feel bad. I don't want to be there. I don't want to. I
don't. Every time my father hugs me, I cringe. You know, I want to pull
back. Pull away. Every time my mother tries to give me a hug or say
something comforting, it does completely the opposite. And then roles
reversed, and I become the doctor. I become the one that brings them
comfort, which I know that's my role now. I'm aware that the older you
get, your relationship changes with your parents, where you become the
parent and they become the children. I'm aware and that's why I'm
there. And there's anger, I have anger and resentment toward that, toward
her for not, for, for, so much. And underlying it all is love, I mean. I
love her. She's a good woman. And she's full of compassion. She's full of
love. I mean, she's, you know, she's a good woman, for the most part.
(46:33)

T121: A moment ago you were, you mentioned about safe sex. Do you have
safe sex?

P121: I mean, I, I'm pretty good, but I fucked up a lot, this past year.

T122: Meaning?

P122: Meaning I didn't have safe sex.

T123: Meaning you let guys fuck you without a condom?

P123: Right.

T124: Why would you do that?

P124: I don't know. Stupid. Stupid. There's no explanation for it.

T125: (Interrupting) Can I assume these are just tricks you're talking about?

P125: No, no. 'Cause like I say I'm risky but I'm not that risky. I mean, I must
say all of them, maybe four guys I slept with in the past year or two I slept
with without a condom. One of them was a one night thing, but in the
moment I caught myself and said okay stop, stop, stop. Put a condom on,
and he did. The other two or three guys were guys that I had been seeing
that I thought were going to move in a proper direction. And there's
something about intimacy, I think, I think that's what it is for me, that I
feel closer to them by losing that condom. And especially with this most
recent guy that, that I was hanging out with. I really liked him and I slept
with him the first night and he stayed for 72 hours, didn't leave. Really
liked each other. And I just, I don't know I—there's no excuses, there's no
explanation. **(48:18)**

T126: You stayed there for 72 hours and how many times did he fuck you
without a condom?

P126: I don't remember, I couldn't even say—four or five times.

T127: Four or five times.

P127: But I saw him—met him in November, October?

T128: What stopped you from seeing him?

P128: He's a douche bag.

T129: Huh?

P129: He's a douche bag. And I knew it. Not a good guy.

T130: What stopped you from saying, "Use a condom. Put it on."?

P130: I tried it. I tried it. I like sex without a condom. It's better. It is. I enjoy it
more. I mean maybe it's partially a physical thing. But, but it's a mental

thing too. You know. You, I never had unprotected sex until my ex-boyfriend, my most recent boyfriend, and, I loved it, you know I loved being that close to him and I feel that I'm looking for that again maybe. I want that closeness, I want that intimacy. And maybe it's just sort of, I'm seeking it—sought, it's the past tense, especially after this whole drama. I sought it in the wrong guy, in being unsafe with guys I, I thought were going to be something more significant than they were. The more time I spent with them, the more I realized you're not a good person. **(50:00)**

T131: What questions haven't I asked you? What things do you think I should know about you at this stage?

P131: Um. My levels of happiness. My levels of depression.

T132: So tell me.

P132: I feel manic. I mean thoughts of suicide run through my mind. Without a doubt.

T133: Thoughts of what?

P133: Suicide.

T134: Uh, huh.

P134: Went through my mind. And they really haven't been this strong since I was a teenager dealing with the whole molestation thing, which is why, also the reason why I went to the doctor ??? But there's also a lot of guilt when I—if someone had told me that my brother was going to die a year ago, I would have thought my reaction would have been to be hysterical and emotional basket case every day—and I'm not. I mean Sunday was miserable, I had a horrible Sunday. I had a horrible Monday. Tuesday, Wednesday, Thursday, no tears. I guess the thoughts are there but I went to a little drinking after work yesterday and I mean it's not that I'm not thinking about him, but he's always there, but—I don't know. I'm not happy in more ways than one. And I want to be happy. (Laughs) **(51:41)**

T135: Let me sum up a couple of things. You've told me about the death of your brother and how hard it's been for you and that you want to be able to find a way to grieve for **David's** death and move on. You told me that your father's possibly molesting you and **David** and about his swindling money from you and God knows who else. And the ambivalent feelings you have toward your family. You told me that you also choose the wrong guy as a boyfriend. And you want to change that. It's interesting that the one thing you didn't say although it's sort of implied and that you really would like to find a boyfriend and settle down with him. Is that something you want? **(53:00)**

P135: Of course I would. I would love it. Who wouldn't? Without a doubt. It would settle me in so many different ways. But I also know that the more you want it the more you're not going to find it—the more you look for it the more you're not going to find it.

T136: OK. Are there any questions you want to ask me?

P136: What's a sexologist?

T137: What is a sexologist?

P137: Kinsey is a sexologist?

T138: Pardon? Is Kinsey a sexologist? Well, not anymore, he's dead.

P138: (Laughs)

T139: You don't know anything about me?

P139: I have to say no. I didn't really do my homework. I got recommendations and I went with you primarily because you're gay.

T140: I've been working with gay people for over thirty years; I've published six books about gay life. I'll give you my card, it has my website. You can look on my website. Google me, get all the dirt you want on me. People who have a lot of difficulties with sex, sexual dysfunctions, but by and large my practice is with gay men with all the variety of problems that they have. **(54:25)**

P140: Well, I'm in the right place then, aren't I?

T141: Let's make an appointment.

P141: OK.

T142: What are your best hours? Let's see if we can get a match here.

P142: You have no weekend hours, right? **(55:00)**

T143: No.

P143: I mean I work Monday through Friday and my hours are a little crazy. So . . . .

T144: I can see you at six o'clock on Tuesday.

P144: This Tuesday? What is that, the date?

T145: Tuesday—next Tuesday would be the eighth.

P145: That should be fine. Could we do 6:30 instead?

T146: No. Because I see someone at seven.

P146: You know what doctor—can I run. Can I call you doctor? Is that what I call you?

T147: Pardon me?

P147: Can I call you doctor?

T148: Or Charles, either one will do.

P148: What do you prefer? **(56:00)**

T149: Hum?

P149: What do you prefer?

T150: Charles.

P150: Can I get my calendar? (Goes to waiting room to get calendar.) Tuesdays, right?

T151: Yes, eight o'clock—I mean Tuesday the eighth at six P.M. Here's my card.

P151: That should be fine, then.

T152: I'll check with—do you know what the co-pay is?

P152: The thing is, I was told through this agency, whatever, employee assistance program that my first eight sessions are entirely covered. And then after that is when my co-pay . . . . **(57:03)**

T153: (Interrupting) This would be an EAP.

P153: Right.

T154: OK. Let me check with them and I'll find out.

P154: OK.

T155: OK. So I'll see you next Tuesday.

P155: Sounds good.

T156: OK. Ah, and next week when you ring my bell outside my office, I'll just buzz you in.

P156: OK.

T157: I won't meet you at the door next time.

P157: Only the first time you get special treatment?

T158: Only the first time you get special treatment.

P158: (Laughs) You can't do that. After that you let yourself in—OK. Well, thank you Charles.

T159: You're welcome. I'll see you next time.

P159: I just unloaded my **30** years of existence on you. Thank you. Have a good day.

T160: You too.

3 The Initial Psychotherapy Interview

Charles Silverstein

Institute for Human Identity, New York, NY, USA

This chapter is divided into two sections. In the first section, I will discuss the procedure of the initial interview, such as greeting the client, gathering information, and the closing. This first section will be somewhat structured because there are important legal and institutional requirements to be fulfilled in addition to gathering information in preparation for psychotherapy or the other forms of treatment covered in this book. The second and longer section will discuss the dynamics of the interview, and especially the relationship between the therapist and her or his client. It is in this second section that my therapeutic bias will be most apparent. While no means an adherent to psychoanalysis, I approach psychotherapy from a psychodynamic point of view, but with a directness that I learned in Gestalt therapy from Laura Perls, and sex therapy with Helen Singer Kaplan. A therapist using a Gestalt or sex-therapy approach is an active participant in the dialogue between patient and therapist. One might argue that much of the discussion in the second section about client—therapist interactions is not of immediate relevance to the initial interview, and to some extent that is true. However, the staff member doing only initial interviews now will inevitably be assigned to work in either short- or long-term psychotherapy, and most therapists in private practice do not distinguish between the initial interview and subsequent psychotherapy. But first, in order for us to have a framework for evaluating the process, let us list the primary goals of the initial interview.

Goals of the Initial Psychotherapy Interview

1. To direct the client to the proper level of care or treatment modality. She or he may need to see a psychopharmacologist, or any of a number of community-based self-help groups.
2. Evaluate the person's suitability for individual, couple, or group psychotherapy.
3. Establish whether the presenting problems are externally caused (such as losing a job) or characterological (such as always pushing loved ones away).
4. Determine whether your clinic (or you if you are in private practice) has the capability of treating this person, and if not, refer the client to a colleague or institution that can adequately serve the patient's needs.

The Initial Psychotherapy Interview. DOI: 10.1016/B978-0-12-385146-8.00003-1

5. Determine whether the client has the financial means to pay for treatment.
6. Write a report or treatment plan that will summarize the findings, identify a diagnosis, and make recommendations for future therapy.

Mental health professionals begin training as either externs or interns at a clinic or hospital associated with their graduate institution. Each of these public clinics or hospitals has a procedure for assigning applicants to an intake counselor, a specific form to be completed during the interview, and a written report summarizing the information and observations by the counselor. Afterward, a supervisor may review the report for completeness, accuracy, writing style, and its timely submission.

Institutions have different intake forms based upon their experience with their patient populations. A drug rehabilitation clinic in New York City, for instance, has a different intake form than, say, a community mental health center in the Midwest, and different still than a mental hospital that serves psychotic and suicidal patients. That is why there is no universal intake form for all mental health professionals to use. Private practice varies even more. The private practitioner has her or his own focus, or the form exists as much in his or her head as it does on paper, learned from many years of experience. Private practitioners, however, are usually not required to write a summary report in addition to their notes, unless she or he is being supervised for licensing.

But when does the interview begin? It is when the interviewer learns that she or he has been given the assignment. There is often preliminary information available, such as name, demographic information, and perhaps a referring source. While we will discuss these written documents later in more detail, by reading whatever information is available, the interviewer may have a reaction to the patient's name, gender, age, sexual orientation, and many other factors that can influence the course of the interview.

The Greeting

A client arriving for her or his first session is usually anxious, and the greeting counselor can alleviate this discomfort with a warm welcome in the waiting room. A simple smile goes a long way toward communicating the office as a comforting environment. This is the first step in making a patient feel safe. You should introduce yourself, shake hands, and make certain that the applicant knows where to put his or her coat. "Please come with me," or something similar might be your next statement as you walk together to the interviewing room. You should tell your client where to sit, even if the choice is obvious. These simple statements carry a meta-message that you are in control of the process and know what you are doing (even if you are new at it and scared to death). It tells the person that you are cognizant of the structure and procedure for the next hour, and that you can be relied upon as a professional. Even though all these points may seem obvious, it is important to state them here because they relieve anxiety in the patient.

How should you address your client, and how should she or he address you? This can be answered only on the basis of how formal or informal you choose to be. Most clinics and hospitals use a more formal structure than private practice therapists, although there is considerable overlap between these two venues. In my practice, I ask the patient. For instance, if Mr. James Jones has arrived at my office, I will ask, "Would you prefer that I call you James, Jim, or Mr. Jones?" In four decades of practice, I have never had someone respond, "Mr., please." Informality is comforting to most people, but severely pathological patients may become highly anxious with it. In that case, I suggest formality until you have a chance to complete the interview. Notice that "James" and "Jim" are not the same and that they each carry information about the person, although you will not understand their differential implications until after the interview, if at all.

"What's good for the goose is good for the gander," is appropriate as a response to your question of how to address your patient. Some clients will immediately respond, "How should I address you?" The question is both a search for information on the patient's part and a meta-message that he or she requests a more democratic, less power differential in the room than one usually finds in traditional doctor–patient relationships. It also demonstrates that the client is an assertive person, but do not confuse assertiveness with aggression. It would be too soon to understand whether the question signals an increased or decreased probability of rapport, but you should keep this assertiveness in the back of your mind as you continue, as it will assist you in the process of hypothesis building.

I generally answer by saying, "It's up to you. Either Doctor or Charles is okay with me." Almost invariably they choose to call me "Charles." On rare occasions, it will be "Charlie," the more familiar form of Charles. Like James and Jim, Charles and Charlie are not the same, and their choice carries another meta-message, although once again it may be too early to understand the implications.

Many patients will not ask. Since I introduced myself as Dr. Silverstein at the door or in the waiting room, they will use my title rather than a familiar form of my name. That too is informative and sometimes diagnostic. Under no circumstances would I suggest the familiar "Charles." Doing so would be an intrusion upon her or his psychological world at an early phase of the interview and could affect its progress.[1]

What if a patient asks who you are? The question is sometimes directed toward students, especially if they are considerably younger than the applicant. Some students on an internship or externship get flustered by the question, and begin their response by hemming and hewing, thereby signaling insecurity and defensiveness. A more comforting response to the question would be a simple and accurate statement of who you are and what your status is at the institution, such as, "I'm a graduate student in social work/psychology, assigned to work here as part of my training." You might add something about supervision if you like, but that isn't necessary unless the client asks about it, or if your state board requires that you disclose it proactively. Then go on with the interview. Adding

---

[1] See Nichols, Chapter 4 for a different approach to the therapist's introduction.

more information than required is a further sign of insecurity. It is defensive, as if one must garner additional arguments to support the interviewer's right to conduct the session.

One basic principle at this point, and throughout the interview, is to use the patient's name often (but not excessively). Because he or she does not know the process of assigning someone to a psychotherapist, this is the place to clarify it. Explain your role, what both of you will be talking about, and what happens after she or he leaves at the conclusion of the interview. This is a very important step because patients will gain an understanding of the time frame required before she or he will be assigned to a therapist *and* who will be calling to arrange for the meeting. (In the best of all possible worlds, you will be the person making the call because the client's primary contact was with you. Clinics and hospitals have their own procedures, however, and your contact with the client may end at the termination of the initial interview.) I suggest following that by asking if he or she understands this process, and if not, to repeat it, and to make a note about the need for repetition in your report.

The Problem(s)

"Well, Mr. Smith, what brings you here today?" is the way many experienced therapists begin, although there are many other opening statements that serve the same purpose. I generally start writing my notes as soon as she or he begins speaking. Some authorities suggest asking for permission. I would not do so because state laws require written notes and you will be in a quandary if your patient responds to your offer by saying "no." While that might be a useful diagnostic sign, it will not help you get the required information on paper. You will have to follow your institution's intake form from this point onward. Avoid closed-ended questions. These can be answered by either yes or no, divulging little information. Open-ended questions are far more informative.

Note-taking can sometimes be a problem, insofar as you will be looking down at your notes rather than at the patient. Remember to stop writing from time to time and look at him or her, especially if she or he expresses some deeply felt emotions. Some clinicians argue against note-taking at all. They suggest that notes should be written after the client leaves, so that the clinician can focus on the person, not the notes. I am sympathetic to their request, as I notice that my contact with the client changes when I am or am not taking notes. Still, it is only the initial interview, not psychotherapy, and the requirements of the clinic and the law may demand that you sacrifice some rapport in order to conform to clinic and state regulations.

The client is likely to respond to the question "What brings you here?" with a specific complaint. After you have listened to it and inquired as to its history, and its effects upon the client's life, I would follow that by asking, "Are there any other problems you need to resolve in psychotherapy?" Some patients have only one, while others have a laundry list.

The Closing

It is good technique to let the patient know when only a few minutes are left to complete the intake session. This is another important characteristic of creating boundaries during the interview. While this will not be of importance to most applicants, it will be very helpful to those clients who suffer from an anxiety disorder. That is the perfect time to sum up what you have learned about her or him and to restate what his or her goals are in seeking psychotherapy. This summary is usually important to patients because it demonstrates that she or he has been heard and understood, and it will encourage the applicant to return for treatment. It is another way to build trust between the patient and the institution or therapist. I suggest ending the session by asking if he or she has any questions. This, too, is important in building confidence in the institution or the therapist in private practice. I would end the session by thanking the client for coming in, showing her or him back to the waiting room, shaking hands again, and saying good-bye. There is one caveat to the preceding statement about shaking hands and saying good-bye. The interviewer should gauge whether the client is comfortable with physical contact. It may simply be too intimate a gesture for some people. If you judge this to be the case, I suggest being more formal in closing the interview. We do not help our clients by scaring them.

The Dynamics of the Interview

Let us step back for a minute and ask a basic question. Why hold a face-to-face initial interview at all? In previous generations, a patient was shy about confiding personal feelings and behavior. Things are different now. Consider those people who appear on national television to ask for help in front of a TV audience of millions, shedding any number of personal problems: infidelity in a marriage, children prostituting themselves, or sexual incompatibility. Even that pales in significance to the ubiquitous use of "profiles" on the Internet. It is now commonplace for some people to upload naked pictures of themselves, advertise the measurement of their genitals, and explicitly request that a potential sex partner do some very juicy things with their bodies. Genital erections, naked butts, shaved testicles in men, and metal rings through the nipples in women are at least as personal as a therapist asking, "What brings you here today?" And up-to-date cell phones (in the hands of up-to-date people) now allow a couple (or more) to instantly transmit electronic pictures of their sexual liaisons to a list of people in real time—whether they asked for it or not. "Tweens" and teenagers are now "sexting" by cell phone, a process in which they photograph their naked bodies and transmit the pictures electronically to friends, unconcerned that those friends may forward the pictures to a different set of friends, and so on. Many of them appear to be unaware that these photographs may return to haunt them in the future.

Given the Internet's penchant for moving the boundaries of the "personal" far beyond what one would have imagined only a few years ago, why not get rid of the face-to-face initial interview? We might devise a carefully constructed online questionnaire instead. We could even have them pay for the online questionnaire by use of a credit card or PayPal. This procedure would have the advantage of not taxing professional time, while providing certainty that we have the information required in order to assign the person to a therapist and that the fee has been paid. And an online questionnaire does not have feelings and reactions as we human do that might muck up the interview. It is also true that some people are far less anxious (even more honest) completing an online questionnaire than in a face-to-face meeting. This is not as outrageous as it may seem, as there are already reports of psychotherapy being conducted on the Internet and via email, although the ethical issues of this venue of professional treatment has not yet been established by professional organizations.

How serious am I about using an online questionnaire as a substitute for the initial interview? The suggestion is partly serious because cell phones, Blackberrys, and emails are now ubiquitous in society. Most people—certainly younger generations—commonly transmit serious and personal information electronically. Most would acquiesce to filling out an online questionnaire as long as they felt that it would be helpful in their subsequent psychotherapy, and that electronic confidentiality would be maintained. There is no reason why an institution could not design a questionnaire to be completed before the interview. We should not, however, confuse a questionnaire's usefulness in collecting data with what we can learn from a face-to-face encounter.

Using an online questionnaire would be perfect for those who believe that the singular goal of an initial interview is the collection of data—facts in the life of a prospective patient. It is not. Facts are sometimes misleading. To illustrate what I mean, consider the following factual experience.

A 9-year-old boy is in the company of a trusted adult family friend. Without warning, the family friend takes down the boy's pants and starts to fondle him. Is this event a sign of psychological trauma? (It can even be noted under "Traumatic Experiences" in the online questionnaire.) But it may be insignificant to the boy's psychological development, since we do not yet know how he felt about it, or how he responded. Let us continue: the 9-year-old boy wrenches himself away, pulls up his pants and runs out of the room. Is that relevant? Maybe, but we still do not know. While we should document these facts, their significance remains elusive. The impatient therapist may already be diagnosing sexual abuse, a hasty and incorrect assumption. (The online questionnaire could even account for this action through the use of conditional questions.) The boy, obeying his parents' frequent instructions, runs to them and reports the abuse. They do not believe him; they call him a liar. I state again that these facts are, *by themselves*, meaningless for the purpose of the initial interview, and for its subsequent psychotherapy.

The boy, now actually over 30 years old, tells this story communicating a sense of pain that is touching to witness. But he is not angry or resentful toward the child abuser. He cries because he feels betrayed by his parents. The boy followed their rules and they punished him for it.

What the online questionnaire cannot do, but what we professionals must, is to find *meaning* in these stories. For this 9-year-old boy, the meaning of the event is betrayal and abandonment by his parents, not the attempted sexual abuse. A child's home must be a place of safety. It was not for this boy; it was a place of danger. He never saw the sexual abuser again, but every day woke up at home and worried about pleasing his parents, and from there to pleasing other parent substitutes in his life.

That is what we mental health professionals do. We look for meaning in a patient's life. The facts are like train stations on a railroad, and we travel along with our clients to the last stop in order to understand their emotional world; to learn where the train ends—the place of personal meaning. It is constructed by feelings and memories and seldom do any two people feel the same about a similar event. A different 9-year-old, for instance, who was not trying to be a good boy might have run away as well, but knew not to report the incident. For that child, the sexual advance might have taken on the greater trauma. (See Gonsiorek, Chapter 8 for more information about sexual abuse.)

Finding the emotional content of a person's experience is something that a questionnaire cannot do because meaning requires a level of communication between two people that the written or electronic word cannot convey. While questionnaires may be helpful in an evaluative and diagnostic sense, they are not useful for the process of psychotherapy. Only a human being with the capacity for empathy can do that. That is what we try to do. This is often called the "therapeutic alliance," and it begins during the face-to-face initial interview. The therapeutic alliance starts there because it is the patient's only experience with the therapist or the institution. It will probably influence whether she or he returns.

The Client and the Therapist

Good technical skills on the part of an interviewer are necessary, but not sufficient in order to conduct the interview competently. One also has to appreciate the emotional vulnerability of a patient who applies for treatment. Therapists-in-training should understand that compassion and an inviting environment are crucial in the consulting room, not only for the patient but, as you will see, for the therapist as well.

There is an implicit power differential between client and professional that influences the communication between them during the initial interview. The client has already admitted defeat. He or she has not been able to solve the problems, and friends are probably tired of listening about them. These clients go to the doctor, who, they believe, can set them on the right path toward happiness. They may or may not know the origin of their conflicts; they may center their problems internally, thinking they did it to themselves, or they may see the problems as externally caused—people out there did them in. But they arrive to be helped and believe that the therapist has the requisite knowledge and ability to heal their pain. They are, therefore, in an inferior position, vis-à-vis power. They also, as in their home of origin, want to please the therapist and be considered a "good patient," a slight displacement from being a good girl or boy, like the previously mentioned 9-year-old boy. In fact, they might be more intelligent, better educated, have a finer cultural background, make more money, and ultimately make a greater contribution to society and the common good than the therapist, but these strengths are subservient to their current feelings of helplessness and failure.

The professional who enters the consulting room and conducts the initial interview has superior status. He or she is the wise one, the healer, knowing what questions to ask, why they are important, and exactly what the answers mean. At least that is what the client falsely believes. It is hoped that the therapist knows that she or he is as vulnerable as the client, lest the therapy become, at the least an exercise in futility, and at the worst, an emotional sado-masochistic relationship. But the interviewer also has expectations. Just as the client wants to be a good patient, the interviewer wants to be perceived as "good." She or he wants to be liked by the client just as she or he wanted to be loved by her or his own parents. Client and therapist, therefore, mirror one another's expectations. While the patient suffers from problems of transference, the therapist suffers from a corresponding counter-transference. *That is what happens when everyone is trying to be good!* This is, therefore, a rather complicated and potentially messy process. How the seasoned interviewer wishes that his or her job could be as easy as checking off responses on a structured questionnaire. Later in this chapter, we will talk about what I call the "gremlins" of the interview, ways in which the personality of the interviewer and her or his feelings and behaviors can influence that of the interviewee. These gremlins keep under cover when conducting a highly structured interview, but they may become energized during unstructured ones.

Transference and Counter-Transference

We should spend more time discussing the concept of counter-transference, especially since its meaning has changed over the years. It began with Freud's observation that his patients often perceived him in the same way as they perceived their parents, and attributed to him the same characteristics that once again belonged to the parents, not to him (Freud, 1905). He believed that this false attribution process was unconscious, and he called it "transference," meaning transferring attributions from the parents to him, the psychoanalyst. Freud further suggested that the therapist could also transfer her or his own unresolved parental conflicts to his or her patients, and he called that process, "counter-transference." To him, not only were these misperceptions unconscious, but they were limited only to unresolved parental conflicts, and occurred only between the analyst and the patient. They were not reality based, meaning that a person's experiences in life, beyond early childhood, were not part of the process. A major goal of psychoanalysis, therefore, was to correct these perceptions of both the parents and the psychoanalyst.

A half-century later, Sullivan argued that both transference and counter-transference were the same thing, and he combined them into the term "parataxic distortion" (Sullivan, 1953). He further suggested that other experiences in life beyond childhood could also result in misperception by the patient or the therapist. In his theory, other problems of living, even in adulthood, could cause perceptual distortion, so that, for instance, a woman who had been sexually molested by a man might feel discomfort with a male therapist for no other reason than his being a man.

Sullivan's theory represented a major theoretical advance in the field of psychotherapy for two reasons. First, he suggested that there were not two forms of these misperceptions, transference and counter-transference, but only one and that both parties could contribute to it. Although this reasoning may seem obvious to the modern mental health practitioner, it represented a major advance in theory and practice. The psychoanalyst lost some of her or his esteemed status.

The second implication of the term parataxic distortion was the rejection of early childhood experience with the parents as the only origin of parataxic distortion. While unresolved parental conflicts still held an honored position in his theory, he suggested that other internal neurotic conflicts could just as easily result in these therapeutic distortions. Sullivan's theory helped to open psychoanalytic practice, which had previously been stuffy with an over-reliance on early childhood, to the recognition that experiences throughout life could morph into these misperceptions in the consulting room.

The concept of parataxic distortion, together with alternative theories about human development, opened the door of psychological treatment even further. Today its definition is very broad. If we look at patient–therapist interactions, we find that our behavior during the interview can profoundly influence the behavior of the patient during the interview, particularly when it is unstructured. Although I will consistently use the term "counter-transference" in this chapter, I mean it to represent the therapist's feelings and reactions in this broader sense, rather than the confined notion of Freud.

When I talk with interns at the Institute for Human Identity, an LGBT counseling center in New York City, I always tell them that, "Being a therapist is hazardous to your mental health." I mean this statement as a reflection of the problems of transference and counter-transference in the consulting room. It is not true that there are only two people present during an initial interview or at the therapy to follow. The room is metaphorically filled with people—it is standing room only—although a camera would capture only the two of them. The others are ghosts, past and present, dead and alive who hover in the air above. They are our memories and feelings of events in our lives that have meaning, people who we loved or did not, or who loved us or did not. They are feelings about our successes and our failures, aspirations met or lost, sexual liaisons good and bad, people who died, lovers, parents, friends—all those who we experienced as harming or abandoning us. And, oh yes, we must consider our spontaneous feelings toward that new person sitting across from us, even though we hardly know him or her. The person in the other chair can evoke feelings of love, hate, anger, fear, jealousy, rage, sexual desire, envy—and all of these before she or he says a word! What other feelings might emerge in us afterward? And what do I do with them? I mean my feelings as the professional. He or she has an excuse for these feelings: the flip side of a lower power position. But the person in power, the interviewer, has to remain strong, an impediment to one's need for empathy. Being good is such a bother!

I am suspicious of goodness in the consulting room, even my own. An interviewer's goodness is sometimes a veneer for manipulation, to make the guy like me for whatever needs there are in my psyche; to feel loved because I believe that my parents did not; to make her need me because I feel useless; to keep him in my practice because of the attractive bulge between his legs, or to hear intimate stories about another person's sexual adventures that are more exciting than my own.

Counter-Transference—Neurotic and Otherwise

The in-training mental health practitioner often asks if there is a sure-fire technique to prevent contaminating the interview with the therapist's own feelings. Yes, there is; leave the profession. Get a job selling stocks or become a professional skateboard rider. If you decide, on the other hand, to continue in our profession, then you will have to join the rest of us who make these errors every day. Do not believe a seasoned colleague who tells you that after years of experience you will not make mistakes. You will, and it is not all neurotic; it is often based upon common human experience. Consider the following: A college-age woman applies for psychotherapy because she was physically and sexually abused by a date who had given her an unknown drug beforehand. She wisely wants to deal with her rage. You might suspect that she may also have to deal with feelings of guilt, and you remember to suggest it in your written report. Presumably you, the interviewer, have your own feelings about physical abuse and the use of drugs during sexual encounters, perhaps even an opinion about an adult's responsibility to say "no." That is already a minefield of counter-transferential problems. But let us salt this interaction a bit more.

Assume that the same thing, or something like it, happened to you. Perhaps it was (unfortunately) during your first sexual experience, and being young and inexperienced, you had no idea what you were getting into. You trusted the nice guy who told you that it was okay to take the pills because "everyone is doing it," and you suffered physically and emotionally for believing his lies.

Won't you remember *your* traumatic experience while your interviewee is telling you about hers? If you try to be responsible and get her to describe her feelings, won't that reactivate feelings about how you felt? You might even see fleeting images in your "mind's eye" while your patient is talking. Only someone inhuman could listen to that story and not be affected by her or his own internal voice. That is not neurotic. There are many other examples of how a patient's experience may activate your own debilitating effect, such as a patient is deciding whether or not to have an abortion, or another who asks you to "cure" his homosexuality (Silverstein, 1977).

The Role of History

This is the time to talk about history and its place during the initial interview. Are a client's past experiences important? As I stated earlier, history per se is not relevant. What one needs to understand in the initial interview, and more so in the subsequent therapy, is to distinguish between the "past" and the "present-past." While this distinction is crucial for your patient's future (and your own for that matter), it is not an easy feat.

The previously mentioned 9-year-old boy experienced two historical events: being molested by the family friend and the actions of his parents. For him, the molestation is in the *past* because it no longer influences or controls his behavior. The actions of his parents, on the other hand, still haunt him, even though decades have passed. It made him more sensitive to issues of abandonment, real or imagined. From a psychodynamic point of view, it is the *present-past*. During the initial interview we attempt to identify historical events that still control the patient's behavior. We are looking for connections between past and present because we theorize that they will also influence the future.

Scott, the subject of this book, entered therapy in order to grieve for his dead older brother whom he deeply loved. Will he no longer grieve after a successful therapy? Is that what we do, take away the pain our patients experience? No, that is not what we do. We do not stop loving people because they died. Scott's pain is real, appropriate, and it always will be. (See Chapters 6 and 11 for a discussion of the normal grieving process.) Our goal in psychotherapy is to make it *past* so that it does not control his behavior in the future. The psychological danger for Scott is that the love for his idealized brother may become the standard upon which potential future lovers will be judged. They will not measure up; how could they against someone who is dead? That would be an example of the *present-past*, a serious impediment toward establishing an intimate long-standing relationship with another man, a goal he desires. But Scott is not going to give up his attachment to his brother any time soon, because doing so would intensify his feelings of abandonment and loneliness. An impatient therapist will drive Scott out of therapy if he moves too quickly here. Scott will determine when he is ready, not the therapist.

Distinguishing between past and present-past is a tall order for an interviewer at an initial interview. There simply is not enough time to track down all the leads in so short a period of time, especially since one also has to get information about the family, coming out, romantic relationships and marriage, drug and alcohol use, physical health, and more, all in an hour or less. And while taking legible notes! Still, there is wisdom in clinical intuition and the interviewer should make clear in his or her report, those historical events that appear to influence the client's current problems. Making a guess about cause–effect relationships will be helpful to the clinician to whom your client is assigned. Will you be wrong some of the time? Yes, but you will sharpen your clinical skills over time by thinking about these issues.

Some of the Gremlins of Interviewing[2]

Gremlin Number One: Identification

Our feelings as professionals often drag us toward counterproductive roads. There are times, for instance, when an interviewer identifies with the client. *Identification* occurs when your feelings merge with those of the patient, as if you are her or him. In contrast, to *empathize* means to feel compassion, while the psychological boundary between the two of you remains intact. To identify means that you have lost that boundary, and you will end up as conflicted as the person sitting in front of you.

Take this example: You interview a 17-year-old boy who tells the following story. A bunch of homophobic students attacked him after school. First they called him the usual pejorative names, such as "fag," or "cocksucker." Then four of them pushed your client to the ground and proceeded to stomp and punch him until he was bloody. No permanent physical damage was done, but the scene was witnessed by hundreds of other students who did nothing to stop the attack. Many of us have experienced the effects of gay bashing, or other forms of discrimination or racism, so it is inconceivable that an interviewer would not feel compassionate toward this young man. Identification with the client occurs when, after hearing this story, we try *to do something to make him feel better, as if it had happened to us.* One telltale clue of identification is that you ruminate about the incident in your head afterward.

What is the difference between expressing compassion for this young man and identifying with him? In the former I might say, "I feel awful because of what you endured," while in the latter I might say, "You should report this to the police," or even worse, "Why don't you ...?" (The theory behind a therapist expressing her or his own feelings during an interview is particularly well presented by Tunnell in Chapter 7.) This instinct to make people feel better is very strong in us; that is why we chose our profession rather than entering a more lucrative industry, such as finance, for example. There are at least two reasons "helping" the client is counterproductive: It takes away the responsibility of solving the problem by himself, and secondly tends to put a "halo" around his head that may interfere with identifying other self-made problems. We identify with the patient as a means to solve our

---

[2] I am indebted to Shea (1998) for suggesting the term "gremlins."

own problems. While the gremlin of identification shines on the "good" side of our counter-transferential feelings, there is a "bad" side as well.

Gremlin Number Two: Interviewer Punishment

We interviewers sometimes punish our clients during the course of an interview. That may sound absurd, but we do it frequently, only subtly, during the initial interview and more profoundly in the subsequent psychotherapy. It is something that we say or do during a counseling session that has the effect of decreasing the probability that our client will confide in us in the future—which can be as short as seconds and as long as the therapy continues. It inevitably leads to an interruption in empathy. This is a common form of counter-transference that ranges from the benign to the blatant. Because we are not irresponsible, we would not slap an interviewee in the face, although I admit that there have been times when I wanted to (see p. 58 this chapter). Nor would we (I hope) tell our interviewee that she or he is a selfish person who deserves his or her current misery, even when that opinion would be seconded by reasonable observers. We do not do these aggressive actions because we have been trained to express positive regard for a client; it would be unprofessional to do otherwise. Therefore, because we are responsible professionals, we may search for subtle ways to encourage clients to talk about what interests or titillates, and to prevent them from discussing topics that upset us. It is the preventing them from talking that I refer to as "punishment" Bandura (1969).

We usually succeed admirably. The average client at an initial interview is keenly aware of our reactions because they want to please us. It might begin this way: A woman mentions that her husband assaulted her during an argument. You ask a question or two, but then let the subject drop, telling yourself that you need other information for the intake form. That may be punishment. You have told this woman that you do not want to hear anything more about violence. It is a meta-message; not the words themselves, rather the underlying communication. We will come back to this later. She is not likely to bring up the subject again during the initial interview, which is forgivable in that context, but deadly in long-term psychotherapy, and even more so in briefer therapies because you have less time in which to recover from errors.

But we can do a better job at punishment. Let us assume that the woman was not assaulted by her husband, but confides that she had an affair with another man. Make her feel guilty; that will shut her up. Send the meta-message of, "Bad little girl, see what you have done?" The usual words out of our mouths are, "Why did you do that?" or, "Did you consider the consequences of your action?" An exceedingly poorly trained therapist might even say, "How do you think your husband will feel when he finds out about the affair?" That last question is a *good* (I like puns) one. You will not have to worry about hearing about an affair again during the initial interview, so you will not have to think about when your spouse (or you) "cheated." *Being the punishing parent works well; it shuts up the patient and gets our feelings off the hook.* I did it at least three times during my interview with Scott. Look at T124, T126, and T130. They are all about safe sex; they are about meaning in my life, not Scott's behavior. Might they refer to the people I loved and lost through AIDS in the 1980s and 1990s? Of course they do.

Here is a brief list of some ways we demonstrate our counter-transference by punishing the patient.

1. Ignoring what the patient says or changing the subject very quickly.
2. Changing the tone of our voice, particularly making it softer.
3. Changing our posture, particularly moving the upper body to convey aggression.
4. Making faces, snarling, rolling the eyes, or looking away.
5. Being parental.
6. Being particularly helpful.
7. Asking a lot of "why" questions.

There are so many impediments in the road to forming a therapeutic alliance during the initial interview and subsequent psychotherapy—so many ways in which the client touches a sensitive nerve in us or violates our sense of morality, social responsibility, or self-esteem. She might be an alcoholic or drug abuser on the verge of getting fired at work, might ask for a lower fee because he is saving up in order to spend the summer in Europe (instead of paying your fee), demand an appointment time that is not available, or tell you that therapy with you has been a failure. He might be HIV positive but refuse to divulge that to sex partners, or she might be a woman you find attractive and you do not want to end the interview. All these conditions may lead you to feelings of depression, guilt, or rage (or all of them), depending upon your unique psychological defenses.

The interviewer's challenge is not getting caught between the twin traps of identifying with, or punishing the client. I suggest that you not punish your interviewee because you could not stop your own trauma. It may be that you cannot work as this person's therapist. It is best to discuss that question with a trusted supervisor or consultant. We could mention other human experiences such as lovers who unilaterally end the relationship (often crudely), family members dying, being unfairly criticized by supervisors—an endless array of possibilities.

Gremlin Number Three: Interviewer Stress

We know that stress is emotionally harmful. Sometimes its effects are greater on the interviewer than on the interviewee. Stress can be either internally or externally caused. Examples of internal stresses are feelings of incompetence (or omnipotence) and emotional reactions to the interviewee. External stress can be created by being overwhelmed with responsibilities such as school and professional practice, disappointments or failures in life, family tragedies or disorder, and conflicts in one's own romantic life. Of course, these examples of internal and external stressors are not mutually exclusive. They are intimately entwined with one another, and the result is that the emotional needs of the interviewer may take precedence over those of the client.

Overpowering stress can sometimes lead a therapist to impulsive behavior, such as punishing a client for not solving her or his problems. At other times it can lead to unethical behavior. The formula goes like this: Stress $\Rightarrow$ Disinhibition $\Rightarrow$ Impulsive behavior. Let us use the example of sexual or romantic attraction as an example of this process. It would be remarkable if an interviewer never found a client romantically or sexually attractive. Occasionally, it is the patient who entices the therapist because that has been a cleverly honed technique of dealing with threat; he or she defends against anxiety by neutralizing the power of the therapist. It is the person's "insurance policy" that she or he will not be emotionally scarred by the experience. More often, however, it is the interviewer who "crosses the line," either by responding positively to romantic fantasies coming from the client or by initiating them.

We know that some psychotherapists, for instance, have had sex with one or more patients. We should talk a bit about that because in a lifetime of practice, each of us could find ourselves in that precarious place. What do we know about therapists who act out their sexual needs with clients? Gonsiorek (1995) informs us that, while such therapists are a diverse group, one of the most common subtypes is the therapist who is not different in training, experience, or competence than the rest of us. They are, in fact, colleagues who have always maintained ethical boundaries through decades of practice. What happens is this: They undergo the effects of significant stress in their lives that change their perception of the patient–therapist relationship. The stress may be some impediment or roadblock in one's own romantic relationships, or academic failures, or financial disaster. Whatever it is, the therapist becomes emotionally needy. While our ethics interpret this behavior as bad, and the law may punish it, the therapist fools himself or herself into believing that she or he does this in the interest of the patient. The Ethics Committee of the American Psychological Association (APA) receives complaints against psychologists for the violation of ethics. Over the years, 15–38 percent of these complaints have been for sexual misconduct by psychologists (American Psychologist, 1993, 1994, 2009).

One could argue that the chance of stepping over this professional boundary is virtually nil during an initial interview, but any student in training now conducting initial interviews will one day be assigned clients for short- or long-term psychotherapy. I think it wise to caution therapists-in-training about this hazard that would have long-term consequences on their careers. Both supervision and personal therapy for the practitioner who falls prey to this gremlin are mandatory.

We should talk a bit more about a therapist's sexual or romantic attraction to a client, because the erotic twitch felt by a therapist carries meaning far beyond those of lust. Elise (1991) has written perhaps the best paper on the experience and implications of erotic counter-transference. She elegantly describes how the process affected her work with clients; for example, "I have spent entire sessions with my hand against my mouth in order to 'hold my face together.' " (p. 64).

There are two variables that are important about a therapist's sexual and romantic impulses. The first is that of gender. In an unpublished study of therapist's sexual fantasies toward patients, I found that men and women had significantly different types of fantasies. Men's fantasies were graphical, genitally oriented, centered upon orgasm, and unconcerned about the feelings of the other person.

Women, on the other hand, generally had fantasies centered upon nurturance, were oriented in time and space, and expressed an egalitarianism seldom found in men's sexual fantasies. There was almost always a power differential in men's fantasies, but that was seldom the case with women. The implications of these findings is that male therapists are *more likely* than women to find themselves sexually attracted to their patients, while female therapists are *more likely* than men to be romantically attracted to their patients. Women therapists are, therefore, more likely to indulge in "rescue fantasies" than men. Of course, there is always overlap between the fantasies of men and women.

The second variable is more complicated. We are not romantically or sexually attracted equally to all of our patients. A sexual attraction, for instance, is not only physical, it is also a meshing of personalities between the two parties. It is likely that you find a certain personality more alluring than others; this is just a different way of saying that we all have our "types." It is often the case that the person toward whom we feel this affinity is also the one who has the physical features and the personality structure that we find most arousing. That situation contains an obvious danger, but it also contains useful clinical information about the client. It reflects some of our needs for affirmation, while at the same time, telling us something about the personality of our client. If, for instance, you are attracted to an emotionally dependent person, it may be a reflection of your need to take care of the person, to take him or her into your metaphorical arms and rescue her or him. Our romantic/sexual fantasies, therefore, give us clinical information about our client that can be useful in treatment, if only we examine their implications. While these attractions may be present during initial interviews, they represent therapeutic danger only in short- and long-term treatment.

Gremlin Number Four: Rescue Fantasies

Rescue fantasies can easily contaminate the initial interview. Exactly what is a rescue fantasy? There are two required components:

1. That you, the interviewer, know the correct solution to your client's problem. Let us say, for example, that your client complains of loneliness and depression. Your client claims not to have any friends and stays home every night (just to prove it). You believe (perhaps correctly) that if he or she participates in some activity, new friends will be found to alleviate her or his loneliness. You do not have to make this suggestion verbally, only that you believe it to be true. In all probability, you will likely convey your attitude through your questioning and nonverbal behavior.
2. That you, the interviewer, have an emotional investment in your client fulfilling your solution to the problem. You receive pleasure when your client finds friends and tells you about his or her change in attitude and reduction of loneliness. You feel a sense of competence when something positive happens, but a sense of failure when it does not. In other words, your self-esteem as a professional becomes dependent upon the behavior of your client. The operative words in this process are your dependency needs.

Therein lies the problem. Mr. Jones, our fictitious client who stays home, isn't likely to change his behavior very soon. That is okay for him because it is a well-practiced behavior. You, however, may experience a sense of failure and frustration, and you may react or retaliate in a way consistent with defensive mechanisms that you have practiced throughout your life. You may, as one example, internalize the frustration, turning it into depression and a feeling of incompetence. At the other extreme, you might externalize the problem, getting angry with Mr. Jones for not fulfilling the requirements of your wise counsel. I repeat—you do not actually have to say these things, only believe them to be true and to suffer emotionally for Mr. Jones' failure to improve his life. Some therapists can be rather heavy-handed in their reactions to someone like Mr. Jones, and retaliate by punishing the patient as a parent would a child. In that case, one's clients are likely to hide future transgressions. Who could blame them for doing so?

The question of rescue fantasies is a big dilemma for us. Consider that we decided to join the helping professions, not to enter the world of business and finance. We expressed an affinity for human rather than financial values. It is a fundamental contradiction for us to hold these values, yet not be invested in our patients' progress. That is why these fantasies are so common in us.

We should not be rigid about the dilemma of rescue fantasies. There may be times when good judgment and professional ethics require us to expose our values to our clients. I will mention a relevant example. During an initial interview of a gay man, I always ask whether he practices safe sex. I know that I want him to say, "Yes."

What if he says "No"? Suppose further that he tells me that he has no intention of practicing safe sex, saying, "The other guy has to take care of himself." He then throws more salt on my wound by telling me that he has anonymous sex many times a week! What is my responsibility? Ask your colleagues, and you will get a set of different answers, from saying and doing nothing to making safe sex part of the therapeutic contract. (See Theodore, Chapter 9, for information about HIV and barebacking.) It is not necessarily that one therapist is right and another is wrong; it is a conflict in values between them. My feeling toward this fictitious patient who does not have safe sex is predicated upon my experience living and working through the worst period of death from AIDS. I witnessed the deaths of many loved ones—and like all medical and nonmedical colleagues, could do nothing to stave it off. It is not necessarily an error of rescue fantasies if I comment upon his not having safe sex, even if I make it a requirement for psychotherapy (which I do not). But it is an intrusion of my value system into the treatment, and the consequence may be the loss of the therapeutic alliance, or even his terminating treatment. We should all have our values, but the rescue fantasy puts our emotional needs ahead of our patients; we become dependent upon them. An old school chum of mine has this saying: "Whenever you feel you have to say something—don't." These are questions to discuss with supervisors and your own therapists.

Gremlin Number Five: Self-Disclosure

If this book had been written 10 years ago, a discussion of self-disclosure would have been relatively straightforward. There is a professional principle involved; it is the ethical requirements of every professional group to distinguish between a practitioner's professional and private lives (see American Counseling Association, 2005; American Psychiatric Association, 2001; American Psychological Association, 2002; National Association of Social Workers, 2008). All these professional groups identify which behaviors on the part of the practitioner conform or violate their ethical standards. They also specifically state that these ethical requirements do not apply to one's private life. Pipes, Holstein, and Aguirre (2005) state this distinction clearly (and colorfully) when comparing a practitioner's private life as compared with her or his professional one.

> *Outside their roles as psychologists, they may ... break confidences, be verbally*
> *abusive to their romantic partners, lie to their friends, evaluate others unfairly,*
> *and generally act like a louse. (p. 326)*

The question of self-disclosure was never a problem in the old rigid days of Freudian psychoanalysis. The neat inviolate rule was never to disclose anything about the therapist, or to answer any question posed by the patient. The theory behind it was that the analyst was supposed to represent a "blank screen" upon which the analysand could project his or her transference. Of course, no one is ever a blank screen, although it took orthodox psychoanalysis half a century to figure that out.

There have been two new dimensions to self-disclosure that have changed the discussion immeasurably: the first are the changes in therapeutic theory, and the second is the powerful influence of the Internet on clinical practice. Modern schools of psychotherapy (like the ones represented in this book) are more relaxed and allow the personality of the therapist to be present in the counseling room. That advance in technique is a two-sided coin that has advantages and disadvantages for the progress of psychological treatment. It has the advantage of aiding in the development of empathy and therapeutic rapport between the therapist and the patient. But the potential disadvantages are awesome. It was easy to know how to behave as a Freudian analyst—just say "No." Because we have opened the door to personal questions from our clients, might we also be opening a Pandora's box, unleashing an entangled web of transference and counter-transference? What questions do we answer, and when do we retreat to the safety of therapeutic boundaries? A story from my past illustrates this dilemma.

I was trained as a clinical psychologist in the psychology department of the City College of New York. In the second year of the program we worked part-time at the college counseling center. I was assigned to do an initial interview with an undergraduate student. He was to be the first client of my career. I arrived at the center with a fresh pad of paper and an outline for conducting the interview. I introduced myself to the student and we walked into the counseling room and sat down. Then before I could say anything, he said, "I want to know how you feel about the Vietnam War." I was dumbfounded. This was not supposed to happen! I was supposed to be in charge! While I sat in turmoil, he said, "I'll only work with you if you agree with me that the war is immoral and should end." For those too young to remember, the Vietnam War was extremely divisive in America, and the war in Southeast Asia was matched by demonstrations on our streets, many arrests, and in a few cases students were shot and killed.

Like other students, I was also against the war, and I had demonstrated on the streets challenging our government to put an end to it. But that was not the point. Did I, a neophyte (tadpole?) therapist have the right to introduce my values into this young man's therapy—and at his demand, to boot? Flying by the seat of my pants, I made my decision based upon how important shared values were to this young man. I said that I was against the war. He responded by thanking me for my answer and began to tell me why he wanted to enter psychotherapy.

Immediately after the session, I ran to my supervisor in order to confess my sin and to ask for absolution. My supervisor was the best on the faculty; he was almost a legend at City College, and I respected his judgment enormously. "He has a right to know about your values," said Dr. Hertzman. He discussed this issue in my supervision class the next day and argued that shared values aid in forming a therapeutic alliance. In the 45 years that have transpired since that day, I have learned that my supervisor was right. Shared values between counselor and counselee represent a fertile foundation for a successful treatment. On the other hand, I have also learned that expressing them carries significant risks. Which values should we share, how often, and when do we stop? This problem of shared values and other personal questions does not come up often during an initial interview, but as I've stated earlier, it is only a matter of time before the neophyte counselor will be handling both short- and long-term clients.

As already mentioned, the patient is entitled to an explanation of the process that she or he is undertaking. In a clinic setting there may be a written procedure; in private practice the therapist usually makes a statement about what she or he is doing and why. Personal questions about the interviewer, on the other hand, are best left unanswered because one cannot in so short a period of time understand what meta-message it will convey to your client.

The only exception I make is to answer a question about my sexual orientation— but only if I am asked. Self-disclosure of one's sexual orientation has often been discussed in the professional literature because it is of importance to LGBT people (Gartrell, 1994; Herek & Greene, 1994; Kooden, 1991; Perlman, 1991). Gay and lesbian therapists have argued the advantages and disadvantages of "coming out" to their clients, and the general consensus is that they should when asked. It is easy to do this in large metropolitan cities, but harder to do so if working in rural clinics, especially those that are religiously funded. Lawyers have a good saying for the problem. It is, "The camel's nose is in the tent," meaning that once you answer (in this case) one question, you may not be able to curtail other client questions that may become more intrusive. Always remember to think in terms of meta-communications; what is the underlying meaning of the question?

While I will divulge my sexual orientation, my client is not entitled to know whether I have a lover, when I came out, where I live, or anything else about my life. One humorous example in my practice was the patient who frequently wanted to put food in my refrigerator during his session, so that he could look over my apartment and learn what kinds of foods I eat (and whether I kept a neat kitchen).

In this day of the Internet, a client may do a search in order to inquire about me, and many of my patients have done so. That is their prerogative. I will not feed the underlying fantasy that motivates the questions, and I do not have enough time to find out about it during an initial interview. The patient who persists in asking personal questions may have serious problems with ego boundaries and that should be noted in a written report. Answering personal questions during the initial interview delivers a meta-message that the future therapist will meet the patient's dependency or control needs. The assigned therapist will not thank you for making her or his work more difficult. These questions relating to the line between one's professional functions versus private life are relatively easy to identify.

Of all the contributors to this book, Nichols (Chapter 4) is the most revealing to her clients about her life, background, and her goals for psychotherapy. Her point of view is passionate and far from the traditional boundaries of psychotherapy. While some colleagues may hail her as courageous, others may feel as if she has strayed too far from traditional boundaries. I admire her ability to self-disclose but to never cross ethical boundaries.

The Internet, however, has changed everything about professional versus private life in clinical practice. Unfortunately professional schools and ethics boards have not yet caught up with the explosion of technology and its implications for practice. This may be due to the fact that students and young practitioners are better versed in these techniques than their instructors. A simple Internet search will reveal many aspects of our lives. Many of us now have professional web pages in which a potential applicant may learn about our education and background, and we construct this source of information in order to advertise our expertise in ways congruent with the ethical guidelines of our discipline. But the same Internet search may also turn up considerably more personal information than we would voluntarily give to a patient.

There is a generation gap here. Prensky (2001) has described "Digital Natives" as a younger generation that has been born to the Internet and views its communication like a second language, while "Digital Immigrants" are considerably older and have (at best) an ambivalent attitude toward modern technology. At least 85 percent of college students own their own computer, some of them having begun to use them between the ages of 5 and 8, and they check their email every day (Lehavot, 2009). Twenty percent of psychology graduate students have Internet profiles, and many of them post photos and information that they would not want their clients to see (Lehavot, Barnett, & Powers, 2010). Almost all of these graduate psychology students were conducting psychotherapy under supervision at their respective schools. A high percentage of them also have profiles on MySpace, Facebook, and other social networking sites, and these are available to other members of the social network community.

But many established psychotherapists are also members of social networking sites, and they too post photographs and personal information for others to see, including current or potential clients. Since this form of technological communication is so new, we do not yet know its implications for professional practice. For instance, should a therapist remove a photograph of himself or herself at the beach wearing a skimpy bathing suit and hoisting a bottle of beer? Should a therapist do a computer search for information about a client in therapy, and is it helpful to the client's therapy if we find a photograph of her or him in a skimpy bathing suit and hoisting a bottle of beer? The normally identified boundary between personal and professional becomes highly permeable under these circumstances.

It has gotten even more controversial with the development of sexually oriented websites on the Internet. We can pose the question this way: Is it a violation of ethical standards for a therapist (male, female, gay, or straight) to join a website whose purpose is to meet another person for a sexual liaison and publish a profile graphically discussing preferred sexual activities, together with nude photographs including their genitals? And is it a violation of ethics for the therapist, knowing that a patient has such a website, to access it and look at his or her physically revealing photos together with other sexual and nonsexual information? Might it be okay for the therapist to do so, if she or he asks for permission? And if that is okay, exactly how would the therapist ask?

These are not theoretical problems because they have already appeared on professional list servers. Some therapists have argued that a therapist has the right to a private life, including membership in sex websites. Others, and here I will count myself among them, argue that once the information and photographs are placed on a public website for all members to see, it is no longer private.

Pipes and associates (2005) state the case well when discussing the issue of ethics for members of the APA.

> Professional associations such as the American Psychological Association (APA) have a vested interest in the behaviors of their members for a number of reasons, including the reputation of the profession, the desire to enhance the education and competency of members, and the aspiration to protect the students, clients, supervisees, organizations, and research participants with whom members work. When individuals enter a profession, a question arises as to what behaviors, if any, they agree to modify or give up as a result of becoming a member of the profession. (p. 325)

They go on to say that by joining the APA, members voluntarily agree to constrain their behavior. They were only discussing social networking sites, not sexual web pages. Within the next few years, all professional organizations and training institutions will be required to come to terms with the ethics of their members participating in sexually oriented websites. Simple participation in social networking sites has already created problems in psychotherapy, even when they conform to ethical standards. Patients viewing naked pictures of their therapists or therapists calling up naked pictures of their patients will unquestionably destroy a therapeutic relationship and could possibly lead to charges of unethical conduct against the therapist by state licensing boards and litigation against the therapist. Advertising for romance, in contrast to sex, while less inflammatory, may create as much havoc in psychotherapy as sexually revealing photographs.

Sophisticated users of these web pages say that privacy controls are available to limit those who see the information posted. While that may be true of sites such as Facebook and MySpace (or may not), it makes no sense to use privacy controls when one is advertising for romance or sex. If you are training to serve the public as a therapist of whatever school of psychotherapy, you will have to give up some of the freedoms that are available to ordinary "civilians." That includes advertising for romance and sex on the Internet. You will have to find other ways to find likely partners.

Conflict of Values

What happens when there is a clash of values between the therapist and the patient? We sometimes have to work with someone whose personal values clash with our own. For instance, narcissistic patients trouble me. The word "reciprocal" does not appear in their vocabulary, and they have endless complaints of how others have disappointed them while communicating a deeply held feeling of entitlement. I once felt the urge to get off my chair and slap a narcissistic patient in the face as retribution for his selfish behavior. Of course I did not, but I thought about this impulse after he left. It was a very curious reaction on my part. Why should I care? So what if he is selfish? These were important questions to ask because I, not my patient, created my feelings. Such a strong, negative counter-transferential reaction is an important issue for all therapists, regardless of their theoretical schools of therapy. I needed to answer it so that *my life* would not be haunted by these feelings, not because I wanted to help my patient. I needed to take care of myself as a person. I did not know (nor particularly care) whether it would help the client. I wanted to stop the "noise" in my head.

As I looked at my feelings about his selfishness, I realized that I was envious of him because I wished that I had the capacity to be so selfish. Envy, therefore, motivated my aggression. It was an important insight. Envy is a very powerful motivator and it shows itself often in psychotherapy, and even during the initial interview. Jealousy and envy are constant companions of mental health professionals, and their effects should not be minimized. A client may have a characteristic that we covet, such as being particularly handsome; or complain about their salary that is three times greater than one's own. Or it may be the braggart who refuses to order a wine at dinner that costs less than $100, but only if other people are around to notice. It may be someone who has (I'm tempted to say "captured") a new sex partner every night. The potential list is obviously endless. It consists of any characteristic of the patient that affects our feelings of jealousy and envy. None of us are immune, regardless of training and experience. These are interviewer reactions that should be discussed with supervisors and one's own therapist.

The Process of Early Hypothesis Building

Scott is an example of hypothesis building before his interview. He phoned saying that his HMO referred him. He specifically said that he wanted to see a gay therapist. Without the slightest hesitation, he asked if I was gay. His voice was strong, clear, and business-like, with no hesitation. What a gold mine of information this was. My hypotheses were these:

1. He is comfortable about being gay.
2. He does not care what others think about his sexual orientation.
3. He gives thought to what he wants in life and goes after it.
4. When he makes a decision, he sticks to it.
5. He probably feels comfortable talking about sex.
6. He is probably not the kind of person who looks back about his decision-making.
7. He will be very assertive during the face-to-face interview.

These were only hypotheses. We all create them (consciously or not) during our initial contact, either with the actual patient or with the form an applicant fills out at a clinic. This valuable information shapes our questioning. These tentative hypotheses may evoke a number of feelings on the part of the interviewer and an ill wind will blow in the form of significant counter-transference if he or she chooses to ignore them. One might as well be explicit about them; otherwise, you may end up projecting your emotional needs upon the patient.

If your clinic has an application form, the manner in which the applicant completes it may be as important as the written answers. For instance a very bright and cultured young man filled out my initial contact form, and I noticed that his handwriting was so severely cramped, that it was almost unreadable. In the place where he was asked to sign his name, he wrote only his first name. With this information I formed the following hypotheses:

1. He was emotionally constricted, what some people would describe as "tightly wound."
2. He was passive-dependent.
3. Spontaneity is very difficult.
4. Feelings of assertiveness are squelched and guilt may be a constant companion.

These hypotheses helped me shape my questioning during his initial interview. I expected that I would have to be more directive with him than with Scott. I also started to wonder what kind of families these men came from (See Datchi-Phillips, Chapter 12). (Incidentally, these two young men would not like one another; their self-esteem and methods of expressing feelings and spontaneity are worlds apart.)

Forms of Communication

As already noted, colleagues differ about the importance of specific information in a patient's life. Some of the contributors in this book believe that it is imperative in order to make a treatment plan, especially on intake forms used in institutions that are publicly funded. Some of the authors of the chapters in this book will emphasize very specific types of information, such as Hellman (Chapter 5) for community psychiatry and Grant and Wingate (Chapter 11) for planning a proper cognitive behavioral therapy (CBT) treatment program. Even Gershoni (Chapter 14) needs some information in order to direct his psychodramas. On the other hand, both

Roughton (Chapter 13) and Tunnell (Chapter 7) believe that only the development of a therapeutic relationship is crucial; information, such as specific facts, are secondary. I suggest that communications from a client are transmitted to us on many levels at the same time. One level is a client's specific words, as one finds in Scott's transcript. But another is the world of nonverbal communication.

Nonverbal Communication

The information you are going to collect will be composed of two factors: the words she or he speaks and the manner of the presentation. The person you meet may be bright eyed and bushy tailed, or stooped over and despondent. The voice may be loud or soft, strong or weak, the words garbled or pronounced carefully. The presentation may show education or the lack of it, so will sentence structure, grammar, and vocabulary. Facial expressions are very important; does he or she look at you when speaking or when you speak, or look away toward somewhere in space or at the feet? What messages do the person's facial expressions convey: depression, helplessness, indifference, rage? The interviewer should note body posture and changes of it during the interview, and especially movements of the hands. Does your client give the impression of being attentive and understand your need to get information in order to help, or has she or he merely found a new person to listen to an endless litany of complaints? Throughout the interview you will be making choices about which verbal and nonverbal statements require documenting. You will be wrong often at first; it takes time to hone those clinical skills.

There is a reason why these nonverbal clues are so useful. The patient has thought about what she or he wants to say and may even have made notes or practiced beforehand. He or she may have had a previous therapist and now must recount her or his story based upon that previous experience. He or she might have rehearsed the *content* of their complaint, but cannot rehearse the *style of presentation*, body posture, how to hold the hands, or the tone of their voice. These are unconscious features of one's narrative and are characterological and not usually subject to conscious control. Your evaluation of these factors plays a crucial role in predicting your client's capacity for establishing a therapeutic alliance. As the initial interviewer, you do not have to make that decision (unless you are in private practice), but by keeping a record of these clues, you will deliver valuable information to those who do, and I can assure you that the assigned therapist will be grateful. Most clients understand that you have to take notes, and invariably consider it a sign of professional conduct. When you ask, for instance, "How long has this been going on?" you write down what she or he says together with all the other clues. When you write your report, you will combine them in more general statements, and always comment on the patient's ability to maintain social contact with you.

Let me show you two ways in which you can learn the power of nonverbal observation. In the first, you will need to work in a clinic or hospital; you can do the second in your private office. Try this experiment if you work in a clinic that has a two-way observation mirror. Have a colleague conduct an initial interview, but turn off the sound. You and another colleague observe the interview and take notes. Discuss your observations with the colleague who observed the silent interview with you. After you form a set of hypotheses about the person, compare them with the interviewer. You will be surprised at how much you will learn. Sometimes you can even make a reasonable stab at a DSM diagnosis. This is a wonderful exercise for therapists-in-training. Not only can you discuss the client under observation, but your feelings about him or her as well as you make your observations.

The other, simpler procedure is to use a video recorder during the initial interview. Get permission from your client to tape the session. It is perfectly reasonable to tell your client that it is for your training, which is true. If she or he is uncomfortable, forego it, but I think you will find your patient will not object when you point the video recorder toward you, not the patient. *Toward you, please.* Afterward, look at the recording twice. The first time, turn the sound off. Study your reactions, your body positions, and facial expressions. What messages are you transmitting? If you can spot your own nonverbal signals, you will be better trained to identify them in a client. Only then repeat the process with the sound on. Listen to what you say and to the tone of your voice, noting how you may be communicating more than you were aware of.

Make sure that your nonverbal messages are congruent with your words. If they are not, the patient will experience mixed messages coming from you and that will be confusing to him or her. It could result in a classic double-bind in which the patient, when presented with conflicting double messages, responds to one of them, then gets punished for not responding to the other.[3] Also observe how your messages influence your client's response. You will accelerate the process of learning about client–therapist interactions if you record some of your interviews and listen to them afterward, preferably with your supervisor or a trusted colleague. Some early career therapists form small peer support groups as an aid to their training, and playing these recordings at a meeting is often helpful to all the participants.

I suspect that the therapist-in-training prays that she or he does not get a supervisor like me! "How do I do all these things and still get the factual information in the other twenty boxes on the intake form my clinic demands? If I do not fill in all the boxes, I get criticized, and if I do not discuss my client's eye contact, I will get criticized. I can't win!" The answer to this complaint is simple; do your best in the time allowed. No one gets everything accomplished in 45–60 minutes.

The Therapist's Nose

This is probably the perfect time to talk about your nose. I assume that you have never had your nose discussed in any of your clinical courses or in your readings

---

[3] The joke goes like this: A mother buys her son two ties for his birthday. The next time he visits her, he wears one of the ties. She says, "Oh! So you don't like the other tie I bought you!" This is a classic double-bind.

about interviewing. It is, however, an extremely important part of your clinical anatomy. Of course, I mean your metaphorical nose, not the one sitting in the middle of your face. Some therapists call it clinical intuition. The experienced psychotherapist uses his or her nose constantly to smell out the personality characteristics and ego defenses of the person being interviewed. While a full discussion really belongs in an advanced course on interviewing techniques, I will touch on it briefly here. The reason it belongs in an advanced course is because using your metaphorical nose is just a hair's width away from significant, full-blown counter-transference. Using the nose insightfully can speed up the progress of the clinical alliance, while using it for uncontrolled counter-transference will end with your patient terminating therapy, or, even worse, by creating a sado-masochistic therapeutic relationship in which you may alternate between rescue fantasies and punishment, making your life miserable and your patient's therapy useless.

The clinical nose can be an important aid in your evaluation of an initial interview. It presents itself as an impression about the person you have interviewed in addition to factual and historical information. It is the sum of all the nonverbal communications by the patient, and the manner in which she or he communicates with you. It is what you sense your client wants from you, but is not necessarily overtly stated. Finally, and this is the most difficult part, it is tuning into your own emotional reactions to the person sitting in front of you. They are the signals from both the patient and from you that coalesce into a coherent picture of your client's needs and wishes. I will give you a successful example from my own practice.

A young man in his twenties was referred to me. His reasons for seeking therapy are not relevant to our discussion. I found myself angry with him at the end of the session, but said nothing. Afterward, I thought about my reaction and decided to tell him about my anger at our next scheduled meeting. I sensed with my clinical nose that he wanted the structure that my words would bring to the session. And I was right. His eyes lit up, moved his body forward and told me how pleased he was to hear my words. Why did he say that? He said that all the doctors he had recently seen for a medical condition treated him like an object. My expressed anger meant that I cared about him; it meant that he could trust me.

Lest you think that I have a crystal ball through which I practice, this example was a successful use of my clinical nose. There have been other times when I made a mess of it. We get better at it as we gain experience, but no practitioner gets it right all the time. What is important for the student in training or the early career counselor is to understand that your clinical nose is "sniffing the air" at all times, even if you are unaware of it. My message is to bring these judgments into your awareness. I would not, however, at an early stage of practice, discuss them with your clients. Better to do so with supervisors or other therapists. While the example I have given is one where I felt anger, it is far more common for interviewers to indulge themselves in a scenario of therapeutically deadly rescue fantasies.

Please keep in mind that your patient also has a nose. Whether she or he uses it the initial interview depends upon that person's personality structure. If a person, on the one hand, is oblivious to one's surroundings and environment, or is extremely narcissistic, he or she will not notice much. On the other hand, some clients are very sophisticated in "smelling" our moods, and even the smallest change in the tone of our voices, how we sit in our chairs, or how we say "hello," will be "read" and interpreted. Such people are often extremely accurate about how we are feeling during the interview.

Sexual Interviewing

Some therapists, particularly those in training and early career counselors, are uncomfortable discussing sexual behavior. That can unquestionably be a problem for your client. Just as you are observing his or her nonverbal clues, she or he is doing the same with you (nose to nose, so to speak). Your client is likely to spot your discomfort, and it is very difficult to know how his or her is reacting to it. On the one hand, your client may believe that you are uncomfortable talking about sex and, therefore, will avoid talking any further about it so as not to offend you. On the other hand, the client who spots your discomfort may interpret it as confirmation of her or his "badness," and avoid talking about his or her sexual experiences. Either way, your client stops talking and that does not bode well for future therapy.

I have seen clients who left previous therapists because they sensed their therapists' discomfort to discuss sexual behavior. If you are uncomfortable discussing sexual behavior, quickly head for either your supervisor or a therapist or both, or your work as a therapist will be limited. This is as true of structured schools of therapy such as CBT (Chapter 11) as it is with psychodynamic ones (Chapter 13). If your discomfort with a particular client is severe enough, you may have to ask your supervisor to assign the patient to someone else. There is no shame in doing so. While that may be a necessary step during your period of training, it will not do for your long-term survival in the profession.

How about the use of profanity? Some patients do not initiate using profanity or describe graphic sexual details until they feel it is permissible. It is perfectly professional to ask, "Do you feel comfortable talking about sex?" If there is a hushed pause afterward, drop it, but you will find that most people today, regardless of sexual orientation, are comfortable using slang language when describing their sexual behavior. There is no rule requiring you to use four letter words in your speech. The question is whether your client feels that she or he can use them without your disapproval. While it may be okay for you to ask, "Are you telling me that you're a bottom?" you deliver a completely different message (actually meta-message) if you ask, "Are you the inserter or the insertee?" If the latter, you are unlikely to hear more about sex, and your patient's tenure with you is likely to be exceedingly short.

Kinsey, Pomeroy, and Martin (1948) have an excellent chapter explaining their sexual interviewing techniques. They found that asking questions directly, to the point, and without hesitation (hesitation suggests interviewer ambivalence) gave them the most valid answers. My training as a sex therapist has only confirmed their observations. Do not beat around the bush, look away, look down, lower your voice, or speak with long pauses between words. And if he or she turns red or hems and haws, say, "If you are uncomfortable talking about this subject, we can do it another time." That takes your client off the hook. Immediately go on to another subject.[4]

Scott's Interview

In P50 Scott states that "we all make mistakes," opening up the subject of making sexual mistakes. Just a few minutes later at P59 he states that his "first intercourse" was at age 17. At P14, he wonders if it is permissible to say "fuck." At P66 he mentions "anal sex" and a few seconds later at P67 he asks, "did he fuck me?" At T69 I respond with "fuck." The meta-message has been delivered; profanity and street language is acceptable. If it were not, he might reconsider his choice of a therapist. It is only at P91 that we learn that he is a bottom and fears the consequence, but he is not clear about it and drops the subject, probably because he is too conflicted to handle it at that particular moment.

In T121 I reintroduce the subject of Scott's sexual behavior since his brother died from AIDS, and in P122 he notes that he did not have safe sex, which is probably the reason why he dropped the subject at P91. My counter-transference is evident in T124, especially my use of the word "why," as it implies that he has to justify his behavior to me. Please try to avoid "why" questions; they are so often about us and not them. It sounds as if you are asking, "Why did you do something as stupid as that?" He already knows it was stupid; that is one reason he came into therapy. He does not need to be browbeaten about it. Avoiding "why" questions is easier to say than to accomplish. Is the interviewer searching for information or expressing a judgment or condemnation? This takes a lot of self-training. I suggest you record one of your intake sessions (or therapy sessions) and check the number of times you ask "why." You may be shocked at the final number and how often it conveys your feelings, not a search for information. You should shoot for the goal of almost never using a "why" question.

As previously stated, I usually ask, "What brings you here today?" Sometimes, such as in the interview with Scott, I ask whether he has had a previous therapeutic experience because it gives me an idea of what defenses the future therapist may have to cope with. In P3 Scott tells me that he did not return to a previous therapist because he did not "like the guy," so he "didn't bother" returning. (The word "bother" stood out.) He had said something different when we talked over the phone previous to our appointment. The discrepancy made me curious, and I wondered whether minimizing his previous therapeutic experience might be a harbinger of his future psychotherapy with me. While I would have wanted to know exactly what he did not like about his previous therapist, in P4 Scott dispenses with my line of questioning and directs the conversation to what is on his mind. By that action he clearly conveys that he is master of his life; a self-starter and in essence telling me to let him run the show. That was okay with me, because if I had

---

[4] See Cerbone, Chapter 15 for a different point of view about sexual questioning.

attempted to redirect the discussion back to his previous therapy we might have entered into a power struggle in the first few minutes of the session. But it deepened my wonder about his previous experience.

The interviewer's choice of words is exceedingly important. Therapists-in-training are usually told to use the patient's vocabulary whenever possible, a good idea. Specific words are important (pauses as well) in order to express empathy toward the interviewee. Empathy is the metaphorical mirror that says, "I understand how you feel." It builds trust and develops the therapeutic alliance. This does not mean that you necessarily agree with your client's actions, only that you understand the underlying conflicts and difficulty in reaching a resolution.

Doing something about it is the province of the therapist who will read your report. Let us suppose, for instance, that you interview a man whose lover or spouse of 8 years just ended their relationship by saying that he is a, "controlling, impossible, selfish bastard—just like your mother." The initial interview is not the time to play Sherlock Holmes and investigate whether he (or his mother) is all of those things, or if not, why he set up house with another person who would want to hurt him like that. You might respond with, "That must have been a terrible night for you. How did it affect you?" You might also want to follow up his answer by asking, "Has this ever happened to you before?" in order to establish whether there is a pattern of failed love relationships.

Do you challenge a statement that sounds wrong or contradictory to what she or he said earlier? Careful here! Feel free to inquire about clarification. I did that any number of times in my interview with Scott, such as in T25 and T28 because he was speaking so quickly that I had trouble keeping up. But before you ask for "clarification," first ask yourself whether you are actually putting your client on the witness chair. You do that when your question implies that he or she must justify or defend her or his actions, such as so often happens with "why" questions. That is called "attacking a defense," and the customary reaction of clients is to respond with a greater defense. That did not happen when I made my mistake with Scott because of his strong sense of self, but it might have closed down another person with lower self-esteem.

When you have enough information in a certain area, move on. The initial interview is evaluative. Of course, in private practice the interviewer can luxuriate with time, but even there, one is likely to miss significant problem areas by not making a comprehensive evaluation. Scott had not said anything about drug-taking after almost 40 minutes. It is possible that if I had not interrupted him, the interview would have ended before I brought up the subject of drug-taking in T107? He responded with a gold mine of information. Was he hiding this drug history during the first 40 minutes? No, he probably did not bring it up because he was not in conflict about it. It was therefore, of tertiary importance to him, but very important to me in planning for his future psychotherapy.[5]

---

[5] Reasonable colleagues will disagree with my comfort at interrupting a patient while he is speaking—no less fifteen times. The disagreement is over how directive an interviewer can be, and to what extent it helps or impedes the therapeutic alliance.

Potential Interviewer Errors and Scott

This is the time to discuss other basic interviewer mistakes. They consist of:

1. Glossing over potentially important material.
2. Letting the interviewee talk incessantly about one particular issue to the exclusion of all others.
3. Subtly preventing patients from talking about subjects that make us anxious.
4. Punishing them for talking about them anyway.

My interview with Scott contains many errors. Let us examine a few of them. (In some of the chapters to follow, my colleagues rightly take me to task for them.) My first begins after only 3 minutes into the interview. In P12 Scott says, "which is why I'm here now." My reply, a few seconds later in T13 is, "So tell me why you're here." What is interesting about this error is that it does not interfere with his exposition of his current crisis. It is a perfect example of how even our mistakes can lead to valuable information.

After 6½ minutes, I repeat the same mistake. In P20 he says, "while I was with him," and in P21 he again says, "while I was with him." My response in T22 was, "Were you there at the time?" Scott excuses my lapse of short-term memory by answering the question more fully. Clients are generally compassionate toward our errors when they believe that we have their best interests at heart. One could reasonably hypothesize that in this early phase of the interview, I was more anxious than my patient!

T25 is not an error even though I interrupt Scott. He is combining events at a fast clip and I interrupt him to evaluate the relative importance of these events. He continues to do this in P27 and my question in T28 is meant to clarify his psychological dilemma.

P30 is very important. Scott tells me about the acting-out behavior of his father. Money is not the primary issue from a psychological point of view; it is the acting out. Instead of dealing with the personal and family problems, the father *does something*, substituting action for feelings. That is what acting out is about. The importance is that Scott is his father's son. While Scott is honest in his financial dealings with people, he may have learned to act out conflicting feelings from his father, and that may be an impediment toward establishing a long-lasting love affair.

P31 is a long and serious exposition of Scott's other family conflicts. My question in T32 is weird. Who cares? Fortunately I get back on track in T33. T53 is clearly a criticism by me of Scott, especially because I say, "Now you tell me ... " My concern is obvious since I still do not know about his vulnerability to HIV and other STDs. The same problem plagues me through much of the interview. I want to know about his susceptibility to HIV, which might also give me information about the men in his life. I also want to learn if he is repeating his older brother's sexual mistakes. Instead of remembering Kinsey's advice about being direct, I went about it too cautiously for someone like Scott.

I begin in T95, "When was the last time you had sex?" The next few minutes are totally off the mark, motivated by my uncertainty about how direct to be. My indirection wastes time, and in T98, I even contradict him. These are clear errors of technique.

It is not until T107 that we get back on track when I ask Scott about alcohol and drugs. In T114 I ask, "*Why* do you think you smoke *so much* pot?" (Emphasis added.) It is far too judgmental and once again the implication is that Scott must justify his behavior to me. It would have been better to ask, "How do you feel when you're smoking pot?" I am back on course by T115. But in P116 Scott mentions "crazy thoughts," and I miss it. T117 misses the opportunity of asking, "What are these crazy thoughts?"

P120 is a long statement by Scott about his mother. He has given me all the information I need to understand her place in his life. He would continue if I let him. I chose to interrupt and I do not think that is an error. Scott spends so much time talking about her because his relationship to her is far less conflicted than with his father. I change the subject in T121 to safe sex. For the first time (it should have been asked 15 minutes earlier) I ask him directly, "Do you have safe sex?" This is a loaded question for both people in the room. I have already mentioned T124, T126, and T130 as punishment for having unsafe sex. Of course Scott expects to be chastised, which is probably why he did not initiate the discussion in the first place.

In P133 Scott uses the word "suicide." He follows it up by saying that he had similar thoughts when he was a teenager. I did not pick up either of these statements. Instead I go on to summing-up the interview. I was at least partially motivated by time. Almost 52 minutes had gone by, and I knew that another 5 minutes were required to wrap up the interview. It was an error. Scott is not going to commit suicide; he uses the word to express how hopeless he feels enmeshed in his family disorganization. (See Datchi-Phillips, Chapter 12.) He wanted to talk about his hopelessness. I should have linked his current and his teenaged thoughts of suicide and then connected them with feeling abandoned by his brother's death. Instead, in T135, I emphasize the totally irrelevant question of finding a boyfriend. This is an excellent example of an experienced psychologist ignoring highly significant information by a patient. Could I have felt worn out by listening to family crises, death, and responsibility? Perhaps.

The audio recording may have contributed to my errors. Scott was relaxed about the audio recording, while I was a nervous wreck! He was the defined "patient," while I was the "wise" therapist, and knew that my words would be read by my colleagues. "How will that sound?" are the words that I heard echoing in my head, and it is likely that they interfered with my concentration.

My desire (is "passion" more suitable?) to produce this book explains the shameless self-promotion in T140. Of a number of initial interview recordings, this one seemed the most promising. By the end of the interview, I knew that I was going to ask Scott for permission to be the subject in the book, and I was obviously trying to keep him interested.

Summary

In order for the initial interview to be successful, it needs to fulfill a number of requirements. To begin, the patient has to feel a warm greeting from the reception staff. Clinic administrative staff members are crucial in conveying a feeling of the clinic as a safe environment. If this does not happen, the initial interview to follow will be contaminated by the impersonality of the reception. This means that non-professional support staff must be trained in how to cooperate with the professional staff in accomplishing this goal.

The greeting by the interviewer is the next step and vital in continuing the patient's experience as a safe one in which to discuss personal problems. By the end of the interview the patient needs to feel as if his or her personal problems have been heard, and that the interviewer understands them. She or he needs to feel a sense of compassion from both the interviewer and from the agency, and to feel as if the patient and therapist have entered a partnership that will end in resolving the problems that led the person to initiate psychotherapy. Minor errors of interviewer technique are not important as long as the patient leaves the office feelings as if a good first step on the path to changing her or his life for the better has been taken. The interviewer needs to be aware of how the characteristics and behavior of a client can affect him or her and, hence, the course of the interview. Issues of transference and counter-transference can profoundly affect the "gremlins" of identification—punishment, stress, rescue fantasies, and self-disclosure—and the competent interviewer takes care to monitor her or his personal reactions to a client. Training exercises such as video recording sessions in conjunction with a small group of other therapists are exceedingly helpful in identifying both verbal and nonverbal forms of communication.

References

American Counseling Association (2005). *Code of ethics.* Alexandria, VA: Author.

American Psychiatric Association (2001). *The principles of medical ethics with annotations especially applicable to psychiatry.* Arlington, VA: Author.

American Psychological Association (2002). Ethical principles of psychologists and code of conduct. *American Psychologist, 57,* 1060–1073.

American Psychological Association, Ethics Committee (1993). Report of the Ethics Committee, 1993. *American Psychologist, 48,* 811–820.

American Psychological Association, Ethics Committee (1994). Report of the Ethics Committee, 1993. *American Psychologist, 49,* 659–666.

American Psychological Association, Ethics Committee (2009). Report of the Ethics Committee, 1993. *American Psychologist, 64,* 464–473.

Bandura, A. (1969). *Principles of behavior modification.* London: Holt, Rinehart, and Winston.

Elise, D. (1991). When sexual and romantic feelings permeate the therapeutic relationship. In C. Silverstein (Ed.), *Gays, lesbians and their therapists: Studies in psychotherapy.* New York: W. W. Norton & Company.

Freud, S. (1905). Fragments of an analysis of a case of hysteria. In S. Freud (Ed.), *Standard edition* (Vol. 7, pp. 7–122). London: The Hogarth Press 1953.

Herek, G. M., & Greene, B. (Eds.), (1994). *Lesbian and gay psychology: Theory, research, and clinical applications.* Thousand Oaks, CA: Sage Publications.

Gartrell, N. K. (1994). Boundaries in lesbian therapist – client relationships. In B. Greene, and G. M. Herek (Eds.), Lesbian and gay psychology: Theory, research, and clinical applications. Thousand Oaks: Sage Publications.

Gonsiorek, J. C. (1995). Assessment for rehabilitation of exploitative health care professionals and clergy. In J. C. Gonsiorek (Ed.), *Breach of trust: Sexual exploitation by health care professionals and clergy* (pp. 145–162). Newbury Park, CA: Sage Publications.

Kinsey, A. C., Pomeroy, W. B., & Martin, C. E. (1948). *Sexual behavior in the human male.* Philadelphia, PA: W. B. Saunders Company.

Kooden, H. (1991). Self-disclosure: The gay male therapist as agent of social change. In C. Silverstein (Ed.), *Gays, lesbians and their therapists: Studies in psychotherapy* (pp. 143–154). New York: W. W. Norton & Company.

Lehavot, K. (2009). "MySpace" or yours? The ethical dilemma of graduate students' personal lives on the Internet. *Ethics & Behavior, 19*(2), 129–141.

Lehavot, K., Barnett, J. E., & Powers, D. (2010). Psychotherapy, professional relationships, and ethical considerations in the MySpace generation. *Professional Psychology: Research and Practice, 41*(2), 160–168.

National Association of Social Workers. (2008). *Code of ethics of the National Association of Social Workers.*

Perlman, G. (1991). The question of therapist self-disclosure in the treatment of a married gay man. In C. Silverstein (Ed.), *Gays, lesbians and their therapists: Studies in psychotherapy* (pp. 201–209). New York: W. W. Norton & Company.

Pipes, R. B., Holstein, J. E., & Aguirre, M. G. (2005). Examining the personal-professional distinction. *American Psychologist, 60*(4), 325–334.

Prensky, M. (2001). Digital natives: Digital immigrants. *On the Horizon, 9,* 1–6.

Shea, S. C. (1998). *Psychiatric interviewing: The art of understanding. A practical guide for psychiatrists, psychologists, counselors, social workers, nurses, and other mental health professionals* (2nd ed.). Philadelphia, PA: Saunders.

Silverstein, C. (1977). Symposium on homosexuality and the ethics of behavioral intervention (paper no. 2). *Journal of Homosexuality, 2*(3), 205–211.

Silverstein, C. (Ed.), (1991). *Gays, lesbians and their therapists: Studies in psychotherapy.* New York: W. W. Norton & Company.

Sullivan, H. S. (1953). *The interpersonal theory of psychiatry.* New York: W. W. Norton.

4 Variations on Gender and Orientation in Scott's First Interview

Margaret Nichols

Institute for Personal Growth, Highland Park, NJ, USA

Introduction

My task in this chapter is unique: to deconstruct the gender and orientation components of the first interview—how would this interview have gone if the client had a
different orientation or gender from Scott, and how would it have been different if
conducted by a female therapist? Because my mission is unusual, I have
approached it a special way: I have literally imagined different clients and written
about them here, and then analyzed the similarities and differences based on gender
and sexual orientation. Moreover, I have imagined myself in Silverstein's role,
envisioning how I might have conducted the interview with Scott and his "alters"
differently. I have tried to focus particularly on the ways my approach would vary
from his because of my gender, and inserted these observations when appropriate.

Why do gender and sexual orientation matter here? On a purely practical level,
they matter because of client preference. Scott specifically requested a gay male
therapist; many psychotherapy consumers want their therapist to be "like them" in
some way they consider crucial, such as gender, sexual orientation, or ethnic,
racial, or religious background. Although psychotherapy researchers debate the relevance of these client–therapist matches, it may be that simply *believing* your therapist understands you increases the therapist–client bond.

Gender and sexual preference also matter because there are real differences
between men and women, gay and nongay clients, which will influence therapeutic
assessment and treatment. For example, if a gay male couple discloses bringing a
"third" into their sexual encounters, it would be helpful for the therapist to know
this is a common practice among some gay men who consider fidelity to be
separate from sexual monogamy and may not even define their behavior as nonmonogamous (LaSala, 2004). Likewise, gender differences can dramatically affect the
therapist's assessment. An adult woman who cries throughout most of a session is
not unusual, and she probably feels better afterwards. An adult male client who

The Initial Psychotherapy Interview. DOI: 10.1016/B978-0-12-385146-8.00004-3

does the same is much less common—and he might feel shame, not relief, at revealing his pain. So therapists should strive to become aware of gender and sexual identity variation to better understand and serve a wide range of clientele.

What of situations where the two conflate, where it is difficult to know when a behavior is the result of gender differences, issues relevant to a gay sexual orientation, both, or neither? The ability to deconstruct gender and sexual orientation is more important than you might think in therapeutic situations. For example, we know that most gender-variant little boys—that is, little boys who want to dress up as girls, to be girls, who at times think they really are girls—do not grow up to be heterosexual males. They mostly grow up to be gay or bisexual, and a smaller percentage transsexual (Green, 1987). We have no good ways to predict which will evolve in what direction. So how does this affect what you suggest to the parents of such a child? This is a real debate among therapists, with some focusing on gender and advocating allowing these natal males to "socially transition" to female at ages as early as 6 or 7 (Lev, 2004), others viewing these boys as gay and recommending a supportive attitude toward the variant behavior as an early sign of homosexuality (Isay, 1997), and still others viewing the gender-variant behavior as pathological and attempt to eradicate it (Zucker & Bradley, 1996).

Even if you are never faced with such complex cases, you are still likely to encounter puzzles about the interaction of orientation and gender. For example, several studies have shown lower frequency of sex in lesbian couples than heterosexual couples (Blumstein & Schwartz, 1983; Nichols, 2004, 2005). Does this difference exist because women are socialized to be sexually receptive and not aggressive, so that when two women are together no one is completely comfortable with initiating? Is it because women in general have a lower sex drive than males, and if that is true, how much is biology and how much socialization? Could it be that our whole concept of how we "measure" sexuality—by frequency of genitally focused interaction, by orgasm—is a completely male perspective? Should we perhaps be "counting" sensual affection that is not genitally oriented? Are heterosexual couples having sex more because frequency is male-driven, with females seeing sex in part as marital obligation? Or, do lesbians have the special burden of internalized homophobia or female sexual shame—times two? These different explanations are important, because if the lesbian couple having little or no genital sexual contact comes to relationship therapy with you, these different perspectives will suggest a wide variety of assessments and corresponding treatment plans, often radically different from one another.

Issues around the interaction of orientation and gender are showing up both in the sexology research literature and the culture, especially lesbian, gay, bisexual, and transgender (LGBT) culture. Chivers, Rieger, Latty, and Bailey (2004), for example, used instruments that measured the biological aspects of sexual arousal and self-report to compare the reactions of gay and straight males and gay and straight females to erotic movies—pornography. They found differences along gender lines to be more salient than differences of sexual orientation. Both the gay male and heterosexual male arousal patterns appeared to be very narrow and limited to depictions of the kind of sex they practiced. Both lesbian and heterosexual women displayed arousal not only to all depictions of human sexual interaction—gay male porn, lesbian, straight—but even to films of erotic play in subhuman primates. So Chivers' research implies that gay and straight men are sexually similar in that they narrow-focus on only literal depictions of the kind of sex they prefer. And both lesbians and straight women are alike in the broadness of their sexual arousal potential. In other words, gender may trump sexual orientation in matters of sexual "orientation." Chivers' research implies that gender differences are so hard-wired, meaning an unchangeable part of brain functioning, that they dominate whatever similarities may exist among men and women who are same-sex oriented.

In fact, some have argued that the *only* thing that gay people have in common is their sexual minority status and their shared history of oppression (Sullivan, 1995) and that when gays are truly equal they will be indistinguishable from nongays (Savin-Williams, 2005). Others have claimed a special "gay sensibility" impervious to changes in culture or historical time period (Warner, 1999).

But even if gay people have only their status as outsiders in common, that constitutes quite a lot. First, discrimination because of sexual orientation does not differentiate on the basis of gender; lesbians and gays have experienced equally bad treatment at the hands of government, military, and private institutions, and this tends to breed solidarity and a sense of "family." Second, in part because of this, gays and lesbians have tended to live together and near each other if not always evenly mixed, thus forming gay communities, especially in urban areas (Katz, 1992). During the early days of the AIDS epidemic, many lesbians, myself included, played leading roles in providing service and agitating for change. Just as Scott and his older brother share a deep bond based on gayness, so do many lesbians, gay men, and bisexuals. So it is important for the clinician to understand the special issues that affect gay people and how lesbians differ from gay men.

And some of these issues involve the intersection of orientation and gender. Modern (Post-Stonewall) gay culture has always tacitly accepted that some gay men are a little like women and some lesbians are a bit like men (Nestle, 1992). As Silverstein surmises, this intersection is the likely source of homophobia, as mainstream society is highly invested in a system of two genders with easily observable differences and relatively rigid roles. Gay culture has evolved over the last 40 years, but some forms of what is sometimes called "gender bending" or "gender queer" has always been an ever-present if sometimes controversial element. There were always drag queens among gay men—men who enjoy dressing as and impersonating women, often for entertainment. And there have always been "butches" and "femmes" among lesbians—some women who present as more male, some as more female (Nestle, 1992). More recently, the ways in which gender and orientation are morphing together are getting more complex and interesting (Nichols & Shernoff, 2006). For example, some transwomen (the term used to signify individuals who would formerly have been termed male-to-female transsexuals) are choosing to identify as lesbian after transitioning; others are living as women without gender reassignment surgery, that is, breasts, female body and presentation, but functioning penis. Others, transmen (formerly female-to-male transsexuals) may have identified as "butch lesbians" before assuming the transidentity, but after transition find themselves attracted to gay men or other transmen. In fact, this phenomenon became common enough in the gay male community, that a few years ago the Saint's "Black Party," an iconic "circuit party" for gay men in New York, used Buck Angel, a transman, as their "poster boy"—and they featured him nude and obviously without having undergone "bottom surgery." These recent trends in the LGBT community highlight the interconnectedness of two attributes of human nature we ordinarily see as separate, gender identity and sexual orientation.

Personal and Professional Biases

Although my job in this chapter does not rely on a particular approach or theoretical school of psychotherapy, it is useful to have at least a thumbnail portrait of my general approach to psychotherapy and in particular my views about sexual orientation and gender.

My techniques are easier to describe than my theoretical views. I am often directive, I give a lot of feedback, and I tend to be self-disclosing unless contraindicated. Unlike Silverstein, I would have done more talking in the session and probably made many more supportive, warm fuzzy statements—in other words, I would have been more motherly, because as a therapist that is often part of my persona. Indeed, I sometimes think of the therapeutic relationship, especially for younger clients like Scott, as a very specialized form of relationship, part parent–child, part objective, nonjudgmental observer, some mentor–mentee, and coaching at times. My techniques are varied and eclectic, and I will mention specific techniques as they become relevant to this case.

I am deliberately atheoretical, even antitheoretical when it comes to psychotherapeutic frameworks. A theoretical orientation is perhaps helpful because, among other things, it aids in organizing and simplifying data. In truly scientific endeavor, theories are testable and rejected if the data does not support the theory. But in psychology, which deals with complex human behaviors, it is not as easy to test a specific. Even when there is data, it is subject to widely differing interpretations. So I hold different theoretical frameworks, including and perhaps especially the *Diagnostic and Statistical Manual* (APA, 2000) of the American Psychiatric Society, very lightly. I am an avid follower of neuroscience research and that has influenced me to see most client problems as a result of a mix of biological and psychosocial factors. My personal experiences lead me to view clients very much in the context of their cultural upbringing and the generation in which they have grown up.

I am a licensed psychologist and a certified sex therapist, living and working in the "queer" community for most of my life. My main area of specialization is work with sexual and gender minorities: since 1983, I have seen hundreds of LGBT clients as well as people living BDSM/kink[1] or polyamorous lifestyles, and my colleagues at the institute I run have seen thousands more. This, of course, informs my perspective.

Because of the nature of Scott's case and the task of this chapter, my views of sexuality in general and sexual orientation and gender are clearly germane. Over the years I have developed a view of sexuality informed both by the "paradoxical perspective" of people such as Morin (1995) and the radical evolutionary biology views of scientists such as Roughgarden (2004). Briefly summarized, I believe that in the "natural" world, including humans, sex serves many functions, most of which do not involve reproduction. For example, we see in nonhuman mammals that sex is used for strengthening affiliation bonds, exercising power, and establishing hierarchies in groups, for fun, play, and so on. If this is true, the major assumption that underlies the pathologizing of sexual outliers is wrong. If the functions of sex are diverse, so should be sexual behavior and sexual orientation. It also follows that, as Morin theorizes, the drivers of sex will not just be warm and gentle, like love and connection, or even the quest for the genetic perfection, but multiple drives, some dark and dangerous, like transgression and dominance. Against the backdrop of biological influenced variations of sexuality along many dimensions, culture shapes the expression of sexuality. So, for example, in some cultures the "outlet" for gender-variant males attracted to other males is "lady-boys" (Thailand) or "berdache" (Native American) (Herdt, 1993); in twenty-first century US culture, the same personal attractions and tendencies might be expressed as transgender, gender-queer, gay drag queens, or simply gay men who make your "gaydar" go off (Savin-Williams, 2005).

I consider most of contemporary research on sexual orientation and gender identity to be fatally flawed. Most researchers are blind to the biases they bring to the table simply in accepting the idea that the goal of sex in mammals is reproduction. It is this "reproductive bias" that dictates that we somehow feel we need an explanation for same-sex behavior but not heterosexual sex, and more dangerously, it is the reproductive bias, historically upheld by Church and State, that pathologizes nonprocreative sexuality. Second, as psychologists, psychiatrists, and sex researchers, we have constructed labels such as "gay" and "heterosexual" to describe *as best we can with limited knowledge* the particular cultural iteration of phenomenon that I am convinced has existed in all times and all cultures—and then we forgot that we made up the labels, and their definitions, in the first place. In fact, not only do I believe that the categories are crude, I am also sure that there are dimensions of sexuality that are quite important that we now only dimly perceive—not just "sexual orientation" or "gender identity," but also dimensions such as fluidity versus stability of sexuality, strength of sex drive, predilection for monogamy, and need for variety and intensity in sexual stimulation.

---

[1] BDSM refers to bondage and discipline and sado-masochistic sex. Kink is a general term for atypical sex, such as one finds in the list of paraphilias in DSM, but without the connotation of being a pathology, only a sexual variation.

In terms of my therapeutic approach, what this means is that when I try to understand my clients, I not only look in terms of symptoms, biological predispositions, family, and peer influences, but also in the context of cultural and subcultural pressures. I look very hard at the role of gender, both biologically and culturally, and also at sexual orientation. I try to look at historical trends as well as the past to predict what kind of world my clients, if they are young, will be living in. I expect the issues of a 50-year-old gay man to be different from the issues of a 20-something gay man; the "complaints" are very culture-dependent. For example, I almost never find a young person needing extensive work to accept her or his gayness, a type of client that was common when I started in the early 1980s. And I think we see far fewer of those clients—the ones with horrible internalized homophobia—because their numbers have decreased in response to cultural shifts toward acceptance of gays. These days, I'm more likely to see a young client trying to figure out if she or he is gay, bi, trans, fluid, or gender queer.

Self-disclosure is natural to many "queer" therapists practicing in the LGBT community, as Silverstein models even before the first session, by forthrightly disclosing his sexual orientation to Scott. Many clients, perhaps especially members of sexual minorities, feel they can achieve the understanding they need only from someone who shares their sexual orientation. This is a powerful reason to self-disclose what might otherwise be regarded as highly personal information.

My first exposures to psychotherapy predisposed me to self-disclosure for other reasons. As a teen in the 1960s, I developed an addiction problem. First, I sought treatment from traditional psychotherapists. I was not helped at all, largely, in my view, because of what I saw as the detached, silent demeanor of these classically, analytically trained therapists. Later, in despair, I located what was then called a "therapeutic community," a drug rehabilitation method that eschewed traditional mental health professionals in favor of "peer counseling." I remained in this atmosphere, first as a client, and then as a "peer counselor," for 6 years. In 1973, I entered graduate school in clinical psychology deeply skeptical of my new profession. I subscribed to the "psychiatry-as-enforcer of cultural-morals" view of psychotherapy eloquently described in *The Myth of Mental Illness* (Szasz, 1961) and the "psychiatry-as-paternalistic" view outlined in Chesler's *Women and Madness* (1972).

Much of my skepticism, if not my in-your-face militancy, remain today. And, like many women who consider themselves, as I do, "feminist therapists," I believe that the power differential inherent in the traditional psychotherapy dyad should in most cases be broken down. One of the ways to do this is to *not* use the term "doctor" to refer to oneself; another method is to liberally self-disclose. This difference—the efforts I would make to shape the interview as more egalitarian, in a way—is perhaps the most obvious way my approach would diverge from Silverstein's, and I feel it is directly related to being a female therapist, more specifically someone who practices feminist psychotherapy.

In this chapter, I self-disclose for a different reason, to let you as the reader/ clinician know pertinent facts of my life that might influence counter-transference in Scott's case. I have already revealed some, my own earliest experiences with treatment and with being a counselor. In addition, I have lived an atypical sexual lifestyle, especially for a woman. Sex was an important part of much of life personally as well as professionally, and my experiences have been not only atypically numerous (again: the caveat "for a woman"; more about that later) but very diverse. I can relate to more than one of the sexual minorities with whom I work. I've been a social activist in mental health areas related to sexuality, for example with AIDS, bisexuality, and BDSM. In general, my lifestyle has been well outside of mainstream culture; for example, my female partner and I had one of the first "turkey baster babies" in the early 1980s,[2] and in addition to forming the Institute for Personal Growth, the group private practice where I still work, I was involved in founding both a feminist women's center and the largest AIDS social service center in New Jersey. I currently have a nontraditional family, which does not include any of the members of my family of origin, so I am perhaps more comfortable than many therapists with the idea that some parents are toxic and should be avoided, something that is of relevance to Scott's case.

One other event in my life affects my view of Scott and particularly my emotional response to his situation. In 2004 I lost a daughter, nearly 10 years old, who died after a difficult 3-month hospitalization following a prolonged misdiagnosis of a brain tumor—a situation not unlike the misdiagnosis of Scott's brother, David. My son was then 20 years old and extremely affected by the death of his sister, to whom he felt closely bonded. So I am a mother who lost a child and watched the sibling go through a very difficult and complicated grieving process. I have a deeper than average, and more visceral, knowledge of this kind of grief. Indeed, my practice now includes a number of bereaved parents and siblings; for example, two young men who lost siblings are in my practice now. This gives me a very special understanding, on one hand, but perhaps makes me less objective, on the other.

My life has been unconventional. I have lived and practiced for decades in a community where diversity is truly celebrated and where ideas considered so radical as to be preposterous by the mainstream are seriously debated, like the need for the death of the two-gender binary, for example, or whether sexual orientation is fluid or stable over time. That informs my assessments and methods in many ways. There is little that shocks me, and my tendency is to de-pathologize clients, sometimes too much. If anything, I err in the direction of seeing clients healthier than they may actually be. My interventions are nontraditional. If I get a client whose sexual preferences are kinky, I try to help that person get rid of their internalized "kink-phobia" instead of trying to "cure" the "paraphilia." I have occasionally suggested experimentation with polyamory or swinging to monogamous couples in therapy.

Unlike other authors in this collection, I have not been tasked with describing a particular therapy approach and contrasting it with other techniques. My job is to imagine the differences in how this interview would have been conducted, and the future directions treatment might take, first if I as a female therapist had done this, and second, if Scott had been a heterosexual female, a lesbian, or a heterosexual

---

[2] A term for babies conceived by a lesbian couple using a sperm donor and at-home insemination.

male. I will start with my view of Scott and how both my perspective on Scott and my interventions in the session would have diverged from Silverstein's. Then I tackle the second task. To accomplish it, I imagined three "alters" and describe them here. Finally, I try to extract general principles of sexual orientation and gender interaction that might be useful in a clinical setting. But before I describe the alters, let me summarize my view of Scott and his problems and point out how my female and feminist perspective informs me.

Scott, Through a Woman's Eyes

Scott is an easy client to like: engaging, intelligent, attractive, interesting, and personable. He is high-functioning with lots of strengths. He has no psychiatric history, a good, if demanding, job he enjoys and that pays well enough to allow him to live in an urban gay area. His plight triggers empathy and compassion, which in my case is probably connected to the fact that he is roughly my son's age. Scott could be a friend of my son's, someone I have hosted in my home. As a woman who is also a mother, I immediately have maternal feelings toward Scott, and I will probably radiate that to him in even this first session. He will see me as his mother's generation, but in his unconscious I may become the mother, his own mother cannot be for him. This transference can help our initial bonding but create complications later on in therapy.

Some of Scott's strengths have been gained from learning to survive in a highly dysfunctional and weirdly abusive family. He appears to be holding his parents together after David's death, especially his mother. However, it is hard to tell how much of Scott's success in life has depended on the support of his older brother David, now dead.

Scott is in a potentially serious crisis. He is dealing with "complicated bereavement." Just as some therapists consider any loss of a child by a parent to be by definition complicated bereavement, I would argue that often the death of a sibling at a young age—and 30 is young—is complex and of major proportions. For one thing, the death of a young person is a shock to a number of illusions we believe, illusions that are usually gradually worn away with age: that life is safe, that it is fair, that you can protect someone you love, and that you have control over your own life. Losing these beliefs may lead to wisdom; in youth, having them suddenly stripped away through unimaginable loss is frightening.

Scott's bereavement is also complicated because he was not just "close" to David. He idolized David and presents himself as being dependent on him—he even calls him "my ego." Moreover, David died as a result of HIV. Although HIV is less feared and stigmatized than it was in the 1980s, it is still seen by many, especially in mainstream society, as the result of sexual promiscuity. Scott undoubtedly sought a gay male therapist in part because he wanted to avoid this judgmental attitude, and he may have been less forthcoming about his own sexuality with a female therapist. If I were conducting this session I might have made a point of mentioning my past AIDS involvement and the fact that I lost beloved friends to the disease.

The death of an adored brother would be a crisis for anyone. But many other issues complicate Scott's situation. First, David made a shocking deathbed revelation, which revived accusations made years earlier that their father had had incestuous, or at least sexually inappropriate, contact with both boys. Scott says his suicidal thoughts "haven't been this strong since I was a teenager dealing with the whole molestation thing" (P134), suggesting the kind of revivification of traumatic memories common in post-traumatic stress disorder (PTSD). Second, Scott implies that he suffers from "a lot of guilt," (P134) connects it to what he suspects is insufficient grief over his brother's death, and then scurries away from this issue. It is likely that Scott suffers from "survivor's guilt," especially strong in sibling survivors. Moreover, Scott has put up with ongoing financial victimization by his father, for reasons in part related to his mother. He has a strong perceived obligation to assume the role of his mother's protector and, now, apparently, he has cooperated with her in helping her stave off grief about her son David's death. Scott feels extremely close to his mother, but their familial roles seem nearly reversed.

Other factors complicate this case. Scott suffers from anxiety and suicidal ideation. He seems dependent on marijuana use, and one senses the possibility for abusing alcohol as well. Scott maintains he wants a relationship—"Of course ... Who wouldn't?" (P135)—but that is unclear. He frames his relationship problems as his poor choices—choosing men who are unavailable. But from his history, it appears he has been nearly as unavailable as the boyfriends he decries. At the point of the first interview, it is hard to assess how much of Scott's expressed relationship difficulty is psychodynamic. It is hard for me to tell how much is even really a "problem," as opposed to, for example, an indicator of his youth and generation, a valuing of career opportunities above relationship ties, or even just an aversion to monogamy. But without knowing more about Scott's relationship patterns, it is still possible to glean from this interview that his interactions with men in the last year appear both desperate and dangerous. Scott is engaging in the most high-risk sexual behavior possible, unprotected receptive anal sex with men. Scott is grappling all at once with complicated grief over the loss of an important older brother, unhealthy engagement with his family of origin, a possible flare-up of PTSD, recent risky behavior, and relationship issues. One senses that Scott has come to therapy because he feels driven almost to the edge of what he can handle, and indeed his plate is much fuller than that of the average person of his age.

If I compare Silverstein's handling of this first session with Scott to what I imagine my own might be, and compare them from the perspective of being a feminist and female therapist, what comes to mind are perhaps more differences in technique than in assessment. Like Silverstein, I might have established my "credentials" on first telephone contact, in my case as someone who has had considerable exposure to gay men and HIV, who is "part of the tribe" if not a gay man herself. But once the session began, my style would have diverged substantially, in part simply because of individual differences in therapeutic styles, but to some extent because of varying perspectives influenced by our different genders.

I would have introduced myself like this, while smiling and extending a hand to shake Scott's: "Hi, I'm Margie. It's Doctor Nichols but I don't 'do' the doctor thing." I would have invited him to partake of candy, cookies, and bottled water left in the waiting room for clients and pointed to the rest room before leaving him with the 10 minutes' worth of paperwork he needed to fill out.

When I brought Scott into my office I would have invited him to sit on the sofa and spent a minute or two in small talk: the weather, how easy or hard it was to find the office, the neighborhood in which my office is located. My goal would be that by the time I began asking difficult questions we would already have made some human connection as *peers*. This, I believe, is a fundamental cornerstone of feminist therapy: that both partners in the dyad are equal. It is not an accident that I call consumers of psychotherapy "clients" instead of "patients." The point is to de-pathologize the consumer and make the relationship egalitarian. Silverstein has done an excellent job of explaining how psychiatry oppressed gay people by pathologizing homosexuality (Silverstein, 1972, 2009). Women have probably suffered even more abuse at the hands of the mental health establishment (Ehrenreich & English, 1978). Central to this abuse was the entrenched belief that the "doctor" was powerful and knowledgeable to know what was "good" for a "patient" despite the "patient's" wishes. So it is not surprising that I, as a feminist therapist, would want to avoid establishing what I view as an unequal, hierarchical relationship with someone seeking my services.

Rather than dissect each of Silverstein's interactions with Scott, let me make some generalizations about what I might have done differently. The cookies and candy are deliberate. I am quite comfortable with the persona I project that some of my clients have described as "earth mother." I see therapy as part science and medicine, but also part village shaman or wise woman, part re-parenting, part mentoring, and part guide to one's interior life. I am comfortable with a type of transference many therapists would discourage, just as I am comfortable with a degree of self-disclosure many would avoid. So Scott would know quite early on that I lost a child and that I have a son near his age who suffered through his sister's loss. I would be much more interactive with Scott, for example, normalizing his grief reaction so as to alleviate some of his guilt, giving him lots of positive feedback about his strengths and the difficulty of the tasks he is facing now. I would establish between us the bond of those who have lost a close family member while the family member is young. I might explain PTSD as a way of helping Scott understand his "manic" feelings and suicidal thoughts, and I might even mention that I use a fast, effective treatment method for PTSD called EMDR.[3] Again, my approach stems from the idea that Scott and I are collaborators right from the beginning, and that he deserves information and feedback.

There is one specific area where my approach is directly informed by my experiences as a woman treating female clients. I would have paid more attention to the allegations of molestation. I will write more about this later, when I tackle

---

[3] EMDR stands for "Eye Movement Desensitization and Reprocessing", developed as a treatment for PTSD.

the concept of Scott's alters. But at the least I would have told Scott that I thought his former therapist had minimized the issue and that this happens commonly when men or boys are molested. Because of my perspective on the impact of child–adult sexual contact, among other things, I would have taken Scott's suicidal thoughts more seriously. Before he left the session, Scott might have signed a no-suicide contract with me, or at least given me a verbal promise of safety, and gotten referrals to support groups for adults abused as children. It seems to me that this divergence from Silverstein's approach is the result of my experience with issues of female sexuality and abuse, both as a woman and as a feminist therapist.

Scott and His "Alters"

The primary task of this chapter is to explore how this initial interview might have been different if the presenting client, Scott, had been heterosexual or a straight or gay woman. Having seen clients representing the widest variety possible of sex and gender expression for over 25 years of practice, I know that there are some clients whose problems transcend identity and cultural background. Scott's case is not one of them. Although some of his problems—the bereavement, the family dysfunction—are arguably mostly "universal," many of them have a particular "spin" associated with his sexual orientation and gender.

This is because many of the problems Scott faces concern sexuality—sexual orientation, sexual abuse, sexual expression, and sexually transmitted diseases. And sexual issues, perhaps more than any other category of difficulties, vary distinctly by gender and sexual orientation. So, for example, as a gay man in the twenty-first century, Scott will see HIV differently than will his heterosexual counterparts—and even his lesbian sisters. And Scott and David's sexual behavior will be judged in certain ways relative to HIV risk precisely because they are gay men. Even sexual abuse, including incest, has different meaning depending on gender and sexual minority status. So Scott's interview provides rich material for an analysis of these variables. A *very* big caveat: By definition, this chapter is all about stereotypes and generalizations. Please be aware as you read that there is more variation of most traits and behaviors within a gender than between genders, and that the same is true of sexual orientation. The broad strokes I paint here risk being caricatures; I have tried to avoid this but in some ways it is inevitable.

In order to write this chapter, I imagined three counterparts, or alters, to Scott: Sarah, a heterosexual woman; Sue, a lesbian; and Sam, a heterosexual man. I encountered my first difficulty immediately: Sarah and Sam probably wouldn't have chosen a gay male therapist in the first place, and Sue might have specifically chosen a woman. So I started my imaginary characters with the assumption that the facts of the alters' lives resembled Scott's as much as possible, and that, like Scott, they sought out a gay male therapist.

I had trouble with some of the "facts," though; for example, that Scott had had only one session in his previous therapy experience. It was nearly impossible for me to imagine sophisticated, educated, urban women, gay or straight, not having gone into therapy for an extended period of time over the allegations of abuse that first surfaced when Scott was a teen. This difficulty is itself an example of gender differences in the treatment of child molestation. One of the legacies of the second wave of feminism was a heightened awareness of domestic violence and the sexual abuse of women, including incest and other sexual molestation of female children (Bass & Davis, 1988). Since the 1980s these have been high-visibility issues for women and ample resources and support, both peer and professional, have been developed. Similar awareness of the sexual abuse of male children has not occurred, or has occurred more recently (Abel & Harlow, 2001).

Because of this, Sue and Sarah might have handled the abuse allegations very differently when they first emerged. First, the showering episodes Scott describes would have been more likely to be seen *as* abuse, by them as they got older but certainly by the therapist they had as teenagers. Hence, both Sarah and Sue might have availed themselves of therapy and self-help groups to work through the allegations of abuse. Sue might be especially likely to consider herself an incest survivor: Lesbians are arguably the biggest consumers of psychotherapy and twelve-step programs of any sex/gender minority, and educated lesbians tend to be very informed about mental health issues (Ryan & Bradford, 1993).

In the end I decided to keep as many of the facts the same as I could, although that broke down when I got to family dynamics, which I will explain later. Before I tell you the stories of Sarah, Sue, and Sam, let me tell you how I believe being a gay man has shaped Scott's story so that you have a basis of comparison.

Scott's Narrative

The first thing I notice that marks Scott uniquely as a gay man is the way he discusses HIV. He is straightforward, matter of fact, and unashamed. While there is some stigmatization of gay men who seroconvert within the gay male community, it pales in comparison with the shame attached to contracting HIV for everyone else. HIV changed from being a terminal illness to mostly a chronic disease (for those who could afford good medical care) at about the time that Scott was a teenager and had his first sexual experience. He may not have known anyone who had died of AIDS/HIV until his brother's death, but he definitely came of age when sex was physically dangerous, and when HIV was still quite visible in the gay male community. On the other hand, *because* he may not have known men who died of AIDS, his attitude about safe sex may have become a bit complacent, which accounts for his attitude about "barebacking," or being the recipient of unprotected anal sex (Shernoff, 2005). It should be said that 20 years ago I would have seen Scott's behavior as flagrantly self-destructive, whereas I would now view it as a mixture of self-destructiveness and denial. Again, behavior must be evaluated in context; Scott's behavior, while risky, is unfortunately somewhat common, and is less risky than it used to be because HIV is so much less likely to be fatal.

This degree of riskiness of behavior also marks him as a gay man. Overall, gay men are *more* conscientious about condom use than heterosexuals; however, they are more at risk when they are *not* conscientious. The fact is HIV isn't easy to transmit. Oral sex has never emerged in any of the many Centers for Disease Control (CDC) sponsored studies as an easy vector of transmission, and vaginal sex isn't nearly as risky as anal sex. In fact, the risk to men from vaginal sex is extremely low and for women far lower than for those who engage in unprotected anal sex, no matter what the gender. Scott has a good deal of awareness of HIV risk because he *has* more risk, at least as compared to white, middle-class, straight people.

Scott's ambivalence about the alleged childhood sexual molestation is reflective of the lower visibility of this issue among men. But one thing stands out: When asked about prior therapy experiences, Scott indicates that David's therapist normalized their father's behavior and even implied that David had sexualized the showering together because of his sexual orientation. And, although it is not clear in this first session, this therapist's opinion may have in part persuaded Scott to see these incidents as "normal," as well. Scott may have blamed himself for sexual contact, or imagining sexual contact with his father. Although he never said this, on some level he may believe these incidents turned him gay. His somewhat driven behavior with male partners in the last year may be a replication of early father–son psychic drama, a manifestation of PTSD. But at least consciously, Scott seems to have minimized the possibility of sexual molestation by his father, and David's deathbed revelation of a "circle jerk" organized by Dad has threatened his compartmentalization of this contact and triggered significant anxiety. This is going to be a significant issue for Scott, as it would for anyone, but it will be complicated in particular by his gender. Because sexual abuse of male children has so little visibility, Scott will get less support and have fewer resources than if he were female.

The fact that Scott and David were both gay makes their bond special, and the bereavement more difficult. Scott makes the men sound almost like twins. In addition, the young men were each other's family support; Scott cannot rely on either parent to support him through his grief, and there are no other siblings. Fortunately, there are good supports for HIV bereavement in the gay male community, especially in urban areas. Although there was no time to assess Scott's support system of friends in this session, it is likely that as a gay man living in a city, it is both strong and accessible.

Scott's relationship with his mother seems quintessentially gay male. Years ago the "theory" about gay men was that they were the product of overprotective mothers (Bieber, 1962). It never occurred to therapists that the mothers of gay boys needed to be protective of them. Scott's mother, although she did not protect them from abuse by the father (if indeed it occurred). She may have protected Scott and David in other ways. Mothers tend to be more accepting of gender-variant boys than are fathers, and this may be in part the source of his protection of her. The flashes of anger Scott professes are appropriate, but he seems to act from guilt rather than rationality. In addition, Scott may identify with his mother as another victim of Dad, and this may drive his "enabling" behavior.

Drug use and sexual impulsivity/compulsivity tend to be more typical of males than females, who are more likely to engage in behaviors like self-cutting or disordered eating. One would expect Scott and his heterosexual male counterpart to exhibit these coping behaviors, and for the behaviors themselves to be somewhat normalized. The same behaviors are more transgessive for women, and thus carry different meanings.

For a gay man, Scott's sexual history is moderate; his first sex was around age 16—a friend of his older brother's—and he describes it as an unambivalently good experience. He had only a few sexual partners until 3 years ago, after the break-up of the second of his two "serious" relationships. Scott reports the number of his total sex partners to be "probably somewhere in the teens" (P94), but it is unclear how many of these encounters have involved unsafe sex. Scott's muted concern about his unsafe sex is all the more striking because of David's death and history of false negatives.

Sarah's Story

If Sarah is Scott's heterosexual female counterpart, she chose an openly gay male therapist because she is culturally liberal, expects empathy about David's death from a gay man, and understands that a gay male therapist will be nonjudgmental about HIV. In addition, an openly gay male therapist would be less likely to trigger father issues, which Sarah undoubtedly has, and a female therapist might provoke her anger at her mother. I imagine Sarah as much more ambivalent than Scott about her mother, for a number of reasons that I will explain in a while.

Because of the high visibility of sexual abuse among women, both Sarah and her lesbian counterpart Susan would have been more likely to begin therapy after the original revelations, and neither would be likely to see showering with Dad as harmless. It is very possible that both women felt some uneasiness when they were young children. Moreover, David's therapist, who apparently saw father–son showering as appropriate, would have been unlikely to normalize father–daughter nudity. Even if Sarah had not continued in therapy, there are extensive networks of "survivor" groups for women from which she could have obtained help. In fact, between the allegations of incest, Dad's gambling problem, and the propensity of women toward psychological self-improvement, both Sarah and Susan might have been involved in Gam-Anon (for those associated with a gambling addict) or Adult Survivors of Childhood Abuse (ASCA) groups. Sarah would be more likely to see herself as a victim of her father, might have a bond with Mom based on their shared abuse at his hands, and might consider herself a victim of the men she dates, instead of just someone who makes bad choices.

If Sarah was neither in therapy nor in any of these groups, I might be more worried about her than about Scott when suicidal thoughts are expressed. I assume that the degree of denial Sarah needed to counteract somewhat common messages in her environment would have been intense, and this use of denial, a somewhat primitive coping mechanism, suggests an underlying fragility. In addition, I would expect Sarah to be wrestling with more sexual shame than Scott, simply because women *have* more shame about sex than men, almost regardless of the issue. Compared to Scott, Sarah's relationships with men seem more likely to be a reenactment of the incest situation. All in all, this is a volatile situation, on top of her losing her idolized and idealized older brother. Although Sarah would not have the bond that Scott and David had as gay men, she might have looked at David as a protector and perhaps fear she could not manage life without him. I might be thinking seriously about suggesting medication to Sarah, fearing more risk of self-harm.

But let us assume instead that Sarah availed herself of self-help groups, which, I believe, can be as effective as psychotherapy. In this case, she might have a healthier relationship with her parents than Scott. She would consider herself a "survivor," and she would be more likely than Scott to have already distanced from her parents, emotionally if not literally. In fact, Sarah might well have sponsors in her ASCA program urging her to cut off her "toxic parents." Sarah might be angrier with Mom for not having protected her from incestuous contact with her father, because, unlike Scott, Sarah has no ambivalence about whether the contact was inappropriate. Sarah is likely to consider Mom an "enabler," a paradigm that would fully justify Sarah's pulling support from Mom and no longer shielding Dad. Sarah might have decided not to prosecute her father for his last credit card fraud act against her, but she would be unlikely to continue this behavior for long. The deathbed revelation would have a less-disturbing impact on Sarah because she has already come to see her father as a sexual abuser, and so in the long run the disclosure will be less shocking to her. I would be less worried about her than I would be about Scott, especially if, as is likely, she has a support system in the self-help community so-called "sexual abuse survivors."

Sarah's sexual history has a different meaning because she is a woman, as well. While it may not be unusual for a man, particularly a gay man, to have had partners "in the teens" at age 30, it is substantially above the national average for women: for females aged 30–44, the average is four (Laumann, Gagnon, Michael, & Michaels, 1994; Peplau, 2003). Arguably, the average is probably a bit higher for single, urban women, and certainly Sarah's "numbers" don't suggest sexual addiction or obviously self-destructive behavior. Sarah may be more sexual than the average woman—but she may also be acting out the incestuous behavior. Certainly, she is more likely to have some shame attached to her behavior, even in this age of *Sex and the City*, and she would not have accepted so easily Silverstein's assertion that the amount of her sex was "not a lot." Moreover, since Sarah is not gay, I imagine her having her first sex with a straight male friend of David's and see it as more significant, because 16-ish is a big young for a straight girl to have intercourse (average age is 17.4 years for girls, Laumann et al., 1994), and having sex with someone that much older is also unusual. So from the start, there is something different about Sarah's sexuality.

Perhaps what differentiates Sarah from Scott the most is HIV. The data shows that heterosexuals are far less likely to be concerned about safe sex than gay men or lesbians. According to the CDC, less than one-third of sexually active heterosexual youth use condoms (Shaw, 2010). Indeed, the term "safe sex" is a gay term, used by gay men and lesbians but not much by heterosexuals. In part, the lack of concern about HIV is a reflection of reality. So for Sarah, what constitutes "unsafe" or "risky" sex is possibly the lack of birth control, and if she is using birth control but not a condom, she is likely to be afraid of contracting genital warts (HPV), not HIV. Sarah would probably be surprised at Silverstein's concern about HIV, even with David's history of false positives. And I would view Sarah's behavior, not as an unconscious death wish, but rather perhaps a wish to get pregnant and sabotage her career, or perhaps a way to enact an unconscious psychodrama involving her father.

Susan, Scott's Lesbian Alter

If it is difficult to imagine Sarah not seeking therapy 12 years earlier for incest allegations, it is even more difficult to imagine this for Susan, because awareness of abuse is so prominent in the lesbian community. Susan's choice of a gay male is unusual; lesbians tend to want female therapists, no matter what their orientation (Ryan & Bradford, 1993). So I imagine she is seeing Silverstein because she has gay male friends and experiences gay men as less judgmental about sex than women. As a lesbian revealing unsafe sexual practice, she might be acutely aware of the possibility of being judged.

Because it is so hard to imagine Susan as an educated, urban lesbian *not* seeking therapy for the incest, I will assume that she has availed herself of the sexual abuse survivor self-help groups ubiquitous in the community. The LGBT Center in New York, for example, houses numerous sexual abuse recovery groups, incest survivor groups, and ASCA groups, but only one incest survivor group for men. Susan, like Sarah, would be more likely than Scott to see showers with Dad as incestuous behavior, to have had clear validation from the lesbian community, and to have resolved it. She may have gone through a period where she had worries that Dad "turned her gay," but she might not care. As a lesbian survivor of father–daughter incest once said to me, "if he turned me gay it's the only good thing the son of a bitch ever did for me."

In general, Susan would be more like Sarah, her heterosexual sister, than Scott, her gay brother. This underscores a theme that I will return to repeatedly in the remainder of this paper: where women are concerned, gender often trumps sexual orientation. So, like Sarah, Susan is likely to have resolved more issues about early sexual molestation than would Scott, and thus less likely to have been thrown into crisis by David's deathbed revelation. Unlike Scott, she would not be ambivalent about whether abuse occurred, she would probably be angrier with both her mother and father and less enmeshed in their dysfunction.

Therefore, Susan is probably ready and willing to ditch the family. Many lesbians and gays have suffered at least temporary estrangement from their family of origin (LaSala, 2010), and thus create nonbiological families composed of ex-lovers and friends. Susan probably has a community to support her, feels much less need for parental relationships in general, and would find a great deal of support for cutting off her relationships with both parents.

If Silverstein's client was a lesbian, her biggest issue might turn out to be her sexual behavior and "unsafe sex." Susan, like Sarah, is a sexual outlier; few women are as sexual as she. She was young to have her first sexual experience and she has had more sexual partners than the average woman, heterosexual or lesbian. What does Susan mean by unsafe sex? Lesbian sex is safe to begin with. Ironically, from the beginning of the HIV epidemic, lesbians have been more vocally concerned about HIV than heterosexuals, while at the same time being the lowest risk group. In fact, there are only a few case reports of woman-to-woman HIV transmission, and most of those cases have other risk factors as well (e.g., IV drug use). But while lesbians turned out in great numbers to lovingly care for their dying gay brothers during the first 15 years of the epidemic, they have tended to be if anything overly cautious about safe sex. And, correspondingly, lesbians can be very judgmental of other lesbians who contract HIV—especially if their exposure was through having sex with men.

As a therapist, Silverstein would have questioned Susan more about her assertion that she has had unsafe sex because her definition of safe/unsafe is not immediately obvious. Given the views about sexual safety that are prevalent in the lesbian community, Susan's statement could have signified her participation in two types of activities:

1. Sexual behaviors that are considered unsafe among lesbians but that in reality are not very dangerous. Susan might have not used condoms on sex toys or sterilized the toys; she might have had sex while she or a partner were menstruating; she could have had oral sex without using dental dams. She may have had sex with bisexual women. If this is the kind of activity Susan is worried about, it might be prudent for the therapist to allay her anxiety with facts. I would have done so, and I might further have encouraged Susan to get an HIV test, making certain to tell her doctor about her brother's tendency to test false negative. But I would not be particularly worried that Susan was HIV positive. The suggestion would be primarily to promote her peace of mind. Susan came to see a gay therapist because she knew he would neither be unduly alarmed nor judgmental about this "unsafe" sex. But the "unsafeness" of her sex would not be something Susan's therapist would be focusing on a lot in future sessions, except as a psychological issue—for example, if she believes these behaviors to be risky, even if they aren't, why is she doing them?

2. Susan might mean something entirely different when she calls her behavior "unsafe." She may mean that she's been having unprotected sex with men while living as a lesbian-identified woman. This behavior would put Susan at about the same level of risk of contracting HIV as Sarah, unless Susan is sleeping with bisexual men. Susan's therapist might have more concern about pregnancy than about HIV. In fact, if this were Susan's revelation about "unsafe sex," the entire focus of treatment going forward would change. Besides the obvious crisis issues of PTSD, suicidal ideation, and complicated bereavement, Susan has another very big problem. She is a self-identified lesbian, living in an urban lesbian community, but sleeping with men. Susan, at age 30, grew up in the age of "LUGs," or "Lesbians Until Graduation," the humorous, slightly negative term used to describe the prevalent bisexual experimentation among college-age and 20-something women and the sometimes fluid sexual identity that younger women exhibit. Diamond (2008) has followed these women and finds that they tend to change sexual orientation identity as they change the gender of their partner.

The problem is that bisexuality has been a divisive issue in the lesbian community for years. As Paula Rust (1995) observes in a study of lesbian attitudes toward bisexuality, "there are a variety of images, both positive and negative, but the negative far outnumber the positive" (p. 93). So if Susan is lesbian-identified and having sex with men, she is likely to be secretive about this and hide it from her lesbian friends for fear of what could be almost a "shunning." Not only will Susan be coping with identity issues, she is probably fearful of being an outcast among her friends if her behavior is revealed, especially if she is not using condoms with her male partners. In this scenario, Susan risks being stigmatized as a "carrier" for HIV, and her opportunities for female partners would drastically decrease. If Susan is having unprotected sex with men, then the dominant treatment themes going forward would be: the health risks of her behavior, primarily pregnancy or non-HIV STDs; the meaning this sexual behavior has for her identity; and the potential for loss of her support system.

If Susan is estranged from her family of origin, which she is more likely to be than Scott, the loss of community could be devastating. One of Silverstein's interventions might well be to encourage Susan to attend the numerous bisexual support groups that exist in most urban LGBT centers. Realistically, she might lose support from lesbians and ultimately she might feel more comfortable with other bisexuals.

The issue of relationship avoidance would be a bit different for Susan as well. Silverstein would be well advised to encourage Susan, like Sarah, to explore her obviously ambivalent desire to be in a monogamous relationship. Susan is a woman, and has been socialized or predisposed to prioritize relationships over individual achievement, to believe that sex is moral in the service of romantic love, and to feel she is not "complete" without a partner with whom she lives in monogamous commitment. To that extent Susan, like Sarah, probably experiences more shame about her sexual behavior than does Scott. So Silverstein will want to explore how much Susan's ambivalence about having a relationship implies difficulties with intimacy or just a desire to remain unattached. Silverstein should validate single-hood as a viable lifestyle; among women (and some men), being single is what happens when you are in between relationships. And he needs to challenge her assumption of monogamous commitment.

There are many forms of nonmonogamy (Taormino, 2008). It is most common among gay men: nonmonogamy was accepted decades ago by most male couples (McWhirter & Mattison, 1984) and the incidence did not really decrease even after the HIV epidemic (LaSala, 2004). Forms of nonmonogamy became visible among heterosexuals briefly in the 1970s as "open marriage" and "swinging" (O'Neill & O'Neill, 1984), but then became subterranean until they resurfaced again, facilitated by the Internet, in the form of the polyamory movement sometime in the 1990s (Anapol, 1997). Similarly, nonmonogamy was promoted among lesbian-feminists in the 1970s and early 1980s (Vance, 1984), only to lose visibility and later reemerge as polyamory (Munson & Stelbourn, 1999). The difference between polyamory and other forms of nonmonogamy is that "poly," as it is called, implies emotional attachment as opposed to purely recreational sex, and sometimes even involves group marriages. It is more suited to many women than are the more recreational forms of nonmonogamy practiced by most gay men and swingers. Gay men rarely consider themselves "polyamorous" and are infrequently found at "poly" events. And even though most people who consider themselves "polyamorous" are heterosexual or bisexual, the average heterosexual is unlikely to know of this community (Nelson, 2010). Lesbians, on the other hand, have always had a small but visible contingency of "sex radicals" (Nichols, 1987) and sexual issues tend to be openly debated. Thus, paradoxically, while Susan might face harsh censure from some lesbians if she has sex with men, she also has easy access to support groups of bisexual women and those who practice alternative lifestyles like polyamory (Munson & Stelbourn, 1999; Taormino, 2008). Susan probably already knows some lesbians experimenting with open relationships and the poly lifestyle could be at some point a potential resolution to her conflict between desire for intimacy and desire for independence.

Sam, the Heterosexual Male Alter

Sam, the heterosexual male younger brother of David, a gay man, undoubtedly overcame his own internalized homophobia years ago in order to be so close to his brother. He is therefore likely to be quite comfortable among gay men and to seek a gay male therapist because Sam would assume that such a therapist would be nonjudgmental, particularly about both HIV and unsafe sex. If Sam refers to "unsafe sex," he may mean condomless sex with a female partner. If this is the case, Sam is at low risk of contracting HIV, both because women who are not IV addicts or the partners of addicts have low rates of HIV infection and because the female-to-male transmission vector is weak. But I can imagine another scenario for Sam that involves exploration of sex with men.

Like David, Sam is more likely to be genuinely unclear about whether incest occurred, so the deathbed story would have great impact on him, probably pushing him to squarely confront the issue of molestation for what may be the first time. The recent stories about priest abuse have helped sexual abuse of boys come out into the open as an issue, but it is still true that estimates are that males are abused at a lower rate than females (Abel & Harlow, 2001) and they are certainly less common users of incest survivor resources. Therefore, Sam could very plausibly have discontinued therapy years before as did Scott, and Sam is arguably even less likely to find support groups for men sexually abused as boys than Scott. So Sam's reaction to what David revealed might activate memories Sam has firmly repressed. Sam, like Scott, is likely to be experiencing full-blown PTSD, as opposed to Sarah and Susan, who likely dealt with their childhood abuse more extensively.

Sam has probably repressed not only memories of possible molestation but also the turmoil that these revelations created in his family 12 years before. His suicidal thoughts may represent a breakthrough into consciousness of fears associated with these incidents, one of which may be that the experiences caused both brothers, not just David, to "turn gay." If Sam has experienced any feelings toward men, this might make him question his sexuality. If his "unsafe sex" is with men, Silverstein will be dealing with serious possibility of HIV transmission and even more prominently, major sexual identity confusion. If Sam is dealing with attractions to men, however, it bodes well that he chose an explicitly gay therapist. Clearly, Sam intends to confront these fears rather than run from them.

But Sam, like Scott, has probably not received help in resolving these childhood incidents of blurred sexual boundaries and molestation. He is, therefore, very unlikely to define himself as an "incest survivor," and very likely to still have a relationship with both parents that is confused, full of ambivalence, and over-involved rather than distant. Sam's relationship with his parents may be very similar to Scott's: close to Mom, protecting her from Dad, angry and disdainful of his father, but not angry enough at his mother's failure to protect him. It will be very helpful for Silverstein, going forward, to direct Sam to male incest survivor groups, which frequently take place in gay centers, for validation, information, and support. Without this direction, Sam is less likely to find these resources by himself than is Scott.

Among Scott and his three alters, Sam is the least likely to have resolved issues related to childhood molestation. But apart from this, Sam is actually the least likely of the four to experience shame about his sexuality. His first sexual experience was just around the median age for boys, his number of sexual partners, while perhaps a tad high at his age for a heterosexual male, would more likely be a source of pride than shame to him. If his unsafe sex is condomless sex with women, he might be oblivious to his own risk of HIV infection; his concern about not using condoms would be mostly fear of contracting herpes or genital warts or the fear of getting a girl pregnant. He would be less likely to be concerned about being single—30 is still not considered abnormally old for a heterosexual man to be single. If Sam's unsafe sex has been with men, the danger of his behavior needs to be addressed rapidly, as Silverstein did with Scott in the first interview, albeit clumsily.

So the most pressing issues for Sam, besides bereavement, depend on whether he is wrestling with sexual attraction to males. If not, he must finally explore and come to terms with the question of his childhood abuse, and he must find a way to extricate himself from the toxic triangle with his parents. Sam, like Scott, must change his role with his mother and put a stop to his father's financial swindling. Like Scott, Sam's habitual protectiveness of his mother may be augmented by survivor guilt. And, as a straight man, he might have identified more with Dad than did Scott, and that may be a complicating factor in the family dynamic. For example, because of this identification Sam might yearn for an earlier close relationship with his father, or he might be worried that he would "turn out like" Dad. Neither Scott nor Susan or Sarah are as likely to experience these conflicts. And if Sam's "unsafe sex" involves sex with men, then Silverstein will be dealing with sexual identity issues arguably more intense and fraught than those Susan will experience if she is having sex with men. Susan is used to being outside the mainstream, and used to creating communities of support for herself among sexual minorities. Moreover, bisexual women's support groups abound. Thus, it is probably easier to go from lesbian to bisexual woman than from heterosexual man to bi or gay man. Fortunately, if this is what awaits Sam, he had the model of his older brother David to guide him, as well as the best therapist he could have chosen to help.

Summary

As I look at Scott and his alters—these sex and gender permutations—I am struck by the following similarities and differences.

Sarah and Susan have the following in common:

- Similar cultural socialization regarding sexuality;
- Similar experience with an incestuous father;
- Similar cultural pressure to be in a monogamous relationship;
- Similar support systems for sexual abuse;
- Similar likelihood that they have dealt with some of the family issues.

What is most different about them—the way that sexual orientation influences the mix—is that Sarah has enjoyed more mainstream acceptance, even in these days of lesbian chic, and that she has not dealt with the sometimes complex sexual identity issues that Susan has faced, and will be facing again if she is having sex with men. This difference of course cascades to other dynamics, but still, my overall impression is that Sarah and Susan are more alike than different.

Sarah and Sam, however, seem to have much less in common, besides heterosexual mainstream identity and lifestyle. Their reactions to every single aspect of this case that involves sexuality and relationships will most likely be different, sometimes starkly so (e.g., shame about multiple partners versus pride).

Sam and Scott have the following in common:

- Similar likelihood that the alleged sexual abuse was never explored, with all the attendant mental health issues that implies;
- Similarly ambivalent attitudes about whether the abuse ever occurred;
- Because of this, similar family dynamics;
- A similarly unremarkable sexual history, up until the riskiness of the past year;

On the other hand, the differences are significant as well. Heterosexual and gay men represent opposite ends of the risk spectrum for contracting HIV. Sam, like Sarah, has always enjoyed heterosexual privilege. He has not experienced life outside the mainstream, nor the stigma that still results from being gay. Sam is less likely than Scott to feel shame about his sexuality, while Scott may have some sexual shame related to internalized homophobia.

As two gay people, Susan and Scott share a common community, one with better resources for incest survivors—much better for Susan—than are available to their heterosexual counterparts. In fact, in general one of the things shared by both lesbian and gay male culture is a more open, explorative, and nonjudgmental attitude toward most aspects of sexuality. For example, lesbians were among the first women to declare themselves "sex radicals" and question negative attitudes toward pornography, kinky sex, gender bending, and nonmonogamy in the feminist movement (Vance, 1984), and variant sexual practices are taken for granted in the lesbian community (Nichols & Shernoff, 2006). So in general, Scott and Susan both will receive more support for sexual issues of all kinds than will their heterosexual counterparts. And, of course, they both experienced "coming out" issues and the struggles of being a stigmatized minority (LaSala, 2010). But the gender differences between Scott and Susan outnumber the similarities attendant to their shared sexual orientation. Everything from the meaning of their sexual histories, the likelihood of contracting HIV, the degree of shame connected to sexuality, their likelihood of having worked through the molestation issues, and the relationships they have with their parents would be different for these two gay people.

In the case of "Scott," gender differences trump sexual orientation, and I would argue that this will often be true when there are sexual or romantic relationship issues of a particular kind: those dominated by paternalistic power differentials, sexual issues in which the "double standard" prevails. These issues throw gender differences into high relief while sexual orientation differences are muted. By contrast, a clinical case without sexual issues, or with sexual concerns of a different nature, might show a different kind of pattern.

Imagine Scott's case, and his three alters, without sexual abuse and without any concerns about sexual behavior. There are few ways such a case would vary by gender or sexual orientation. In bereavement, perhaps the males would be more likely to express their grief as irritability and the females as sadness. The women might be more likely to be the parents' caretaker than the males, particularly Sam, the heterosexual male alter. But these are not major differences. A case with no sexual or intimate relationship issues might actually be a gender and orientation-blind case, or the closest we come to it in reality. In that case, not much specialized knowledge of either gender differences or sexual orientation would be required on the part of the therapist; being gay affirmative, for example, might have been sufficient, as opposed to gay-knowledgeable.

Our perceptions of child sexual abuse vary by gender because they stem directly from our general beliefs about the differences between male and female sexuality. We know that males are more sexually active than females in nearly every way and at an earlier age (Laumann et al., 1994). Moreover, men seem more able to separate sex and romantic love than women. It is hard to deny that a cultural double standard still exists, that we reward men for being sexual and punish women for being sexual except under narrowly constrained circumstances, such as when sex is part of a romantic relationship. Anyone who has raised teens of both genders knows this: The sexual behavior my son engaged in to enhance his "reputation" as a teen would lower my adolescent daughter's "reputation."

Upon reflection, I realized that my own initial reaction to Scott's showering story was influenced by gender bias. I thought, "Maybe it *was* innocent. Maybe the boys' discomfort *was* rooted in their early recognition of male-sexual attractions." My doubts about the meaning of the father—son showering led me to have doubts about the deathbed story as well, wondering whether this was a "real" event or a distorted "recovered memory." But when I imagined Sarah and Susan, I had no such thoughts. I felt instinctively that the showering was inappropriate, and that it might indicate greater abuse. David's story seemed more plausible, too: a man who sexually abuses children very often abuses girls and boys alike.

Some of my reaction simply reflected the heterocentric cultural value that it is "okay" for persons of the same sex to be naked in each other's company, but not for opposite sex children or adults. But there is also gender bias. What is our reaction to the idea of a mother showering with her 7- or 8-year-old son? It makes most of us uncomfortable, and we might think of the mother as "smothering" and "lacking boundaries." But many of us would not automatically think of the mother as a sexual predator, as we might a father who showers with his daughter.

The other sexual issues in this case that make gender differences so salient involve sexual activity and STIs (sexually transmitted infections). Here, the double standard prevails. Heterosexual men brag about, even exaggerate, their sexual exploits. Gay men flaunt their "sluttiness." But few women, gay or straight, can take open pride in having large quantities of sexual partners or sexual activity, and many women see STIs not simply as health problems but as a cause for shame and proof of their "dirtiness."

There are some areas of sexuality where gay men and lesbians are more similar to each other than their heterosexual counterparts. Gay people deal with other gender and sexual variations better than heterosexuals. Among gays and lesbians, especially in urban areas, BDSM and nonmonogamy/polyamory have such high visibility and such a relatively high frequency of occurrence that there is little stigma attached to these forms of sexual behavior. Even bisexuals and transgender people, who confront some discrimination within the gay community, are more easily accepted there than they are within mainstream heterosexual society (Nichols, 1994).

The dynamics of intimate couple relationships vary at times by gender, at other times by sexual orientation. On one hand, considerable research has found that both gay male and lesbian couples are more egalitarian than heterosexual couples (Gottman, 2010; Schwartz, 1994). Gay couples, like heterosexual couples, establish roles within the relationship that may appear similar to heterosexual gender roles. But the roles taken by gay couples lack the consistency usually found in opposite sex pairings: the gay man who does the cooking may be the "top" in bed; the "lipstick lesbian" may be the one who grouts the tile in the bathroom. Moreover, there is no inherent assumption of a power differential that follows gender. An example of this comes from the literature about heterosexual versus gay/lesbian parents. Heterosexual couples leave the bulk of parenting *and* home chores to women, even when both partners are working, thus privileging the father. Gay and lesbian couples share more equal distribution of these tasks, regardless of which partner appears to be more feminine or masculine (APA, 2010; Bryant & Demian, 1994).

On the other hand, there are ways in which same-sex couples seem to exhibit extremes of gender-stereotypic behavior. Gay male couples are frequently successful in negotiating nonmonogamy; perhaps this is because both partners have the male ability to compartmentalize sex. Long-term lesbian couples have arguably less sex than heterosexual or gay male relationships but more affection (Blumstein & Schwartz, 1983; Nichols, 2005); this could be seen as an expression of a female sexual ideal. Another female trait, prioritizing couple relationships, is caricatured in this joke ubiquitous in the gay community: Q: What does a lesbian bring to the second date? A: A U-Haul. Moreover, as Gottman (2010) observes, gay couples are often more effective in communicating and resolving conflict because, as two males or two females, they "speak the same language."

Of most interest to me are questions that involve the interaction of gender and sexual orientation. For example, based on personal experience, it did not surprise me to learn that researchers had proven gay and lesbian parents to be more egalitarian than heterosexual parents. What I am interested in is how the lesbian and gay parents differ from each other. To the extent that same-sex couples sometimes magnify gender-stereotypic behavior (lesbian cuddling versus gay male nonmonogamy), their behavior can tell us something about male and female behavior when it is unconstrained by someone with opposing role behaviors. For example, lesbian sexual encounters, which typically last longer, involve more nongenital touching, and result in a higher percentage of orgasms than do heterosexual encounters, may represent unrestrained female sexuality, just as gay male nonmonogamy probably represents an ideal for males.

In Scott's case, examples of these intersections of gender and sexual orientation seemed minor. Unless Silverstein deliberately used a stereotype to throw readers off the track of Scott's true identity, his choice of a "creative profession" is one such case. So, to me, was his exceptionally close relationship to his mother, which seems more characteristic of gay men than of heterosexual men. The closeness may have been based solely on the other family dynamics, but it may also stem from Scott's partial identification with his mother as a gender-variant boy.[4]

Scott's case is interesting because at first reading it appears to be "all about" male homosexuality: two gay brothers, a gay therapist, and HIV. But in the end, the gender-related issues surrounding sexual abuse and the cultural double standard regarding sexual behavior may turn out to dominate the problems related to sexual identity, gender trumping orientation just as it frequently does in everyday life.

References

Abel, G., & Harlow, N. (2001). *The stop child molestation book*. Bloomington, IN: Xlibris.

American Psychiatric Association (2000). *Diagnostic and statistical manual of mental disorder: Text revision* (4th ed.). Washington DC: American Psychiatric Association.

American Psychological Association. (2010). *APA Amicus brief: Lesbian and gay parenting*. www.apa.org/pi/lbgt/resources/parenting.aspx#.

Anapol, D. (1997). *Polyamory: The new love without limits*. San Rafael, CA: Intinit.

Bass, E., & Davis, E. (1988). *The courage to heal*. New York: Harper & Row.

Bieber, I. (1962). *Homosexuality: A psychoanalytic study of male homosexuals*. New York: Basic Books.

Blumstein, P., & Schwartz, P. (1983). *American couples: Money, work and sex*. New York: William Morrow.

Bryant, A., & Demian, N. (1994). Relationship characteristics of American gays and lesbians. *Journal of Gay and Lesbian Social Services, 1*, 100–117.

---

[4] If he was gender variant as a child—there is not enough information in this first interview to determine that, and certainly not all gay men were gender variant as children.

Chesler, P. (1972). *Women and madness*. New York: MacMillan.

Chivers, M., Rieger, G., Latty, E., & Bailey, J. (2004). A sex difference in the specificity of sexual arousal. *Psychological Science, 15*, 736−744.

Diamond, L. (2008). *Sexual fluidity: Understanding women's love and desire*. Cambridge, MA: Harvard University Press.

Ehrenreich, B., & English, D. (1978). *For her own good: Two centuries of experts' advice to women*. New York: Anchor Books.

Gottman, J. (2010). *The 12 year study: Gay and lesbian couples research*. http://www.gottman.com/SubPage.aspx+spdt_id=100842&spt_id=1.

Green, R. (1987). *The sissy boy syndrome and the development of homosexuality*. New Haven, CT: Yale University Press.

Herdt, G. (1993). *Third sex, third gender: Beyond sexual dimorphism in culture and history*. New York: Zone Books.

Isay, R. (1997). Remove gender identity disorder from the DSM. *Psychiatric News, Nov.*, 3−4.

Katz, J. (1992). *Gay American history* (revised ed.). New York: Plume.

LaSala, M. C. (2004). Extradyadic sex and gay male couples: Comparing monogamous and nonmonogamous relationships. Families in Society. *The Journal of Contemporary Human Services, 85*, 405−412.

LaSala, M. C. (2010). *Coming out, coming home: Helping families adjust to a gay or lesbian child*. New York: Columbia University Press.

Laumann, E., Gagnon, J., Michael, R., & Michaels, S. (1994). *The social organizations of sexuality: Sexual practices in the United States*. Chicago, IL: University of Chicago Press.

Lev, A. I. (2004). *Transgender emergence: Therapeutic guidelines for working with gender-variant people and their families*. New York: Haworth Clinical Practice Press.

McWhirter, D., & Mattison, A. (1984). *The male couple*. Englewood Cliffs, NJ: Prentice-Hall.

Morin, J. (1995). *The erotic mind*. New York: Harper Collins.

Munson, M., & Stelbourn, J. (1999). *The lesbian polyamory reader: Open relationships, non-monogamy, and casual sex*. New York: Haworth Press.

Nelson, T. (2010). The new monogamy. *Psychotherapy networker, 34*(4), 20−28.

Nestle, J. (Ed.), (1992). *The persistent desire: A femme−butch reader*. Boston, MA: Alyson.

Nichols, M. (1987). What feminists can learn from the lesbian sex radicals. *Conditions Magazine, 14*, 152−163.

Nichols, M. (1994). Therapy with bisexual women. In M. P. Mirkin (Ed.), *Women in context: Toward a feminist reconstruction of psychotherapy* (pp. 149−169). New York: Guilford.

Nichols, M. (2004). Lesbian sexuality/female sexuality rethinking "lesbian bed death." *Sexual and Relationship Therapy, 19*, 353−372.

Nichols, M. (2005). Sexual function in lesbians and lesbian relationships. In J. Goldstein, C. M. Meston, S. Davis, & M. Traish (Eds.), *Female sexual dysfunction* (pp. 307−313). London: Parthenon Publishing.

Nichols, M., & Shernoff, M. (2006). Therapy with sexual minorities: Queering practice. In S. Leiblum (Ed.), *Principles and practices of sex therapy* (4th ed.). New York: Guilford.

O'Neill, G., & O'Neill, N. (1984). *Open marriage*. New York: M. Evans and Company.

Peplau, L. (2003). Human sexuality: How do men and women differ? *Current Directions in Psychological Science, 12*(2), 37−71.

Roughgarden, J. (2004). *Evolution's rainbow*. Berkeley, CA: University of California Press.

Rust, P. (1995). *Bisexuality and the challenge to lesbian politics: Sex, loyalty, and revolution*. New York: NYU Press.

Ryan, C., & Bradford, J. (1993). The National lesbian health care survey: An overview. In N. Garrets, & D. Kimmel (Eds.), *Psychological perspectives on lesbian and gay male experiences* (pp. 541–556). New York: Columbia University Press.

Savin-Williams, R. C. (2005). *The new gay teenager*. Cambridge, MA: Harvard University Press.

Schwartz, P. (1994). *Love between equals*. New York: Simon & Schuster.

Shaw, R. (2010). *Condom compliance why aren't all the adults doing it?* http//sexuallysmarter. blogspot.com/2010/04/condom-compliance-why-arent-all-adults.html.

Shernoff, M. (2005). *Without condoms: Unprotected sex, gay men, and barebacking*. London: Routledge.

Silverstein, C. (1972). *Behavior modification and the gay community*. Paper presented at the Annual Convention of the Association for the Advancement of Behavior Therapy, New York City, October.

Silverstein, C. (2009). Letter to the Editor: The Implications of removing homosexuality as a mental disorder. *Archives of Sex Behavior*, *38*(2), 1–3.

Sullivan, A. (1995). *Virtually normal*. New York: Random House.

Szasz, T. (1961). *The myth of mental illness: Foundations of a theory of personal conduct*. New York: Hoeber-Harper.

Taormino, T. (2008). *Opening up: A guide to creating and sustaining open relationships*. San Francisco, CA: Cleis Press.

Vance, C. (Ed.), (1984). *Pleasure and danger: Exploring female sexuality*. London: Routledge.

Warner, M. (1999). *The trouble with normal: Sex, politics, and the ethics of queer life*. Cambridge, MA: Harvard University Press.

Zucker, K., & Bradley, S. (1996). *Gender identity disorder and psychosexual problems in children and adolescents*. New York: Guilford.

5 Institutional Aspects of the Initial Interview

Ronald E. Hellman

South Beach Psychiatric Center, Brooklyn, NY, USA

Introduction

This chapter focuses on the gay person receiving outpatient institutional care, a generic term for a wide range of services typically provided by large, health-care organizations that operate within the public or private domain. Most are mainstream institutions, but some smaller institutions provide services exclusively to a gay clientele. The chapter explores issues of common concern at the time of the intake with a gay man seeking help in mainstream, institutional settings such as the academic university medical center, the general hospital center, the public or private clinic, the community mental health center, and the private institute.

When patient encounters occur in an institutional setting, there are additional considerations that may distinguish this experience for a gay patient, such as the nature of the institution and its impact on the patient, the therapist, and the warmth or formality of the initial session. From a sexual minority perspective, the mainstream institutional setting stands out as an exclusively, or predominately, heterosexual environment. Past reactions from the heterosexual world to a gay identity can influence expectations about the institution. For the new patient who is gay, this can raise fears and questions about what is to be anticipated from this "new family." A new, dyadic relationship occurs between the institution and the gay individual even before an interpersonal relationship is established with an intake clinician. The client initially has a fantasy of what the institution will be like, and typically will interact with secretaries by telephone and direct contact, and possibly other personnel before meeting with the clinician. There will be an initial impression of the physical setting, and projections about other staff and patients.

Institutions, therefore, have the opportunity to orient themselves to their gay clientele at every level, from the systemic, to the individual clinical encounter, to the telephone call with a secretary, to the physical environment of the building. When each of these areas is reviewed and addressed, the gay person's ability to engage and the quality of the working relationship is more likely to be enhanced.

I have organized this chapter with a focus in three areas, beginning with an overview of how systemic change came about in my institution, followed by a

The Initial Psychotherapy Interview. DOI: 10.1016/B978-0-12-385146-8.00005-5

description of some general issues when outpatient institutional care is directed toward the gay person, and concluding with a look at how the case of Scott might be approached within the defined role of the psychiatrist in my institution.

Systemic Transformation: A Personal Account

My experience on the subject of this chapter derives from 30 years of work in a mainstream community mental health setting. It was here that I became aware of shortcomings in the provision of care to sexual minority individuals with major, disabling psychiatric disorders.

The modern gay civil rights movement began with the Stonewall uprising in 1969. Although I had been involved with gay health care since then, it would be years until a confluence of influences would provide the ingredients necessary for me to mobilize an entire mainstream community mental health center. These changes require some perspective, because it took 16 years from the time of my employment for this to happen.

In 1980, when I began as a staff psychiatrist at South Beach Psychiatric Center (SBPC) in Brooklyn, New York, 11 years had passed since the Stonewall uprising, and 7 years from the American Psychiatric Association's declassification of homosexuality as a mental illness. During this remarkable period, pathological models of treatment gave way to gay affirmative therapies.

Yet, to my knowledge, the first reference to the term "affirmative" in relation to those with a same-sex orientation seeking treatment, did not appear in the professional literature until 1982 in an article by Malyon (1982). Just 4 years earlier, in a review of these yet to be named, novel approaches, Coleman (1978) noted how radical it still was for a therapeutic intervention *not* to have a shift to heterosexuality as its goal. Psychiatric institutions, understandably, did not have clear standards of care for their gay patients during this transitional time.

As a knowledge base developed, gay affirmative practices were gradually adopted, but this was occurring on an individual, nonorganized basis in the mental health field. There were no government mandates to ensure provision of services, no accreditation requirements certifying that mental health institutions provided credible services to their sexual minority patients, and no public funding to support initiatives. Furthermore, progress was eclipsed and derailed by the explosive onset of the AIDS epidemic. In the gay community, this deadly illness had a massive impact, and got most of the attention and funding for many years.

In New York State, an organized effort to obtain public funds for lesbian, gay, bisexual, and transgender (LGBT) mental health services did not occur until 1994. That year, LGBT social service organizations throughout the state formed a coalition entitled the LGBT Health & Human Services Network, which was coordinated by the Empire State Pride Agenda Foundation. However, it was not enough for the coalition to request government support for *LGBT* social services. HIV funding had been so pervasive, funding requests also had to specify that they were for *non-HIV* social services. This distinction, and the broad, professional push, finally merited the government's attention as to the many other needs within the LGBT community.

A second crucial aspect of the funding picture in New York had to do with the passage of the *Community Mental Health Reinvestment Act of 1993*. This major reform allowed money that had been saved from the downsizing or closing of old state inpatient hospitals to be designated for community mental health programs. These funds would play a crucial role in the development of our LGBT program.

With gay affirmative therapies, and now funding initiatives in place, the stage was set for change in the public institutional sector. But it was a third factor that catalyzed the mobilization of my institution, leading to the development of our LGBT program model. This was the growing influence of cultural psychiatry.

Major, chronic, and disabling psychiatric disorders uproot people because they shift their lives into the world of psychiatric hospitals, clinics, day programs, residences, and rehabilitation programs, while inducing discomfort and creating burdens that distance others from the afflicted. By the early 1990s, I had observed time and again how major mental illness could tear LGBT patients away from their community and culture. If and when they were well enough to venture back, they were often shunned because of their symptoms and disabilities, and their sexual identity conflated this stigma. Worse, disabling psychiatric disorders inhibited many from even attempting to reconnect.

To my dismay, the hope I had pinned on the burgeoning LGBT affirmative therapies as the means to address and resolve this breach was not congruent with the outcomes I was witnessing. For example, I recall a gay man who I saw for medication management, who told me that he really appreciated the work his therapist was doing with him, and how well she understood him, but he felt that something was still missing in his life.

He wanted a romantic relationship and gay friends, but he found that people lost interest when they learned he was a 40-year-old man on disability living with his brother. He lost contact with a new acquaintance after having a psychiatric relapse. He was actually relieved to have a low libido on his medication. For a long time, he never admitted to sexual side effects when assessed by his caregivers, because he found the challenges of a relationship and the fear of being shunned overwhelming. Libido, for him, was a door to rejection and further isolation. The outside world, even the LGBT world, seemed unforgiving. His refuge became his individual gay affirmative therapy sessions, and the time he spent with his brother.

Over the transitional years between the 1970s and 1990s, many of our clinicians had adopted LGBT affirmative approaches on an individual basis. Yet, I observed that while these practices helped LGBT patients develop a more positive and integrated sense of self, and greater ability to cope in a world with mixed attitudes toward them, these approaches could not restore that lost cultural connection.

I had to acknowledge that *psychosocially* oriented, gay affirmative therapies alone were insufficient for those who were too disabled or stigmatized to reintegrate within their own cultural community. Without a relevant *sociocultural* program, the LGBT patient with major mental illness spent years adapting to generic, predominately heterosexual settings, where they were always in the minority, where their role as "patient" was more likely to predominate, and where they were again, more subject to the homophobia, genderphobia, and heterosexism that spurred them to seek out an LGBT community before mental illness disrupted their personal development.

Without a place for these patients to turn, I felt that it was up to our institution to create the cultural space that these patients had lost or avoided. It became clear how an institution could have a significant advantage over a private practice setting, for only an institution had the resources to create a program that could provide for both the psychosocial aspects of treatment and the sociocultural need.

A cultural program is different from a gay therapy group. Clinicians run therapy groups in both private practice and institutional settings, but they do not fill the cultural gap because they are forms of *therapy* that address interpersonal and social issues. They are not the real world living out of a social life within a cultural framework. In fact, many therapists admonish patients *not* to socialize with each other outside these groups.

These insights gave me the basis to shape a model for a program, with the support and input from concerned administrators, executives, and clinicians at my institution. To provide a complete range of services, LGBT affirmative psychosocial therapies would be formalized within the program for those enrolled in the institution, while sociocultural programming would be open to LGBT patients from outside the clinic as well. There was no reason why patients who were already receiving psychosocial therapies elsewhere could not continue to do so. So that outside patients could participate in cultural programming without having to enroll in the clinic, this component was developed as an affiliated program within the continuum of care. Individuals seeking these resources had to be enrolled as *patients*, either in our institution or through outside care, while all could enroll as *members* in the cultural program. By developing an open cultural program, greater numbers could attend, ensuring that it would more likely approximate an actual cultural community.

A physical space within the institution was designated as a safe and private social space for ongoing social and cultural activities. Potentially, however, the entire institution could be transformed. For example, a generic elevator could become part of that cultural space if it routinely posted notices of planned LGBT events. A generic waiting room could be redefined with LGBT signifiers such as a rainbow decal, posters, and brochures. These signifiers were more than "theatrical props" because they linked to the substance of the programming offered. As the program developed, it was anticipated that LGBT patients would begin to recognize each other, and a generic waiting room could become an extension of their LGBT social space.

Initiating the South Beach Program

SBPC is one of the largest community mental health centers in New York State, providing services to those with serious, persistent mental disorders who have low or no income, and who have no or limited health insurance coverage.

In 1995, SBPC organized a meeting to review the status of its multicultural services. At that meeting, I shared my observations and insights regarding our LGBT patients. I noted that without financial resources or private health insurance, they had little choice but to be in mainstream mental health settings such as ours, and I shared my thoughts regarding the need for relevant cultural service provision to these clients. I maintained that they were less likely to identify with our services without such a resource, more likely to be nonadherent with treatment regimens, and more likely to suffer from the complications of recurrent illness and the impact of insufficiently recognized stigma.

Based on this meeting, interested staff volunteered to form a group to develop recommendations for a program. We were initially unaware of funding sources, and it was unlikely that we would have been awarded major funds for an unproven program. We began on a small scale, utilizing existing clinical resources. A drug company provided a small grant to print brochures and business cards. The program began in February 1996, at first targeting in-house clients. Through feedback from patients and referrals from the hospital and other agencies, we knew that the program was gradually achieving its goals. We grew and matured over time to become a resource for both the psychiatric and LGBT communities in New York City.

Today, the LGBT Affirmative Program (LGBTAP) provides a full range of core psychiatric services in a culturally sensitive and affirmative environment for LGBT-identified patients. In-service educational presentations are provided for staff as well as clinical supervision. Training opportunities are available during the academic year for psychology student externs and social work interns. Research, professional papers, and a book, *Handbook of LGBT Issues in Community Mental Health* (Hellman & Drescher, 2005), have been published that we trust have contributed to an enhanced understanding of this unique population.

Rainbow Heights Club (RHC) functions as the cultural, support, and advocacy program. It is funded through public and private resources. It is a separate entity affiliated with the LGBTAP. RHC provides a full range of adjunctive services that are available daily, evenings, and weekends. (See www.rainbowheights.org for more detail.) RHC began in September 2002 as a semiautonomous program with its own director and funding. In-kind space and basic facilities are provided by the clinic.

LGBTAP and RHC illustrate the distinct role that mainstream institutions can play in the provision of mental health services to sexual minority individuals. But, institutional care has had a wide-ranging evolution, and its interface with LGBT culture has had a mixed history.

A Brief History of Institutional Care

Psychiatry and surgery were the earliest forms of institutional medical care provided in the United States. Psychiatry first developed in this country in the form of public institutional tutelage through the asylum system of the 1800s. This changed dramatically during World War II and the period thereafter, not only with the advent of modern psychotropic medications for the more severely ill but also with the demonstration that community care was less likely to disrupt social and cultural connections (Grob, 2004). Mental health services subsequently expanded into a variety of community institutional settings.

Attention to the cultural groups in the communities now served by these local mental health programs gave rise to the new discipline of cultural psychiatry. Its prism would eventually shed light on the need for, and the validity of, gay affirmative therapies as a contemporary LGBT community and culture blossomed following the Stonewall uprising in 1969 and the declassification of homosexuality as a mental disorder in 1973 (Silverstein, 1976–1977). Gay affirmative therapies begin with the idea that differences in sexual orientation are not manifestations of pathology, but normal variations within the human constitution. If there is distress associated with sexual orientation, it is thought to arise from the negative valuation by others. These principles can be incorporated into the spectrum of existing therapeutic methods.

Psychiatric institutions differed in their ability to assimilate these changes. Divergent clinical perspectives were emphasized in different schools, which competed to understand and treat the various forms of mental suffering. Some institutes became known for a particular approach, while others endeavored to incorporate and synthesize a wide range of interventions within a cohesive framework.

In recent years, concerns about the utilization of psychiatric resources and the economics of mental health care have reshaped the nature of institutional services. These changes, summarized below, affect all recipients of care including the gay patient.

Regulatory agencies that accredit institutions increasingly demand evidence supporting the achievement of concrete goals, while payment systems influence clinical management in the direction of greater efficiencies. While this has resulted in the ability to establish, influence, and document basic standards of care, it has also deflected from direct time spent with patients, leaving at least some therapists feeling overwhelmed and more detached from their work. Direct patient contact, chart documentation, clinical indication, and economic reality vie for the clinician's attention. Pressures to increase efficiency and productivity may affect policies that determine the availability of services. And economic conditions can impact clinical staffing and patient load when staff attrition and layoffs occur in times of restricted budgeting.

SBPC experienced more referrals during the economic recession of 2007–2010, as some outpatient services in New York closed due to lack of funding. Despite these strains, clinical decision-making continued to be primarily based on empirical data and outcome measures. Core services were retained given certain economies. For example, dance and art therapists in my clinic were replaced on their retirement with staff conducting individual and group psychotherapy.

At SBPC, who is treated is governed by the New York State Mental Hygiene Law and the Office of Mental Health (OMH). Directives from OMH guide how SBPC is to interpret the Mental Hygiene Law. Thus, although a public community mental health facility in New York cannot discriminate on the basis of ability to pay, the priority is to treat the indigent, the uninsured, and those on Medicaid and Medicare. Although Medicaid fee-for-service authorizes a fixed number of visits per year before further review is required, New York State offers disabled Medicaid patients receiving intermediate and long-term psychiatric care enrollment in a Medicaid-managed care plan, the Prepaid Mental Health Plan (PMHP), that does not stipulate a fixed number of visits.

Not every gay person seeking our services is accepted into the program. There must be a primary psychiatric diagnosis, excluding a principal diagnosis of mental retardation or drug dependence. The exclusions are acceptable as secondary diagnoses. A dual diagnosis that includes drug dependence is allowed if the drug abuse is in remission. Patients not accepted into our program are referred to other mental health agencies.

In private practice, the only oversight might involve documentation of need for treatment by managed care insurance plans authorizing visits. Licensing and registration renewals may inquire only about malpractice, suspension, or revocation of a license. Since 2006, however, all newly certified psychiatrists must pass a recertification examination every 8 years. Many institutions require documentation of continuing medical education to qualify for reprivileging. To help guide patients in evaluating an institution, accreditation summaries are now available on the Internet (online Accreditation Quality Reports, issued by the Joint Commission on Accreditation of Health Care Organizations, can be found under Quality Check at www.jointcommission.org).

These core features of institutional functioning, including the institutional perspective, the population served, the type and availability of services offered, and credentialing provide a framework for the appropriateness and quality of patient care when mental health treatment is being sought by the gay consumer.

Advantages and Disadvantages of a Clinic Setting

Clinics have certain advantages and disadvantages for the gay person seeking help. Public mental health organizations are available to those who do not have the financial resources or insurance coverage to see a private practitioner, as are some private institutes that assign supervised therapists-in-training to clients. With the passage of the *Community Mental Health Act of 1963*, public community mental health centers were mandated to be widely available, but each may serve only a particular geographic zone, known as a "catchment area." The community served is designated by its physical location and not a particular cultural community, although geographic exceptions are sometimes made when a specialization is only regionally available. Theoretically, institutional settings must provide culturally competent care to the clientele it serves; however, there may be considerable variation in the level of culturally appropriate services that are provided.

The institutional setting has the advantage of furnishing a clinical team that can offer both psychological and biological treatments under one roof. This setting tends to be more structured than a private practice setting, where the individual clinician is the sole arbiter of treatment. My institution treats patients who are more severely ill or disabled. Such patients are referred to designated institutional settings mandated for that purpose, while other institutes may target a clientele with more modest concerns or higher functioning. These constraints can affect the role of the practitioner doing the intake, who may initially function primarily as a gatekeeper in order to determine if the client is appropriate for the setting.

The institutional setting tends to have a wide-ranging staff of specialists that can identify and treat co-occurring disorders. Mental health organizations are usually extensively networked with other mental health and social service resources, although links to relevant gay resources may vary considerably.

Institutional environments also vary from impersonal, to warm and empathic, and from generic to multicultural. The clinician in private practice is the sole person responsible for the tenor of the setting, whereas the culture of the institution itself may compete with, or complement, the institutional clinician's predilections. Institutional organizations can hinder or facilitate the capabilities of staff, affect clinician morale, and impact the relationship between the patient and provider. Clinicians tend to see a wider variety of patients from various cultural backgrounds in the institutional setting, and they need to have both a general strategy in their approach to cultural differences as well as more specific competencies in regard to a particular patient's cultural background and needs.

The Treatment Alliance with a Gay Patient

There are some factors particular to the gay patient when establishing a therapeutic bond. For example, how likely is it that a request for a gay therapist would be met in a mainstream institutional setting?

A 2001 survey found that only a third of 274 therapists felt that a gay patient had a right to a gay therapist, and only 1 of 218 therapists in that survey admitted that they were gay (Bartlett, King & Philips, 2001). There appears to be reluctance on the part of clinical providers in the mainstream setting to be open about their own sexual minority status. The availability of gay staff appears to be quite limited. The study also suggests that there is a limited understanding of the potential benefits of referral to a gay therapist.

Is the treatment and well-being of the gay client jeopardized from the start in this setting? It is a crucial question for many gay clients, because they see "straight" culture, including "straight" therapists, as having a different worldview from their own. This, in itself, can be enough to inhibit a sense of identification with a potential treatment resource. When the horizon of treatment providers is also perceived to include negative biases, judgments, and misunderstandings, further resistance to help seeking will be engendered (Lucksted, 2004). Distancing, mistrust, and self-censorship during the evaluation and treatment process are the result. Lack of full participation and involvement in therapy inevitably leads to poorer outcomes.

In one of the few studies to compare how gay patients rate providers by discipline, Liddle (1999) found that psychiatrists tended to rate lower than psychologists, social workers, and other counselors. Psychiatrists were not perceived as helpful in addressing sexual orientation, and significantly more psychiatrists were likely to disregard a gay identity than in the other disciplines. Surprisingly, 70 percent of nonpsychiatrists were rated as very helpful, suggesting that mainstream therapists are able to address the issue of disenfranchisement and alienation and can work effectively with the gay patient.

More recently, Neville and Henrickson (2006) found that many gay patients report that their health provider assumed they were heterosexual. There can be a reluctance on the part of the gay person to correct this assumption because of lingering stigma associated with homosexuality. A 2008 study found that 39 percent of men who had sex with men do not disclose same-sex attraction to their medical provider (Bernstein et al., 2008). Provider assumptions, stigma, and unspoken patient concerns about provider knowledge and competencies can easily conspire to create a clinical situation where the gay patient feels it is not safe to talk, resulting in suboptimal care.

Such findings have spurred the development of gay-focused programming in some mainstream agencies (Hellman & Klein, 2004), but the ability to find a culturally appropriate, institutional mental health setting can be a challenge. Institutional practitioners should understand that the mainstream nature of their mental health setting can be a barrier for a gay man who prefers to be in a gay setting, but cannot find or afford to see a gay therapist privately, or is compelled to seek treatment in the mainstream setting because of mental health issues, complications, and other comorbid disorders that a private practice or gay-identified institute is not equipped to manage.

Issues of trust, comfort, and confidentiality can be more acute for the gay person in this setting and will need to be addressed. It should be anticipated that the gay person may be concerned about the level of understanding and acceptance she or he will find and the competency of staff available to work with them. Nevertheless, it appears that the clinician in the institutional setting can be a useful and effective resource. If the request for a gay therapist cannot be honored, the gay person can still be helped if there is a sincere clinical effort and not a superficial attempt at engagement.

The Initial Interview with a Gay Client in the Institutional Setting

Basic functions of the initial interview in any setting are to establish rapport; obtain information on core signs, symptoms, and personal history that will assist in developing a differential diagnosis; and gather content and observational data in order to forge an initial assessment. The assessment forms the basis for a treatment plan. In its most comprehensive form, the initial interview provides the data necessary to begin a broad synthesis of the person, in order to gain a comprehensive understanding of the dimensions of the distress requiring attention, as well as potential emotional, cultural and relational barriers, and factors that may aid in achieving goals (American Psychiatric Association, 1994; Margulies & Havens, 1981).

The interview proceeds in stages (Haley, 1989) that include an initial social exchange of greeting and introduction, and an effort to make the client comfortable, all while establishing an initial impression from observations of the patient's appearance and behavior. The inquiry stage can begin by clarifying how the patient was referred and by conveying what is already known about the patient, and proceeds with elaboration by the client.

This phase of the interview presents the opportunity to preemptively address stigma-related barriers by sharing information related to the patient's sexual identity that may have been introduced during the referral process from permissible background materials, prior communication with referral sources, or the reiteration of information provided by the patient.

Three relevant variables are operating during what, otherwise, appears to be a dyadic interaction: the mainstream clinic setting, the interviewer, and the gay patient. The institutional setting can reinforce the power imbalance between client and clinician, between a mainstream authority and a minority newcomer (Altman, 1995). If it is not perceived as gay-friendly, it may not be sensed as anything more than superficially welcoming at best, and intimidating at worst. A bird's-eye view of these interacting variables should be part of the clinician's awareness for the valuable information contained in these early cross-cultural aspects of the interview.

The following is an example from my caseload in a mainstream mental health center with gay cultural programming. A new client began by saying, "I was referred here by the gay community center but this doesn't look like a gay clinic to me." I reasonably assumed that the client was gay-identified, had a cultural affiliation with the gay community, had an expectation from past experience of what a gay clinic should look like, was comfortable enough to be open about gay concerns with me, and was expressing some disappointment and hostility possibly rooted in distrust of mainstream heterosexual environments.

I experienced some defensiveness evoked by the patient's stance, was aware that this could threaten a budding treatment alliance, and mentally noted the need to further explore the meaning of the setting for this person. I hypothesized that the client harbored a need to separate from heterosexual environments at this stage in their development, in order to individuate further within a gay cultural world. I suspected that cognitive dissonance was also in play for a person struggling to grasp how there could be a safe, gay space within a mainstream, "heterosexual" setting.

The initial interview typically precludes the possibility of exploring these issues in any great detail, because the interviewer must direct and limit the extent of inquiry in any particular area, in order to obtain the information necessary to develop a broad sketch of the patient. But the issue cannot be ignored. Here, the challenge and art of interviewing emerges in the effort to balance the informational requirements with the task of developing a helpful relationship with a gay individual harboring certain anxieties, fears, and expectations.

What constitutes a helpful connection early on with a gay patient will vary. In the example above, the institutional variable predominated for the client, and if neglected, would likely be experienced by the patient as potentially negating, exacerbating the patient's hostility, and possibly resulting in an irreconcilable breach with the patient not returning. Clarification and reassurance may be all that is necessary in the brief time available.

The concluding stage of the interview provides the opportunity for the clinician to determine if the main areas of concern have been covered, summarize an understanding of the case, and lay out a course of action.

Gay Institutional Transference

Transference in traditional psychoanalysis refers to feelings between the analyst and his patient. In our experience with LGBT patients, we have learned that an institutional transference also exists and can have a profound effect upon the patient. It is particularly clear during the early stage of the intake.

Gay institutional transference involves an emotional feeling evoked by what the institution represents. For example, a gay man's reaction to a church, a gay center, or a clinic may be quite different, because each symbolizes a history of what that organization is perceived to represent in the eyes of a gay person. Each embodies and represents the past ideas and attitudes of numerous individuals. These can unconsciously influence the expectation as to whether the present institution is likely to be gay-friendly, gay-hostile, or gay-indifferent.

Gay institutional transference differs from the traditional concept of institutional transference in which the patient seems more attached to the institution, over time, than with any individual therapist (Gage & Gillins, 1991; Gendel & Resier, 1981; Safirstein, 1967). Gay institutional transference involves a projection onto the institution that is rooted in past social reactions to a gay identity. This generates an emotional reaction that can play out in the early relationship with the intake clinician. The hostility I felt from the patient in the case I described in the previous section is an example. This patient initially and unconsciously saw me as a member of a type of mainstream institution that previously pathologized gay people and is largely constituted by heterosexual individuals. Even if that person knew I was gay, he, nevertheless, reacted as if I was one of "them."

Gay institutional transference can generate hypotheses about character and culture, and how the personal and the institutional connect the past and present. What is the significance of the reaction? Is it rooted in the family relationship, classroom, or place of worship where they were judged, dismissed, shamed, or negated as a gay person, or does it evoke an environment where they were understood and unconditionally accepted? Or, something in between? Would a gay man feel more vulnerable in this setting because the experience of the institution kindles an earlier sense of alienation at a time of need? Or, would he feel comforted as, perhaps, he did when under stress by understanding, benevolent, heterosexual parents.

We normally don't think of transference reactions in relation to institutional elevators and waiting rooms, but these physical elements can reinforce unconscious alienation, or affirm cultural identification and self-esteem. All staff and clients use institutional hallways, elevators, and waiting rooms. They become testing grounds outside a designated LGBT cultural space, where an internal awareness occurs of feeling either like an outsider or one who belongs and equally shares that physical space. A person's reaction may be overt, as in the example in the previous section, or go unspoken. In the latter case, prompting gives the reluctant patient permission to relate her or his experience more openly and critically. An example: "Institutions can feel intimidating or comforting. What has been your experience here?"

Institutional Roles of the Clinician and the Gay Client

The role of the clinician in the institutional setting is broader than in private practice, and each role component provides the opportunity to help or hinder the development of a good therapeutic bond with a gay patient. In their clinical provider role, the clinician must have dual competencies, including the ability to evaluate and diagnose a new patient, and the knowledge and skills to approach the cultural challenge. This would be true in any practice setting.

As a matchmaker, the intake person will need to focus on clinician–patient cultural dyads (Carter, 1995), guided by whether a therapist shares the same sexual orientation or has similar attitudes and expertise regarding sexual minority issues. The sole clinician in private practice must decide if the fit is good, or if the client should seek help elsewhere. Institutional settings are more likely to have choices in-house. As an ambassador between the patient and the agency, the institutional clinician is responsible for conveying the strengths and weaknesses of the organization regarding competencies and resources available in the area of gay concerns. As a facilitator, the clinician endeavors to create a positive, welcoming environment for the gay person. The institutional setting can be more challenging because the clinician is not the sole arbiter here. But, if the client is connecting with the setting and the ancillary staff, then the institutional alliance enhances the possibility for a good connection with the clinician.

As team players, institutional practitioners consult with administrators and staff, and make additional referrals for further assessments and treatment. Institutional clinicians with gay expertise may be called upon to supervise and train other staff and ancillary personnel, including secretaries who are often the first contact. They may also function as advocates, ensuring a safe and secure environment for the gay client given the numerous staff and clientele in the facility.

Finally, the clinician may function as a specialist with proficiency in a specific area. Some institutions may be funded to study and treat such focused concerns, or there may be a staff clinician with a specific interest that would identify them as a resource in a particular subspecialty.

At SBPC, these roles are facilitated by the presence of LGBTAP and RHC, where the situation is more analogous to that of a client seeking out a private practitioner already known to have expertise on gay issues. If the patient's sexual orientation is not known, and they are assigned to a generic intake worker, the program remains a resource that any intake clinician can reference, thereby enhancing an early cultural connection.

Matchmaking is facilitated at SBPC because of LGBTAP and RHC, but there are times when the process is less than ideal. This occurs when caseloads of designated therapists are full. Even in this circumstance, it is usually less of an issue with time because all therapists in the clinic are increasingly exposed to the program over time due to its physical location within the clinic, overlapping staff, patient participation, ongoing communication, discussion of cases, clinical support, and ongoing LGBT continuing education presentations.

LGBTAP and RHC routinely post informational notices on elevators that serve the clinic, while posters and brochures in the waiting room convey a gay-friendly message before any dialogue occurs with an intake clinician.

The therapist is usually the only contact the patient has in a private practice setting. At SBPC, exposure to ancillary staff and other patients presents a greater risk for perceived slights that can be experienced as homophobic. Breaches of confidentiality and situations that exacerbate issues around stigma are also more likely. Examples include patients who would not want a secretary to verbally articulate a confirmation that they are there for the "gay group," and patients who are reluctant to reveal details about their gay identity or behavior to anyone other than the therapist. Secretaries have been coached to refer to the facilitator's name running groups, to Rainbow Heights Club as "The Club" or "RHC," and the psychosocial program as "The LGBT Program," which is more likely to be ambiguous to non-LGBT clients in the waiting room.

On occasion in our clinic, the referral process is not benign for the gay person. Referral to a group, for example, may reawaken memories of being mocked by childhood peers who sensed the difference in their temperament and excluded them from the social network (Shelby, 1994). Even the groups in LGBTAP and RHC can be experienced in this way, and group facilitators must constantly ensure that a supportive and inclusive atmosphere is maintained.

LGBTAP and RHC are located in one of seven outpatient clinics of SBPC. This clinic is differentiated from the others in providing this service. Within the program, staff are known for their interest and expertise on particular aspects of gay life, and they also function as specialists/consultants to the other clinics.

Self-Disclosure in the Institutional Setting

When a patient requests to work with a gay therapist, she or he charges the clinician with the responsibility to understand the circumstances under which they would choose to disclose or conceal their sexual orientation. Not only when and why, but where disclosure takes place can be an issue in a large organization. The therapist may or may not be inclined to be open about their sexual orientation for a variety of personal and professional reasons, and the relative need for discretion regarding whom they are open with may, in part, be dictated by the institutional environment.

The ethics of clinical practice necessitate the confidentiality of patient sessions and materials, but *there is no requirement that patients maintain confidentiality regarding the therapist.* Because institutional therapists maintain a relationship with the institution, their coming out with other staff and management may influence judgments about coming out to patients. Administrators and members of the treatment team have legitimate access to confidential clinical materials, and patients may develop clinical or social relationships with other patients and staff where information about the therapist may be disclosed. These factors can impact clinical decision-making in ways that would not occur in a private practice setting.

That said, disclosure of sexual orientation (but not personal details) can be seen as qualifying the therapist in the eyes of the patient. It may promote a sense of understanding and trust (Sophie, 1987). Because gay people often find that they could not tell the truth to others or even themselves, self-disclosure by the therapist has special significance. It is a vote of confidence and a sign of affirmation in the eyes of the patient (Coolhart, 2005).

For therapists that do not disclose, studies indicate that the clinician is often perceived as distant and aloof, which can result in a weak therapeutic alliance and client self-censorship regarding intimate personal concerns (Hanson, 2005; Knox & Hill, 2003). Openness, honesty, and an expression of willingness to learn about, understand, and support the gay client may be enough reassurance to establish a credible therapeutic bond. However, the therapist that employs obfuscation, rather than transparency, is likely to exacerbate distrust.

Whether or not heterosexual staff has extensive experience with gay issues, self-disclosure of sexual orientation can also begin a process that addresses heterosexual stereotypes that the gay person may harbor. For the heterosexual therapist, some variation of the following response may be appropriate: *Although I'm not gay, I've worked with many gay patients, and I know there can be real concerns about being judged or stereotyped, as well as discomfort talking about sexual details. Are any of these of particular concern to you?*

At SBPC, self-disclosure is encouraged but is an individual decision. A supportive environment for gay staff has been nurtured over the years. Administrators and staff are out at all levels of the organization, and same-sex partners are routinely invited to staff social gatherings. Openness is reinforced in other ways, as well. Domestic partner and marital status are now recognized in New York State for state and city employees. Employees who are open about same-sex partners are eligible to have them covered on their health insurance plan. In LGBTAP and RHC, clinical providers are informed that they must be willing to discuss their sexual orientation or qualifications to work with LGBT clients.

How Scott Would Be Assessed at SBPC

The case of Scott focuses on a gay man in mourning. The extent to which the mourning process will be facilitated in an institutional setting will depend on the degree to which the patient feels understood, and the extent to which he can identify and connect with those attempting to provide support.

Historically, the gay patient has had an ambivalent relationship with institutional mental health settings. With few exceptions, this environment was not a place where the gay person could have an affirmative therapy experience during a substantial period of psychiatric practice. When psychiatric care shifted from the asylum to the local community, it continued to embody a pathological bias toward gay individuals until the formal declassification of homosexuality in 1973. Despite the emergence of gay affirmative therapies, the gay patient was, and still is, a minority individual in mainstream mental health organizations where most patients and staff are heterosexual. Gay patients are, therefore, less likely to identify and connect unless steps are taken to ensure that social disenfranchisement is addressed.

Although we cannot know with certainty how Scott would have reacted to an institutional setting, we do know that he was hesitant to be open with his physician about his sexual orientation and practices. He perceives his medical doctor to be heterosexual (P51–P53). We also know that he was not about to reach out to just any therapist. The therapist's sexual orientation was of paramount concern. It is reasonable to conclude that in a largely heterosexual, mainstream community mental health center, he would also exhibit this anxiety, discomfort, and avoidance. We might reasonably speculate that he would not have reached out for help at all if a generic clinic setting was his only option. At SBPC, LGBTAP and RHC were developed to address such concerns.

Because LGBTAP is a formal component of SBPC, the initial evaluation is governed by legal and institutional requirements, and is a highly differentiated process that can take several weeks and three individuals to complete. RHC has its own intake protocol and requires additional time with an RHC staff person. Contrast this with the private practice evaluation of Scott, which occurred in the course of one session with one evaluator.

Standardized New York State OMH forms are completed by the intake team. Adapting the interview process to a gay client, therefore, depends on the training and skills of the interviewers. Because Scott made it known at the time of referral that he wanted a gay therapist, his intake would be assigned to a gay-identified or experienced, gay-sensitive team.

The procedure, however, begins before the actual interview process. Scott would be given priority for evaluation at SBPC if he lacked private insurance coverage and adequate financial resources to pay for visits. An administrator would determine this during the initial telephone contact. Scott would be asked to bring in documentation of a recent, complete physical examination, and he must sign a consent form allowing previous caregivers to release information to the clinic. If Scott had been referred from another treating agency, a copy of records would be requested that included the results of a psychiatric evaluation, psychosocial evaluation, current medications, if any, and the results of a recent physical examination. Scott would be asked to complete a form eliciting demographic information. The clinic is also legally mandated to provide him with patient rights, voter registration, and patient privacy act forms.

During the registration period, Scott would have entered the building on at least one occasion, and he would have been exposed to LGBTAP/RHC postings in elevators, posters in the waiting room, and brochures about these services. Given Scott's anxieties about a therapist, this exposure would have communicated early on that he had come to a place where he was likely to feel comfortable.

Phases of the Intake Process

1. The first phase of the intake is scheduled once the registration process is completed. This component of the intake is the first of three parts, beginning with an interview with an administrator who validates received information (which often contains errors). Using clinical judgment, the administrator then hones in on major topics of concern, highlighting issues that will need attention by clinicians that will subsequently be assigned to the case. There is a brief assessment of symptoms, level of insight about symptoms and/or problems, attitude about mental health treatment, and a brief review with the patient of what therapy can do. Information about LGBTAP and RHC may be reviewed at this time. From this interview and referral materials, a screening note is synthesized.
2. The administrator then arranges an appointment with a staff psychiatrist. This interview focuses on psychiatric signs and symptoms. Past psychiatric history is reviewed, and a brief history taken. Past treatment interventions are reviewed. A mental status examination is completed, a differential diagnosis formulated, and further evaluation and treatment recommendations summarized (American Psychiatric Association, 1994).
3. The third part of the intake is arranged by the administrator with a psychologist, social worker, or student therapist under supervision. A psychosocial evaluation is conducted. Core aspects of this interview include assessment of mental and physical functioning, rehabilitative functioning in regard to work, school, and the living situation, and the nature of interpersonal supports.
4. The case is finally assigned to a therapist with a psychology or social work background affiliated with LGBTAP. This person develops and initiates a master treatment plan based on the three component evaluations. If medication is indicated, the psychiatrist continues to follow the patient. Patients will then undergo an evaluation with staff from RHC if they wish to become a member. This can occur at a later time if they require stabilization.

Because the private practice intake of Scott coincided with a single, initial session, the pressure to prioritize and ration the line of questioning in that time frame was undoubtedly more acute. The strategy in the single, private practice setting is probably most akin to the first part of the SBPC interview.

One priority supersedes all phases of the intake at SBPC. SBPC clinicians are trained to identify and prioritize potential areas of high risk. Scott had strong thoughts of suicide that he revealed late in the interview (P131–P134). At SBPC, the level of any imminent risk would be immediately assessed further, and a plan of intervention recommended. We use the New York State OMH "Routine Suicide Risk Screening" to assess the potential for self-harm. When a patient is a potential danger to themselves or others, this concern takes precedence over all other aspects of the initial interview.

My participation on an SBPC intake team would involve phase II of the interview process, targeting signs and symptoms, completing a mental status examination, developing a differential diagnosis, and providing further evaluation and treatment recommendations. The art of the interview involves transforming this potentially rote procedure into an empathic experience for a gay patient.

I would first note the initial contact observations from phase I of the intake. Here, Scott makes known from the outset that he is gay and is seeking a gay therapist to address the death of his gay brother. I would review this information with him, and inquire as to whether he had contacted the clinic because he had heard about the LGBT program. If he had not, I would mention that I was a gay psychiatrist and had initiated the program. Ordinarily, this brief interaction is enough to establish initial rapport. (In situations where an institutional LGBT program is lacking, an interviewee can establish rapport by confirming Scott's sexual orientation concerns, and by being prepared regarding the issue of self-disclosure.)

I would then add a question inviting brief elaboration of any acute concerns related to his sexual orientation, as well as a brief question verifying Scott's comfort with his male birth gender, which quickly rules out any transgender concerns. Because transgender individuals can be gay, straight, or bisexual, we have found that it is important to make this distinction.

An essential task for the psychiatrist interviewing Scott would be to differentiate grieving from major depression (Clayton, 1990; Prigerson, Bierhals & Kasl, 1996). Another task would be to clarify the extent of any post-traumatic stress disorder (PTSD) related to his incestuous concerns and the father's financial indiscretions. Specific questions and a directive approach are usually necessary to obtain the needed information.

This material was not available in the original interview. To obtain it, I would first share with Scott that all members of his treatment team confidentially communicate with each other about his case in order to be as helpful as possible. I would then follow a line of questioning in an attempt to differentiate grieving from depression. With sensitive topics like incest, I would first inquire as to his comfort level discussing this area of concern, provide reassurance, and indicate that I wanted to clarify the extent of any emotional impact in the present. I would then pursue inquiry regarding symptoms of PTSD and its complications.

With awareness of the behavioral observations noted at the first contact (strong, steady voice, handshake, smile, well-related), I would be attuned to any change in Scott's demeanor during the second phase of the intake with me. The first contact observations are consistent with an absence of major, overwhelming depression, but they are incongruent with Scott's later reference to depression and suicide (P131, P133).

As had been noted, Scott does not mention suicide or depression until virtually the end of the interview, and this may never have come up given the therapist's focus elsewhere. Suicidal preoccupation can be deeply disturbing to patients who fear it is a sign of a serious malady, or fear they will be hospitalized if they mention it, and they may avoid its discussion unless there is specific inquiry. Scott's initial behavioral presentation, and the late timing of this admission, hints at just such an effort to hide the extent of his fears and distress.

I would document the potential for any actual risk of harm to himself or others, elaborate on the nature of his depression, and also discern if there is a history suggestive of previous major depression or bipolar disorder. I would make a mental note to recommend that the therapist further explore issues of shame and self-esteem related to experiences of incest that could contribute to depression and suicidal ideation. I would elicit Scott's feedback as to how concerned I should be regarding any imminent desire to harm himself, and I would have him articulate a commitment not to do any harm. I would then review an intervention plan should suicidal intent become imminent. This would include a brief exploration of his fears if hospitalization was ever necessary. When the practitioner is not a psychiatrist, the presence of suicidal ideation and depression should trigger referral to a psychiatric colleague for consultation.

During the interview, Scott used the term "depression" (P131). Because the term has long been in the casual lexicon of the layperson, it can have a different meaning for a patient than it does for the mental health professional. I would, therefore, clarify what he means when he uses the term, in order to differentiate whether he is just upset, dysthymic, grieving, or in the thick of a major, clinical depression (Clayton, 1990; Oerlemans-Bunn, 1988; Prigerson et al., 1996; Siegel & Hoefer, 1981).

Grief, depression, and PTSD can affect cognitive status. This would be routinely evaluated at this phase through brief assessment of concentration, memory, orientation, and intellectual level. Minor impairment would warrant explanation, reassurance, and further observation.

Transient psychotic symptoms can occur during a period of grieving. Those in mourning sometimes think they hear the voice of the dead person, feel their presence, or see them. Without specific inquiry, the person may fear they are "going crazy," but are too frightened to say so. I would introduce the topic by stating that these questions address some unusual symptoms that sometimes normally occur during a period of grieving but sometimes occur for different reasons.

Loss, grieving, and trauma are stressors that can trigger other psychiatric disorders in susceptible individuals. I would pursue risk factors such as past psychiatric and drug abuse history, and obtain greater detail regarding his family history of such disorders. For example, the original interview does include inquiry about past psychiatric intervention (T1–T4), but it does not clarify if symptoms of other psychiatric disorders have occurred in the past. Scott makes reference to suicidal thoughts in his mother (P120), but there is no elaboration.

Once the information is gathered, a differential diagnosis, assessment, and treatment recommendations can be proposed. The lack of crucial information in the original interview, as discussed above, precludes any evidence-based accuracy in these formulations until that data is collected. Nevertheless, the case demonstrates how a culturally relevant institutional setting can serve as an important, even critical resource for a gay man. He is the son of a gambling father with inappropriate sexual boundaries, and he is now experiencing bereavement, relational issues, possible major depression, suicidal ideation, drug abuse, and possible PTSD.

He may require medication should there be significant symptoms of depression or PTSD. He may require hospitalization or intensive observation if the suicide risk was determined to be high. Other than these acute concerns, the opportunity to work with a gay therapist should promote a level of trust and identification that can ensure a progressive and productive treatment alliance. RHC membership could be offered once his acute distress was stabilized. This might not be a necessary option for someone who continues to function within the larger community, but the opportunity for further self-reflection in a healing cultural environment may be just the right therapeutic complement.

Concluding Remarks

The initial interview is a unique moment in the therapeutic encounter, when patients anticipate what the new setting will be like, and when their first impressions of the surroundings and initial sense of what is to be expected are fresh, vivid, and now starkly juxtaposed with the concerns that bring them into the institutional environment.

The history and predispositions of the patient, therapist, and institution interact in ways that can distract and threaten, or facilitate the task of evaluation and treatment. The first interview is a time for mutual first impressions of the facility and its personnel and other patients, of the intake therapist, and of the patient. Information gathering is not the sole province of the therapist, but a de facto process between all participants. But it is the singular task of the clinician to understand this complex of elements within the context of the patient as a person reaching out for help.

In the case of the gay patient, it is also the task of the intake clinician to recognize when the institutional setting or therapist evokes preconceptions that may create early barriers to the formation of a treatment alliance based on sexual minority experience. In clinical work with gay clients in the institutional setting, therapists need to know not only the strengths and limitations of their own qualifications but also the strengths and weaknesses of the institution regarding its ability to engage, evaluate, and treat gay clients.

The novice clinician tests and refines basic interviewing and treatment skills during each encounter. As knowledge and technical skills integrate and mature, they are inevitably applied more creatively and strategically. Learning about gay issues, exploring one's own biases, and finding a knowledgeable and trusted supervisor are part of what it takes to get started. It is a process of learning from one's mistakes and successes. In the institutional setting, this process also includes the development of a perspective on the role played by the practitioner's institution, and the myriad ways in which it can influence the therapeutic encounter. Not to worry. The art of practicing culturally competent therapy in an institutional setting is advanced and refined over a professional lifetime.

Evaluation and intervention in the institutional setting is a highly coordinated process, utilizing a team of specialists with resources not available to a solo practitioner. But even here, caution is warranted. The patient that is the subject of this book had suicidal ideation and discomfort with heterosexual settings. It should be clear that the LGBT cultural component in an institutional setting can make the difference between engagement and detachment, which can mean the difference between life and death.

Welcoming the troubled gay person into a healing environment in itself lets light shine through. It shines from the humanity and skills that we bring to the clinical encounter, and it shines from what we learn about who they are. In the institutional setting, it shines the brightest in those organizations that have the strength to reflect on their effectiveness, encourage and promote the talents of its staff, and in the particular case of the gay client, to know how to involve that person in a process and experience of well-being.

Wider institutional adaptation of LGBT-inclusive cultural and affirmative practices, at all operational levels, can reduce barriers to treatment, improve the quality and relevance of care provided, impart professional pride in the ability to reach out to diverse social groups, build a reputation for the institution as a true community resource, expand the horizon of administrators and staff, and, most importantly, enhance treatment outcomes with this population.

For More Information on Community Psychiatry, the Author Recommends

Garnets, L. D., & Kimmel, D. C. (Eds.), (2003). *Psychological perspectives on lesbian, gay, and bisexual experiences* (2nd ed.). New York: Columbia University Press.

Hellman, R. E., & Drescher, J. (Eds.), (2005). *Handbook of LGBT issues in community mental health.* New York: The Haworth Press.

Lim, R. F. (2006). *Clinical manual of cultural psychiatry.* Washington, DC: APPI.

Rosenberg, J., & Rosenberg, S. (Eds.), (2006). *Community mental health challenges for the 21st century.* New York: Routledge.

Thornicroft, G., & Szmukler, G. (Eds.), (2001). *Textbook of community psychiatry.* New York: Oxford University Press.

Acknowledgments

The author wishes to thank Eileen Klein, Jack Martin, Jean Okie, Susanne Shulman and David Wilson for their thoughtful suggestions during the preparation of this chapter.

References

Altman, N. (1995). *The analyst in the inner city*. Hillsdale, NJ: The Analytic Press.

American Psychiatric Association (1994). *Diagnostic and statistical manual of mental disorders* (4th ed.). Washington, DC: American Psychiatric Association.

Bartlett, A., King, M., & Philips, P. (2001). Straight talking. *British Journal of Psychiatry*, *179*, 545–549.

Bernstein, K. T., Liu, K. L., Begier, E. M., Koblin, B., Karpati, A., & Murrill, C. (2008). Same-sex attraction disclosure to health care providers among New York City men who have sex with men. *Archives of Internal Medicine, 168*, 1458–1464.

Carter, R. T. (1995). *The influence of race and racial identity in psychotherapy*. New York: John Wiley & Sons.

Clayton, P. J. (1990). Bereavement and depression. *Journal of Clinical Psychiatry*, *51*(Suppl.), 34–40.

Coleman, E. (1978). Toward a new model of treatment of homosexuality: A review. *Journal of Homosexuality, 3*(4), 345–359.

Coolhart, D. (2005). Out of the closet and into the therapy room: Therapist self-disclosure of sexual identity. *Guidance and Counseling, 21*, 3–13.

Gage, K., & Gillins, L. (1991). Institutional transference: A new look at an old concept. *Journal of Psychosocial Nursing and Mental Health Services, 29*, 24–26.

Gendel, M. H., & Resier, D. E. (1981). Institutional countertransference. *American Journal of Psychiatry, 138*, 508–511.

Grob, G. (2004). The ambivalent character of American psychiatry. *Journal of Health Policy and Law, 29*, 515–525.

Haley, J. (1989). *The first therapy session*. San Francisco, CA: Jossey-Bass Audio Programs.

Hanson, J. (2005). Should your lips be zipped? How therapist self-disclosure and non-disclosure affect clients. *Counseling and Psychotherapy Research, 5*, 96–104.

Hellman, R. E., & Drescher, J. (Eds.), (2005). *Handbook of LGBT issues in community mental health*. New York: The Haworth Press.

Hellman, R. E., & Klein, E. (2004). A program for lesbian, gay, bisexual, and transgender individuals with major mental illness. Treating LGBT patients in the public sector. *Journal of Gay and Lesbian Psychotherapy, 8*(1–2), 67–82.

Knox, S., & Hill, C. E. (2003). Therapist self-disclosure: Research-based suggestions for practitioners. *Journal Clinical Psychology, 59*, 529–539.

Liddle, B. J. (1999). Gay and lesbian clients ratings of psychiatrists, psychologists, social workers, and counselors. *Journal of Gay and Lesbian Psychotherapy, 3*, 81–93.

Lucksted, A. (2004). Lesbian, gay, bisexual, and transgender people receiving services in the public mental health system: raising issues. In R. E. Hellman, & J. Drescher (Eds.), *Handbook of LGBT issues in community mental health*. New York: The Haworth Press.

Malyon, A. K. (1982). Psychotherapeutic implications of internalized homophobia in gay men. In J. C. Gonsiorek (Ed.), *Homosexuality and psychotherapy*. New York: The Haworth Press.

Margulies, A., & Havens, L. L. (1981). The initial encounter: What to do first? *American Journal of Psychiatry, 138*, 421–428.

Neville, S., & Henrickson, M. (2006). Perceptions of lesbian, gay and bisexual people of primary healthcare services. *Journal of Advanced Nursing, 55*, 407–415.

Oerlemans-Bunn, M. (1988). On being gay, single, and bereaved. *The American Journal of Nursing, 88*, 472–476.

Prigerson, H. G., Bierhals, A. J., & Kasl, S. V. (1996). Complicated grief as a disorder distinct from bereavement-related depression and anxiety: A replication study. *The American Journal of Psychology, 153*, 1484–1486.

Safirstein, S. (1967). Institutional transference. *Psychiatric Quarterly, 41*, 557–566.

Shelby, R. D. (1994). Mourning within a culture of mourning. In S. A. Cadwell, R. A. Burnham, & M. Forstein (Eds.), *Therapists on the front line.* Washington, DC: American Psychiatric Press.

Siegel, R. L., & Hoefer, D. D. (1981). Bereavement counseling for gay individuals. *American Journal of Psychotherapy, 35*, 517–525.

Silverstein, C. (1976–1977). Even psychiatry can profit from its past mistakes. *Journal of Homosexuality, 2*(2), 153–158.

Sophie, J. (1987). Internalized homophobia and lesbian identity. *Journal of Homosexuality, 14*, 53–65.

Part Two

Problem Behaviors

6 Death and Bereavement

Michael C. Singer

Private Practice, New York City

Grief over the recent death of his brother is the reason Scott gave for seeking therapy. While there are no reliable statistics on the reasons for psychotherapy-seeking activity, we know that bereavement, as a traumatic yet normative experience, often generates a search for new meanings in life, a process that is a core component of psychotherapy.

In this case, bereavement includes feelings of pain, loneliness, and anger. It has also raised many troubling questions for Scott about his own life thus far, and has cast a pall over his view of the future. Circumstances and issues that previously might have seemed manageable, or merely a part of life's inexorable flow, have taken on potentially ominous meanings. In the audio recording of the initial interview, Scott's pain was palpable. Its intensity ebbed and flowed as he and the therapist ranged over the major domains of his life. His grief at various moments was intermingled with sadness, anger, and numbness, as well as with what we assume was Scott's usual degree of self-assurance, humor, and buoyancy. Therapist and patient raised questions of immediate concern, and did some exploration around other major issues of family, relationships, and sex, indicating potentially useful directions for the treatment.

The patient's personality is complex and it is not yet clear how grief influenced Scott's self-awareness and presentation during that initial hour. One's overall impression is of a man who has adaptive defenses and can manage his grief sufficiently to focus on other issues, when necessary. However, Scott displays a limited awareness of his family history and its likely impact on his current life. As a result, we may generate a series of questions about him at the time of the intake: How much were his expressions of anger and yearning amplified or diminished by grief? Which coping mechanisms have remained intact, and which have been compromised? Have more primitive defenses been brought to bear under the stress of bereavement? The nature and trajectory of these state-specific adaptations will have ramifications as his grief becomes more manageable and Scott works through the complexities of his loss.

Because death figures prominently in this initial session, there will be an unavoidable connection with the therapist's own experiences of bereavement and other traumatic losses, as well as his reactions to them, and his self-awareness regarding these counter-transference issues (Schaffner, 1997). The therapist is also

The Initial Psychotherapy Interview. DOI: 10.1016/B978-0-12-385146-8.00006-7

gay and we would expect patient and therapist to have some traumatic experiences in common that are normative for gay men. The importance of this cultural commonality will be elucidated later in the chapter.

The following section will give a brief account of the theories that this writer finds useful when working with and thinking about bereavement. Examples from Scott's intake will illustrate how these ideas add information to the therapist's understanding. The subsequent section will examine the specifics of Scott's initial presentation as it pertains to bereavement and will be followed by comments on the therapist's handling of the session and suggestions for alternative lines of questioning.

Theories of Bereavement

There have been numerous contributions to the professional literature about bereavement (cf. Bowlby, 1980; Freud, 1957; James, 1961; Jung, 1959; Klein, 1948). Among these, the following have been useful to this writer in defining an empathic and effective psychotherapeutic approach.

Psychological thinking in the area began with Freud (1957), who wrote extensively about the differences between normal and pathological mourning. Freud (1953) originated the idea that significant relationships were internalized as part of each person's inner life, along with the strong feelings that accompanied them. He thought that more significant relationships, which would naturally be associated with strong feelings, would evoke powerful experiences of separation and loss. In this initial session, it is not easy to gauge the depth of Scott's feelings about his brother's death. One assumes they would be powerful, yet he presents in a subdued and controlled manner 3 weeks after the loss. Scott did not weep during the session. This was not explored further during the intake.

Freud observed that the bereaved would first over-connect and then gradually disconnect from her or his internal representations of the deceased, a process later designated *grief-work*. He described the goal of bereavement as detaching from the deceased, in a sense withdrawing the individual's emotional investment, through a concentrated and often painful examination of memories and feelings. In this case, Scott frequently reviews his memories of David and his feelings toward him. He feels guilty about some (P45) and warmly nostalgic about others (P34). While Scott is not overtly angry at his dead brother, he does speak angrily about his father's (P24) and mother's (P120) current lack of success as caregivers, while indirectly criticizing his brother's choice of an HIV-positive partner (P18).

In Freud's view, the significance of the loss, the ambivalence of the associated feelings, and the survivor's predisposition to depression, are all factors that impact the outcome of bereavement (Freud, 1957). In this case, Scott has suffered the loss of a significant relationship, expresses some ambivalence about it (P45), and may well have a predisposition to depression that arises from his childhood sexual abuse (P24) and its denial (P27). While Freud thought that anger was not exhibited in normal mourning, it is now generally agreed that anxiety, anger, and despair are its basic components, and it is this very particular mixture of feeling that makes mourning so painful and also so liable to give rise to pathology (Bowlby, 1961). While Freud conceptualized pathological mourning specifically as melancholia, or chronic severe depression, in current psychodynamic discourse, the term refers to bereavement that does not ultimately lead to a resumption of everyday activities and a pre-morbid level of satisfaction. Whether mourning will be pathological or not depends on several variables, including: extent of emotional maturity, availability of support, psychic structure of the bereaved at the time of loss, ability to express and process feelings, and individual capacity to symbolize experience (Aragno, 2003). Given the extreme nature of Scott's family history, his limited awareness of its significance, the questionable support he currently receives, and his as yet unknown ability to make use of psychotherapy, we would have some serious concerns about bereavement outcome.

Freud initially believed in the finite duration of grief-work, and the importance of giving up the lost relationship completely to make way for future relationships. However, theory is also shaped by personal experience, and Freud's subsequent self-examination after his loss of a child and a grandchild suggested to him that mourning might lessen but never end, and further, that it might be unrealistic to imagine the survivor finding a replacement for the deceased. He suggested in a letter to a friend that some gaps were not meant to be filled (quoted in Rothaupt & Becker, 2007). This was a first indication that bereavement itself could be better conceptualized in terms of attachment and loss than as depression or other psychopathology.

It is now an accepted part of psychological thinking that even healthy survivors will continue to feel emotionally engaged with the deceased for an indefinite period, and may experience an ongoing internal relationship for the rest of their lives. Thus, the notion of *managing* or *adapting to loss* has replaced *recovering from loss*, which is now considered to inaccurately imply a medical model of disease and cure (Stroebe & Schut, 2001). This is not just abstract terminology, but rather a stance toward patients in bereavement that can help the therapist remain flexible and growth-supporting during the treatment. It is not uncommon for bereaved patients such as Scott to report hearing the deceased's voice, feeling her or him near, or even reporting visual hallucinations of the deceased. However, it is important to assess for impaired reality testing. For example, when Scott reports that his brother is always with him (P33) and that he regards David as his "ego" (P23), the therapist would want to know how concrete the experience is for him.

Melanie Klein (1948) understood bereavement as a phase of psychic disorganization and reorganization that results in psychological compensation for the loss: the work of mourning produces symbol formation that installs images and memories of the loved one in the bereaved's inner object world. The work of mourning allows survivors to transform their relationship to the deceased into a permanent inner reality, which facilitates continuity of the self, acknowledgment of the importance of the deceased, and reinvestment in external connections. Klein made an additional observation that may be particularly relevant to Scott's case, that this grief response is closely related to responses to previous losses; moreover, that the success of this psychic reorganization is largely determined by the successful resolution of these earlier losses (Klein, 1948). Scott's confusion and possible dissociation in the aftermath of sexual molestation (P7) and continuing anger at his mother's failure to protect him afterward (P27) are likely to have had a negative impact on his ability to reorganize himself and seek further intimate connections.

Bowlby's attachment theory (Bowlby, 1961, 1980) provides an overarching explanation for grief as the natural response to loss of a significant relationship. Bowlby thought of attachment and its complementary behavior, caregiving, as having evolved in many species because it increases parental proximity, and thus, the survival of offspring. This frame of reference helps therapists understand the propensity of human beings to create strong emotional bonds with significant others and explains the many kinds of emotional distress and personality disturbance, including anxiety, anger, depression, and emotional detachment, that result from unwilling separation and loss. Attachment style develops in infancy and remains relatively stable throughout life. Bowlby predicted, and recent research confirms (reviewed in Shaver & Tancredy, 2001) that individuals who are insecurely attached are at higher risk for elevated traumatic grief symptoms than securely attached individuals. Scott reports being unable to be consoled by his family, feeling angry and exploited instead (P24). Another study (Lyons-Ruth & Block, 1996) indicates that emotional dissociation in parents leads to disrupted attachment and experiences of loss in their children. This may be relevant for both of Scott's parents. The father's sexual molestation of the boys (P11) and his physical overtures during bereavement (P120), as well as the mother's denial of the abuse (P27) and continuing expressions of anger toward the dead brother (P120) suggest dissociative processes at work, perhaps the result of their own early experiences of abuse or neglect. Clearly, both children experienced disrupted attachment, while Scott continues to express yearning for the support and safety that were missing from the family.

Bowlby (1980) used his observations on attachment, separation, and loss to develop a *four-phase theory of the mourning process*. It should be noted that, like many other stage theories, including Kuebler-Ross' (1969) stages of death and dying, these stages are rarely discrete, and we would expect Scott to display aspects of more than one stage at a time and move back and forth between stages as his bereavement proceeds. His blunted feelings throughout the session may indicate a lingering of numbness and shock, the adoring statements about David suggest a yearning for his lost brother (P23), while his seeking therapy so soon after the loss indicates a push to get on with his life.

In the first phase, survivors are numb, shocked, and uncomprehending. This phase usually lasts from a few hours to a week, and may be interrupted by outbursts of intense distress and/or anger. Reactions of disbelief, inability to understand, or receiving the news as if one were having a dream are all typical of this first phase. The second phase is characterized by yearning and searching for the lost figure, often angrily, which may last months or years. The reality of the loss begins to be taken in by the survivor and is marked by periods of tearful crying and pining for the deceased. Intense feelings that the deceased is present, or vivid dreams in which the deceased is alive, followed by a distraught awakening, may occur. There is both yearning for reunion and acceptance of loss, with the former gradually ceding ground to the latter. During this time, for various reasons that will be explored later in this chapter, the circle of supporters around the bereaved, such as family, friends, significant others, and therapists may be at risk for offering encouragement to move on, rather than comfort and support. These missteps may result in anxiety or anger in the bereaved and can be the source of lasting recrimination, long after the bereavement period has passed. During this period of my own bereavement, I yearned for connection with those closest to me, but was also frightened and disorganized by this need. I found it very difficult to listen to certain pieces of music, with which I have always had a deep connection, feeling that the connection itself was too painful to be experienced, when my deepest connection had just been irrevocably lost. While this protective avoidance gradually diminished in the course of bereavement, the now-familiar window into loss and remembrance evoked by music has become a precious, if painful, pathway.

Bowlby's third phase is one of disorganization and despair. Here, loss and its negative consequences are accepted and acknowledged. This is followed by a greater or lesser degree of psychological reorganization in the fourth phase. In order for mourning to be successful, and of course, the definition of *successful* will vary, the bereaved must be able to tolerate all of these powerful, unpleasant feelings.

Interpersonal and relational theories of bereavement (Shapiro, 1991, 1996) suggest that the self is always in transition, continually influenced and changed through the many contexts in which a person interacts with others. These theories add to attachment theory a focus on how relationships are represented internally, and how these representations continuously adapt and reorganize to changing conditions over the life span. One aspect of this evolution is the dialectical tension between holding on and letting go of the lost object during bereavement. Memories of the deceased may be tightly held and examined by the survivor, while simultaneously being placed in historical context. For Scott, the dialectical tension may include the recent catastrophic loss, as well as his protracted and unresolved despair over the family's life-long failure to provide safety and love (P24, P27, and P28). *Psychotherapists will be advised to tread carefully in this complicated situation of multilevel loss, so that the bereaved patient feels safe to explore the emotional breadth of the relationship, as well as the long-term idealization of the family's functionality.* Psychotherapeutic work may ultimately facilitate the patient's ability to separate from both kinds of grief and also to transform both. This mourning over family inadequacy is also at the core of psychotherapy with survivors of childhood sexual abuse (Davies & Frawley, 1994), and with gay patients, who frequently experience rejection, isolation, and a general failure of understanding on the part of their families. In Scott's family, his brother appears to have faced significant hostility from the parents in connection with coming out (P45). We would expect that these kinds of long-standing family failures would exacerbate and complicate bereavement.

Loss can engender further loss within a family, and a central task of psychotherapy around bereavement issues can be to explore the potentially disruptive effects of bereavement on the ability of the family to remain functional and effective. This work may be particularly complicated within families that functioned poorly even before a bereavement, as in Scott's family, where understanding and trust have been undermined by abuse and deceit. It has been observed that many people who experience loss do not reach out any further than their immediate families. This "keeping things within the family" may occur whether or not the family actually meets the bereavement needs of its members. Preexisting shame, secret-keeping, and other dysfunctional features can increase enmeshment after a loss and prevent family members from reaching out. Scott's family, for example, has been relatively paralyzed for many years since the father's molestation of the boys. Although affirmed by both boys (P11), the sexual abuse has never been openly acknowledged by the parents (P27); moreover, the mother withheld consolation for the boys' distress and consistently upheld the prohibition against disclosure (P28). The shaming secret festered within the family for 20 years, and its potency was reaffirmed by the boys at David's deathbed (P25). Now, during bereavement, the mother is unable to let her vulnerable feelings about the loss be known, unable to obtain comfort from her surviving son, and unable to provide any honest comfort to him (P120). As far as we know from the initial interview, except for Scott's seeking a psychotherapist, the family circle would have remained shut against intruders.

Some families provide adequate comfort or support during bereavement. Individual members may exhibit a synchronization of post-loss activity that is sufficient to provide an acceptable level of solace. In other families, however, this synchronization fails to occur, as various family members display different and perhaps discordant coping styles (Stroebe & Schut, 2001). In Scott's family, the father seems distraught and needy (P120), for reasons that will be discussed later. He displays his feelings indiscriminately, without attempting to address the lifelong mourning in the family that his sexual abuse set into motion years before. He has no ability or authority to comfort his wife and son, and describes his wife as "stoic" (P120). The mother also presents as needy, and vents some feelings of anger at the deceased brother to Scott (P120), which keeps him from getting closer to her, except when he feels weak and needy. Scott himself seeks solace and comfort from them, although he would likely claim that he seeks it solely from his mother, while being forced to remain in contact with his father as the price of his mother's presence. He becomes a doctor to his mother (P120), trying to cure her or satisfy her in some unknown way (P119). Scott claims to have kept the family intact after his father's swindling, by not pressing charges, but ultimately this act of mercy also seems to be a denial that the family has ceased to function (P31).

A theory of incremental grief has been developed to explain how discordance leads to secondary loss, in the form of deteriorating relationships between family members. This deterioration increases the stress experienced by the survivors, as their customary styles of providing and obtaining comfort break down. For example, the death of a sibling might cause a change in the relationship between the remaining sibling and a parent, possibly leading to more serious estrangement, which is yet another loss. The parents' relationship may founder, which would be a third loss. In another family, deterioration could lead to more serious enmeshment between the survivors, or between discordant idealized feelings about the deceased, either of which would tend to complicate the bereavement process. In Scott's family, the death of his gay brother, whose homosexuality had been a source of parental anger, also serves as a flashpoint for further discordant coping, as Scott experiences despair (P23), while his mother remains angry and denying, and his father indiscriminately needy (P120). One would predict a less effective adaptation to grief in families in which discordant grieving occurs, while more compatible coping styles would predict a better trajectory of bereavement. In Scott's family, the members are being further isolated by their incompatible responses to David's death, enlivening old hurts and unresolved hostilities. There does not appear to be enough unity to produce mutual comfort or support.

The AIDS Holocaust

While HIV/AIDS is discussed in depth in another chapter of this book, no chapter about a gay man's grief over the death of another gay man, especially a beloved brother, could fail to mention the catastrophic effect of HIV on our population. The statistics are well known and have been reported elsewhere (Centers for Disease Control, 2007). More than a quarter century after the emergence of HIV and its transformation into the world's leading health crisis, psychotherapists still struggle to understand how this intrusion of sickness and death into the everyday lives of gay men has altered the way in which they tolerate intimacy, form durable relationships, plan for the future, and maintain feelings of efficacy and self-worth (Blechner, 1997).

Like other overwhelming realities, HIV is often ignored or denied, and the fear it engenders is dissociated. The effect of this dissociation is not immediately discernible, since it is not conscious. One would expect, in theory, that psychotherapists would be in an advantageous position to help their patients understand these dissociated feelings, because they are trained to look for currents of feeling outside of awareness. Yet, under the extreme circumstances of HIV, psychotherapists also experience radiating feelings of powerlessness and vulnerability. These countertransference feelings may be more intense for gay therapists, in particular, who have likely experienced similar AIDS-related trauma, as well as earlier stigmatization and rejection by their families and communities, all of which are normative for gay men. Therapists who were trained in the twentieth century also survived varying degrees of homophobia in their training institutes (cf. Drescher, 1993; Singer, 2002). Like their patients, psychotherapists may or may not acknowledge the effects of these losses, repeated traumas, and stigmatization on their treatment relationships. Sometimes a therapist will withdraw from bereaved patients, overloaded by his own thoughts of death and reminiscences of trauma evoked by the treatment (Blechner, 1997). A therapist may respond counterphobically, going forward into an exploration in which the patient experiences too much anxiety and despair. It is essential for a psychotherapist to examine his own feelings and fantasies about death when embarking on a treatment with a patient who is bereaved. This self-examination can mitigate the possible derailing of the treatment by the therapists' various fears, worries, and denials (Schaffner, 1997). Years after my own HIV-related bereavements, I occasionally experience feelings of despair and hopelessness in response to bereavement material presented by patients. However unsettling this can be, these feelings also open a window of connection for me, both to my own past, and to the patient's feelings in the moment.

There has been much written about therapists' disclosure of personal information to patients (cf. Greenberg, 1995; Jacobs, 1999). Although I have not disclosed my own HIV bereavement status to a patient, some therapists may feel that a supportive treatment should include disclosure of this information when a patient is particularly frightened, isolated, or shamed by his feelings.

Survivor guilt is another issue. First identified with respect to survivors of the Nazi holocaust, survivor guilt can be a factor not only in those who have been bereaved by AIDS but also in the psychotherapists who treat them. Blechner (1997) describes survivor guilt as widespread among people who engaged in risky sexual activities before HIV was identified, yet somehow managed to survive. Twenty-five years later, while there is no written confirmation within our profession, we have seen that survivor guilt afflicts many survivors, regardless of their behavior in the early days of the epidemic. To simply be alive, in the face of so much death, can arouse guilt feelings, which are often, as well as feelings of relief, that are often denied and thereby exacerbated. We would expect a surviving gay brother to feel some intense survivor guilt after the death of his beloved gay brother. Scott disclosed some information during the interview that suggests this kind of guilt, including his continued unsafe sex practices (P121), failure to obtain a full workup of HIV tests (P50), and annoyance at his mother for idealizing him (P120). This is an area that the therapist will no doubt explore.

It may seem curious to highlight HIV in this way, since the bereaved patient under consideration in this book may or may not be HIV positive. Moreover, the relevance of HIV/AIDS has been discussed in a separate chapter of this book. Yet, it seems important to note some possible effects of HIV on how gay men live their lives and think about death. It would be impossible for a psychotherapist to examine intimacy difficulties, unprotected sex and other high-risk behavior, self-harm, and bereavement, without also examining how a gay patient has been affected by the proximity of suffering and dying, as well as by his membership in the group most consistently tainted by the stigma of AIDS. As mentioned earlier, these issues are as personally relevant for therapists as they examine counter-transference feelings, as they are for their work with patients, and have a particular relevance for gay therapists working with gay patients.

Scott's Intake Interview

People from dysfunctional families spend their lives yearning for the love and support they never received (Klein, 1948; Golden & Hill, 1991). This ongoing grief would locate them in a life-long sense somewhere within Bowlby's second phase). For people who were raised in more or less intact families, experiencing the death of a loved one can shatter their basic beliefs that they live in an orderly, understandable, and meaningful world. What is the experience of grief for those whose beliefs in meaning and order are already tenuous? Scott has always been yearning and searching for closeness and safety, which he experienced only with his brother (P7, P11, P14, P18, P23, P28, and so on). Now, we might ask how these feelings of long-standing yearning are being affected by his recent bereavement. David's death has closed down some customary avenues of engagement, both healthy and pathological. Scott seems to seek psychotherapy in the hope that other avenues of engagement may be discoverable, as well as for a possible quick fix for his intense feelings of mourning.

As psychoanalytic ideas might suggest, Scott has begun to manage his grief, in the sense of looking at his loss and attempting to describe it and incorporate it into what is left of his life. He has acknowledged David's death verbally, and has even created a symbol of the death to remind himself and others that David is always with him (P33). As stated above, survivors often feel the deceased nearby and experience the heightened emotional proximity of the deceased as an almost physical reality for a very long time. Scott has also concretized his brother's death through the tattoo (P33), the creation of which caused some physical pain that may have either added to or distracted from his emotional pain. Since we know the family is Jewish from Scott's mention of "Jewish guilt" (P48), we wonder about this expression of loss, given the unique relationship between Jews and tattoos created by the Holocaust: specifically, other kinds of self-punishment and persecution the tattoo represents. Surely, both brothers had ample experience as childhood victims of their father's molestation and swindling and their mother's betrayal to make this Holocaust association feasible. Victimization, masochism, defiance, and even atonement are possible meanings for the tattoo. It is notable that Scott asserted his brother was always with him, yet still required the tattoo as a further substantiation. At this initial moment in the treatment, the tattoo is the physical equivalent of the loss and the therapist likely made a correct decision not to question Scott further about it, which might have been experienced as an intrusion and a failure of empathy for the bereavement. There will be ample opportunity to explore these multiple meanings of victimization and survival contained in the tattoo, which will unfold during the course of treatment.

Scott is invested in the grief-work of the bereavement: He thinks about his brother frequently, recounts their shared history to his friends, and wonders what his life will be like alone. There are hints that this is not a smooth process for him. Freud (1957) warned about the development of melancholia in cases where the idealization of the deceased prevented the survivor from expressing ambivalent feelings directly. In death, David has become a hero for Scott, who described him as "my protector—he was my Number One. He wasn't just my brother. You know he was my ego. ... he had so much love to give me. It was unconditional" (P23).

Although we know the brothers were very close, this characterization is extreme. It is difficult, especially perhaps for a psychotherapist, to understand what Scott means when he says David was his "ego." Does he mean that David was his rational part, which is a commonly held idea about the ego, or does he mean that his brother was a repository or support for Scott's own sense of self or self-worth? The answer is unclear. One must remember that this relationship was set amidst a troubled, poorly boundaried, and abusive family. The brothers clung tightly to each other as mutual protection against the father's molestation and swindling, on the one side, and the mother's betrayal, on the other. The details of how the brothers may have tried to shield each other during these ongoing traumas have not yet been revealed. Shielding may not have been their only activity. It would have been just as natural for abused children to sacrifice each other, if it meant possible escape from further abuse. The only hint of less-than-altruistic behavior in the session is the retelling of how their parents were informed by David that Scott was gay, which Scott immediately recognized as his deceased brother's attempt to deflect potential bad feeling onto him (P45). One might wonder whether there were many more scenes like this when they were younger and the family situation was more "dog eat dog."

The patient expressed several reasons for being angry at his brother, including choosing an HIV-positive partner, putting himself at risk, getting sick, and finally, dying and leaving Scott to cope with their troubled parents all alone. At this initial session, Scott is able to express some guilty feelings about not supporting his brother's choice of a partner who was HIV positive and some further self-blame about having always been their parents' "slightly preferred" child (P120). This guilt may indicate the anger turned inward that characterizes melancholia and it may also indicate survivor guilt: Not only has Scott not died from AIDS, but he is the sole survivor of the family's dysfunctionality. We might speculate that he has projected some of this anger onto his mother, who he presents as ungrief-stricken and furious at the brother for putting himself at risk (P120). It will be part of the therapist's inquiry to help Scott flesh out the origins of his reaction formation in anger and disappointment, so that he can work to clarify his ambivalent feelings toward David. In a family with sexual abuse, psychotherapists assume that feelings of anger and fear have been dissociated and may be experienced as shameful when they surface during treatment.

We can already begin to observe the relationship between Scott's life-long yearning for the love not received from his family, and his immediate grief over his brother's death. The reaction formation that developed during his youth to keep his mother intact as "a good woman," (P120) who continued to love him, in spite of her betrayals, resembles his idealizing feelings toward David (P23). The two idealizations may be mutually exclusive. It will be difficult to idealize David, while also continuing to idealize his mother. We can see this in the juxtaposition of highly ambivalent feelings toward his mother that include severe criticism of her anger toward the brother, Scott's attempts to maintain her goodness, his disappointment in her dependence on the father, his praise at her overflowing love, and his anger at his mother's inability to offer comfort and solace during their bereavement (all in P120).

As Bowlby suggested, there are elements of more than one stage of grief in this session. There is numbness and disbelief as Scott describes his brother's hospital ordeal and quick death (P20, P21), while yearning and searching are communicated through his attempts to convey David's centrality (P18) to his own psychic well-being. The pain of losing his brother and the questions it engenders about the future are still inextricable so soon after his brother's death. There can often be a retelling of specific details from the death story in an apparently numb or affectless manner, but from which occasional outbursts of weeping or anger break through. This is the mixture of stages.

Scott spoke about his older brother in the initial session as a benevolent primary attachment figure (P23). While this would be expected of an older brother with whom he shared so much, it becomes more complicated when viewed within the setting of Scott's ambivalent relationship with his parents. We might predict that bereavement following the loss of an ostensibly secure attachment would ultimately lead to robust functioning; however, Scott's relationship with each of his parents is insecure and has been periodically cut off (P31). The father's depredations, the mother's early failure to protect her children from him, and her angry defense of the father against the boys' accusations (P28), have all contributed to the boys' extreme need to rely only on each other for love and safety. We would expect David's death to further complicate this ongoing grief in Scott.

Scott seems determined to maintain the idealized image of his family. He has tried to create some façade of family functionality, in a family that has been largely unworkable. He has dissociated his yearning, yet still performs the gestures of trying to convince his mother to stand up to or leave his father. The strain in his strange repeated proclamation that she is "a good woman" (P120) also contains the seed of recognition that she has never been a good mother. The family does appear to be changing since David's death, but not toward greater efficacy. Scott complains, "...there are times when I want to be with my parents to get that solace, comfort from them and they don't bring it. In fact they give the complete opposite" (P23). There is evidence throughout the session that some currents of anger that have remained obscure or indirect in the past are being stirred up and given direct expression by his brother's death (P120). His repeated attempts to obtain comfort and solace have not been any more successful since David's death than they were previously (P15). If anything, the result has been less solace, while Scott's isolated efforts at repair seem obsolete now (P120), as he takes the decisive step to seek a psychotherapist. The task of the psychotherapist will be to guide Scott into an acknowledgement of his despair. In a successful treatment, one has the expectation that he will realize that his yearning for love and protection will not be fulfilled within the family. It is in this sense that the working through of his current bereavement may help Scott finally explore the sequelae of his childhood molestation and move beyond the overshadowing needs for love and safety.

The notion of incremental grief provides a further insight into the discordant responses of the family. The family members appear distraught, and there has not been any synchronization of needs between them (P120). Scott's father is indiscriminate, as he has always been, offering nothing to the others, while trying to steal what comfort he can, the way he has swindled them of other possessions on other occasions (P120). The mother ostensibly gives her husband what she has always given: She stays with him and keeps quiet (P119, P120). Now, in her bereavement, mother has moved away, into what appears to be a demanding isolation. She may want some genuine comfort from the husband that he cannot provide, as the molester and swindler of her dead child. The mother is in an untenable position now, pulling away from both her husband and son. The father is distraught without her. Scott also appears to be experiencing this secondary loss very directly, extorted into becoming his mother's doctor to maintain connection and comfort. The family has come apart.

In his grief, when he needs her as if he were a child, Scott experiences the loss of his mother again, but now it may be less tolerable, both because of his brother's death and because Scott is now a rather insistent adult. He is angry about this loss (P119) and his idealization of her appears to be breaking down. This process of maintaining his mother as "a good woman" has been familiar to him for many years and it requires a very strong force to be displaced. This force is the death of his brother, who, in his turn, is now idealized as a hero, nurturer, and "ego." For Scott, bereavement and therapy may provide an opportunity to gain some deeper understanding of these very complicated and painful dynamics that he has carried for so long and perhaps to establish new and deeper connections with others.

This chapter began with some important ideas about bereavement from a number of theoretical orientations in psychology. These ideas were mainly originated within the psychodynamic school, which provides ways of understanding human thought and behavior that may occur either within or outside of conscious awareness. It has been the goal of the chapter to apply these ideas to Silverstein's findings during Scott's intake interview, and to do so in as simple language as possible, so that psychotherapists with diverse training and styles of working will find them helpful in working with bereaved patients. *When working in this area, which is commonly occupied by extreme combinations of sadness, anxiety, and anger, it is the hope of this writer that therapists will pay close attention not only to their patients' feelings, reactions, and well-being, but also to their own.*

The following section contains some thoughts on Silverstein's specific technique of inquiry during the intake session and offers some after-the-fact criticism and suggestions for improvement.

Reactions to the Intake Session

A great deal was learned during the intake. The therapist was very interested in Scott's sexual habits, even though that was not the presenting problem. In the luxury of hindsight, I would likely have altered the distribution of time during the intake to give more to bereavement and abuse, less to sex, although I do not deny its importance in any way to psychological inquiry. While new patients are often reluctant to talk about one or more of these areas, Scott seemed willing to follow any line of inquiry, with the exception of exploring his closeted relations with his straight medical doctor.

The first area of the session deals with the father's molestation. Scott's responses were somewhat vague, and it remained unclear what he remembered, the duration of the abuse, or whether Scott was now in a position to affirm what specific activities had taken place. This is such an important area, with particular bearing on the course of bereavement, that further clarifying questions would have been helpful at T8, such as: "Was he in the shower with you?" or "The three of you were in the shower?" and "It sounds like you mean he touched you in a sexual way?" and "Did your father also touch himself during these times?" and "Were you aware of your mother's whereabouts at these times?" At T10: "You sound a bit uncertain. Maybe you can tell me what that's about." I would especially have wanted to know more about the brothers' conversations about the abuse: At T12, I would have deferred asking demographic questions and would instead have wondered: "Could you tell me more about your conversations with David about the abuse?" and "Did the two of you deal with it similarly or differently?" and "How has it been to have that abuse on your mind over so many years?"

At P12, Scott brings up his brother's death as his presenting problem. He seems ready to talk. Instead of going with that, the therapist responded in a somewhat distanced manner, simultaneously inviting Scott to go on and changing the subject: "Okay. We'll get back to this later. So tell me why you're here. Your brother is named...?" A more encouraging comment might have been: "I'm so sorry for your loss. How has it been for you over the past 3 weeks?" Scott is relatively at ease disclosing his guilt feelings and at T19, the therapist might have asked more about them: "Sounds like you feel guilty about getting scared. Maybe you could say some more about that."

At P24 the abuse motif returns concerning David's deathbed disclosure about the circle jerk. I might have asked: "It sounds like it was difficult hearing this when you were so worried about David. Sounds like a kind of confession," and "When you and David spoke about the abuse over the years, what were your other conversations like?"

At P27 the abuse motif changed and an increasing vagueness crept into Scott's narrative. I might have asked: "I'm a little confused. You just said 'allegations', and you didn't say that before," and "When you and David spoke about these events over the years, did you have different takes on what happened?"

At T32 I might have asked: "What was it like seeing your father again?" At P33 a more intense version of the bereavement appears. I might have been unsure whether to be supportive or find out more information. For example, I would have been curious to know what Scott meant by "really emotional" and also what he meant by "...put up a façade and I'm fine or I think I'm fine." I might have asked: "When you say 'really emotional', could you tell more about what you mean?" and "what kind of façade do you put up?" On the other hand, it might have been more appropriate to support this difficult moment in the session by saying: "Sounds like you've been finding a way to cope during such a difficult time."

At P45 there is a further possible reference to guilt, which offered an opportunity at T47 to ask about his denial of anger or resentment, possibly: "How did you feel about it at the time?" or "It must have been difficult to be put on the spot like that."

Beginning at P51, Scott shows his only refusal of the session, by making excuses for his closeted approach to his new medical doctor and disclosing that his

HIV tests were conducted at an anonymous public clinic. The reasons for this are unclear, and the therapist expressed some astonishment and disapproval beginning at T52, which may have exacerbated Scott's anxiety.

Finally, there is Scott's peroration at P119 and P120, which contains so much rich material that has been drawn on for this chapter on bereavement. It is this moment that seems to signal the beginning of a therapeutic alliance. A simple question about Scott's mother unleashes many feelings, including love, frustration, despair, and anger, and really sums up the patient's life and hopes at the moment. Scott seems to drop his "façade" and become more real, less controlled and edited. We can feel the relationship come alive. With time running out, the therapist turns the subject to safe sex, suicidal ideation, and scheduling. Both patient and therapist seem ready to move forward in a hopeful and committed treatment.

For Further Reading About Death and Bereavement

Aragno, A. (2003). Transforming mourning: A new psychoanalytic perspective on the bereavement process. *Psychoanalysis and Contemporary Thought, 26*, 427–462.
Blechner, M. (Ed.), (1997). *Hope and mortality: Psychodynamic approaches to AIDS and HIV.* Hillsdale, NJ: The Analytic Press.
Bowlby, J. (1980). *Attachment and loss. Vol. 3: Loss.* New York: Basic Books.
Kuebler-Ross, E. (1969). *On death and dying.* New York: Scribner.
Singer, M. C. (2004). Being gay and mentally ill: The case study of a gay man with schizophrenia treated at a public mental health facility. *Journal of Gay & Lesbian Psychotherapy, 8*(3/4), 115–125.

References

Aragno, A. (2003). Transforming mourning: A new psychoanalytic perspective on the bereavement process. *Psychoanalysis and Contemporary Thought, 26*, 427–462.
Blechner, M. (1997). Psychodynamic approaches to AIDS and HIV. In M. Blechner (Ed.), *Hope and mortality: Psychodynamic approaches to AIDS and HIV.* Hillsdale, NJ: The Analytic Press.
Bowlby, J. (1961). Processes of mourning. *International Journal of Psychoanalysis, 42*, 317–340.
Bowlby, J. (1980). *Attachment and loss. Vol. 3: Loss.* New York: Basic Books.
Centers for Disease Control (2007). *HIV/AIDS surveillance report.* Atlanta, GA: US Department of Health and Human Services.
Davies, J. M., & Frawley, M. G. (1994). *Treating the adult survivor of childhood sexual abuse: A psychoanalytic perspective.* New York: Basic Books.
Drescher, J. (1993). *Psychoanalytic attitudes toward homosexuality.* Paper presented at the meeting of the American Academy of Psychoanalysis, New York.
Freud, S. (1953). Three essays on the theory of sexuality. In J. Strachey (Ed.), *The standard edition of the complete psychological works of Sigmund Freud* (Vol. 7, pp. 125–245).

London: The Hogarth Press and the Institute of Psychoanalysis (Original work published 1905).

Freud, S. (1957). Mourning and melancholia. In J. Strachey (Ed.), *The standard edition of the complete psychological works of Sigmund Freud* (Vol. 14, pp. 239—260). New York: Norton (Original work published 1917).

Golden, G. K., & Hill, M. A. (1991). A token of loving: From melancholia to mourning. *Clinical Social Work Journal, 19*(1), 23—33.

Greenberg, J. (1995). Self-disclosure: Is it psychoanalytic? *Contemporary Psychoanalysis, 31*, 193—205.

Jacobs, T. (1999). On the question of self-disclosure by the analyst: Error or advance in technique? *Psychoanalytic Quarterly, 68*, 159—183.

James, W. (1961). The sick soul. In W. James (Ed.), *The varieties of religious experience 114—142 (Original work published 1902)*. New York: MacMillan.

Jung, C. G. (1959). The soul and death. In H. Feifel (Ed.), *The meaning of death* (pp. 3—15). New York: McGraw-Hill.

Klein, M. (1948). Mourning and its relation to manic-depressive states. In *Contributions to psychoanalysis, 1921—1945*. London: Hogarth Press.

Kuebler-Ross, E. (1969). *On death and dying*. New York: Scribner.

Lyons-Ruth, K., & Block, D. (1996). The disturbed caregiving system: Relations among childhood trauma, maternal caregiving, and infant affect and attachment. *Infant Mental Health Journal, 17*, 257—275.

Rothaupt, J. W., & Becker, K. (2007). A literature review of western bereavement theory: From decathecting to continuing bonds. *The Family Journal, 15*(1), 6—15.

Schaffner, B. (1997). Modifying psychotherapeutic methods when treating the HIV-positive patient. In M. Blechner (Ed.), *Hope and mortality: Psychodynamic approaches to AIDS and HIV*. Hillsdale, NJ: The Analytic Press.

Shapiro, E. R. (1991). Grief in interpersonal perspective: Theories and their implications. In M. S. Stroebe, R. O. Hansson, W. Stroebe, & H. Schut (Eds.), *Handbook of bereavement research: Consequences, coping, and care*. Washington, DC: American Psychological Association.

Shapiro, E. R. (1996). Grief in Freud's life: Reconceptualizing bereavement in psychoanalytic theory. *Psychoanalytic Psychology, 13*, 547—566.

Shaver, P. R., & Tancredy, C. M. (2001). Emotion, attachment, and bereavement: A conceptual commentary. In M. S. Stroebe, R. O. Hansson, W. Stroebe, & H. Schut (Eds.), *Handbook of bereavement research: Consequences, coping, and care*. Washington, DC: American Psychological Association.

Singer, M. C. (2002). Reenfranchising psychoanalysis. *Psychoanalytic Psychology, 19*(1), 167—181.

Stroebe, M. S., & Schut, H. (2001). Models of coping with bereavement: A review. In M. S. Stroebe, R. O. Hansson, W. Stroebe, & H. Schut (Eds.), *Handbook of bereavement research: Consequences, coping, and care*. Washington, DC: American Psychological Association.

7 An Attachment Perspective on the First Interview (Accelerated Experiential Dynamic Psychotherapy)

Gil Tunnell[*]

Department of Counseling and Clinical Psychology, Teachers College, Columbia University, Accelerated Experiential Dynamic Psychotherapy (AEDP) Institute, New York City, NY, USA

Silverstein's first interview with Scott immediately brings to mind how multiple attachment-related traumas can contribute to a patient's distress. Accelerated Experiential Dynamic Psychotherapy (AEDP), developed by Diana Fosha (2000), is the first model of psychotherapy based solidly on attachment theory (Bowlby, 1969, 1973), not only in terms of positing how psychopathology develops but in explicitly using the therapist/patient relationship to form a secure attachment dyad so that the individual can safely express affects long warded off. From the first session with the patient, AEDP understands the patient's problems as attachment-related, and utilizes the therapeutic relationship in that first encounter to begin to form a new attachment bond, this time with a sensitive and responsive caregiver, so that the patient may viscerally experience, and cognitively integrate, difficult emotions.

John Bowlby's (1969, 1973) attachment theory has long offered developmental psychologists a theoretically rich account of mother–infant attachment, which, when it goes well culminates in "secure" attachment. Secure attachment leads to the individual not only becoming independent, autonomous, and secure within himself but also secure within relationships, being able to enjoy interpersonal closeness and interdependency, feeling neither suffocated nor clingy. Secure attachment is the optimal outcome from the attachment bond, which Bowlby (1969, 1973) describes as having four characteristics: (a) proximity maintenance (both mother and infant desire to be near one another); (b) separation protest (both mother and infant dislike periods of separation), (c) secure base (the mother offers physical protection as well as emotional security by encouraging, accepting, and

[*]The author thanks Dr. Jenna Osiason and Dr. Diana Fosha for their feedback on this chapter.

The Initial Psychotherapy Interview. DOI: 10.1016/B978-0-12-385146-8.00007-9

affirming the infant's feelings), and (d) safe haven (the mother functions as a safe port as the infant independently explores the world away from her, welcoming him upon his return).

In the last decade, there has been an explosion of interest in applying attachment theory to adult relationships (Cassidy & Shaver, 1999), following Bowlby's (1979) dictum that attachment systems are active "cradle to grave." Moreover, emotion—how it gets expressed and regulated—is intricately involved in attachment relationships. As Bowlby (1979) noted, some of our most intense emotional experiences arise within attachment bonds: As the bond forms, we experience "falling in love." We experience anxiety, anger, or grief when the bond is disrupted or lost. We experience relief and joy when the bond is renewed.

How emotion gets processed is significantly influenced by what transpired in the original mother/infant attachment bond. As the "secure base" characteristic suggests, it is the adult caregiver's reactions to the earliest expressions of the infant's affect that teach infants how emotions are to be dealt with. Fosha has argued that it is in the original attachment dyad that the infant develops the rudiments of "an affective competence" (Fosha, 2000, p. 49), which develops by adulthood into a capacity within the self to regulate emotional ups and downs and to have fully processed affective experiences (Fosha, 2001). Left on its own, the infant does not have the capacity to regulate emotions. However, in a well-functioning attachment dyad, the attachment figure, by responding with presence, empathy, and support, helps the child manage, accept, embrace, and make sense of his emotional states. Trauma results when the child is left *alone* with unbearable negative emotional states. Affect then goes underground into the unconscious, which leads to the development of anxiety, defenses, and other psychological symptoms.

Positive and negative affects occur naturally as part of the emotional hardwiring of all human beings, but individuals show wide variability in how emotions are expressed and regulated. Thus, the outcome of the infant's relationship to attachment figures (usually the mother) can have dual life-long implications for (a) how the individual regulates emotions, by embracing them, fearing them, or being unable to control them; and for (b) how the individual relates to significant others, either authentically, warily, or ambivalently.

Affect is therefore entwined with the capacity to form and maintain close interpersonal relationships: One cannot experience real emotional intimacy with another unless she or he can express her or his authentic self and true feelings (Greenan & Tunnell, 2003). The full expression of affect—and its receptivity by the other—strengthens the attachment bond. Individuals who attain a "secure" attachment style have a positive view of affect and are confident enough to reveal it in close interpersonal relationships; moreover, when they are distressed, they acknowledge it and turn to others for support (Feeney, 1999). Secure individuals emerge from childhood with an expectation that in close relationships one can have both individual autonomy and close emotional connection with the other; neither needs to be sacrificed.

In less-perfect childhoods, which include the majority of individuals, children develop one of three insecure attachment styles: avoidant, anxious/ambivalent, or disorganized (Ainsworth, Blehar, Waters, & Wall, 1978). As adults, *avoidant* individuals exhibit a rather extreme "affect phobia" (McCullough, 1997), restrict revealing their feelings to others for fear of judgment or reprisal, and pride themselves on being stoic and independent. Attachment theory holds that avoidant individuals develop self-reliance as a way to cope with rejecting or insensitive early caregivers. Connection being unreliable, they overvalue autonomy and are dismissive of attachment experiences. In contrast, *anxious/ambivalent* adults display higher levels of affect as a way to gain the attention of the current attachment figure, presumably because their early caregivers were inconsistent. In behavioral conditioning terms, when faced with attachment figures who responded only sometimes to their emotional needs, these children ramped up their levels of distress, sometimes with success, which reinforced expressing higher levels of distress in the future. As adults, anxious/ambivalent individuals are preoccupied with the attachment figure, may pursue romantic others with verve partly because they fear being alone, yet often either choose inappropriate partners or become suspicious when others are in fact emotionally responsive, thus revealing their ultimate ambivalence about close connection: *They desire it but don't trust it.* Because they have difficulty being autonomous, they pursue connection as a way to manage their "abandonment anxiety." Finally, *disorganized* attachment is thought to develop from serious early trauma such as physical or sexual abuse where the primary caregiver is simultaneously the abuser (Lyons-Ruth & Jacobvitz, 1999). The one on whom the child is totally dependent is also the one harming him. As adults, those with disorganized attachment are extremely conflicted about close relationships, act out both their love and anger toward the other, and have a tendency to form and maintain relationships that are violent or abusive. They feel "stuck" in them because they are utterly unable to be independent and autonomous, yet at the same time cannot be at peace within relationships because their experience has taught them that close relationships are inherently unpredictable. Disorganized attachment style is characterized by an inability to contain and regulate affect.

Longitudinal studies have shown attachment style, which gets crystallized by early childhood, to remain moderately stable and robust throughout adulthood (Feeney, 1999), yet is amenable to change if and when the individual experiences a more secure attachment bond with another person, or with a therapist. That is, attachment style can change from disorganized to organized, and from insecure to secure, and often does, given the right conditions. These corrective emotional experiences in later life can occur in romantic relationships, close friendships, with siblings or other family members, and in a therapeutic relationship. That said, simply because two people are involved in a close relationship does not necessarily mean that a secure attachment bond has formed. Because their very nature requires mutual trust and safety, attachment bonds take time to develop; they do not form quickly. Moreover, adult attachment bonds need to satisfy adult versions of Bowlby's four criteria: some degree of proximity maintenance and separation protest, and large degrees of secure base and safe haven.

Although all psychodynamic therapies have as their goal helping the patient gain access to the unconscious to uncover unresolved conflict or buried emotions, few models explicitly encourage the full expression of affect early in treatment as a mechanism of healing. AEDP does. AEDP assumes that every individual is hard-wired for transformation and healing, to be self-righted and to resume impeded growth, "the letting down of defensive barriers and the dismantling of the false self" (Ghent, 1999). The AEDP therapist works from the very first interview to create the conditions of safety so that this innate motivation, called "transformance" by Fosha (2008a), is activated and released. Moreover, creating safety in the first interview takes priority over obtaining a comprehensive patient history.

Focusing on healing rather than psychopathology, AEDP puts the bodily experience of affect front and center so that the patient may have, in the presence of the therapist serving as a secure attachment figure or "true other," a corrective experience. Thus, from the first session on, AEDP is a somatically based treatment. As the patient talks, the therapist engages in moment-to-moment tracking of the patient's body, attending to nonverbal cues (i.e., a heavy sigh, swallowing hard, wetting of the eyes, shift in gaze) that the patient is experiencing some bodily feeling. These cues alert the therapist to help the patient attend to what is happening in the body, as in, "That was a heavy sigh, what were you feeling then in your body?" As affect deepens, the therapist remains present, matching her or his affect with the patient's, responding with empathy and support. The AEDP therapist is exquisitely emotionally attuned to the patient, encouraging and welcoming the patient's deeper feelings.

Fosha, as in other short-term psychodynamic therapies (Davanloo, 1980) utilizes Malan's (1979) triangle of conflict, which she calls the *triangle of experience*, as a clinical roadmap. At the top corners of the (inverted) triangle (see Figure 7.1) are defenses and anxiety that serve to protect the individual from what lies at the bottom of the triangle: unresolved feelings, impulses, or core affects, which the individual, when he begins treatment, finds difficult to access. Defenses, including the defense against interpersonal closeness, were formed early in life as a way to cope with emotional distress. When defenses are working, the patient feels neither anxiety nor core affects. When defenses fail, the patient begins to feel anxious.

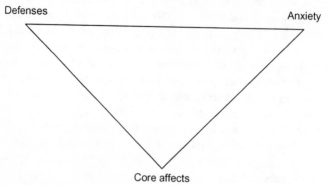

Figure 7.1 Triangle of experience.

In Davanloo's Intensive Short-Term Dynamic Psychotherapy (ISTDP), the goal is to break down defensive structures quickly, even in the first session, to get to the bottom of the triangle rapidly. The ISTDP paradigm holds that the superego with its punitive guilt keeps the patient from experiencing deep affect, particularly socially unacceptable aggression and rage. With the ISTDP therapist taking the role of a provocateur, the early phase of treatment is quite confrontational to break down the patient's resistance, with the typical patient becoming very anxious and eventually responding in anger, either at the therapist, at past significant others, or both. Once the patient has had a breakthrough of viscerally feeling anger, rage, or aggression, he then experiences softer feelings such as loss, grief, tenderness, sadness, and compassion.

Following Freud's dictum to identify, confront, and work through the patient's negative transference to the therapist (which Freud considered the path to a successful treatment outcome), and specifically in the first session the patient's resistance toward closeness with the therapist, Davanloo's more confrontational model essentially speeds up this process. Moreover, again following Freud, Davanloo's ISTDP model does not address explicitly the patient's positive transference.

Fosha's AEDP model does exactly the opposite, accentuating and explicitly building the patient's positive emotional responses to the therapist, in an effort to build a strong attachment bond from the get-go, and "softening" any initial resistance or negative transference. "Softening" means that the therapist accepts as valid any negative feeling the patient is having toward the therapist, but the therapist neither interprets nor judges it. This is in contrast to Davanloo's confrontational approach that intensifies the patient's negative transference once it emerges.

In the first interview, rather than the ISTDP therapist meeting the patient's narrative with challenge and confrontation of what they are avoiding affectively, the AEDP therapist offers affirmation, support, and empathy—in other words, safety, acceptance, and validation, rather than confrontation. Working at the top of the triangle, which is where most patients are at the beginning of treatment, the AEDP therapist tries to "melt away" the defenses, even in the first session, by continuously responding actively with verbal and nonverbal signs of compassion, empathy, warmth, reassurance, and affirmation as the patient tells her or his narrative. The therapist also tracks the patient's response to her or his empathic support: "Do you notice the tears in my eyes as you tell me this? What do you think I am feeling as you tell me this?" For many patients, this type of response from a therapist, in and of itself, is an entirely new experience: Not only to have their emotions received and accepted but also to experience real empathy from another person. Most patients beginning AEDP therapy experience a sense of relief, as well as a sense of relational connection to the therapist, and the treatment is off to a good start. Other patients, unfamiliar to such interpersonal receptivity, are stunned and may defensively resist the relational connection, saying to the therapist, "I don't want to burden you with my feelings. Are you getting too involved with me?" Such a reaction is a significant clue to the therapist about the patient's attachment history, that is, that the patient has rarely experienced true empathy from significant others without it being fraught with negative consequences. The AEDP therapist accepts and explores the patient's reaction.

For patients who talk without exhibiting much affect at all, the therapist makes attempts to get the patient into her or his body, by asking, for example, "What are you feeling in your body as you say that?" and tracks that further, "What does that tightness in your chest feel like? If it could speak, what would it say?"

If and when the patient becomes anxious, instead of encouraging deeper feeling, the AEDP therapist engages in anxiety-regulating interventions such as helping the patient breathe deeply, asking the patient to notice in the body where the anxiety is and exploring what that feels like, asking if the anxiety could have words what might it say, or suggesting simply that the patient try to set the anxiety aside and observe what happens.

AEDP obviously requires that the therapist develop real, positive feelings toward the patient. What if the therapist working within the AEDP model instead feels negative counter-transference toward the patient, particularly in the first interview? Traditional clinical wisdom suggests that the therapist strives to identify within herself or himself, perhaps with the help of a therapist or supervisor, the source of the negativity. Simply knowing the source of this negativity can often allow the therapist to continue to work with such a patient. If the AEDP therapist finds it almost impossible to develop liking, warmth, and empathy for the patient, traditional clinical wisdom again applies: It is probably not a good therapeutic match, and it may be best to refer the patient elsewhere. That said, one of AEDP's working assumptions is that the patient at all times, in or out of session, is doing the best she or he can to cope using her or his current resources. Moreover, the AEDP therapist expresses empathy *for that*, and, appealing to her or his transformance motivation, to support her or his desire to change.

Especially in the first session, it is important that the patient leave feeling affirmed and supported. Without conditions of safety and trust, the therapy that has as one of its goals to build a secure attachment bond, would be off to a shaky beginning. The AEDP therapist, accepting the patient's current coping strategies, may say near the end of the initial interview, "I am impressed by how you, on your own, have been dealing with a very tough situation, and together, we are going to work toward your feeling better."

As sessions continue and the attachment to the therapist is experienced by the patient as ever more safe, the therapist does whatever anxiety-regulating is necessary for the patient to tolerate more uncomfortable feelings that lie at the bottom of the triangle, attempting as much as possible to "bypass" defenses and psychopathology. When anxiety emerges as the patient's usual defense fails, this is a signal to the therapist that something is happening bodily within the patient. The goal of anxiety regulation is not necessarily to help the patient be completely rid of anxiety, but to regulate or reduce it sufficiently so that she or he can get beneath the anxiety. The therapist's use of self as a very attuned and present caregiver and attachment figure not only validates the patient's emotional experience, but the emotional experience also becomes shared rather than being borne alone. In so doing, the AEDP therapist provides the patient with a corrective emotional experience.

In Fosha's model, the rationale for getting to the bottom of the triangle is not just for the sake of it, but that these deep feelings lead the way to authenticity and a "truth sense," are an entry to the individual's resilience and untapped resources, in essence helping the patient engage in a self-righting process. In short, emotions have functional value. What Fosha calls "core affects" are the categorical emotions recognized by researchers (Lewis, 2000; Tomkins, 1962a,b)—joy, sadness, disgust, anger, fear, pride, embarrassment, shame, guilt—as hardwired into all human beings. Moreover, each core affect has associated with it an "adaptive action tendency" that was evolutionarily designed to help the individual survive. For example, when we experience fear, we move away from the frightening situation; when we experience guilt, we act to make amends.

Psychopathology, in the AEDP model, is the result of the individual not being able to express these naturally occurring affects, usually because early attachment figures could not tolerate them or were otherwise unavailable to serve as a "secure base." To keep the attachment bond on which she or he so depends, the individual represses core affects. Over time, as defensive structures rigidify, the individual comes to fear rather than embrace affect (McCullough, 1997), in effect, depriving the self of these useful guides to adaptive living (Frederick, 2009).

For gay men, repression of affect is more problematic and complicated. Gay males become particularly adept at creating an inauthentic false self in order to navigate a heterosexist society (Greenan & Tunnell, 2003). When young boys discover they are attracted to other males, they soon realize, from the actual or imagined responses of others, that their inclinations are unacceptable, therein internalizing the homophobia of majority culture. The young gay boy, to keep whatever attachment bond he has with his parents, adapts by keeping his same-sex interest a secret. Not only is his homosexuality kept secret, but other emotions go underground as well, because being more authentic about one's other feelings carries the risk that he will be found out about his homosexuality. Expressing authentic emotions becomes a slippery and risky slope. Many gay males learn not to get too close to other people, particularly other males, who are likely to shame and stigmatize him (Tunnell, 2006). In deliberately creating a false self, the gay male becomes increasingly adept at impression management, all the while becoming increasingly inauthentic (Greenan & Tunnell, 2003). Mohr (1999) has argued that insecure attachment interferes with gay identity development, and may delay a gay man coming out to his parents and others because he so fears their rejection. Isay (1989) has expertly articulated how many fathers, once they sense their son may be gay or gender-atypical, begin either passively distancing from the son or more actively shaming or stigmatizing him, but that the young gay boy also has a role in keeping the father distant out of his own self-protection; he adopts a guarded attitude of "the less you know about me, the better."

Fosha (2000) has written that once the authentic self and its affects go underground, it is a "Faustian bargain": "The individual must choose between preserving the integrity of her or his attachment ties and that of her or his affective self experience ... giving away the affective soul in exchange for a measure of security" (p. 33). AEDP is a model of treatment that helps the patient regain her or his affective soul in the context of a secure relationship with the therapist.

Again, as a somatically based therapy, the AEDP therapist works to engage the patient to feel affect physically in the body. As Fosha (2008b) explains, the central agent of change in AEDP is the patient's "viscerally experiencing previously feared-to-be-unbearable emotions in the context of an emotionally engaged relationship with a trusted other, and being able to process these to completion until their adaptive action tendencies are released" (p. 4). AEDP treatment proceeds through several "state" transformations, often within a single session, beginning with the creation of safety by the therapist, so that defenses dissolve or are momentarily pushed aside, followed by the experience of bodily feeling and expressing of core affect, with the therapist guiding and helping the patient go deeper into the body, from which emerges resilience, hope, and relief, and finally the transformation into "core state": "openness, compassion and self-compassion, wisdom, generosity, kindness, understanding deeply, clarity, the sense of things feeling 'right,' capacity to construct coherent and cohesive autobiographical narrative" (Fosha, 2008c). The experience of "core state" is profoundly satisfying and pleasant, and, in fact, reinforces the experience of having felt one's feelings. Core state is a shared experience of calm between patient and therapist.

A clinical intervention that occurs throughout all the state transformations and that is unique to AEDP is *meta-processing*, which has two forms: (a) Asking the patient continuously to reflect on what just happened emotionally within himself ("What was it like feeling your anger just now?"), which typically deepens the affect even more; and (b) Asking the patient to reflect on what it was like to have the emotional experience with the therapist ("What was it like for you going through this *with me?*"), which deepens the attachment to the therapist whom the patient comes to regard as more and more safe. This latter type of interpersonal meta-processing is essential to help undo the patient's previous state of aloneness and to entrain more secure attachment.

Meta-processing is the mechanism by which AEDP sessions tact back and forth between emotional experience and reflection. In meta-processing, the implicit is made explicit so that deeper integration can occur. Not only does meta-processing deepen the "right brain" emotional experience, but it also helps the patient integrate her or his emotional experience cognitively in the "left brain," all of which leads to a more complete integration and character transformation from defensive to more authentic functioning.

Meta-processing is utilized in the first session of AEDP treatment. As the patient gives the narrative of what brings her or him there and what she or he is suffering, the therapist actively responds with presence, empathy, and support. It is important to gauge, as the session goes along, the patient's response to having been "emotionally received" by the therapist. The therapeutic alliance is made much more explicit in AEDP than in other types of therapy as a vehicle to build secure attachment between patient and therapist. As discussed previously, near the end of the first session when the AEDP therapist explicitly makes a statement of affirmation of the patient, it is important to meta-process with the patient her or his reaction to being affirmed. For many patients, this may be the first time they have felt affirmed. How did that feel to them? Affirmation makes some patients uncomfortable at first and they cannot quite trust it; it may be novel to them and they don't know what to make of it. Can they begin to "take in" viscerally the therapist's regard for them?

Finally, although the model is rooted in attachment theory and research, AEDP therapists do not formally assess the patient's attachment style.[1] As treatment progresses, the patient's attachment style emerges, with the therapist making accommodations to the patient's style. For example, patients who show avoidant attachment may have more difficulty accessing their emotions, so the AEDP therapist may have to do more work "at the top of the triangle" regulating anxiety, restructuring defenses, and simply moving more slowly. Anxious/ambivalent patients may find it difficult to accept the therapist's affirmation and support, but that too is "grist for the mill" and meta-processed during treatment. Patients with disorganized attachment (often seen in severe borderline character pathology) can be treated in the AEDP model, but the work is much slower because their emotions are difficult for them to regulate, manage, and contain, so the therapist must first instill some ego-building and resilience-building resources.

Case Material

Two primary strengths of Silverstein's interview are how safe Scott already seems to feel with the therapist and how much information Silverstein gathered, which is beautifully articulated back to Scott at the end of the session:

> You've told me about the death of your brother and how hard it's been for you and that you want to be able to find a way to grieve for David's death and move on. You told me that your father's possibly molesting you and David and about his swindling money from you and God knows what else. And the ambivalent feelings you have toward your family. You told me that you also choose the wrong guy as a boyfriend (T135).

Silverstein obtained a thorough sexual history, a coming-out history, as well as substance-use history. The fact that he spent so much time collecting information on sex, coming out, and substance use is particularly important in a first interview with a single gay man living in a major metropolitan area. These questions demonstrate to Scott that Silverstein knows the lives of young gay men and is totally at ease talking about their issues, all of which help Scott begin to feel safe. In this respect, Silverstein's first interview of a gay patient is very different from that of a straight patient.

At the very end, Scott reveals symptoms of anxiety, depression, a feeling of mania, suicidal ideation, and racing thoughts. The way Scott speaks of these symptoms, however, does not suggest bipolar disorder, major depression, or even attention deficit disorder (ADD), but rather major anxiety. Given what Scott has been through in his "30 years of existence," and most especially in the previous 3 weeks,

[1] Adults may be assessed for attachment style through the Adult Attachment Interview (see Hesse, 1999).

the anxiety he is experiencing at the time of the interview is quite expectable and normal.

An Attachment Perspective

The interview reveals significant attachment breaches with both parents: Major betrayals by the father (sexual molestation, financially swindling his son), and an almost complete inability of the mother to accept and support Scott's feelings historically and presently. Scott also appears to have been betrayed by at least one boyfriend, the Parisian who did not value their 2-year relationship enough to encourage Scott to live with him (P78). Finally, Scott's first experience with his only therapist prior to Silverstein did not go well, because she or he did not take the allegations of molestation seriously (P11); Scott did not go back after one session, presumably because he did not feel safe or validated in a fundamental aspect of his experience.

The more pressing attachment-related trauma, clearly, is the recent death to AIDS of Scott's brother David, also gay, only 2 years older than Scott, who seems to have served as more of an attachment figure to Scott than either parent did. Older siblings can indeed serve as attachment figures (Cassidy, 1999), and given the small age difference between the brothers, David and Scott most likely developed a "pair bond" attachment, which adolescent peers often do as they separate from their parents (Hazan & Zeifman, 1999). Scott is struggling presently with strong feelings of grief (and some guilt) over the death of his brother, which he literally witnessed, and appears not to know how to express or manage his feelings. He longs to grieve with his family, but those relationships are "fucked up" (P14). In addition to his sadness and grief over his brother's death, Scott has long-standing anger at his father. Scott's mother is unable to help him with either his grief or his anger. The mother did not emotionally support Scott when the accusations of molestation by the father emerged years ago, instead choosing "to stand by her man," not by her son. In short, almost all the important attachment figures in Scott's life have failed him.

What makes either death or sex abuse traumatic is not so much the horror of the event itself, but being left to deal with one's feelings alone. Scott is certainly in that situation now, and rather than face the feelings, he medicates himself by smoking marijuana daily. His current pursuit of other men seems more about combating loneliness and avoiding affect than seeking sex or romance.

While it is difficult to gauge "attachment style" from one interview, Scott clearly shows evidence of insecure attachment, most likely anxious/ambivalent, and possibly even disorganized attachment, given the sexual abuse by the father. We do not yet know how comfortable Scott is with affect, because Silverstein does not push him when glimmers of affect emerge (T23–P23; T33–P34). Scott minimizes the emotional significance of past intimate relationships, for example, in describing the breakup with the Parisian boyfriend who urged him to stay in Paris rather than join him in San Francisco, Scott says, "So we broke up, but we are friends now. So it's okay" (P81). Yet this was the longest and possibly most intimate relationship Scott has had, and Scott must have had strong feelings of loss and anger when this man chose unilaterally to end it because he had other priorities, claiming it was better for Scott to keep his current job than relocate with him (P78, P80).

When Scott talks about relationships, he says he wants "that closeness...that intimacy" (P130) yet seeks "it in the wrong guy" with the hope they were "going to be something more significant than they were" (P130). Yet later the patient reveals that he may have a role in pushing those very people away:

> I'm a big believer in passion. And having that attraction and having that desire, and I find often that when it's too easy, when they're easy to obtain, when they really go that extra mile to show that they're there for me. Or they would be good for me. I don't like it. *I like a struggle ... I don't like that from the get-go when it's easy because it's boring* (P86) (emphasis added).

More securely attached individuals don't find it a struggle or that it's boring. Scott's statement is a rather apt description of "anxious/ambivalent" insecure attachment. Later in his description of his interaction with his father, he puts it more succinctly: "Every time my father hugs me, I cringe. You know, I want to pull back. Pull away" (P120). Further evidence of anxious/ambivalent attachment is Scott's telling Silverstein how he closely monitors the men he is attracted to: "What their reactions mean. What does that mean? What does that movement mean?" (P115).

Scott's strong aversion to being hugged by his father now is understandable given how unreliable and "shady" his father has shown himself to be in the past. Assuming Scott's memories of the molestation are accurate as are the other accounts of the father's unscrupulous dealings with money, the father's current attempts to get closer to his son continues to give Scott a very mixed message, which again, would contribute to Scott's "push me/pull me" attitude toward male closeness. Can men be trusted?

The "ending dance" that Silverstein and Scott do together suggests that Scott already feels comfortable with "Charles," and that they are off to a good start, with Charles serving as an older, wiser attachment figure. Scott seems quite engaged in answering the many questions Silverstein asks about his sexuality, which demonstrates Silverstein's comfort about matters sexual and thus Scott can feel safe. At the end, Scott asks "What's a sexologist?" in what seems a friendly attempt to relate to Charles, as well as a reaction to all the questions on sexual history. Having the therapist so comfortable talking about sex explicitly seemed to make Scott, like most other gay male patients, feel safe and understood.

An AEDP Perspective

The patient's overall presentation nicely illustrates Fosha's concept of "transformance" motivation: Not only does Scott convey a friendly, direct demeanor toward Silverstein throughout the session, has good eye contact, and talks openly with little defensiveness, but also he has purposely chosen Silverstein because he wants a gay therapist, presumably to feel safe. (In contrast, Scott is not open with his physician because he does not entirely trust a straight physician.)

In "transformance" terms, Scott is searching for conditions of safety where he may heal and do some self-righting. He has sought therapy to help him process some traumatic emotional experiences that he has been unable to do on his own. An AEDP therapist forges a strong attachment relationship from the get-go, emphasizing that the patient is no longer alone and that, together, they will face the patient's feelings and issues.

For an AEDP therapist, what is striking about the interview is Scott's level of anxiety (in the audio version of the transcript he talks rapidly with a staccato lilt), which puts him at the "top of the triangle" of experience (see Figure 7.1). AEDP treatment would aim to get to the bottom of the triangle (the core affects), which could have occurred possibly in this first interview. Silverstein does inquire directly about Scott's affect twice. The first is when he learns about the brother's recent death to AIDS, and asks, "But what was that experience like for you?" (T23), but as Scott begins to talk about his loss, very quickly Silverstein goes back to content, gathering more information about the parents' lack of solace (T24).

The second time Silverstein asks a potentially more affect-arousing question (T33), "So how have you dealt with David's death?", Scott begins to open up: "(David) never leaves, he's always here, he's always with me, thoughts always with me. I mean I miss him incredibly. How to deal with it, I don't know. I just feel like, you know it's a day by day thing. I'm here, I'm living, and I'm breathing" (P33). This moment of Scott opening up illustrates what Fosha calls "dropping down," demonstrating a capacity for affect tolerance ("I miss him incredibly") and a capacity for relational connection ("he's always with me, thoughts always with me").

Silverstein's next question (T34) is interesting, "what made your relationship with David so close?" which is once again a more information-gathering, cognitive question rather than staying with Scott's emerging affect, though it is asked with much empathy on Silverstein's part. The question might have yielded some affect, but Scott replied in kind, giving a rational, cognitive answer, such as, we were very close in age, similar interests, both gay. To which Silverstein then asks another information-gathering question, "When did you find out you were gay?" (T35).

In the sequence above, when Scott reveals how much he misses David on a daily basis, an AEDP therapist would have been more emotionally attuned and expressive, perhaps even tearing up if the therapist felt truly moved, and perhaps reflecting back the sadness Scott must be feeling right now. Upon hearing how the brothers were so close (P23), an AEDP therapist would amplify the feeling of loss, as in, "Mmmmm ... he was so important to you, and now he is gone, and, as you say, you've lost your Number One, your angel. This is very sad." It is only 3 weeks since David has died and Scott is struggling to grieve, entirely on his own. The AEDP therapist would want him to explore how he is feeling the loss and to begin to express his grief viscerally, and Scott, at this point in the interview, appears to be giving the therapist "a green light" to do so. Even in first sessions, AEDP therapists attempt to access affect. First sessions become something of a trial therapy to see if the patient has the capacity to go into deeper affective states, and to assess how comfortable he is in doing that relationally with the therapist.

But here, whenever emotional material emerges, Silverstein tends either to shift topic or ask a more content-oriented or intellectual question, which in a first interview is understandable in the therapist's attempt to gain as much information as possible in a short time frame. Most therapists "go for content" in meeting a patient for the first time and seek to contain or even minimize affect for fear of destabilizing the patient. However, in AEDP it is possible and even desirable to "go for affect" in the first interview. As Fosha (2009) has written, in AEDP, "we don't just seek a new ending: From the onset we are also seeking a new beginning" (p. 81). Moreover, as described above, Scott, at several points, seems to be giving the therapist a "green light" to do so. Another example is, after Scott describes, with some distress, seeing his estranged father for the first time in 6 months at David's hospital bed (P31), it would have been possible for the therapist to ask what that was like for him, how did it feel, rather than asking, "Where did (your parents) live?" (T32) Here, an AEDP therapist might have mirrored back, "That must have been very complicated and uncomfortable for you, an awful scene as your brother is so sick, with your being still so angry at your father. Can you say more about what that was like for you emotionally?" Such clinical interventions would encourage the patient to tap into his feeling.

In this first interview, it is clear that underneath the patient's anxious presentation are the core affects of sadness and grief. Scott's description of how unavailable either parent is at the time (as they are undoubtedly struggling with their own grief over losing their son) is heartbreaking. An AEDP therapist not only follows the patient's narrative but also actively "leads" the patient (Fosha, 2009) to go deeper into the feeling behind the narrative, matching it with her or his own "affective resonance," in contrast to most psychodynamic therapy where the therapist is more likely to sit back and wait for the patient's feelings to emerge on their own. Here the AEDP therapist might have gone deeper, "So what does that feel like to you . . . that your parents aren't able now to help you grieve?" Alternatively, the AEDP therapist might have engaged in some "anticipatory mirroring," (Fosha, 2000), saying something like, "That must be very sad for you that you so alone in this, that they can't be there for you when you have lost your special brother."

To be sure, AEDP runs counter to everything psychologists have learned in our training not to self-disclose our own emotional reactions to what the patient is saying, and instead be neutral at all times. In AEDP, the therapist's judicious self-disclosure of affect is essential in deepening the connection between therapist and patient; the therapist self-discloses her or his own feeling state not simply for the sake of it, but to initiate a shared emotional experience in order to help normalize and regulate the patient's own affect. AEDP therapists are not neutral and do not attempt to present a "blank screen" on which the patient projects. AEDP is very different because its goal is different: To provide the patient with a safe emotional experience in the presence of a caring therapist, even in the first interview.

AEDP orients the therapist to be vigilant about attending to affect, both the patient's and her own. Because Silverstein is not an AEDP therapist, he stays neutral in his reactions to what the patient says. He adopts an analytic neutral stance of "you can tell me anything you want here, and I will accept it." An AEDP therapist, in contrast, self-discloses affect much more, responding verbally and nonverbally as the patient talks, mirroring emotionally what the patient is, or might be, experiencing. If we err, the patient will edit and correct us. (Again, some patients with a strongly avoidant attachment style do not welcome such active efforts on the part of the therapist, and AEDP therapists explore that too through meta-processing and may accommodate by "toning it down" so as not to be experienced by the patient as intrusive.)

Scott has a very complicated and ambivalent relationship with his father, which I would have not explored in the first interview any further than what Silverstein did. The patient is unquestionably enraged at this man who fondled and molested him, as well as attempting to swindle him out of thousands of dollars (and as Silverstein says, who knows what else?). Yet the father showed unconditional acceptance of Scott's homosexuality when David outed him at age 17 (P48), and the father now makes attempts to hug him (P120). Yet Scott cringes when the father hugs him. Assuming the therapy takes off, an AEDP therapist would explore in depth Scott's ambivalent feelings toward the father in later sessions. This process will take much more time for the patient to feel safer with the therapist and because these affects are much more complex: Along with the rage at his father is a son's guilt for feeling rageful toward a parent he is supposed to love.

Scott reveals two significant risk-taking behaviors to Silverstein: substance abuse and unsafe sex practices. An AEDP therapist probably would be nonjudgmental here in the first interview, as Silverstein is, because any sort of reprisal at this point is likely to shut down the patient opening up or returning. When Silverstein asks, "Why do you think you smoke so much pot?" (T114), Scott answers insightfully, "There's something about it that numbs me, where I get dumb and I'm just able to mellow out, stop thinking" (P114). An AEDP therapist might possibly have made a more affirming response to that answer: "That was insightful of you. You know a lot about yourself, that you are trying to numb yourself from thinking and feeling." The therapist would carefully observe the patient's response to this affirmation, and "meta-process" it: "What was it like for you to hear my recognition of your self-awareness?"

Silverstein asks Scott several pointed questions about his unsafe sex practices: (a) "... you let guys fuck you without a condom?" (T123); (b) "Why would you do that?" (T124); (c) "You stayed there for 72 hours and how many times did he fuck you without a condom?" (T126); and (d) "What stopped you from saying, 'Use a condom. Put it on?'" (T130). By this point it is absolutely clear that Silverstein thinks Scott's behavior is unwise. An AEDP therapist might have asked Scott near the end of that part of the interview if he feels anything about the therapist "pressing" him on this. Suppose Scott was indeed angry at Silverstein here. As discussed previously, AEDP does not ignore the patient's negative feelings toward the therapist. Indeed, they are respected and validated. Here, given Silverstein's strong reaction to Scott's having unsafe sex, it seems imperative to "meta-process" Scott's reaction to Silverstein's questions. In other words, it's better to head off negative transference by discussing it in the here and now, rather than allowing it to build up in the patient and perhaps sabotage treatment. On the other hand, Scott, instead of feeling angry at Silverstein, may have felt cared for. We simply do not know.

Both the excessive substance use and unsafe sex need to be monitored in future sessions. What if neither stop? Simply because the AEDP model is premised on the therapist facilitating a secure attachment bond with the patient by expressing positive affect toward him does not mean that the therapist must be wholly supportive of every behavior the patient engages in. Indeed, in mother—infant attachment, the mother is compelled to step in and protect the infant from harm. Excessive marijuana use will indeed impede the therapy because, as the patient insightfully says, smoking pot numbs his thinking and feeling.

Continuing to practice unsafe sex must also be addressed, without judgment but with empathy: "You matter to me, I am concerned about your well-being and don't want anything bad to happen to you. Can we talk again about why you aren't using condoms?" Given Scott's experience of losing his brother to AIDS, the therapist might decide to return to processing further David's death to AIDS specifically. Is Scott himself worried about HIV? Why or why not?

In AEDP the therapist has greater freedom not only to disclose her or his own feelings but also personal life experiences if they are relevant to the patient's experience and can be clinically useful to the patient. Here with Scott grieving the death of his brother to AIDS, if the therapist has lost relatives, close friends, and acquaintances to AIDS, it may be helpful for the therapist to disclose those losses briefly ("I have also lost people close to me to AIDS so I know something about what you are going through"). At that point, the patient may well ask the therapist, "Oh, what did you go through?" There are several ways to respond: (a) "Why don't you first tell me a bit more what you are going through and then I'll tell you my experience?"; (b) immediately meta-process: "What is it like for me to tell you that I have lost someone to AIDS?"; or (c) simply tell the patient *briefly* what he went through affectively. Obviously, the therapist must be extremely judicious about such self-disclosures. If the therapist does self-reveal, the general goal is to help the patient feel his own emotional reactions are normal and valid, as well as to make way for other feelings the patient has yet to express. (In this situation of losing a loved one to AIDS, the therapist and the patient may have felt not only grief and loss but also anger and survivor's guilt.) In any event, if the therapist chooses to self-reveal incidents from her or his personal life, it is extremely important to meta-process with the patient what it was like for the therapist to share something so personal (Prenn, 2009). The few instances where I have done this have never backfired, but instead have led to a greater opening up of the patient and later a feeling of gratitude that my experience was shared.

Silverstein asks Scott another bold question: "If you seek guys that are unavailable, why do you do that? Why not some guy who is available?" (T86). Presumably he is accessing the patient's capacity for insight (which Scott demonstrated somewhat by agreeing with the observation), to see if the patient gets curious about his behavior, or to see how defensive the patient may become when challenged. From an attachment perspective, the explanation undoubtedly has a lot to do with Scott not being able to trust men. After all, what should have been the strongest male figure in his life—his father—is the man who most betrayed him. For an AEDP therapist, however, having an insight about choosing unavailable men because one's father was emotionally unreliable is insufficient in helping the patient change. For truly transformational change to occur, it will be necessary for Scott (a) to explore deeply and viscerally his feelings toward his father (most likely anger and rage, but also grief and sadness that his father so failed him), and (b) in the presence of a (male) therapist who is safe and reliable, thus giving him a truly corrective emotional experience that men can be trusted. And in "meta-processing" that emotional experience, the patient will begin to integrate insight with affect, and past with present. Often when the patient realizes she or he is benefiting from an entirely different interpersonal experience, albeit with a thera-pist, there is gratitude but also a deeper mourning of all she or he didn't get.

Scott mentions at the very end of the session other potentially serious symptoms (mania, suicidal ideation, racing thoughts). Silverstein does not explore these here. These symptoms, in context, sound more like anxiety than anything else. An AEDP therapist might have attempted to "normalize" these feelings given what he has been going through the last month, and even express some admiration for the fact that he is still "living and breathing"; for example, "Yes you are indeed still here, living and breathing, after everything you have been through. You have survived," and followed by meta-processing of the therapist making such an affirmation of the patient: "What is your reaction just now to my calling you a survivor?"

What does a therapist make, at this point, of the relationships Scott has formed with other gay men? He says he has had "several boyfriends," and acknowledges, as Silverstein points out, that they are often on "other continents" and "emotionally unavailable." Scott (P86) claims he wants passion and "a good person" all rolled up into one. (Don't we all?) I suspect Scott is looking for friends rather than boy-friends, and gay men often begin life-long friendships by having sex first (Nardi, 1999). Nowhere in the interview does Scott mention friends, nor does Silverstein ask. Probably his brother David was his closest friend. He and David were emo-tionally intimate: Each had been molested by the father, had bonded around that experience in addition to both being gay, and were able to talk openly about their gayness and the molestation. David served as Scott's guide to gay life (P72), and, indeed, Scott's first sexual encounter was with a friend of David and occurred with David was in the car and later down the hall in the family home. David seems to have provided Scott some semblance of safety and "guardian angel" caregiving. (Maybe David failed Scott here: Did he counsel Scott about practicing safer sex, particularly after David himself seroconverted?)

Silverstein asks Scott at the very end if he "would really like to find a boyfriend and settle down with him. Is that something you want?" (T135) Scott's syntax is revealing: "Without a doubt. It would *settle me* in so many different ways" (P135) (emphasis added). His use of the phrase "settle me" is significant to me: This young man is looking for a safe haven and a secure base. He may be fortunate to find it in a romantic relationship, but I think he is more likely to find it first with an understanding and empathic therapist.

Finally, although Silverstein maintained a neutral stance with almost no self-disclosure of his own feelings about what Scott is relating to him, Scott seems to feel safe with Charles, so the therapy has a good beginning. Interestingly, Silverstein does not ask Scott at the end what the session has been like for him, which an AEDP therapist would do. But Scott tells him anyway near end of the interview: Anxiety (P103). Other than to suggest that it's the interview that is making him anxious, Silverstein does not explore further the feeling of the patient's anxiety and what's beneath it (T104—T107), which an AEDP therapist would do, as with, "So you are feeling anxiety right now. What part of our meeting do you think made you anxious? Where exactly in your body do you feel the anxiety? Can you describe it?"

Given that Scott most likely has an anxious/ambivalent attachment style, I would predict some testing or doubting on his part of just how accepting Silverstein is. Individuals with anxious/ambivalent attachment find it difficult to really believe that a trusted other could truly be there for them. It is particularly important that Scott be in therapy with a *man* he comes to trust, because distrust of men seems to be his primary psychological issue. I think, in this situation, the gender of the therapist does matter. Still, if a male therapist is conducting a traditional psychodynamic therapy, he will most likely wait until there is evidence in the transference that the patient does not entirely trust him before the trust issue gets explored. In AEDP with its attachment perspective, the therapist will actively engage in interventions that explicitly build trust, so that the patient, from the first session onward, feels the therapist at his back, entirely supportive and empathic. Moreover, the therapist is continually meta-processing how the patient is experiencing this type of supportive relationship, so that the attachment bond between the two of them is openly acknowledged and deepened, thus providing Scott with a truly corrective emotional experience with a man.

If You Want to Learn More About This Approach

Fosha, D. (2000). *The transforming power of affect: A model for accelerated change.* New York: Basic Books.
Fosha, D. (2001). The dyadic regulation of affect. *Journal of Clinical Psychology/In Session, 52*(2), 227—242.
Frederick, R. J. (2009). *Living like you mean it.* San Francisco, CA: Jossey-Bass.
Tunnell, G. (2006). An affirmational approach to treating gay male couples. *Group, 30,* 133—151.

References

Ainsworth, M. D. S., Blehar, M. C., Waters, E., & Wall, S. (1978). *Patterns of attachment: A psychological study of the strange situation.* Hillsdale, NJ: Erlbaum.
Bowlby, J. (1969). Attachment and loss: Vol. 1. *Attachment.* New York: Basic Books.
Bowlby, J. (1973). Attachment and loss. Vol. 2. *Separation.* New York: Basic Books.

Bowlby, J. (1979). *The making and breaking of affectional bonds*. London: Tavistock.

Cassidy, J. (1999). The nature of the child's ties. In J. Cassidy, & P. R. Shaver (Eds.), *Handbook of attachment: Theory, research and clinical applications* (pp. 3–20). New York: The Guilford Press.

Cassidy, J., & Shaver, P. R. (1999). *Handbook of attachment: Theory, research and clinical applications*. New York: The Guilford Press.

Davanloo, H. (Ed.), (1980). *Short-term dynamic psychotherapy*. New York: Jason Aronson.

Feeney, J. A. (1999). Adult romantic attachment and couple relationships. In J. Cassidy, & P. R. Shaver (Eds.), *Handbook of attachment: Theory, research and clinical applications* (pp. 355–377). New York: The Guilford Press.

Fosha, D. (2000). *The transforming power of affect: A model for accelerated change*. New York: Basic Books.

Fosha, D. (2001). The dyadic regulation of affect. *Journal of Clinical Psychology/In Session, 52*(2), 227–242.

Fosha, D. (2008a). *Emotional experience processed to completion*. Handout.

Fosha, D. (2008b). *Healing affects and healing interactions in AEDP*. Sixth Annual Level 1 AEDP Immersion Course. Austin, TX, October 22–26.

Fosha, D. (2008c). Transformance, recognition of self by self, and effective action. In K. J. Schneider (Ed.), *Existential-integrative psychotherapy: Guideposts to the core of practice* (pp. 290–320). New York: Routledge.

Fosha, D. (2009). Emotion and recognition at work: Energy, vitality, pleasure, truth, desire & the emergent phenomenology of transformational experience. In D. Fosha, D. J. Siegel, & M. F. Solomon (Eds.), *The healing power of emotion: Affective neuroscience, development, and clinical practice*. New York: Norton.

Frederick, R. J. (2009). *Living like you mean it*. San Francisco, CA: Jossey-Bass.

Ghent, E. (1999). Masochism, submission, surrender: Masochism as a perversion of surrender. In S. A. Mitchell, & L. Aron (Eds.), *Relational psychoanalysis: The emergence of a tradition* (pp. 211–242). Hillsdale, NJ: The Analytic Press.

Greenan, D., & Tunnell, G. (2003). *Couple therapy with gay men*. New York: Guilford Press.

Hazan, C., & Zeifman, D. (1999). Pair bonds as attachments: Evaluating the evidence. In J. Cassidy, & P. R. Shaver (Eds.), *Handbook of attachment: Theory, research and clinical applications* (pp. 336–354). New York: The Guilford Press.

Hesse, E. (1999). The adult attachment interview: Historical and current perspectives. In J. Cassidy, & P. R. Shaver (Eds.), *Handbook of attachment: Theory, research and clinical applications* (pp. 395–433). New York: The Guilford Press.

Isay, R. A. (1989). *Being homosexual: Gay men and their development*. New York: Farrar Straus Giroux.

Lewis, M. (2000). The emergence of human emotions. In M. Lewis, & J. M. Haviland-Jones (Eds.), *Handbook of emotions* (2nd ed., pp. 265–280). New York: Guilford Press.

Lyons-Ruth, K., & Jacobvitz, D. (1999). In J. Cassidy, & P. R. Shaver (Eds.), *Handbook of attachment: Theory, research and clinical applications* (pp. 520–554). New York: The Guilford Press.

Malan, D. H. (1979). *Individual psychotherapy and the science of psychodynamics*. London: Butterworths.

McCullough, V. L. (1997). *Changing character: Short-term anxiety-regulating psychotherapy for restructuring defenses, affects, and attachment*. New York: Basic Books.

Mohr, J. J. (1999). Same-sex romantic attachment. In J. Cassidy, & P. R. Shaver (Eds.), *Handbook of attachment: Theory, research and clinical applications* (pp. 378–394). New York: The Guilford Press.

Nardi, P. M. (1999). *Gay men's friendships: Invincible communities.* Chicago, IL: University of Chicago Press.

Prenn, N. (2009). I second that emotion! On self-disclosure and its metaprocessing. In A. Bloomgarden, & R. B. Menutti (Eds.), *The therapist revealed: Therapists speak about self-disclosure in psychotherapy* (Chapter 6, pp. 85–99). New York: Routledge.

Tomkins, S. S. (1962a). Affect, imagery, and consciousness: Vol. 1. *The positive affects.* New York: Springer.

Tomkins, S. S. (1962b). Affect, imagery, and consciousness: Vol. 2. *The negative affects.* New York: Springer.

Tunnell, G. (2006). An affirmational approach to treating gay male couples. *Group, 30,* 133–151.

8 Understanding Self-Report of Sexual Abuse in an Initial Clinical Interview

John C. Gonsiorek

Argosy University/Twin Cities, Eagan, Minnesota, USA

Introduction

In this chapter, I spend a fair amount of time reacting to the interview, exposing my thought process as a clinician and behavioral scientist attempting to make sense of this client's self-report of sexual abuse. The first and last sections of this chapter describe my reactions with use of critical thinking analyses. The middle section, the analysis of the intake, is in a looser, almost free-association style, where I think out loud as I might do with myself, were I conducting the interview. On the surface, these styles seem discordant, but they represent different yet important components of the clinical process. The goal is to join critical thinking and scholarship with a disciplined intuitive response to the human interaction that is the interview.

In cases where a history of sexual abuse is reported, I have a number of goals, including:

1. Understanding how the abuse has affected this person's life and functioning.
2. Understanding the sense this person makes of this experience, the meaning of the abuse, and the meaning of the self-report of the abuse.
3. What psychological processes does this person bring to bear now, and in the past, to manage these experiences?
4. What does this person mean by abuse?
5. How does this meaning affect self-report of the experiences called "abuse"?
6. What is the natural history of how this person has understood and made sense of the experiences called "abuse" over time?

As readers will soon see, I do not finally resolve this ideal wish list. There are more pressing clinical concerns that take precedence over abuse, but which also are an integral part of preparing for treatment of abuse aftermath. There are also many issues about the nature of information in intake, and other clinical concerns that warrant discussion.

The Initial Psychotherapy Interview. DOI: 10.1016/B978-0-12-385146-8.00008-0

Also, none of the above questions genuinely addresses whether the abuse objectively occurred. This "objective" event is an important consideration, but not necessarily the central concern. First, the ability of mental health professionals to effectively discern objective truth is not strong. Also, it is not always necessary. Mental health professionals as a matter of course regularly base diagnoses and treatment plans on self-report, even though we know empirically that self-report is of limited accuracy, which deteriorates further as the issue discussed is more psychologically "hot" or socially sanctioned. For instance, clients may report sleep patterns such as early morning awakening with approximate accuracy (presumably this is a fairly neutral topic), but they are likely to report drug and alcohol use, sexual behavior, embarrassing family history, and their own unnerving symptoms with less accuracy.

The Limitations of Self-Report

Such self-report limitations exist throughout health care, and while not optimal, health-care providers muddle through, usually well enough to get the tasks of diagnosis and treatment done. We can do this effectively to the extent that we focus on pattern detection. Any single bit of information has an inherent error rate, and predicting from that sole piece of data will never surmount that error rate, no matter how clinically experienced or credentialed is the professional engaged in prediction. When multiple data at one point in time, however, are evaluated for their consistency and coherence, and especially when compared to multiple data from other points in time, patterns that may or may not be consistent with diagnostic and theoretical ideas may emerge. Such patterns are almost always more robust, reliable, and accurately predictive than any one component of the pattern. The accuracy of any particular piece of information can then be evaluated relative to this more robust pattern.

For example, consider clients who describe themselves as "depressed" in the initial interview. It might seem that they have provided a useful shorthand that facilitates therapist assessment and treatment planning. But people use words in idiosyncratic ways, and nonclinicians use "clinical" words in ways that track imprecisely on anticipated clinical meanings. So, "depressed" might mean clinically diagnosable depression; symptoms that might more accurately be obsessional or anxiety spectrum in nature; having had a rough day at work; or any number of personalized interpretations of that word. The clinician who assumes such clients mean by the word "depressed" what the clinician means by the word will have a high error rate.

If, instead, the clinician were to carefully assess the current symptom picture and past history of symptoms, accuracy is improved. It could be improved further still if a standardized objective measure of depression such as the Minnesota Multiphasic Personality Inventory (MMPI) Depression Scale or the Beck Depression Inventory (BDI) were administered. Further accuracy might be obtained with a review of past records, collateral interviews with family members, and so on, although there rapidly comes a point of diminishing returns from unnecessarily zealous assessment in most clinical situations. But if verbal self-description of being "depressed" is embedded in some matrix of reasonably reliable information, the chances of ascertaining its true meaning are greatly improved.

Health-care providers who "shoot from the hip" and base conclusions on unnecessarily narrow data such as a self-report of sexual abuse without thorough evaluation, may look brilliant when they are occasionally accurate; but most of the time, their recklessness leads to a needlessly high error rate, misunderstanding of clients, and, as a result, inadequate treatment.

It must be emphasized that all sources of information and data have an error rate, without exception. Different data sources have different error rates, however, and effective health-care providers weigh them accordingly. Someone may report feeling feverish, but a thermometer reading has higher accuracy. But the thermometer, while the stronger measure, is imperfect. It may be malfunctioning, be calibrated improperly, or have other flaws. Similarly, clients vary in the degree to which their reports of feeling "depressed" may be accurate. Objective standardized measures are likely more accurate, but still imperfect. Client reading level, or variation by culture or social class may affect the understanding or social desirability of individual items, and other factors can all impact accuracy. Mental health disciplines are especially prone to these kinds of inaccuracy because we remain heavily reliant on informal self-report of symptoms and history, and structured self-report, as in many paper and pencil tests. Other health-care disciplines with a wider array of measurements often have improved measurement accuracy. But perfectly accurate measurement does not exist, and even highly accurate measurement is embedded in fallible theory and other assumptions about knowledge on which it relies for its epistemological meaning.

With regard to sexual abuse history in particular, it is a false dichotomy to view the clinical challenge as merely one of self-report "distortion" versus "objective" facts. Some events are simply more objective by nature than others. Reports about an adult engaging in particular defined sexual acts with a child have a potentially high degree of objectivity, in the sense that different observers, had they been present, may have demonstrated high reliability across their reports about whether certain acts occurred. The raters will likely be less in agreement regarding how they name or understand the acts in question, about what these behaviors mean for the mental state and intent of the adult engaging in the acts, and less still in predicting long-term effects on the child.

But other experiences lack even this minimal degree of potentially reliable agreement about the acts in question. Consider an adult who persistently finds reasons to talk with and gaze upon a latency age child who is bathing. How much of this behavior is "too much"? How much conversation with the child about her or his body is intrusive? How much gazing upon the child is improper? Is this behavior "abusive"? Here agreement among raters about the objective facts is more tenuous, because the behaviors are less distinctive and noteworthy, and are more closely tied to judgments about the meaning and labeling of these behaviors.

For example, whether an adult touched a child's genitals is relatively discrete and objective; while whether an adult is looking inappropriately at a child involves questions about how much is too much and what is qualitatively improper.

Under these circumstances, predicting mental state or intent of the adult is even more difficult because the target behavior involved is less stable. None of this speaks to experience of the child, who may attribute a wide range of meanings to the adult's behavior, ranging from benign (the adult likes me, finds me interesting to talk to), to highly aversive (the adult is hurting me, the adult is judging my body), and a range of possibilities in between. Further, the child's perception may change over time, depending on developmental level, changes in the adult's behavior, comments from peers and other adults, and a host of other possibilities. The behavior shapes the meaning ascribed to it, and the meaning shapes perception of the behavior. Only at the most objective end of the behavioral possibilities (behaviors with a high reliability of being perceived as abusive, and ongoing patterned behavior) do the relationships between behavior and meaning approach becoming linear and predictable.

Readers interested in this approach to understanding clinical phenomena can consult Cronbach and Meehl (1955), Grove and Meehl (1996), and Meehl (1954, 1973). This clinical approach is itself informed by philosophy of science considerations exemplified by the work of Kuhn (Kuhn, 1996; Conant and Haugeland, 2000) and Popper (1963, 1992).

The Literature on Sexual Abuse

It is a truism that clinicians are expected to be well-versed in the empirical and theoretical literature in the issues they treat. Sexual abuse is no different, except that extra cautions are in order: This literature in this area is confusing, unusually partisan, and contentious. For example, a controversial review of the literature on the effects of child sexual abuse by Rind, Tromovitch, and Bauserman (1998) generated much media attention, usually negative, and a condemnation by the US House of Representatives. Despite critiques (see Dallam, Gleaves, Cepeda-Benito, Silberg, Kraemer & Spiegel, 2001; Ondersma, Chaffin, Berliner, Cordon, Goodman & Barnett, 2001) and a rebuttal of the critiques (Rind, Tromovitch, & Bauserman, 2001), the net result seems to be that more heat than light was generated, and no one seems to have been convinced or enlightened.

The cautious, critically thinking approach described here rests heavily on applying broader behavioral science knowledge to issues of sexual abuse, and to deliberately avoid treating it as a mature area of scientific inquiry where a body of knowledge can be relied upon. The study of sexual abuse is simply not at that level of certainty and maturity. But clinicians must start somewhere in approaching sexual abuse with any specificity and precision. This can be done, albeit tentatively, provided wishes for certainty, theoretical elegance, and, most importantly, clear dogmas are left at the door. Finkelhor's (1990) thoughtful review (strangely ignored in the flurry of analyses, critiques, and rebuttals noted above) and my review of the literature on male victims of abuse (Gonsiorek, Bera, & LeTourneau, 1994, see chapter 3) are attempts to strike this balance. Both are somewhat dated, although the conclusions of both generally remain consistent with more current literature. Clinicians approaching this literature should be aware of distortions from both radical victimologists who espouse overly broad and vague definitions of abuse and uniformly grim sequelae of abuse; and abuse deniers, who minimize both prevalence and effects (see Gonsiorek et al., 1994, chapter 2 for an analysis, and read between the lines in the four articles noted above in the more recent controversy). Both distortions are primarily political and not scientific or clinical in their approaches, and both warrant a plague on their houses.

The Role of Intake

The dialectic between assessment and intervention is a useful one. It is a common human tendency for clinicians to draw conclusions both too quickly and on an excessively restricted data set. A primary function of clinical training is to slow down the process, broaden the data set, engage in pattern detection, and differentially weigh data of varying quality. The assessment and/or diagnosis then create a foundation for a treatment plan. The operationalizing of the treatment plan may and often does generate new information that triggers a reformulation of the assessment, which triggers a revised treatment plan, until the client is reasonably well, or at least not symptomatic.

As useful as this dialectic is, it is also partially false. All assessment functions on a more covert level as an intervention, and all interventions provide additional assessment data, occasionally in terms of truly new and different information, and minimally in terms of what works and what does not, which has implications for the coping abilities of the client, as well as the efficacy of the therapy provided.

With this perspective in mind, the manifest purpose of the intake is to obtain the data necessary to assess and plan in an efficient manner. Yet, on a more covert level, this process should minimally convey that the client is valued and important; that the therapist is responsible, concerned, cautious, orderly, conscientious, and benign; and that the therapy environment is a safe place to explore and express difficult concerns. Clinicians can often discern or create opportunities in intake to stretch the envelope: to pose questions or challenges that move clients beyond their typical ways of understanding themselves, to alter their self-narrative, to observe how they cope with challenge and disagreement and how their defenses operate, and to see what they are capable of. These are interventions as much as assessment strategies.

A challenge in this approach is that the therapist must be vigilant about not moving clients too far beyond their typical ways of understanding before they are ready. The goal in the intake is for the client to be psychologically activated or primed, but not scared off, or provoked to a level where they are more distressed than relieved. There may well be times later in the therapy where more distress than relief is clinically useful; but this requires an established level of trust and viable working relationship.

My preferred intake style is active and goal-oriented, and when the situation allows, straddles this assessment/intervention dialectic. Alternate styles exist, and perhaps the mirror opposite style is a classically psychodynamic one in which the clinician structures the intake minimally or not at all, allowing information to unfold in its own internal rhythm, based on the belief that this style results in the most productive and uncontaminated clinical material, and the most viable therapeutic alliance. While this approach has a certain theoretical elegance, I ultimately reject it as clinically and socially irresponsible.

I perceive myself as operating clinically within a cognitive-behavioral therapy (CBT) perspective primarily, but informed by psychodynamic and system theories. Consistent with this orientation, I approach intakes in a structured manner, seeking to obtain current client concerns and presenting problems and history sufficient to begin formulating a diagnosis and treatment plan. There is a short list of crucial topics about which I inquire whether or not the client offers information on them. These include past mental health history and treatment, alcohol and drug use patterns, general health and risk factors, history of physical or sexual abuse, risk of harm to self or others, relationship status and history, work status and history, significant medical history and current medications, and others depending on what else emerges. My rationales in pursuing such information directly include: needing to know quickly if emergent or high-risk situations are present, efficiency in diagnosis and treatment planning, and heuristic value in opening up areas of inquiry that have a high likelihood of fruitfulness. For example, learning early on that clients have had past psychotherapy cues me to learn what problems for which they sought earlier treatment, and their reactions to the past therapy. This makes my diagnostic process more focused, and alerts me to how they might be experiencing our current interaction. As suggested above, I take issue with unstructured approaches because I believe these place clients at unnecessary risk (if there is an undisclosed emergent issue) and also slow down gathering of information important for diagnosis and treatment. From both clinical and cost-effectiveness viewpoints, I believe structure is warranted in the intake process.

Analysis of the Intake

(Throughout the entire Analysis of the Intake section, "S" stands for Dr. Silverstein, and Scott is Scott.)

Introduction. Curious to know more why he wanted a gay therapist. His default assumption is likely to be that the therapist is likely not homophobic, but sometimes clients have other reasons. His quick agreement to recording the session is somewhat surprising, given the content that follows; does this suggest a lack of self-care, liking attention, something else? His immediate comfort and confidence are also surprising, for clients new to therapy in general, and especially for someone who is about to make the disclosures he does. Similar with his "bold ... brash" response style. Not sure what to make of it, but it is noteworthy.

(P4) Very early mention of sexual abuse, and he gets right to the point with use of the word "molestation." Unusual presentation, most people build to it, offer it in more tentative way. Counter-phobic defensive style? Attention-seeking?

(P7) Uses a "hardcore" word like molestation, but then modifies it, backs away from it, makes it more vague. This is more typical, but the initial decisive presentation of it remains puzzling.

(P11) Suddenly, he gets relatively inarticulate about the abuse, less sure of himself, the confidence cracks. It is as if he takes a flying leap to get the issue on the table, then stumbles with it. I wonder if his style is similar with other difficult issues?

(P14) Echoes of the same style—strong language with "fucked up," but then backs away from it.

(T15) S stokes the fire, exactly what is meant by therapist activities that are both assessment and intervention.

(P18, P19, P20), Brother David, a nurse, takes a risk of exposing himself to HIV, and does contract HIV. Maybe bad luck, maybe lack of self-care runs in the family?

(P23) "Protector"? From what? Or whom? Scott talks about David's unconditional love as if it is not much present in his life otherwise. Wonder what that's about? His parents don't provide solace for the grief about David. Have they ever provided it? Interesting that this is his first substantive portrayal of them, failing him after the vague "screwed up relationship" in P15, and his initial report of abuse.

(P25) Scott seems to be describing that his brother, when a child, happened upon public sex between men, which the brother viewed, but otherwise did not participate in. This is puzzling in that it is hard to imagine adult men knowingly exposing themselves to a minor without physically engaging the minor; and unclear why Scott seems to label this event as molestation of Scott (phrased decisively again) by the father (P24). What actually occurred to the brother is quite unclear. It has somewhat of a fantastic quality, but then again, this is Scott's recollection of his brother's recollection as an adult of childhood events. Lots of room for distortion. The only thing that is clear is Scott's distress about it.

(P30) Here is egregious and serious criminal behavior by the father toward Scott, but it is credit card fraud, not sexual abuse. Assuming this account is accurate, it is hard to imagine the father not having significant character pathology.

(P31) This is noteworthy in the way it speaks to Scott's decision-making. A simple analysis might conclude that he does not adequately stand up for his own interests, and some element of that may well be present. On the other hand, he is also engaging in complicated cost−benefit analyses of how differing courses of action might affect his mother, father, and himself. Scott is a complex man, a mix of different functioning levels.

(P33) The tattoo seems almost ... romantic? "... he's always with me." Earlier, he called David "a sweetheart" (P18) and "my ego" (P23). Curious.

(T33) S stokes the fire again. Nice move!

(P34) "... the molestation thing ... brought us closer." Scott gets vague again, something's up. Were he and his brother sexual? How did the "molestation" of

David, which seemingly consisted of David observing men having sex, bring them closer?

(T37) One interpretation of this is that both Scott and David seemed excessively sexualized at a young age? What does this mean? On the other hand, the mists of time can be quite foggy. . . . Again, S pokes the bear.

(P40) The make-out in the car. It is noteworthy that this occurs with his brother's friend and in the presence of his brother. Again, the interaction with the brother might seem sexualized.

(T42) S pokes the bear, but more gently this time. Keep the flow of material coming without provoking panic?

(P43) A complex response. Scott seems to be saying that he and David engaged in sexual touching, but that it was somehow not sex, and that others have wondered if their relationship was sexual. It is decidedly *not* typical that "People do ask that quite often . . ." Why would they do that? What did they observe to make them pose such a low-probability question?

(T44) Even S is surprised by the nonchalance of this unusual statement.

(P44) Wall goes up. Scott has now positioned it as a straight versus gay issue, in what seems like a hard defensive response, and follows it with humor. He's reached his limit exploring this issue.

(T45) S sees that, enough poking the bear, switch topic. Don't want to risk a broader defensive shutdown. Nice.

(P45) Maybe this just happens to be merely factual, or maybe . . . Scott can't keep himself from focusing on David. And the information on David is unflattering, in that David outs Scott to their parents. It certainly sounds like it was done in anger, and that David does not have the firmest boundaries. Scott is quick to rationalize this, however, as an attempt to increase closeness and "just a deflection," even though he paradoxically ends with what seems to be an acknowledgment that it was done in anger.

(P46) Scott is still needing to emphasize that David is blameless and that he holds no anger or resentment. And if you believe that one, there's this Bridge in Brooklyn . . . .

This section raises questions about how accurate versus distorted Scott's take on David is; that is, has he deeply idealized David?

(P48) One wonders how distorted much of this is as well. I'm having trouble seeing the father who commits felony fraud to his son to the tune of $20,000, and the mother who minimizes this, as the same parents who were so "very supportive" about Scott's coming out, and were "great" and "fantastic" to boot. What does this mean about Scott's self-report more broadly?

(T52, T53) S points out this discrepancy regarding Scott's assertiveness and self-care in the way he approaches mental health services with the lack of these in the way he approaches medical services. But Scott sidesteps the discrepancy, twice (P53 and P54).

(T55) S pushes it a bit.

(P55) Scott retreats into compliant good boy mode. S then lets it go.

(P81) Scott is again quick to deny anger.

(P82) Scott seems quick to turn lovers into friends.

(P84) He quickly acknowledges that he keeps intimacy at length, but does so in an intellectualized manner; it is unlikely there has been much emotional integration of these "insights."

(P86) Passionate? I wonder if that is a code for something else, some other psychological process. He continues intellectualizing his problems with intimacy.

(P96, P97, P98) Again questions about the accuracy of his self-report seem reasonable here.

(P103, P104, P105) A similar pattern as earlier: a strong statement, followed by backing away, modification.

(P107) Clearly describes marijuana abuse.

(P114) Scott seeks numbing ... why? Difficulty quieting himself is more another way of saying it, rather than an explanation.

(P115) "That fucking loser that I've been seeing." Where does that come from? Statement has an abrupt quality, as if erupting. All his problem areas seem to get thrown together; he becomes disorganized, and seeks numbing.

(P120) Complex family cauldron emerges. Mother is confidante, friend, "I tell her everything" but he does not "want to be there."

(P121, P122, P123) Given his brother's infection and death from HIV, this behavior seems unusually self-destructive. Does he want to join his brother in death?

(P124) Continued self-destructive themes.

(P125) Death-defying risk = intimacy for Scott, and poor boundaries and sense of self suggested—spending 3 days with someone after the first night together might be developmentally understandable immaturity in a 20-year-old; in a 30-year-old, it suggests a weak sense of self.

(P128, P129) Intimate feelings worth risking one's life for quickly turn to dislike!

(P130) Again, risk = intimacy for Scott.

(P132, P133, P134) A classic end-of-session bombshell, and a big one—suicide! Is it suicide, need for attention? Why does S not assess it? See discussion below.

(P140/T141) I'm puzzled why S sidesteps what seems to be an obvious need for reassurance.

(P157) Scott continues to want reassurance or something more.

(P159) I wonder if he feels a bit taken aback at himself.

Further Assessment and Treatment Plan Ideas from the Intake

Further Assessment

I come away from this intake with four hypotheses, or more accurately, areas of curiosity, as these are not precise enough to be labeled hypotheses.

First, while Scott has reported that he has been "molested," what, if anything, occurred to *him* is entirely unclear. What we have is his belief that his father molested him, but when he describes that, he reports what his brother described: that as a child he (brother) observed adult men having sex, and/or participated in it, and/or was the desired sexual object of their group masturbation. The brother clearly stated that their father was not part of this. How does this relate to Scott's belief that he (Scott) was molested, and by the father?

Second, Scott has been seriously financially exploited by his father, to a level of significant criminality. Does this relate to Scott's perceptions of sexual abuse by the father, and if so, how? Additionally within the family, Scot gives conflicting information about his mother, describing himself as a friend and confidante, expressing great closeness with her, but also expressing a need for distance. He reports his muted response to his father's financial fraud of him as being driven by a wish to protect her.

Third, Scott's relationship with his deceased brother David is deeply idealized, perhaps romantic, even though Scott reports that it was not sexual. He reports that others have speculated about a low base rate guess: that he and David were sexual. Sibling incest is not something people typically consider. It is unclear what is going on, but there certainly seems to be more sexual cathexis between Scott and his brother than anywhere else in Scott's history.

Finally, Scott appears to have a dangerously self-destructive streak—he knowingly exposes himself to possible HIV, despite his brother having died from precisely such behavior. One wonders if this is an extreme form of identification with the brother, perhaps wanting to join him in death. At the least, it raises questions about what exactly is the nature of their relationship. Scott ends the session with a dramatic suggestion that he might be suicidal. His use of marijuana is at a level of clinical concern, in that initial information suggests a use pattern that may be consistent with substance abuse or dependency. If further information bears out this concern, this may be an aspect of self-destructiveness, an attempt to numb painful affect, both, or serve other functions as yet unclear.

A First Wave of Interventions

Based on these four initial ideas, my initial interventions would be structured in the following manner. These are listed in order of importance. As noted above, these are primarily interventions, but contain assessment components as well.

Of primary importance is a dually focused safety plan. One aspect includes assessment of his suicide risk, a plan for ongoing assessment of suicidality, and Scott's agreement to a no-harm plan if there is significant risk. I would approach this issue directly, stating that whenever there is a possibility of suicide, I evaluate carefully. This includes inquiring about suicide plans, means, intent, past history, and risk factors such as active substance use, medical problems, and others. I am also frank about my ethical, legal, and moral obligations to prevent client suicide and my intention to meet these. For readers desiring more information, Bongar's work is a sound introduction to these issues (Bongar, 2002; Bongar, Berman,

Maris, Silverman, Harris & Packman, 1998), and there is much other useful literature as well (e.g., Packman, Marlitt, Bongar, & Pennuto, 2004; Sanchez, 2001). If
this exploration uncovers imminent danger, and if this risk does not seem reliably
containable, hospitalization may be in order. I would be surprised if the suicide risk
is significant, and even more so if it was imminent. But due diligence requires a
careful assessment, and the ability of clinicians to estimate such risk without such
assessment is weak. I fault Silverstein for not assessing the risk of suicide.

My clinical intuition is that Scott's report of feeling suicidal is more dramatic
than substantive. I am unclear if it is manipulative. But these speculations are beside
the point: They change nothing about the need for assessment and, if anything, such
speculations pose risk for the clinician in that they can deflect attention from the
needed assessment. Even if the talk of suicide were in fact primarily manipulative
(which cannot reliably be determined), I would continue to argue that this changes
nothing. There are myriad ways to manipulate; the selection of this method suggests
a depressive frame of mind, which leads back to the need to assess suicide risk.

This assessment process also serves as an intervention: it demonstrates that the
therapist is cautious, orderly, takes Scott's safety seriously, ... and is also willing
to call his bluff, if that is what is occurring. As with any therapist behavior or non-
behavior, this approach has consequences that require management. Such directive
interventionist approaches elicit client transferences as strong and variable as non-
directive approaches. The increased demands on the therapist of having to manage
a high-risk situation so early in the interaction typically elicit therapist counter-
transferences as well. All of these require exploration and effective management.

The second aspect of the safety plan involves developing strategies so that Scott
can establish behavioral control such that he ceases to expose himself to HIV, and
that his substance use is further evaluated. This would take the form of the therapist
strongly recommending that they engage in a classic cognitive-behavioral evaluation and treatment of his risk-taking sexual behavior and to screen for substance
use problems, and treat these if necessary. Obviously, all this cannot be accomplished in the initial interview. Rather, the therapist would recommend that evaluation and management of these two areas of risk behavior be part of the ongoing
treatment plan. Depending on the therapist's areas of competency and available
community resources, these may be accomplished in future sessions and/or involve
external referrals for these limited tasks. Such use of auxiliary resources as part of
an overall treatment plan is consistent with cognitive-behavioral approaches, but
may not blend so easily with other approaches. The meta-message from the therapist is essentially: "You're not going to be killing yourself, overtly or covertly, on
my watch, if I can at all help it." This is decidedly not a neutral stance, and likely
will have ramifications, discussed below.

This active interventionist style is compatible with some approaches to ethical
theory and decision-making models, and a weaker fit with others. (See Bersoff,
2008, chapter 3 for an introduction to these.) I am most comfortable with it because
of its emphasis on client safety and relatively rapid assessment of important areas;
I believe these are central to quality care, and are squarely a therapist's responsibility. But no approach is without vulnerabilities, and maintaining support for client

autonomy is a challenge in this approach. Assiduous informed consent and therapist transparency (again, easily compatible with cognitive-behavioral approaches) are the necessary solutions.

Establishing safety is not merely about literal safety of Scott and managing risk, although these are primary. It is also about creating a therapeutic environment in which it is safe to divulge difficult disclosures of any variety. If Scott cannot count on his therapist to respond seriously to expressed suicide potential, sexual behavior that is potentially life-threatening, and possible substance problems, why would he feel safe enough to pursue exploration of whatever happened that is included in what he terms "molestation"? The failure to pursue a suicide risk assessment and to clearly state an opinion that high-risk behavior warrants serious therapeutic efforts are errors in this intake, I believe. This derives both from a general standard of care framework, but also from a specific intention of creating a safe therapeutic container.

Some may disagree and reply that the emergence of expressed suicidality at the closing moments of the intake may well be consciously or unconsciously attention-seeking or manipulative, and that if the therapist extends the interview to perform a suicide risk assessment and make whatever response that demands, then the door has been opened for the client to bend the rules of the therapeutic environment.

I disagree with this perspective. This client is unknown to the therapist; therefore, there is no reliable basis for judging the motivations of the disclosure about suicidal feelings, as there might be with a client well into therapy. It simply cannot be reliably discerned. One could make a counter-argument that because suicidality was not specifically evaluated earlier in the interview, it was a sign of health that the client would make certain it was mentioned before the session ended. There is also the possibility that the client was not fully aware of the depth of his suicidal feelings, and the discussion of his brother's death, his troubled family and personal relationships, and other issues elicited these feelings in an abrupt fashion. It also *is* entirely possible that the disclosure is attention-seeking or manipulative in a way that potentially undermines the integrity of the therapy.

I would argue that the cost−benefit analysis can best be understood in the following manner. On the one hand, by evaluating the risk and commenting on the self-destructive sexual behavior, I increase the likelihood the client remains alive. One cannot treat the dead. I have signaled to him that this therapy takes his welfare seriously, that self-destructive acting out is not trivial, that any substance problems will be taken seriously, and that he can feel safe in this environment with other issues as well. On the negative side, I may have created a precedent for his bending the structure of therapy, which I will need to manage later if it recurs. There are many positives, and the negative I can manage.

On the other side, by not responding to the risk, I have increased the likelihood of the admittedly low probability possibility of suicide, given him a confusing, mixed message about the importance of his safety in general and his self-destructive sexual behavior in specific, and taken the risk that the therapy may not be seen as a reliably safe environment. But I have managed what might be manipulation—or not. Many serious negatives, one dubious positive. The choice is clear; the former is clinically sound, the latter, too risky.

Admittedly, as someone who acts cognitive-behaviorally, but thinks in a hybrid CBT/psychodynamic style, this is relatively easy for me to say. My predominant therapeutic style accommodates and thrives on direct goal-oriented management of issues arising in therapy. It also illustrates why I am partisan about this style: it readily enables me to operate in a "First, do no harm" manner.

This issue of safety, then, is the first order of business. Once it is adequately managed, the next issue is to further evaluate Scott's description that he was molested. I would approach this directly, commenting that I was unclear how his description of whatever happened to his brother in the gym, relates to his perception that he was molested, and by his father. I would ask for behavioral descriptions of events, his intuitions and hunches, all of it. The point of this is understanding, not "proof." While I am interested eventually in obtaining as accurate a history as is possible, at this point, I am more curious about the inner reality of someone who so decisively describes being molested by his father but then produces as evidence a relatively tangential story about one unclear event experienced by his brother involving strangers. I suspect this issue will be revisited a number of times.

It is entirely possible that in the future Scott will report a history of relatively clear abuse or near abuse, and he was just not ready to disclose it initially. Perhaps "molestation" is a calling card to discuss other issues, such as financial exploitation, emotional neglect, or family dysfunction. Frankly, I do not have a clear estimate what might emerge in this regard. That is fortuitous: Genuine curiosity without expectation (or rather, with so many possible expectations that they are unfocused) is an ideal stance.

Exploring the relationship with his brother is another important issue, and one that reflects the two concerns of safety and sexual abuse. Do Scott and his brother share self-destructiveness? Is Scott emulating his brother's risky behavior sexually in an attempt to connect with him? Was their interaction sexualized or sexual, and does this play a role in Scott's self-destructiveness? Again, I have many questions and no answers. I am as interested in learning the answers to these as I am in observing the process of inquiry and what Scott and I might learn about him as these questions are pursued. Similarly, I am interested in exploring his relationship with both parents.

Early in the treatment, I would follow up on my concerns expressed in intake about his unsafe sexual behavior, and strongly recommend that he avail himself of behavioral approaches within our therapy, community educational and support resources, and any other methods that might prove effective in establishing consistently low risk/safe sexual behavior. This will be tricky: It is very difficult for gay men in this society to reach adulthood without incorporating some degree of societal disparagement about their sexuality and sexual behavior (see Gonsiorek & Rudolph, 1991). The risk for the therapist is that this concern about Scott's risky sexual behavior will be seen consciously or unconsciously as punitive. Consistent with the approach described here, transparency and informed consent shape my response. I would explain to Scott that I have a dilemma, in that I am concerned that his sexual behavior poses substantial medical risk for him, and I wish to see him healthy and happy if at all possible. At the same time, I worry that this concern might be misconstrued as a negative judgment about him, his sexual orientation, or sexuality in general. Therefore, while my concerns about his risky sexual behavior and my recommendations to change that remain, I want to engage in an ongoing dialogue with him about his reactions to my doing so.

This behavioral change would take precedence over exploring and understanding the meaning of his risky behavior. Again, I would be transparent about this, explaining that unmanaged patterns of current risky behavior make understanding and resolving historical issues more difficult, and might pose a risk of increased risk behavior if behavioral management is not stable. Once behavioral goals are stably established, this exploration would be engaged. Concurrently, evaluating and, if necessary, arranging for treatment of any substance abuse issues would occur.

Possible Later Developments

I anticipate that some shoes will drop as a result of the focus on safety issues. If Scott has a long-standing pattern of self-destructiveness, the therapist acting in the best interests of his safety may well provoke this pattern, and it may show itself in other ways—which will illuminate its workings, and may make it more clearly manifest to Scott. On the other hand, if the self-destructiveness is not entrenched and is, for example, a recent reaction to his brother's illness and death, then the management of the current safety issues solves the problem. In either way, it is informative. I would put my money on a pattern, but his behavior, not my hunches, will tell the tale.

I am unclear what to expect regarding the sexual abuse. If a clear history of abuse does not emerge, it may be that the "molestation" by the father is code for other things. For example, if the relationship with the idealized brother was sexual, the discomfort from that could have been displaced onto the father. Alternatively, the father's financial exploitation coupled with the need to protect his mother may have eventuated in a conclusion that his father treated him very badly, and sexual abuse is the worst he can imagine, so that must be it. These are weak speculations with a low degree of confidence.

It is more likely, I suspect, that the relationship with his brother will open avenues to understanding his perception that he was molested, his self-destructive behavior, his seeming tendencies to distort interpersonal situations, and other clinical dilemmas. Exactly how is unclear.

As it now stands, Scott's description of the molestation by his father is idiosyncratic, to say the least. He describes his brother witnessing sexual activity of adult men, not his father, as *his* molestation. This may not be as distorted at it seems: Scott may have gotten lost in the rush of material that emerged in this intake; he may have been reluctant to divulge his own history and was testing the waters with lesser issues first; or he may construe "molestation" in unusual ways. Or his account may be as distorted as it seems, or even more distorted once more information is disclosed. All bets are off.

Final Thoughts

Some readers may think it odd that I as a psychologist who has worked extensively in the area of sexual abuse of males has spent much discussion focused on issues other than sexual abuse. This is true in part, for both clinical and theoretical reasons; but it is also only partially true. Let me explain.

Clients presenting for therapy with a possible history of sexual abuse rarely present solely with this history. First, abuse (the damaging events) and trauma (the psychological response of being overwhelmed and unable to create meaning from the events, see Haughn & Gonsiorek, 2009, for a discussion) tend to cluster: neglect, family dysfunction, and any earlier abuse or trauma typically create vulnerability that makes it more likely that more trauma and abuse will occur. How this happens is complex. Some abuse perpetrators have well-developed abilities to perceive who is vulnerable and to test limits to verify this. Equally important, vulnerable children often act in ways that telegraph that vulnerability to the world and, additionally, in ways that expose them to further harm and risk. Further, as vulnerable children incorporate the negative evaluations of themselves that are consistent with their history and experience, they often move away from positive experiences that might disconfirm their negative self-images. Simply stated, they are familiar dealing with adversity and believe it is their due, and uncomfortable dealing with the positive. Similarly, a history of trauma increases the likelihood that future adverse events will be overwhelming and traumatizing. Not surprisingly, intimacy, love, and sexual relationships, with their emotional intensity, possibility of disappointment, and capacity to mobilize earlier history, are often exquisitely affected by a history of abuse and trauma.

It does not always occur this way. Sometimes, children with no discernible preexisting vulnerability are merely unlucky and are abused not because they lack self-care or were "read" by a perpetrator as vulnerable, but because they happened to be in the wrong place at the wrong time, or because perpetrator behavior is governed primarily by response to particular physical features. It appears that when abuse occurs with such children, they may be more adept at extricating themselves, and their family/personal/community resources may also be more effective at minimizing or even reversing the adverse effects of the abuse. This is how meta-analysis of researched effects of sexual abuse can conclude that a quarter to one-third of children known to be sexually abused display no measurable adverse effects (Finkelhor, 1990). They are not denying or repressing effects. Rather, they came into the abuse with enough psychological resiliency, and were able to access appropriate resources after the abuse, such that they successfully managed the psychological challenges presented by the abuse experience.

But for the children with vulnerabilities or inadequate post-abuse resources (or more classically, both of these), these factors dovetail, grow over time, feed off each other, and fester. These are the people who become the classic sexual abuse "victims." By the time an adult abused as child presents for psychotherapy, she or he often has accumulated layers of problems. The earliest layer might be those issues of neglect, family dysfunction, and other issues that created the initial vulnerability. Lacking habits of self-care, this group often is abused longer and more severely. Fewer ameliorating resources are available post-abuse. After the abuse ends, this group is prone to developing mood problems, substance abuse, self-destructive behaviors, self-esteem problem, chronic relationship difficulties, eating disorders, and sexual behavior problems. The sexual abuse history comes wrapped in a clinically complex and symptomatic package.

One of the unfortunate legacies of the earlier victimology movement has been to conceptualize treatment of sexual abuse as a separate area of specialty, the implication being that it could be conceptualized and treated on its own. Given the way those with the most significant sexual abuse sequelae present, nothing could be further from the truth. Sexual abuse is inextricably bound up with and embedded in any earlier vulnerabilities, and the accumulated history of symptomatic reactions to it and habits of insufficient self-care. For readers interested in these ideas of resiliency, competence, and their relationship to psychopathology, see Cicchetti and Lynch (1995); Cicchetti and Valentino (2006); Masten and Coatsworth (1995); and Masten, Burt, and Coatsworth (2006).

Much of what sexual abuse is clinically bound with and embedded in is itself challenging and dangerous: suicidality, self-destructive behavior, substance abuse, and the like. Much of the treatment of sexual abuse involves unpacking and systematically resolving or managing these other issues. The "remaining" sexual abuse issues cannot be clearly perceived until these are accomplished, and the flurry of symptoms they produce subsides. Further, it can be clinically inefficient and sometimes dangerous to substantially address the sexual abuse until stability or resolution has occurred with these behavioral symptoms. Discussion of any abuse history is typically upsetting, and if any existing self-destructive behaviors are not well-managed, there is risk of resurgence and strengthening of these behaviors as a mechanism to distract from this upset.

In the case of Scott, then, assessment and management of issues involving suicide risk, unsafe sexual behavior, substance problems, and others are precisely the first order of business in treating the sexual abuse. The parameters of the abuse will be unclear until headway is made on these, and until these are resolved, primary focus on the abuse is clinically risky. By the time Scott is no longer suicidal, is no longer engaging in unsafe sexual behavior, and is not abusing substances, he will be ready to deal with whatever sexual abuse and family dysfunction is here. Along the way, the therapist will have learned a good deal about what psychological assets and liabilities Scott brings to challenges, as will Scott. The accuracy and style of his self-report will be clearer than it now is. A number of therapeutic successes will be accomplished, enhancing the therapeutic relationship. The role of the sexual abuse in fueling the self-destructive behaviors will likely become clearer to both the therapist and Scott, providing a natural bridge to examining all the ways the sexual abuse has affected him. After all this, the sexual abuse issues can be approached with the highest likelihood of success.

The remaining issues in resolving the sexual abuse vary from case to case, but a reasonable expectation is that many if not most interpersonal relationships were affected, especially those involving intimacy and sexuality. Self-concept and self-worth, and the myriad ways these express themselves behaviorally are also likely candidates.

References

Bersoff, D. N. (Ed.), (2008). *Ethical conflicts in psychology* (4th ed.). Washington, DC: American Psychological Association Press.

Bongar, B. (2002). *The suicidal patient: Clinical and legal standards of care* (2nd ed.). Washington, DC: American Psychological Association Press.

Bongar, B., Berman, A., Maris, R., Silverman, M., Harris, E., & Packman, W. (Eds.), (1998). *Risk management with suicidal patients.* New York: Guilford.

Cicchetti, D., & Lynch, M. (1995). Failures in the expected environment and their impact on individual development: The case of child maltreatment. In D. Cicchetti, & D Cohen (Eds.), *Developmental psychopathology, Vol. 2: Risk, disorder and adaptation* (pp. 32–71). New York: John Wiley & Sons.

Cicchetti, D., & Valentino, K. (2006). An ecological-transactional perspective on child maltreatment: Failure of the average expectable environment and its influence on child development. In D. Cicchetti, & D. Cohen (Eds.), *Developmental psychopathology, Vol. 3: Risk, disorder and adaptation* (2nd ed., pp. 129–201). New York: John Wiley & Sons.

Conant, J., & Haugeland, J. (Eds.), (2000). *The road since structure: Thomas S. Kuhn.* Chicago, IL: University of Chicago Press.

Cronbach, L., & Meehl, P. E. (1955). Construct validity in psychological tests. *Psychological Bulletin, 52*, 281–302.

Dallam, S. J., Gleaves, D. H., Cepeda-Benito, A., Silberg, J. L., Kraemer, H. C, & Spiegel, D. (2001). The effects of child sexual abuse: Comment on Rind, Tromovitch, and Bauserman (1998). *Psychological Bulletin, 127*, 715–733.

Finkelhor, D. (1990). Early and long-term effects of child sexual abuse: An update. *Professional Psychology: Research & Practice, 21*, 325–330.

Gonsiorek, J. C., Bera, W. H., & LeTourneau, D. (1994). *Male sexual abuse: A trilogy of intervention strategies.* Newbury Park, CA: Sage Publications.

Gonsiorek, J., & Rudolph, J. (1991). Homosexual identity: Coming-out and other developmental events. In J. Gonsiorek, & J. Weinrich (Eds.), *Homosexuality: Research implications for public policy* (pp. 161–176). Newbury Park, CA: Sage Publications.

Grove, W., & Meehl, P. (1996). Comparative efficiency of informal (subjective, impressionistic) and formal (mechanical, algorithmic) prediction procedures: The clinical–statistical controversy. *Psychology, Public Policy, and Law, 2*, 293–323.

Haughn, C., & Gonsiorek, J. C. (2009). The *Book of Job*: Implications for construct validity of posttraumatic stress disorder diagnostic criteria. *Mental Health Religion and Culture, 12*(8), 833–845.

Kuhn, T. (1996). *The structure of scientific revolutions* (3rd ed.). Chicago, IL: University of Chicago Press.

Masten, A., Burt, K., & Coatsworth, J. D. (2006). Competence and psychopathology in development. In D. Cicchetti, & D. Cohen (Eds.), *Developmental psychopathology, Vol. 3: Risk, disorder and adaptation* (2nd ed., pp. 696–738). New York: John Wiley & Sons.

Masten, A., & Coatsworth, J. D. (1995). Competence, resilience and psychopathology. In D. Cicchetti, & D. Cohen (Eds.), *Developmental psychopathology, Vol. 2: Risk, disorder and adaptation* (pp. 715–752). New York: John Wiley & Sons.

Meehl, P. E. (1954). *Clinical versus statistical prediction: A theoretical analysis and a review of the evidence.* Minneapolis, MN: University of Minnesota Press.

Meehl, P. E. (1973). *Psychodiagnosis: Selected papers.* Minneapolis, MN: University of Minnesota Press.

Ondersma, S. J., Chaffin, M., Berliner, L., Cordon, I., Goodman, G., & Barnett, D. (2001). Sex with children is abuse: Comment on Rind, Tromovitch, and Bauserman (1998). *Psychological Bulletin, 127,* 707–714.

Packman, W., Marlitt, R., Bongar, B., & Pennuto, T. (2004). A comprehensive and concise assessment of suicide risk. *Behavioral Sciences and the Law, 22,* 667–680.

Popper, K. (1963). *Conjectures and refutations.* New York: Routledge & Kegan Paul.

Popper, K. (1992). *The logic of scientific discovery.* New York: Routledge (Originally published as *Logik der Forschung* (1935). Vienna: Verlag von Julius Springer).

Rind, B., Tromovitch, P., & Bauserman, R. (1998). Meta analytic examination of assumed properties of child sexual abuse using college samples. *Psychological Bulletin, 124,* 22–53.

Rind, B., Tromovitch, P., & Bauserman, R. (2001). The validity and appropriateness of methods, analyses and conclusions in Rind et al. (1998): A rebuttal of victimological critique from Ondersma et al. (2001) and Dallam et al. (2001). *Psychological Bulletin, 127,* 734–758.

Sanchez, H. (2001). Risk factor model for suicide assessment and intervention. *Professional Psychology: Research & Practice, 32,* 344–345.

9 Sex, Drugs, and HIV (Clinical Issues and Assessment Strategies)

Peter S. Theodore

California School of Professional Psychology, Los Angeles, at Alliant
International University, Alhambra, CA, USA

Sexuality, substance use, and HIV are intricately woven together into a complex system of relationships that challenge both our patients and ourselves. As a clinical psychologist I integrate various theories and clinical skills in order to treat gay and bisexual men coping with HIV-related issues. Using a cognitive-behavioral framework, I facilitate a process through which patients learn to alter negative core beliefs and maladaptive thoughts that fuel their psychological distress and drive HIV-related risk behaviors.

In this chapter, I will:

1. Examine relevant psychological models that help to explain the intersection of sexual behavior, substance use, and HIV transmission among gay and bisexual men.
2. Apply the resulting conceptual framework to the case of Scott.
3. Review guidelines and strategies for assessing drug use and sexual risk behaviors using applied examples from the case of Scott.
4. Highlight potential ethical and legal challenges that can complicate psychotherapy with gay and bisexual men addressing HIV-related risk behaviors.

The Fusion of Sex and Drugs

Sexual transmission remains the primary route of HIV-infection among gay and bisexual men. Drug use and sexual behavior become inextricably linked through multiple cognitive-behavioral mechanisms including classical and operant conditioning. Classical conditioning (Pavlov, 1927) refers to the evolution of a paired association between two variables through repeated experiences. In the case of sex and drugs, as the strength of the association increases, sex and drugs can become "triggers" for one another such that it becomes increasingly difficult to have sex without being intoxicated or high, or to use drugs without inevitably craving sex. Operant conditioning (Skinner, 1963) refers to the principle that a behavior is likely to be repeated if the behavior is followed by a pleasant or reinforcing experience, while that same behavior is less likely to be repeated if followed by an unpleasant

The Initial Psychotherapy Interview. DOI: 10.1016/B978-0-12-385146-8.00009-2

or punishing experience. More specifically, reinforcement can be broken down into two distinct types—positive reinforcement and negative reinforcement—both of which will prove important to understanding the link between sex and drugs.

Positive reinforcement refers to the process in which a behavior (e.g., drug use) is followed by the onset of "positive," rewarding experiences (e.g., feeling euphoric, happy, energized). Negative reinforcement, although the term seems counterintuitive, refers to the process in which a behavior (e.g., drug use) is followed by the removal or attenuation of "negative," adverse experiences (e.g., reductions in anxiety, depression, and fatigue). In this manner, the avoidance of psychological pain and withdrawal symptoms through sex and drug use constitute forms of negative reinforcement.

Many theories have been proposed to help explain how substance use has become an important part of gay men's sexual lives (Lewis & Ross, 1995; Shoptaw & Frosch, 2000; Stall & Purcell, 2000). Social venues revolving around alcohol and other drug use have historically served a central role in the social networking of gay men. They represented safe havens where otherwise stigmatized gay men could go in search of friendship, lovers, and sex-partners. Today, they remain vital parts of the gay male social scene, although Internet sites have rapidly begun to replace them as meeting grounds for sex-partners (Fernandez et al., 2007; Parsons, Severino, Grov, Bimbi, & Morgenstern, 2007). Behaviorally, gay men are socialized in each of these forums to pair sex with alcohol and drugs through the placement of sexually charged ads, pictures, videos, and/or go-go dancers. With repeated exposure to these stimuli, sex and drugs become classically conditioned triggers for one another, and the likelihood of meeting a partner with whom one has sex while intoxicated or high increases. From then on, each subsequent experience of having sex under the influence of drugs or alcohol strengthens the conditioned association.

Focusing our attention on operant conditioning, it is helpful to look more closely at the particular reward systems that motivate alcohol and drug use. Many of us have used alcohol or other drugs because of their initial, pleasurable effects that can range from a sense of peace and relaxation to profound energy, self-confidence, and sexual excitement. These sensations drive the process of positive reinforcement, encouraging continued use as the effects of the substance(s) fade. On a deeper level, substance use helps some gay and bisexual men avoid psychological pain engendered by social and cultural ideologies that perpetuate heterosexual masculinity (Herek, 1986). Growing up with few or no role models in a society that normalizes heterosexuality (see Cerbone, Chapter 15), many gay and bisexual men come to feel isolated, invisible, and inferior. Struggling against a cultural paradigm that supports heterosexuality as a fundamental condition of manhood, and equates masculinity with power and respect, those who fail to meet these standards can develop feelings of shame, guilt, and anxiety about their same-sex desires (Mayfield, 2001); this is also called internalized homophobia (Malyon, 1982; Shidlo, 1994). As a result of internalized homonegativity, they may develop core beliefs that they are "damaged" or "unlovable" and suffer from low self-esteem and poor self-image.

Given this set of issues, the effects of substance use create a powerful, if temporary, sense of relief for gay and bisexual men. In this manner, substance use decreases the psychological distress of its user, encouraging continued use through the process of negative reinforcement. For some, substance use circuitously progresses to abuse as positive reinforcement (i.e., the physical pleasure, euphoria, energy, self-confidence, sexual excitement) gives way to negative reinforcement (i.e., the removal of negative feelings/withdrawal symptoms such as anxiety, depression, and shame). In other words, while the substance "user" initially uses in search of a buzz or high, the substance "abuser" more commonly seeks to avoid distress (e.g., anxiety, depression, loneliness, anger, fatigue) and the withdrawal symptoms characteristic of his drug of choice.

Minority Stress Model and Internalized Homonegativity

The minority stress model and its relation to internalized homonegativity afford a fuller understanding of the associations between sex, drugs, and HIV among gay and bisexual men (Meyer, 2003; Meyer & Dean, 1995). Extrapolated from various stress and social psychological theories, Meyer has expanded the minority stress model to explain the evolution of health disparities among sexual minorities. The model specifically describes a process through which a combination of chronic, minority stressors (i.e., acts of antigay discrimination and victimization) predispose gay and bisexual men to internalize homonegativity. The model links higher levels of internalized homonegativity to increased rates of mood and anxiety disorders, substance use, and risky sex among gay and bisexual men (Frost & Meyer, 2009; Hamilton & Mahalik, 2009; Yi, Sandfort, & Shidlo, 2010). As gay and bisexual men learn to shroud their same-sex attractions, they become increasingly lonely and vulnerable to substance use and risky sex. In the absence of meaningful relationships, gay and bisexual men seeking a sense of belonging may turn to substance use. Similarly, some gay and bisexual men turn toward sex, particularly unprotected sex, as a source of connectedness and intimacy.

Minority stress and internalized homonegativity are greatest among select groups of sexual minorities, such as gay and bisexual men living in suburban and rural towns. They remain relatively isolated and marginalized (Preston et al., 2004). Bisexual men have an increased risk stemming from having to contend with biphobia—the double stigma cast by gays and lesbians in addition to heterosexuals—that presumes bisexuals are less capable of commitment relative to others. Similarly, gay and bisexual men of color experience increased levels of minority stress, mental health issues, and HIV-risk behaviors (Centers for Disease Control and Prevention, 2006; Fernandez, Bowen, Varga, Collazo, & Perrino, 2005; Hart & Peterson, 2004). In essence, gay and bisexual people of color must cope with a larger set of minority stressors that in turn helps explain the elevated rates of mental health issues, drug use, sexual risk, and HIV-infection seen in these communities.

A note on women and mental health disparities. Because the purpose of this chapter is to understand the links between substance use and sexual behavior within the context of HIV-related risk and apply this understanding to the case of Scott, the bulk of material discussed will focus on gay and bisexual men rather than lesbian, bisexual, or heterosexual women. However, it is not my intent to suggest that sexual minority women do not also experience forms of chronic minority stress and adversity that elevate their risk for particular mental health issues. In reality, quite the opposite is true.

Research supports an interaction between sexual minority status, gender, and links to mental health disparities (Cochran & Mays, 2011). Regarding mood and anxiety disorders, women in the general population have been found to be at greater risk compared to their male counterparts. Regarding substance-use disorders, however, gender-based differences vary based upon sexual minority status. While males in general tend to have higher rates of alcohol and substance-use disorders, this disparity disappears when comparing alcohol use more specifically between sexual minority males and females. By pooling estimates of 1-year prevalence rates across numerous studies, Cochran and Mays found higher rates of alcohol dependency among sexual minority women compared to heterosexual women.

Furthermore, Cochran and Mays (in press) cite literature supporting that within the population of sexual minority women, bisexual women are most at risk for mental health issues—particularly suicide attempts, alcohol misuse, and mood and anxiety disorders (Burgard, Cochran, & Mays, 2005; Kertzner, Meyer, Frost, & Stirratt, 2009). While the greater prevalence of these issues among bisexual women relative to other sexual minority women may help explain the interactions present between gender, sexual minority status, and mental health disparities, knowledge of the underlying reasons for such disparities remains limited and understudied.

Culturally Relevant Factors among Gay and Bisexual Men

The existence of a gay male culture with unique values and practices is well documented as contributing to a sense of community and collective identity (Flores, Mansergh, Marks, Guzman, & Colfax, 2009; Harper, 2007). Relative to their heterosexual counterparts, more gay and bisexual men tend to embrace the idea of polyamory[1] and nonmonogamy. Some enter into open relationships that permit sex with multiple partners in the context of their primary relationship. Other gay and bisexual men frequent commercial sex venues such as sex clubs and bathhouses for sex with casual or unknown partners. While less conventional, it is important to consider that each of these practices, if performed in the absence of substance use, can become part of a healthy and fulfilling sexual life. It is also important to appreciate the wide range of sexual behavior that exists among some gay and bisexual men while acknowledging that others adhere to traditional norms.

Research and clinical evidence suggest that some gay and bisexual male communities place considerable emphasis on physical appearance and sexual

[1] The state of being in love with multiple partners simultaneously.

marketability, with self-image and perceived acceptance significantly influenced by body image and sexual desirability (Hospers & Jansen, 2005; Martins, Tiggermann, & Kirkbride, 2007; Ricciardelli & McCabe, 2004; Siever, 1996). Through a process of sexual objectification, many gay and bisexual men modify their lifestyle in an effort to maximize their sex appeal—developing diet and exercise rituals, and coming to see themselves as sexual objects. The perceived failure to meet increasingly narrow standards of masculinity is significantly related to mental health issues including poor self-esteem, depression, and body dissatisfaction.

Peer norms related to drug use and sexual novelty in certain gay and bisexual male communities also have direct relevance to HIV-related risk behavior (Flores et al., 2009). Debate surrounds use of the term "recreational" to describe any form of drug use given the toxic effects and addictive potential of most street drugs and the tendency of some users to adopt this term in denial of a deeper problem. Still, recreational drug use is referenced in the HIV-prevention literature to describe a pattern of episodic, poly-drug use, around major club events or party weekends, that involves any combination of cocaine, ecstasy (MDMA), GHB, ketamine (K), and methamphetamine (crystal meth) (Fernandez et al., 2005; Halkitis & Parsons, 2002; Mattison, Ross, Wolfson, Franklin, & HNRC Group, 2001; Morgenstern et al., 2009). Accordingly, the terms "club drugs" and "party drugs" have become popular in the scientific press and media.

Examination of the psychopharmacological properties of these club or party drugs helps explain why recreational drug use has become socially normative in the sexual lives of many who use (Freese, Miotto, & Reback, 2002). Similar to alcohol, these drugs impact certain regions of the brain—the prefrontal cortex, which governs logic and reasoning, and the limbic system, our pleasure and reward center that governs our sexual impulses and responses. For some users, lowered inhibitions and increased sexual cravings foster a state of arousal in which sexual urges overshadow the ability to make safer sexual decisions.

The aforementioned properties are considerably pronounced and associated with HIV and other sexually transmitted infections (STIs) among gay and bisexual men who use methamphetamine (Halkitis, Green, & Carragher, 2006; Hirschfield, Remien, Walavalkar, & Chiasson, 2004; Shoptaw & Reback, 2006). While prevalence rates vary, recent findings support the presence of a small yet significant portion of gay and bisexual men who use methamphetamine (Morgenstern et al., 2009; Nanin & Parsons, 2006). For these men, behavioral changes associated with methamphetamine use increase the likelihood of risk of exposure to HIV and other STIs (Freese et al., 2002). Methamphetamine use rapidly increases levels of dopamine and serotonin (i.e., chemicals in the brain called neurotransmitters), producing a profound "rush" in which the user feels euphoric, energetic, and confident. For some, this translates into feeling more attractive, desirable, and confident of one's prowess. Patients commonly report that methamphetamine makes them feel "sexier." Methamphetamine use has also been associated with sexual stimulation, prolonged arousal, delayed orgasm, and lengthy periods of continuous sex that may include unprotected anal intercourse.

Perhaps the most alarming issue related to HIV-risk among gay and bisexual men is the phenomenon of barebacking, the intentional decision to have unprotected anal intercourse (Berg, 2009; Wolitski, 2005), although the majority of gay and bisexual men do not intentionally engage in unprotected sex. Recent studies have found that within the minority of gay and bisexual men who bareback, the trend is more frequent among those already HIV-positive (Grov et al., 2007; Parsons & Bimbi, 2007).

Some gay and bisexual men identify as part of a bareback community that normalizes and celebrates unprotected anal sex (Berg, 2009). Various theories have been proposed to explain the paradoxical emergence of the bareback community (Berg, 2009; Wolitski, 2005). The growth of bareback forums on the Internet has engendered a community replete with opportunities for sexual networking, role models who sanction bareback sex, and peer norms that oppose safer sex.

In their respective literature reviews, Berg (2009) and Wolitski (2005) suggest the broadening demographic of HIV and growth of government funding for HIV-prevention programs may cause some gay and bisexual men to view HIV as less personally relevant, and to perceive gay-specific prevention campaigns as shaming and homophobic. These perceptions can in turn propagate bareback sex as a political statement and act of rebellion against perceived sexual repression.

Bareback sex has also been connected to perceptions of heightened masculinity and the desire to define and celebrate one's manhood (Haig, 2006; Ridge, 2004). As a reaction to homonegativity, gay and bisexual men who feel emasculated may intentionally engage in unprotected sex as a means to prove one's manhood. "Raw" sex can serve both literally and symbolically as an expression of strength, power, and endurance.

Festinger's (1957) theory of cognitive dissonance provides an alternative explanation for bareback sex, suggesting that some men who bareback experience dissonance (e.g., anxiety or guilt) related to their decision to have unprotected sex, and consequently rationalize their behavior by developing beliefs that assuage their anxiety or guilt. Research suggests that bareback sex may relate to HIV-treatment advances, reductions in viral loads and concomitant beliefs about HIV-transmissibility, and the perception that HIV has become a chronic, manageable illness rather than a terminal, progressive, disabling condition (Gold, 2004; Huebner, Rebchook, & Kegeles, 2004; Kalichman, Rompa, Austin, Luke, & Difonzo, 2001; Kelly, Hoffman, Rompa, & Gray, 1998). The advent of medications such as protease inhibitors has coincided with a growing sense of relaxation of safer sexual behavior.

Additional issues that contribute to the phenomenon of barebacking are "safer sex fatigue," "AIDS burnout," and "fatalism"—the belief that one will inevitably contract HIV (Carballo-Diéguez & Bauermeister, 2004; Yi et al., 2010). The combination of prolonged efforts to adhere to safer sex and the internalization of decades of HIV-prevention campaigns may lead some gay and bisexual men to feel angry, overwhelmed by responsibility, or resigned to the idea of becoming HIV-positive. To understand the evolution of these issues, it is helpful to think about their historical context. Older generations of gay and bisexual men survived the "Pre-Stonewall" era only to live through the onset of HIV/AIDS (Morrow, 2001).

The emergence of HIV in the early 1980s created a resurgence of antigay stigma coupled with an unprecedented fear of death among gay and bisexual men. Renewed levels of shame, fear, and anger mixed with profound experiences of loss, grief, and trauma secondary to the death of multiple loved ones engendered an unfathomable state of emotional turmoil (Villa & Demmer, 2005). Issues of complicated grief and re-traumatization can understandably help to explain feelings of fatigue, burnout, and resignation that may fuel bareback sex for some gay and bisexual men.

Within the younger generation of "Post-Stonewall" gay and bisexual men, HIV-related optimism and fatalism have different bases of origin. Most gay and bisexual men born during the Post-Stonewall era do not share the older gay or bisexual man's traumatic burden of having had to bury friends and lovers. Instead, younger gay and bisexual men have benefited psychologically from the scientific advances in understanding and treating HIV. These trends help explain the growth of HIV-related optimism among many gay and bisexual youth and young adults, which translates for some into complacency and a decreased need to practice safer sex. For a small but significant minority of young gay and bisexual males, fatalistic beliefs surrounding HIV develop in response to being born amidst the HIV epidemic and having to contend with the threat of HIV throughout their entire life (Yi et al., 2010).

Individual, Intrapersonal Factors

Research assessing gay men's motivations for having recently engaged in unprotected anal intercourse revealed three major reasons: seeking physical pleasure, seeking an emotional connection and sense of intimacy with their partner, and rebelling against safer sex norms (Halkitis, Parsons, & Wilton, 2003; Mansergh et al., 2002). To enhance pleasure is the most literal and easily understood explanation for unprotected sex.

A growing body of literature supports the idea that unprotected anal intercourse represents a symbol of love, trust, and intimacy for some gay and bisexual men (Appleby, Miller, & Rothspan, 1999; Cannold, O'Loughlin, Woolcock, & Hickman, 1995; Meyer & Dean, 1998; Remien, Carballo-Diéguez, & Wagner, 1995; Theodore, Durán, Antoni, & Fernandez, 2004). While many gay and bisexual men have been able to develop healthy, committed relationships, other gay and bisexual men suffer significant damage, internalize the negative belief that gay and bisexual men cannot develop loving and committed relationships, and ultimately come to fear that they are incapable of intimacy. Some of these men in turn forego condom use in an effort to assuage their fears and feel connected to others. Across repeated acts, unprotected anal intercourse may become associated with intimacy while condoms may come to represent a barrier to intimacy.

Findings from my own research of HIV-positive men in primary relationships— defined as an emotionally committed relationship of at least 3 months—support these symbolic representations (Theodore et al., 2004). In our study, intimacy between primary partners helped explain unprotected "insertive" intercourse for participants in serodiscordant relationships (i.e., within our sample, greater intimacy increased the risk that an HIV-positive participant would "top" his HIV-negative partner without using a condom). As part of our study, we also asked participants to report the three most common reasons for not using a condom during their most recent act of unprotected sex with their primary partner, and found that the participants whose partners were HIV-negative felt the unprotected sex carried a message of intimacy and trust. Together, our findings suggested that for these participants, the act of unprotected anal intercourse appeared to be perceived as a deeply intimate expression of love and trust conferred by their HIV-negative partners.

Beyond all the factors discussed thus far in the chapter, researchers have also found that low self-esteem (Stokes & Peterson, 1998), and personality-based factors such as impulsivity and sensation-seeking (Horvath, Beadnell, & Bowen, 2006; Kalichman et al., 1994; Semple, Zians, Grant, & Patterson, 2006) are associated with unprotected anal intercourse among gay and bisexual men.

The Case of Scott: Theoretical Conceptualization

Scott is a 30-year-old, HIV-negative, white, single gay man who presents with concerns about anxiety, depression, grief over the recent death of his brother to AIDS, marijuana use, and risky sexual behavior. Scott also reports an alleged history of sexual molestation and fraud by his father.

Scott's outward appearance is that of a confident and assured young man. Given his self-referral and the level of emotion with which he describes the events surrounding his substance use and sexual and relationship histories, I believe his public persona masks that of an anxious, less secure private self. From a cognitive-behavioral perspective, my focus turns toward specific events described and statements made by Scott that suggest the origin of his negative thoughts, feelings, and beliefs. It is clear that Scott harbors significant anger and resentment against his father, and more recently is coping with conflicting sets of emotions toward his mother. Scott's reported history (i.e., reports of fraud, identity theft, and concerns of possible molestation perpetrated by his father; anger toward his mother for "not supporting her children" and protecting them from these events; recent death of his brother representing the loss of his "protector" and the one relationship Scott perceived as "unconditional") helps explain the origin and maintenance of conflicts involving abandonment, lack of trust, and fear of intimacy. Some statements made by Scott during early portions of his initial interview signify these themes:

> **P23:** (*Describing the meaning of his brother in his life*) ... I lost my, my
> protector—he was my Number One. He wasn't just my brother. You know
> he was my ego. He was my Number One—he had so much love to give me.
> It was unconditional . ...

P23: (*Switching focus to his parents*) ... but there are times when I want to be with my parents to get that solace, comfort from them and they don't bring it. In fact they give the opposite.

P28: ... having sort of anger toward my mother—her reaction when it all came out and not supporting her children and quickly going to his [*Scott's father's*] side, and not even hearing us out.

With subsequent sessions and exploratory work, I would not be surprised to learn that Scott thinks of himself as vulnerable, others as untrustworthy and undependable, and his world as unsafe. I also suspect we might eventually learn that such negative thinking is rooted in core beliefs that he is damaged, powerless, and/or unlovable. While he does not exhibit insight regarding these thoughts and beliefs, I suspect that these cognitive structures are at the root of his anger, anxiety, and depression, and that he uses marijuana to calm his anxiety, quiet his mind, and escape his depression.

Portions of Scott's intake lead me to believe that experiences of cultural and institutionalized homonegativity confirm the negative thoughts and beliefs described above. Scott apparently was aware from the age of 5 of social disapproval and the need to remain secretive and vigilant about discussing his same-sex attractions:

P35: ... we [*referring to Scott's brother*] would talk about having crushes on our counselors, our male counselors, but we knew to never talk about it beyond the two of us.

Evidence of such vigilance continued into adolescence as Scott described feeling trapped by heterosexual norms well into high school:

P70: ... I had been hooking up with girls. Knowing that I was gay, just going through the motions of girls ... feeling like I had to, when I knew I didn't want to.

So where do Scott's intimacy issues fit into the picture? Struggles with loneliness, sex, and intimacy recur throughout Scott's intake. Scott exhibits such a profound sense of loneliness and desire to feel loved, he confuses sex with love repeatedly throughout his search for intimacy. As I understand Scott, he exhibits a pattern of rushing toward intercourse that began with his first sexual experience at the age of 17 and has continued with recent casual sex-partners and men whom he has dated.

P59: ... The first guy I was with I did everything [in the same night], my first kiss with a guy, my first intercourse, my first everything was [at] 17 years old.

This pattern suggests a chronic sense of urgency to gain intimacy and connectedness. Attempting to do so, he overestimates the depth and meaning of his relationships based upon the type of sex (i.e., anal sex, protected or unprotected) he has with his partners. I believe Scott views sex, particularly unprotected sex, as a symbolic expression of intimacy and closeness and as a source of hope and optimism that he will find that perfect, romantic love whom he refers to as "the one" (P78). This symbolic association becomes both clear and alarming when Scott struggles to rationalize recent acts in which he engaged in unprotected, receptive anal sex with a casual partner on the first night. In addition to describing the physical pleasure he connects with unprotected sex, he emphasizes the cognitive and emotional value:

> **P130:** ... but it's a mental thing too ... I never had unprotected sex until my ex-boyfriend ... and, I loved being that close to him and I feel that I'm looking for that again maybe. I want that closeness, I want that intimacy.

The strength of this association and its relevance to Scott's HIV-risk must not be underestimated.

Despite Scott's desire for romance and love, I believe he holds a conflicting fear of intimacy that may stem from core beliefs that he is damaged and unlovable. I suspect Scott's intense anger toward his father stems from a sense of betrayal based on his father's reported abuses. We know that Scott resents his mother for siding with Scott's father over her own children. Logically, we can infer that Scott feels wounded by his father, and emotionally abandoned and rejected by his mother. Survivors of trauma and abuse, in their struggle to make sense of their experiences, commonly take responsibility for the abuse and develop beliefs that they are damaged and unlovable. Such beliefs would certainly explain Scott's vulnerability toward abandonment and rejection in his romantic relationships. Consider how Scott describes his two serious relationships during his interview. When describing his second and most recent relationship, Scott's initial hope and promise for romance is quickly replaced by anger and cynicism:

> **P78–P81:** ... I thought he was the one. And I was wrong. We were together for two years ... he was quite romantic. It was great ... [but] it ended up not working out. He had priorities, *his career ... He didn't even give me even the choice to make up my mind, and say what I want .... So I said look I'm not going to push myself ....* [*Italics* indicate tone of anger and resentment—conveying a sense of abandonment.]

Sensitivity toward abandonment and rejection frequently underlies difficulty managing true intimacy within relationships, causing some to seek out relationships they know are likely to fail. When describing his first serious relationship, which occurred during his junior year of college, Scott remarked that his boyfriend was "emotionally unavailable (P82)," yet ironically shared that *he* initiated their break up upon preparing to go abroad for a semester and not wanting to feel emotionally obligated to someone living back home. Prompted by an observation of Silverstein's, Scott ultimately acknowledges a pattern in which he seeks out "emotionally unavailable" men.

> **P84:** I see the pattern ... I know that I choose, I choose men ... that are *emotionally unavailable.* They give themselves to a degree and then it stops,

and that's what I'm attracted to. I've seen it time and time again. That's what I desire the most.

T86: ... Why do you do that? Why not some guy who is available?

P86: I don't know. I don't know. I don't know .... I'm a big believer in passion. And having that attraction and having that desire, and I find often that when it's too easy ... when they really go that extra mile to show that they're there for me. Or that they would be good for me. I don't like it. I like a struggle. ...

From an approach-avoidance perspective, Scott desires and moves toward passion and romance, yet distances himself from true emotional intimacy and its inherent risk of getting hurt. Unfortunately, the emotional expense of repeating the above pattern strengthens his negative thoughts. Each time a long-term relationship fails to materialize, I suspect that Scott feels increasingly despondent, desperate, and frightened that he will end up alone. In a cyclical pattern, Scott enters into the very emotional state that makes him vulnerable to unsafe sex and risk for infection with HIV and other STIs. I further suspect that amidst Scott's grieving over the profound loss of his brother, his most important attachment figure, Scott's struggles with loneliness, anxiety, and issues of abandonment will intensify—magnifying his drive to use marijuana and seek nurturance, comfort, and support through unprotected sexual intercourse.

Diagnostic considerations. Many have questioned the existence of marijuana abuse and dependence independent of recreational use. Early studies documented a withdrawal syndrome associated with high levels of marijuana use and including anger, irritability, insomnia, restlessness, nervousness, and decreased appetite (Budney & Wiley, 2001). Historically, however, these symptoms have been downplayed as mild in comparison to those associated with "harder" drugs such as cocaine, methamphetamine, heroin, and even alcohol. This has led many to ignore marijuana as a potentially disabling and addictive substance. A recent issue of *Monitor on Psychology*, the official journal of the American Psychological Association, published an article in which psychologists expressed concern that approximately 10 percent of marijuana users eventually develop dependence, and advocated for the importance of addressing treatment needs (Munsey, 2010). Research also has documented that marijuana use has been associated with abuse and dependence on other substances, and has been associated with more than twice the risk of engaging in unsafe sex among gay and bisexual men (Ross et al., 2001). I suggest exercising caution and using motivational interviewing techniques (see Bux, Chapter 10) to assess for actual abuse or dependence when working with patients like Scott who label themselves using derogatory terms and express concern about how much and how frequently she or he uses. (P107: I'm a pothead. I smoke pot. Way too much. Almost every day.) Given these statements and Scott's description that he continues to smoke pot as a way to manage his anxiety despite awareness that the pot sometimes worsens his anxiety, I believe Scott meets criteria for marijuana abuse. I suspect that, if further assessed, Scott would likely meet criteria for marijuana dependence.

Scott's description essentially amounts to a cycle of substance use propelled by negative reinforcement—smoking pot daily to quiet his mind—to "numb," "mellow out," and "stop thinking." I also suspect that Scott may have an underlying anxiety condition such as generalized anxiety disorder (GAD) which causes him to ruminate and self-medicate with marijuana. The following segment of the transcript provides some evidence for this working diagnosis:

> **T115:** Well, what thoughts are racing through your mind if you're not smoking pot?
>
> **P115:** I mean it's work related ... or it's men .... What their reactions mean. What does that movement mean? ... Or it was mostly something about my brother. Or it was the drama with my parents. Money ... the molestation thing ... thoughts that kind of flood my mind ....

While the breadth of Scott's anxiety seem to support GAD, a diagnosis would depend upon the assessment of additional information regarding the intensity, frequency, and duration of his anxiety. It is also possible that Scott's symptoms could warrant a diagnosis of substance-induced anxiety disorder (i.e., cannabis-induced anxiety disorder). Regardless of whether Scott has a distinct anxiety disorder, issues pertaining to anxiety and substance abuse or dependence would certainly be important to explore during subsequent sessions.

Assessment Guidelines and Strategies

In the spirit of LGBT-affirmation, it is exceptionally important to ask questions in a manner that affirms your patients and contextualizes their sexual behavior and substance use. Furthermore, it is important to remain sex-positive and to monitor any biases and feelings of discomfort that may arise. Issues of counter-transference are inevitable regardless of the level of clinical experience. As mental health professionals, we want to encourage open and honest exploration of our patients' sexuality and to validate the existence of sex separate from love. While continually assessing for signs of distress in our patients that may indicate the fragmentation of sex, love, and intimacy, we must remain vigilant of our own verbal and nonverbal cues that may unintentionally convey shame or judgment.

Understanding your patient's sexual identity. As a mental health professional, it is important to distinguish between a person's sexual identity and sexual behavior. Various terms such as gay, bisexual, and queer may be used by a patient to label or describe his sexual identity, but these labels are not always consistent with what would be expected based solely on the person's sexual behavior. It is possible that a male may identify himself as gay based on his attraction to other men without actually having had sex with another man. It is also possible that a male who has had sexual experiences with one or more other men may not identify as gay or bisexual and instead identify himself as heterosexual. Because a person's actual sexual identity does not always conform to behavioral definitions or societal expectations, it is best to avoid making assumptions and instead ask your patient directly about his sexual identity. The simplest and most direct question to ask is, "Do you identify as gay, bisexual, heterosexual, or do you identify with another term I have not mentioned?" Considering the variability in public disclosure of one's sexual identity (e.g., how open or "out" to others a particular patient might be about his sexual identity), I also find it important to ask patients, "How open to others are you about being (*self-reported sexual identity*)?" or "Do most other people in your life know you identify as (*self-reported sexual identity*)?"

For some patients who identify as gay or bisexual, greater disclosure of their sexual identity correlates to an increased sense of belonging to the greater gay community and lower levels of internalized homonegativity. For others, level of openness and disclosure of one's gay or bisexual identity has less to do with community affiliation and/or internalized homonegativity, but may reflect the realities of a hostile or unsafe environment in which they live, or reflect a personal or cultural orientation toward privacy. For all gay and bisexual men, issues of social support, environmental/contextual demands, internalized homonegativity, and sociocultural values should be considered but not assumed while assessing sexual identity and level of disclosure.

Sexual roles. In addition to sexual identity, issues related to sexual roles may be significant. Some gay and bisexual men identify themselves according to the sexual role they perform during anal intercourse. Those who exclusively or usually perform the insertive role during anal sex with another man sometimes identify as a "top" while those who exclusively or usually perform the receptive role during anal sex with another man sometimes identify as a "bottom." Some gay and bisexual men enjoy performing both sexual roles and identify as "versatile."

Self-identification as a "top" or "bottom" can sometimes convey multiple layers of information beyond just one's preferred sexual role. For these gay and bisexual men, identifying as a "top" may represent an attempt to resolve significant conflicts they experience between their sexual identity and gender role (i.e., their perceived sense of masculinity). Gay and bisexual men who hold more traditional views about gender roles may feel inferior as men, and need to label themselves as "tops" in a conscious effort to reaffirm their masculinity. As a potential sign of internalized homonegativity, labeling oneself a "top" may further represent a conscious effort to reduce any shame or guilt connected to being gay or bisexual.

The reverse of this issue applies to gay and bisexual men who prefer the receptive role during anal intercourse but do not feel comfortable identifying as a "bottom." For some, a reluctance to identify as a "bottom" or to endorse a preference for the bottom role stems from shame, stigma, and internalized homonegativity. For others, the shame and stigma affiliated with performing the receptive role (i.e., weaker, more effeminate position) is internalized deeply enough that anger and defensiveness surface in the face of being labeled a "bottom" by someone else.

For these reasons, while it is important to be familiar with these labels, I recommend against asking a gay or bisexual male patient, "Do you identify as a 'top' or 'bottom'?" If a patient seems familiar with these terms, I may instead ask, "Do you usually take on the role of a 'top' or a 'bottom' during anal sex?" Alternatively, albeit more formally, for patients who have not themselves introduced the label "top" or "bottom," I would advise asking "Do you usually perform the insertive role or receptive role when having anal sex?" Ultimately, of course, the level of formality you use will depend on your clinical judgment about the tone of the interview and the comfort level of your patient.

Getting to know your patient's language. Beyond sexual role labels, it is also important to familiarize yourself with other street-based and culturally relevant terms for gay and bisexual men. Doing so will help you to affirm your patient's experiences, establish rapport, and consequently encourage an open dialogue between you and your patient. This will help your patient in return feel a greater desire to open up and help you understand his life—including his sexual life.

In the following segment of Scott's transcript, Silverstein reflects the patient's language in the subsequent question.

T66: So what did you do that first night? You kissed?
P66: We had sex, we had oral sex, and anal sex.
T67: Both ways?
P67: You mean did he *fuck* me? ... No ....
T69: You *fucked* him. So that was the first time you ever did that?

In the above segment, Silverstein's matching of Scott's language (i.e., use of the term "fuck") illustrates his active listening for Scott's preferred terminology and demonstrates his desire to connect with him.

I generally recommend using informal language when discussing sexual experiences. In the previous example, Scott's use of the term "fuck" essentially gave Silverstein permission to use the term. The choice of whether to use more formal or informal language can also be based on your impression of the tone of the interview up to that point, your patient's style of communication, and your overall clinical judgment. Scott's use of informal, bold, and obscene language from early on in the interview (e.g., P14 "a lot of shit happened to me this year") gave Silverstein further permission to use informal, slang terminology, and helps to establish a strong therapeutic rapport.

Contrary to Scott, some patients regardless of their sexual identity will present as more formal and concerned with social etiquette, and may shut down in response to the use of informal, sexual slang. With more formal patients, I recommend asking the patient directly what terms he prefers to use when discussing sex with others (e.g., "What terms do you typically use with your sex-partners or friends when discussing sex?"). This helps give the patient a sense of comfort and control over how the discussion progresses. Extremely shy and private patients may respond by telling you, "I don't really talk about sex with others." In such instances, it is best to respect patients' boundaries by asking them if they feel comfortable enough to answer a few questions about their sexual history. I also recommend normalizing the patient's discomfort as something experienced by many and reminding the patient about your responsibility to maintain confidentiality.

Behavioral specificity and level of sexual risk. Learning to translate your patient's sexual language into precise behavioral terminology is very important in allowing you to evaluate your patient's level of risk for HIV and other STIs. Specifically, your patient's sexual risk depends upon the type of sexual behavior, frequency of sexual behavior and use of condoms, and number of sexual partners. In general, level of HIV-risk among gay men is based upon exposure to blood or seminal fluid (including pre-cum) containing the virus, with unprotected receptive anal intercourse (i.e., having anal sex without a condom as the bottom), followed by unprotected insertive anal intercourse (i.e., having anal sex without a condom as the top), representing the two riskiest sexual behaviors. Providing oral sex to, and receiving oral sex from, another man without using a condom are less risky for HIV transmission but carry risk for the transmission of other STIs such as oral and genital herpes simplex virus (HSV), gonorrhea, and chlamydia. While rubbing against one another naked, massaging another's penis and fingering one's anal cavity are considered relatively safe with respect to HIV, genital and anal warts (i.e., symptoms of human papilloma virus—HPV) are easily transmitted via skin to skin contact. Understanding the behavioral risks for exposure to STIs beyond HIV has important implications for HIV disease progression and potential reinfection among those who are already HIV-positive, and for the efficiency of transmission of HIV and other STIs themselves.

The following few examples from Scott's interview help illustrate the importance of behavioral specificity, precision and detail when evaluating a patient's level of sexual risk. In the first segment, Silverstein seeks to clarify which sexual role Scott performed when he references having had "consistent anal sex."

P90: ... he was really the first person with whom I had consistent anal sex ....
T91: You're talking about fucking him?
P91: No, fucking me.

Understanding that Scott was consistently assuming the receptive, bottom, role became very important later during the interview when it became apparent he was talking about his most recent boyfriend with whom he began to have unprotected sex.

The next two examples illustrate the importance of precision and detail when obtaining information about a patient's frequency or amount of sexual activity:

T126: You stayed there for 72 hours and how many times did he fuck you without a condom?
P126: I don't remember, I couldn't even say—four or five times.

In the above example, notice that even a single sexual situation may contain multiple sexual acts. Although not relevant for Scott, it is important to remember that patients who pair drugs such as methamphetamine with sex, commonly engage in prolonged periods of sex containing serial acts of intercourse that cumulatively increase the risk of exposure to HIV and other STIs. The second example pertains to the relationship between risk of exposure to HIV and other STIs and number of sexual partners. In this example, by seeking clarification on what Scott means when using the phrase "a lot of sex," notice how Silverstein obtains more accurate information about Scott's actual number of sexual partners and changes in Scott's sexual activity over time.

> **T93:** What do you mean by I've had a lot of sex?
> **P93:** It's all relative.
> **T94:** Exactly, that's why I'm asking.
> **P94:** I mean, prior to him I guess I had slept with maybe three or four guys, and since him the numbers have tripled, so probably somewhere in the teens . . ..

When assessing a patient's recent and past sexual activity, important information is also found in the contextual details surrounding the activity. Identifying the cognitive, emotional, and situational/environmental factors that precede and follow sex—particularly unprotected sex—is considerably useful when seeking to understand patterns of sexual risk. A simple, direct set of questions you might ask to obtain such information about a specific episode of sex follows:

> **T:** What thoughts went through your mind just before you had unprotected sex with [sex-partner's name]?
> **T:** How did you feel just before you had unprotected sex with [sex-partner's name]?
> **T:** And how did you feel after you had unprotected sex with [sex-partner's name]?

Patients who have limited insight about such matters may require more indirect methods of assessment. For such patients, it can be useful to ask the following:

> **T:** Tell me more about the events leading up to the sex you just described. What was going on around you just before you and [sex-partner's name] had sex? [*Listen for situational and environmental factors.*]

This type of question facilitates recall and may elicit details the patient did not initially think were important. Another useful question is to ask the patient to think about specific factors that prevented him from practicing safer sex. Silverstein demonstrates this during Scott's interview when he asks, "What stopped you from saying, 'Use a condom. Put it on.'?" (T130) Alternatively, when possible, it can also be useful to ask a patient to select two distinct sexual situations—one in which he had unsafe sex and another in which he had safer sex—and then ask him to contrast the two situations:

> **T:** What was different for you during the time you had unsafe sex versus the time you had safer sex?

Gathering an overview of your patient's sexual history. Your ability to obtain a comprehensive overview of your patient's sexual history will vary depending on your patient's age, age at the time of his first sexual experience, and quantity of sexual partners since that first sexual experience. When working with a patient who has had a large number of casual sex-partners or romantic relationships, I recommend that you just get a snapshot of the more important sexual experiences and relationships for your patient. In such cases, ask your patient to "approximate" their total number of lifetime sexual partners, total number of boyfriends (*or patient's preferred term*), and number of sexual partners in the past month, but limit the more detailed assessment of relevant thoughts, emotions, and contextual factors to your patient's earliest sexual experience and most recent sexual experience. Silverstein does this when asking Scott, "When was the first time you had sex with a man to orgasm?" (T57) and later when asking, "Well, when was the last time you had sex?" (T95)

Counter-transference issues. When conducting sexual histories with gay and bisexual men, we must anticipate the possibility of hearing reports of unprotected anal intercourse or intentional barebacking, and the variety of counter-transference issues (i.e., emotional reactions) that may surface in response to such reports (Cole, 2007; Shernoff, 2004). Counter-transference responses I have wrestled with when working with patients on issues pertaining to unprotected sex include various combinations of anger, disappointment, judgment, anxiety, alarm, and concern. Which emotions will surface for you in response to reports of unprotected anal intercourse will likely vary depending upon your sexual identity, your HIV status, your patient's HIV status, and your patient's age/generational cohort (e.g., Pre-Stonewall versus Post-Stonewall). The greater the similarity in demographics and experiences between ourselves and a patient, the greater the risk of over-identifying with that patient, developing intense personal reactions toward them, and losing our ability to remain neutral when assessing highly stigmatized and controversial sexual behaviors.

In the face of anger and disappointment, we become more likely to lose our patience and become irritable, to inadvertently judge our patients, and to ask questions in a manner that causes them to feel guilty, ashamed, and defensive. In addition to damaging therapeutic rapport, we risk our patients shutting down and withholding important information regarding sexual risk and potential drug use. In the face of anxiety, we may struggle out of concern and alarm with the impulse to "correct" our patients' sexual behavior, to "rescue" our patients from themselves, and to "protect" their sexual partners from potential harm. Such impulses certainly may influence the manner in which we ask interview questions and the level to which we dissect the sexual risk scenario. If not careful, we risk developing a tone of authority and discipline that once again may elicit guilt or shame in our patients.

The following examples from Scott's initial interview will allow us to more fully examine how counter-transference can influence the assessment of sexual risk behaviors. Revisiting the following segment from Scott's transcript, the bracketed and italicized portions represent areas where I detected signs of counter-transference I believe impacted the content of Scott's responses.

T93: [*Interrupting*] What do you mean by I've had a lot of sex?
P93: It's all relative.

T94: Exactly, that's why I'm asking. [tone of frustration]

P94: I mean, prior to him I guess I had slept with maybe three or four guys, and since him the numbers have tripled, so probably somewhere in the teens ....

T98: So you're saying that you had a lot of sex. *This doesn't sound like a lot of sex. [nurturing, paternal tone]*

In the above segment Silverstein's interruption of Scott and tone of frustration represent products of anger and concern that may have surfaced in reaction to Scott's reported increase in receptive anal sex (e.g., bottoming) with casual sex-partners. It illustrates why it is so important to monitor our personal reactions to what patients tell us. We want to avoid letting our own emotions unintentionally influence our tone of voice and phrasing of statements and questions formed while clinical interviewing. If, as I suspect, Silverstein was experiencing a mixture of anger and concern for Scott, it is possible that in his effort to clarify a discrepancy in reported sexual behavior, Silverstein was fulfilling his own need to manage his anger and concern by reassuring himself that Scott was not having a lot of sex. An alternative method to clarify discrepant information that carries less risk of appearing argumentative, judgmental, or paternal is to reflect one's confusion and ask for clarification through inflection:

T: I'm a little confused by something you said Scott. You noted that you have had a lot of sex recently but now it sounds like you have only had sex once in about 3 months (*ending this statement with an inflection that suggests a question*).

A separate segment of the interview illustrates the reciprocal influence between Scott's transference and Silverstein's counter-transference relative to Scott's sexual risk behavior. It also demonstrates the ease with which even experienced therapists can unintentionally exacerbate issues of guilt and shame within their patients when discussing issues related to sex and HIV.

T121: ... Do you have safe sex?

P121: I mean, I, I'm pretty good, but I fucked up a lot, this past year.

T122: Meaning?

P122: Meaning I didn't have safe sex.

T123: Meaning you let guys fuck you without a condom?

P123: Right.

T124: Why would you do that? [tone of disapproval]

P124: I don't know. Stupid. Stupid. There's no explanation for it.

T125: (Interrupting) Can I assume these are just tricks you're talking about?

P125: No, no. 'Cause like I say, I'm risky but I'm not that risky ....

Guilt and shame felt by Scott is reflected at the outset of the above segment when Scott proclaims "I fucked up a lot this past year." These emotions are projected (e.g., transferred) onto Silverstein who follows up with a question that casts judgment—"Why would you do that?"—to which Scott replies with increased guilt, shame, and self-deprecation—"I don't know. Stupid. Stupid. There's no explanation for it." Silverstein's next response, which contains an assumption that Scott had unprotected sex with a series of "tricks," increases Scott's sense of perceived judgment to which Scott recoils in defense by stating, "... I'm risky, but I'm not that risky," and subsequently rationalizes his behavior as less risky because he allows himself to have unprotected sex only with partners whom he is dating and for whom he feels the promise of a developing relationship.

Substance use, abuse, and dependence. Analogous to obtaining a sexual history, assessment of substance use is a complex task that requires sensitivity toward perceived shame and judgment, and a high degree of behavioral specificity. It is important to understand the sequence of thoughts surrounding the substance use. If a patient uses a term with which you are unfamiliar, do not be afraid to ask what he means and simply make a note of it. Some of the more common terms used among gay and bisexual male substance users of which I am aware include "Crystal," "Meth," and "Tina" for methamphetamine; "Coke" for cocaine; "G" for GHB; "K" or "Special K" for ketamine; and "E" or "X" for ecstasy.

I suggest reviewing the criteria sets contained within the DSM-IV-TR for the criteria in order to diagnose substance use, abuse, and dependence (APA, 2000). Sometimes, the specific quantity and frequency of substance use will serve as a clue that a substance-use disorder exists. Regarding alcohol, *more* than sixty drinks per month (i.e., *more* than two drinks per day) is a red flag (Morrison, 2008). The best way to approximate the average number or drinks per month is to ask the following and multiply the two responses:

> T: In an average month, on how many days would you say you have at least one drink of alcohol?
> T: On an average day when you drink, how many drinks would you say you have?

In calculating the number of drinks per month, keep in mind that a 12-oz. beer, a 5-oz. glass of wine, and a 1.5-oz. shot of 80-proof hard liquor contain roughly the same alcohol content. The same set of questions can be used to approximate the average quantity and frequency of use of other drugs by substituting your patient's drug(s) of choice for alcohol, and using the street terms referenced earlier.

Diagnostically, the presence of a substance-use disorder relates more to the consequences of substance use on your patient's life and functioning than the specific quantity of the substance used. For patients who endorse a history of substance use, regardless of the amount they use, follow up with questions about any current or past medical, legal, psychological, social/interpersonal, and/or job-related difficulties experienced in connection with their substance use as these represent signs of "abuse." Some examples, alternating between substances for illustrative purposes only, follow:

> T: Have you ever experienced any shakes or tremors hours after drinking? How many times has this happened?

T: Do you tend to get into more arguments or fights with people when you have been drinking?

T: Have you ever felt more anxious or had a panic attack when you have been stoned?

T: Do you find yourself feeling significantly depressed when coming down from meth?

T: Do you find yourself calling out from work on days after you have partied with meth?

A brief assessment tool that can aid in screening out whether a patient's substance use meets the criteria for abuse or dependence as defined in the DSM-IV-TR (APA, 2000) is to ask four questions that line up with the acronym CAGE (Ewing, 1984). A response of "Yes" to any of the following questions indicates a high probability that your patient has a substance-use disorder:

C: Have you ever tried to *cut down* how much you drink?

A: Have any friends or family ever become *annoyed* and expressed concern to you about your drinking?

G: Have you ever felt *guilty* about your drinking?

E: Have you ever had a drink *early in the morning* to chase away a hangover?

Considering the strong associations of substance use, sex, and HIV-related risk for some gay and bisexual men, the following set of questions is also quite important. Particularly true of chronic methamphetamine users, remember that some patients may have difficulty remembering a time that they have had sex while they were not under the influence of methamphetamine or some other drug. Several important questions related to this issue, some purposefully closed-ended, follow. One or more of these questions may be asked as appropriate:

T: How often do sex and drugs go together for you? [Provide the following response options: Never, Rarely, Sometimes, Often, or Always]

T: Can you remember a time when you had sex without *Drug X*?

T: When you get high on *Drug X*, do you find yourself thinking a lot about sex? If so, what thoughts pop into your mind?

T: When you get high on *Drug X*, have you ended up having sex? If so, describe what type of sex you have had and whether or not you used a condom?

T: Tell me about any differences you have noticed in your thoughts and feelings before you have sex without *Drug X* compared to when you have sex drunk or high.

When working with the subset of gay or bisexual men for whom drug use and sex are strongly linked, keep in mind that HIV-related risk is most elevated among those who are indigent and homeless, and/or have been involved in commercial sex-work (e.g., worked as escorts, hustlers, or prostitutes). Therefore, it is extremely important to listen for information that reveals a history of having sex in exchange for money, drugs, or housing. On this one set of topics, however, I would refrain from asking direct questions during the first interview without sufficient reason.

The challenges of underreporting, resistance, and denial. When assessing substance use, patients commonly underreport their frequency and quantity of substance use. Stigma, criminalization, and subsequent guilt and shame help explain this tendency. For example, consider Scott's descriptions of his marijuana and alcohol use during the intake:

> **P107:** I'm a pot head. I smoke pot. Way too much. Almost every day. Um, I'm a drinker but I'm not an uncontrolled drinker ... I'm very controlled ....

To increase openness and comfort for your patient to discuss substance use, it is helpful to phrase questions in a manner that helps normalize substance use and facilitates discussion. When transitioning into the Drug and Alcohol History portion of an intake, I usually avoid beginning with closed question such as "Have you ever used drugs?" because they invite short responses and increase the likelihood of the patient answering "No" out of social desirability. Instead, I rely upon "open" questions that invite self-disclosure and exploration of "experimentation" with drugs. For example:

> **T:** What drugs you have used or experimented with in your life?

Silverstein offers a variation of this question when transitioning to the substance use history portion of Scott's intake (T107: What about your history of alcohol and recreational drugs?). Some patients will openly respond with a description of the first, and possibly only, time they used drugs or they may tell you that they have never used drugs. In the latter case, it is a good idea to elaborate that you are interested to know about alcohol, over-the-counter and prescription drugs, as well as street drugs. This opens the door for patients who may have intentionally or unintentionally overlooked pain medications and more socially sanctioned drugs such as alcohol and marijuana. In Scott's case, his defenses came out in response to Silverstein's first question when he proclaimed that his drinking is "very controlled" (P107) and shortly after seemed irritated when he reported: (P109). "I don't think anything is wrong with having a drink or two by myself before I go out or if I'm going to stay home alone." Such responses are insightful for you as a clinician in better understanding the patient's potential judgments and morals surrounding substance use, and can open the window for exploring such views in subsequent sessions.

For patients who do report a history of drug use, I recommend asking several follow-up questions because it is important to understand the cognitive, emotional, and environmental factors surrounding the substance use. Requesting a narrative of their first experience with drugs can be quite helpful toward this goal. For example:

> **T:** You told me that you have tried pot a few times. Tell me about the first time you ever tried pot.

Depending on the details shared by your patient, you can then follow up with the sets of questions described earlier to assess more fully the patient's current level of use. In Scott's case, Silverstein's question to Scott (T114: Why do you think you smoke so much pot?), elicited a wealth of information about his thoughts and feelings connected to marijuana, his duration of use, and the value he attributes to using.

> **P114:** ... I love it, I mean I've been doing it since I was 13 years old.... I find it very, very difficult to quiet myself, to relax, and my mind's always racing. And marijuana is like the one thing that just stops everything.

During the process of assessing a patient's substance use, it is also important to make note of how the patient self-identifies. In Scott's case, he rapidly identified himself as a "pot head," but remember that he was very quick to make sure Silverstein was aware that he doesn't have a drinking problem (i.e., as he is reportedly "very controlled" in his drinking). Many people, gay or not, when first entering treatment have difficulty applying the terms "alcoholic" and/or "addict" to themselves, and will be equally turned off by the label "problem drinker." With this type of patient, you are likely to get more information by simply and directly asking the patient to describe his current level of use of drugs or alcohol, or presenting the patient with a variety of choices from which he may choose to describe his current level of use. You can then reflect the choice back to your patient and ask him to elaborate the meaning of his choice. Consider the following scenario:

> **T:** Would you currently describe yourself as a nondrinker, a social drinker, or concerned about your drinking?
> **P:** I'd say more of a social drinker.
> **T:** Okay. Tell me why you feel you're a social drinker. What does the phrase "social drinker" mean to you?

Legal and Ethical Challenges and Controversies

Substance use and sexual behavior among gay and bisexual men are shadowed by layers of legal and ethical issues that mandate careful adherence to professional ethics boards, national and state-specific legal statutes, and considerable reflection of one's personal set of morals, especially how one's own HIV status affects the course of the interview. I highly recommend that you seek supervision throughout your training and consult as necessary once you are licensed.

Perhaps one of the most pressing issues for mental health providers concerns the recognition of suicidal and homicidal ideation. While a full discussion of risk management is beyond the scope of this chapter, it is important to consider these issues within the context of HIV and sexual transmission. The overarching question is do we have the legal and ethical responsibility to report an HIV-positive patient to legal authorities if we have knowledge that he has had or intends to have unprotected sex with another person? In the state of California, licensed psychologists may reveal a patient's HIV status only if she or he has knowledge that the patient has *willfully lied* about his status to his sex-partner, and the patient has communicated malicious intent to harm his sex-partner (i.e., to transmit HIV to a reasonably identifiable person). Simply knowing that a patient has not disclosed his HIV status to a sex-partner yet plans to have unprotected sex with that partner is not legal grounds in and of itself to violate a patient's confidentiality. In such a scenario, it is possible that the patient's sexual partner did not ask about his HIV status and the patient did not wish to volunteer the information. Here the idea of mutual responsibility becomes important as the patient, or you, the mental health provider, can make the argument that the HIV-negative partner has an equal responsibility to protect himself from possible infection by requiring his partner(s) use a condom.

So what about the reverse scenario in which an HIV-negative man intentionally has unprotected sex with someone he knows is HIV-positive or whose status is unknown? Throughout this chapter, I have reviewed evidence suggesting that while this occurrence is rare, it is a significant issue. With such a patient, we must consider the variety of psychological issues discussed in the section on barebacking such as HIV-related fatigue, safer-sex burnout, resignation about becoming HIV-infected, HIV-related optimism, and the desire for intimacy and love regardless of HIV-risk. Legally and ethically, however, we must also explore the possibility that the patient is depressed, hopeless, and no longer values life. In this context, some mental health professionals have conceptualized barebacking as a self-destructive impulse that borders on suicidal behavior. Regardless of where you stand on this issue, I am unaware of any legal precedent that supports reporting someone as actively and imminently suicidal based solely on the decision to have unprotected sex with someone who is HIV-positive. Personally, I lean in favor of protecting such a patient's confidentiality with the hope of keeping the patient in treatment. While I would certainly monitor for signs of depression and assess for suicidality, in their absence, I would rely on motivational interviewing (Miller & Rollnick, 1991) and the transtheoretical model (Prochaska & DiClemente, 1986) to facilitate movement toward safer sexual behavior (see Bux, Chapter 10).

If You Want to Learn More About Sex, Drugs, and HIV

Berg, R. C. (2009). Barebacking: A review of the literature. *Archives of Sexual Behavior*, *38*, 754−764.

Finnegan, D. G., & McNally, E. B. (2002). *Counseling lesbian, gay, bisexual, and transgender substance abusers: Dual identities*. New York: Haworth Press.

Morrison, J. (2008). Sensitive subjects. In *The first interview* (3rd ed., pp. 92−109). New York: The Guilford Press.

Shoptaw, S., & Frosch, D. (2000). Substance abuse treatment as HIV prevention for men who have sex with men. *AIDS and Behavior*, *4*(2), 193−203.

References

American Psychiatric Association (2000). *Diagnostic and statistical manual of mental disorders* (4th ed., text revision). Washington, DC: Author.

Appleby, P. R., Miller, L. C., & Rothspan, S. (1999). The paradox of trust for male couples: When risking is a part of loving. *Personal Relationships, 6*, 81–93.

Berg, R. C. (2009). Barebacking: A review of the literature. *Archives of Sexual Behavior, 38*, 754–764.

Budney, A. J., & Wiley, J. (2001). Can marijuana use lead to marijuana dependence. In M. E. Carroll, & J. B. Overmier (Eds.), *Animal research and human health: Advancing human welfare through behavioral science* (pp. 115–126). Washington, DC: American Psychological Association.

Burgard, S. A., Cochran, S. D., & Mays, V. M. (2005). Alcohol and tobacco use patterns among heterosexually and homosexually experienced California women. *Drug & Alcohol Dependence, 77*(1), 61–70.

Cannold, L., O'Loughlin, B., Woolcock, G., & Hickman, B. (1995). HIV as a catalyst for positive gay men's desire for clarification, enhancement and promotion of intimacy in significant relationships. *Journal of Psychology and Human Sexuality, 7*(1/2), 161–179.

Carballo-Diéguez, A., & Bauermeister, J. (2004). "Barebacking": Intentional condomless anal sex in HIV risk contexts. Reasons for and against it. *Journal of Homosexuality, 47*, 1–16.

Centers for Disease Control and Prevention (2006). Racial/ethnic disparities in diagnoses of HIV/AIDS—33 states, 2001–2004. *MMWR Weekly, 55*, 121–125.

Cochran, S.D. & Mays, V.M. (2011). A systematic review of sexual orientation and the prevalence of mental health disorders: Implications for research and mental health services. In C. J. Patterson & A. R. D'Augelli (Eds.), *Handbook of psychology and sexual orientation*. London: Oxford University Press.

Cole, G. W. (2007). Barebacking: Transformations, dissociations, and the theatre of countertransference. *Studies in Gender and Sexuality, 8*(1), 49–68.

Ewing, J. A. (1984). Detecting alcoholism: The CAGE questionnaire. *Journal of American Medical Association, 252*, 1905–1907.

Fernandez, M. I, Bowen, G. S., Varga, L. M., Collazo, J. B., & Perrino, T. (2005). High rates of club drug use and risky sexual practices among Hispanic men who have sex with men in Miami, Florida. *Substance Use and Misuse, 40*, 1347–1362.

Fernandez, M. I., Warren, J. C., Varga, L. M., Prado, G., Hernandez, N., & Bowen, G. S. (2007). Cruising in cyber space: Comparing internet chat rooms versus community venues for recruiting Hispanic men who have sex with men to participate in prevention studies. *Journal of Ethnicity in Substance Abuse, 6*(2), 143–162.

Festinger, L. (1957). *A theory of cognitive dissonance*. Palo Alto, CA: Stanford University Press.

Flores, S. A., Mansergh, G., Marks, G., Guzman, R., & Colfax, G. (2009). Gay identity-related factors and sexual risk among men who have sex with men in San Francisco. *AIDS Education and Prevention, 21*(2), 91–103.

Freese, T. E., Miotto, K., & Reback, C. J. (2002). The effects and consequences of selected club drugs. *Journal of Substance Abuse Treatment, 23*, 151–156.

Frost, D. M., & Meyer, I. H. (2009). Internalized homophobia and relationship quality among lesbians, gay men and bisexuals. *Journal of Counseling Psychology, 56*(1), 97–109.

Gold, R. S. (2004). Explaining gay men's unrealistic optimism about becoming infected with HIV. *International Journal of STD and AIDS, 15*, 99−102.

Grov, C., DeBusk, J. A., Bimbi, D. S., Golub, S. A., Nanin, J. E., & Parsons, J. T. (2007). Barebacking, the internet and harm reduction: An intercept survey with gay and bisexual men in Los Angeles and New York City. *AIDS and Behavior, 11*, 527−536.

Haig, T. (2006). Bareback sex, masculinity, silence, and the dilemmas of gay health. *Canadian Journal of Communication, 31*, 859−877.

Halkitis, P. N., Green, K. A., & Carragher, D. J. (2006). Methamphetamine use, sexual behavior, and HIV seroconversion. *Journal of Gay and Lesbian Psychotherapy, 10*(3/4), 95−109.

Halkitis, P. N., & Parsons, J. T. (2002). Recreational drug use and HIV-risk sexual behavior among men frequenting gay social venues. *Journal of Gay and Lesbian Social Services, 14*(4), 19−38.

Halkitis, P. N., Parsons, J. T., & Wilton, L. (2003). Barebacking among gay and bisexual men in New York City: Explanations for the emergence of intentional unsafe behavior. *Archives of Sexual Behavior, 32*, 351−358.

Hamilton, C. J., & Mahalik, J. R. (2009). Minority stress, masculinity and social norms predicting gay men's health risk behaviors. *Journal of Counseling Psychology, 56*(1), 132−141.

Harper, G. W. (2007). Sex isn't that simple: Culture and context in HIV prevention interventions for gay and bisexual male adolescents. *American Psychologist, 62*(8), 806−819.

Hart, T. A., & Peterson, J. L. (2004). Predictors of risky sexual behavior among young African-American men who have sex with men. *American Journal of Public Health, 94*(7), 1122−1124.

Herek, G. M. (1986). On heterosexual masculinity. *American Behavioral Scientist, 29*, 563−577.

Hirschfield, S., Remien, R. H., Walavalkar, I., & Chiasson, M. A. (2004). Crystal methamphetamine use predicts incident STD infection among men who have sex with men recruited online: A nested case-control study. *Journal of Medical Internet Research, 6*, 41.

Horvath, K. G., Beadnell, B., & Bowen, A. M. (2006). Sensation seeking as a moderator of internet use on sexual risk taking among men who have sex with men. *Sexuality Research and Social Policy: A Journal of NSRC, 3*(4), 77−90.

Hospers, H. J., & Jansen, A. (2005). Why homosexuality is a risk factor for eating disorders in males. *Journal of Social and Clinical Psychology, 24*, 1188−1201.

Huebner, D. M., Rebchook, G. M., & Kegeles, S. M. (2004). A longitudinal study of the association between treatment optimism and sexual risk behavior in young adult gay and bisexual men. *Journal of Acquired Immune Deficiency Syndrome, 37*, 1514−1519.

Kalichman, S. C., Johnson, J. R., Adair, V., Rompa, D., Multhauf, K., & Kelly, J. A. (1994). Sexual sensation seeking: Scale development and predicting AIDS risk behavior among homosexually active men. *Journal of Personality Assessment, 62*(3), 385−397.

Kalichman, S. C., Rompa, D., Austin, J., Luke, W., & DiFonzo, K. (2001). Viral load, perceived infectivity, and unprotected intercourse. *Journal of Acquired Immune Deficiency Syndromes, 28*, 303−305.

Kelly, J. A., Hoffman, R. G., Rompa, D., & Gray, M. (1998). Protease inhibitor combination therapies and perceptions of gay men regarding AIDS severity and the need to maintain safer sex. *AIDS, 12*, F91−F95.

Kertzner, R. M., Meyer, I. H., Frost, D. M., & Stirratt, M. J. (2009). Social and psychological well-being in lesbians, gay men, and bisexuals: The effects of race, gender, age, and sexual identity. *American Journal of Orthopsychiatry, 79*(4), 500−510.

Lewis, L., & Ross, M. (1995). *A select body: The gay dance party subculture and the HIV/AIDS pandemic*. New York: Cassell.

Malyon, A. K. (1982). Psychotherapeutic implications of internalized homophobia in gay men. *Journal of Homosexuality*, 7(2), 59–69.

Mansergh, G., Marks, G., Colfax, G. N., Guzman, R., Rader, M., & Buchbinder, S. (2002). 'Barebacking' in a diverse sample of men who have sex with men. *AIDS*, 16, 653–659.

Martins, Y., Tiggermann, M., & Kirkbride, A. (2007). Those speedos become them: The role of self-objectification in gay and heterosexual men's body image. *Personality and Social Psychology Bulletin*, 33, 634–647.

Mattison, A. M., Ross, M. W., Wolfson, T., Franklin, D., & HNRC Group (2001). Circuit party attendance, club drug use, and unsafe sex in gay men. *Journal of Substance Abuse*, 13, 119–126.

Mayfield, W. M. (2001). The development of an internalized homonegativity inventory for gay men. *Journal of Homosexuality*, 41(2), 53–76.

Meyer, I. H. (2003). Prejudice, social stress and mental health in lesbian, gay and bisexual populations: Conceptual issues and research evidence. *Psychological Bulletin*, 129(5), 674–697.

Meyer, I. H., & Dean, L. (1995). Patterns of sexual behavior and risk taking among young New York City gay men. *AIDS Education and Prevention*, 7(Suppl.), 13–23.

Meyer, I. H., & Dean, L. (1998). Internalized homophobia, intimacy, and sexual behavior among gay and bisexual men. In G. M. Herek (Ed.), *Stigma and sexual orientation: Understanding prejudice against lesbians, gay men, and bisexuals* (pp. 160–186). Thousand Oaks, CA: Sage.

Miller, W. R., & Rollnick, S. (1991). *Motivational interviewing: Preparing people to change addictive behavior*. New York: The Guilford Press.

Morgenstern, J., Bux, D. A., Parsons, J., Hagman, B. T., Wainberg, M., & Irwin, T. (2009). Randomized trial to reduce club drug use and HIV risk behaviors among men who have sex with men. *Journal of Consulting and Clinical Psychology*, 77(4), 645–656.

Morrison, J. (2008). Sensitive subjects. In *The first interview* (3rd ed., pp. 92–109). New York: The Guilford Press.

Morrow, D. F. (2001). Older gays and lesbians: Surviving a generation of hate and violence. *Journal of Gay and Lesbian Social Services*, 13, 151–169.

Munsey, C. (2010). Medicine or menace? Psychologists research can inform the growing debate over legalizing marijuana. *Monitor on Psychology*, 41(6), 50–51.

Nanin, J. E., & Parsons, J. T. (2006). Club drug use and risky sex among gay and bisexual men in New York City. *Journal of Gay and Lesbian Mental Health*, 10(3), 111–122.

Parsons, J. T., & Bimbi, D. S. (2007). Intentional unprotected anal intercourse among men who have sex with men: Barebacking—from behavior to identity. *AIDS and Behavior*, 11, 277–287.

Parsons, J. T., Severino, J. P., Grov, C., Bimbi, D. S., & Morgenstern, J. (2007). Internet use among gay and bisexual men with compulsive sexual behavior. *Sexual Addiction and Compulsivity*, 14(3), 239–256.

Pavlov, I. P. (1927). *Conditioned reflexes*. New York: Oxford University Press.

Preston, D. B., D'Augelli, A. R., Kassab, C. D., Cain, R. C., Schulze, F. W., & Starks, M. T. (2004). The influence of stigma on the sexual risk behavior of rural men who have sex with men. *AIDS Education and Prevention*, 16(4), 291–303.

Prochaska, J. O., & DiClemente, C. C. (1986). Toward a comprehensive model of change. In W. R. Miller, & N. Heather (Eds.), *Treating addictive behaviors: Processes of change* (pp. 3–27). New York: Plenum.

Remien, R. H., Carballo-Diéguez, A., & Wagner, G. (1995). Intimacy and sexual risk behavior in serodiscordant male couples. *AIDS Care, 7*(4), 429−438.

Ricciardelli, L. A., & McCabe, M. P. (2004). A biopsychosocial model of disordered eating and the pursuit of muscularity in adolescent boys. *Psychological Bulletin, 130,* 179−205.

Ridge, D. T. (2004). "It was an incredible thrill": The social meanings and dynamics of younger gay men's experiences of barebacking in Melbourne. *Sexualities, 7,* 259−279.

Ross, M. W., Rosser, S. B. R., Bauer, G. R., Bockting, W. O., Robinson, B. E., & Rugg, D. L., et al. (2001). Drug use, unsafe sexual behavior, and internalized homonegativity in men who have sex with men. *AIDS and Behavior, 5*(1), 97−103.

Semple, S. J., Zians, J., Grant, I., & Patterson, T. L. (2006). Methamphetamine use, impulsivity, and sexual risk behavior among HIV-positive men who have sex with men. *Journal of Addictive Diseases, 25*(4), 105−114.

Shernoff, M. (2004). Barebacking and challenges to therapeutic neutrality. *Journal of Gay and Lesbian Social Services, 17*(4), 59−68.

Shidlo, A. (1994). Internalized homophobia: Conceptual and empirical issues in measurement. In B. Greene, & G. M. Herek (Eds.), *Lesbian and gay psychology: Theory, research, and clinical applications* (pp. 176−205). Thousand Oaks, CA: Sage.

Shoptaw, S., & Frosch, D. (2000). Substance abuse treatment as HIV prevention for men who have sex with men. *AIDS and Behavior, 4*(2), 193−203.

Shoptaw, S., & Reback, C. J. (2006). Associations between methamphetamine use and HIV among men who have sex with men: A model for guiding public policy. *Journal of Urban Health, 83*(6), 1151−1157.

Siever, M. D. (1996). The perils of sexual objectification: Sexual orientation, gender, and socioculturally acquired vulnerability to body dissatisfaction and eating disorders (pp. 223−247). In *Gay and lesbian mental health: A sourcebook for practitioners.* New York: Haworth Park Press.

Skinner, B. F. (1963). Operant behavior. *American Psychologist, 18*(8), 503−515.

Stall, R., & Purcell, D. W. (2000). Intertwining epidemics: A review of research on substance use among men who have sex with men and its connection to the AIDS epidemic. *AIDS and Behavior, 4*(2), 181−192.

Stokes, J., & Peterson, J. L. (1998). Homophobia, self-esteem, and risk for HIV among African-American men who have sex with men. *AIDS Education and Prevention, 10*(3), 278−292.

Theodore, P. S., Durán, R. F., Antoni, M. H., & Fernandez, M. I. (2004). Intimacy and sexual behavior among HIV-positive men-who-have-sex-with-men. *AIDS and Behavior, 8*(3), 321−331.

Villa, D. P., & Demmer, C. (2005). Exploring the link between AIDS-related grief and unsafe sex. *Illness, Crisis & Loss, 13*(3), 219−233.

Wolitski, R. J. (2005). The emergence of barebacking among gay and bisexual men in the United States: A public health perspective. *Journal of Gay and Lesbian Psychotherapy, 9*(3), 9−34.

Yi, H., Sandfort, T. G. M., & Shidlo, A. (2010). Effects of disengagement coping with HIV risk on unprotected sex among HIV-negative gay men in New York City. *Health Psychology, 29*(2), 205−214.

Part Three

Treatment Modalities

10 Motivational Interviewing for Health Behavior Problems

Donald Bux

Montefiore Medical Center, Bronx, NY, USA

This initial session with Scott covers a great deal of ground, and many important issues were revealed in a single hour. Nevertheless, any two therapists will inevitably move a given session in different directions depending on their respective experience and training. From my perspective as a specialist in motivational and cognitive-behavioral interventions for substance abuse and HIV risk, Scott's case immediately draws my attention to his feelings and attitudes about these behaviors, and more specifically to the specific motivational strategies that might be applied to enhance Scott's chances for positive change in these areas. In this chapter I will focus my discussion on my impressions of Scott from the perspective of interventions for substance abuse and HIV risk behaviors, with a particular emphasis on interventions most useful in the early sessions of treatment, namely, motivational interviewing (MI) (Miller & Rollnick, 1991).

MI for Health Behavior Problems

Particularly in the initial interview, when the therapist is confronted with substance abuse or other problem behaviors, MI is a powerful approach that can establish a positive therapeutic environment and maximize the chances that the client will embrace change. MI constitutes a set of strategies and techniques that are designed to help the client resolve her or his ambivalence about—and enhance her or his intrinsic motivation to change—problem behavior. MI assumes that all individuals facing decisions concerning changes in health behaviors (including weight loss, smoking, drinking or drug use, or risky sex) are ambivalent about change, and it is the therapist's task to help the individual resolve this ambivalence and move toward making a solid commitment to change.

MI is based on the Stages of Change model originally proposed by Prochaska and DiClemente (1986). Individuals presenting with problem behaviors such as substance abuse or HIV risk behavior can be reliably classified according to their psychological readiness for change, with the specific stages being as follows: *precontemplation* (the client is not considering change because she or he does not perceive a problem); *contemplation* (the client is aware of a problem and is

The Initial Psychotherapy Interview. DOI: 10.1016/B978-0-12-385146-8.00010-9

considering change, but remains ambivalent and has not made a commitment to change); *preparation* (the client has made a decision to change and is considering her or his options and evaluating specific goals); *action* (the client has decided on a change plan and has begun to implement it); and *maintenance* (the client is actively involved in sustaining change achieved during the action phase). The model also accounts for *relapse* as a normal part of the change process that most individuals experience once or more on the path to sustained change.

It is the explicit goal of MI to help the client move from early stages of change readiness (principally precontemplation and contemplation) to actual change (action and maintenance). The broad therapeutic goals of MI include:

1. Effective *expression of empathy* for the client's point of view, including both sides of her or his ambivalence toward change; it is through the demonstration of empathy that the therapist helps the client to fully articulate not only the obvious (and socially desirable) reasons to change a particular behavior but also the often hidden or poorly elaborated factors that undermine motivation to change at the moment when she or he must make the choice to engage or not engage in the particular behavior.
2. To develop or *heighten discrepancy* within the client between her or his current behavior and her or his personal goals and/or values, and to increase psychic tension in such a way that change becomes a more salient need.
3. To *avoid confrontation and argumentation* in order to reduce resistance on the part of the client and minimize the client's urge to "dig in their heels" in response to pressure from the therapist.
4. To *"roll" with resistance* rather than push back against it, meaning the therapist responds to resistance by backing away from whatever intervention was being pursued, allowing the client "space" to approach the idea of change again on her or his own terms.
5. Perhaps most critically, the MI therapist *supports the client's self-efficacy for change* by identifying the client's strengths and reflecting these back to her or him, expressing confidence in the client's ability to change that the client may not share.

To accomplish these goals, MI relies upon a set of basic therapeutic strategies best remembered by the acronym OARS:

1. *Open*-ended questions.
2. *Affirmation* of the client's current efforts and abilities.
3. *Reflective* listening.
4. Frequent *Summarization*.

These strategies together can be used to effectively draw out and clarify the client's ambivalence concerning change, and to highlight strengths the client may under-appreciate that may be marshaled in the service of change. Used effectively, these techniques are critical in early sessions to establish a positive change environment and open communication between the therapist and client.

The therapist's goals early in MI center on the elicitation from the client of "change talk" and "commitment talk." More specifically, the therapist's aim is to draw from the client so-called "DARN-C" statements:

1. Statements of *Desire* for change;
2. Statements conveying belief in the *Ability* to change;
3. Identification of concrete *Reasons* why change is important;

4. Statements expressing a *Need* for change; and
5. Statements of concrete *Commitment* to change.

On the surface, with its focus on active listening and affirmation of the client, MI may appear in its implementation much like Rogerian psychotherapy. However, the approach is actually quite distinct, in that the therapist, far from adopting a neutral stance, is an active proponent of change in her or his implementation of MI. For example, the therapist chooses carefully and strategically which material to reflect and highlight, in order to use the client's own statements to highlight the need for change; for example[1]:

> **P:** I don't know ... I mean I really have a great time when I party, but I guess there are times when I kinda go overboard and lose control.
> **T:** It scares you that you can't always seem to control your drug use.

The therapist using MI techniques is thus always listening for statements from the client that support the argument for change, and will often selectively reflect those statements in order to magnify their salience to the client. It is of critical importance to MI, however, that the therapist never supply the arguments for change to the client; for example, in Scott's case a therapist might be tempted to say the following:

> **P114:** I love [pot] ... there's something about it that numbs me, where I get dumb and I'm just able to mellow out, stop thinking.
> **T:** Well, but don't you think there are healthier ways to cope with stress than being dependent on a drug?

Here the hypothetical response by the therapist conveys an obvious, negative opinion of the patient's behavior: His use of marijuana to "mellow out" is unhealthy, and the therapist's expression of this opinion is clearly negative and judgmental, and likely to trigger defensive and argumentative response from the patient. For this reason argumentative, confrontational, or judgmental statements by the therapist are strictly avoided in MI, a key characteristic that distinguishes it from many traditional approaches to substance abuse and HIV risk-reduction counseling.

Likewise, although skills-based approaches such as cognitive-behavioral therapy (CBT) certainly play an important role later in the change process (i.e., once the client has endorsed a change goal), motivational interventions strictly avoid advice-giving or the provision of skills training toward a change goal, because this puts the therapist in the position of an expert dispensing instructions to a client who may not have completely "bought into" the therapist's agenda:

> **P107:** I'm a pot head. I smoke pot. Way too much. Almost every day.

---

[1] Throughout this chapter, I make use of quotes to illustrate various clinical points. If these reference actual quotes from the session with Scott, these will be denoted by a line number following "P" or "T"; otherwise in hypothetical exchanges "P" and "T" will be used alone to denote "Patient" and "Therapist," respectively, without line references.

    T: Well, why don't we talk about some strategies you can use to cut down on your smoking?

    P: Well, but I really enjoy having a joint at the end of the day. It's my version of a martini when I get home from work.

Here, the therapist's (hypothetical) premature suggestion of behavior change triggers resistance in the form of backpedaling by the patient. The reason that the principles of nonconfrontation and nondirectiveness are so central to MI is rooted in a basic understanding of human nature: When one is pushed in a particular direction, one's first instinct is often to push back in the opposite direction, even if one may have been considering moving in that direction oneself before that point. Why this is so—the need to assert one's autonomy, an unconscious rebellion against the therapist as a parent figure—is beyond the scope of this chapter and probably of MI itself. It suffices to understand that the idea and impetus for change must originate in the patient: Irrespective of how painfully obviously and self-evidently necessary change may be to the therapist, it is critical to avoid falling into the trap of expressing implicitly or explicitly such sentiments to the client, as this will only engender resistance and shut down communication.

When the MI therapist encounters resistance to an intervention, it is important to recognize the reaction as such. This can be more challenging than it seems, in that resistance is often subtle and can be mistaken for part of the simple give and take of a conversation, as in the fictitious exchange below:

    P: I don't know ... I mean I really have a great time when I party, but I guess there are times when I kinda go overboard and lose control.

    T: It scares you that you can't always seem to control your drug use.

    P: Well, I mean it's not like I'm totally off the deep end. I'm not going off for days at a time or anything like that.

Note that the client's second statement is not just a correction of the therapist's reflection or a clarification of position, but *an expression of resistance to the direction the therapist has attempted to take the conversation.* The patient is saying that he is not ready to acknowledge being "scared" about the drug use, and so responds by retreating from his previous statement and staking out a less pro-change position.

The appropriate response to resistance of this type is to immediately retreat from the intervention being pursued, not simply to a neutral stance but actually to a position that is even *further* from change than that expressed by the client; in other words, the therapist overstates the degree of control that the client is expressing. This puts the client in the position of needing to correct the therapist, and again be the one arguing for change, as in the following fictitious exchange:

    P: Well, I mean it's not like I'm totally off the deep end. I'm going off for days at a time or anything like that.

    T: OK, so you feel that you actually *are* able to control your drug use. So when you say "going overboard," you don't really think of that as a problem in any way.

P: I don't know ... I guess I just mean there are times when I get carried away having fun and I end up using way more than I wanted to ... way more than I should ... so I either end up broke or just really regretting it the next day.

T: So there are times when your using kind of gets away from you, and you don't always like how you end up feeling afterward.

P: Yeah, maybe that's more like it. I don't know if it's a problem, but I guess I wonder sometimes.

T: It concerns you.

The specific MI techniques being discussed here generally presume a client who is not yet ready to make a commitment to change behavior, but rather one who is ambivalent about change. Once the client has shifted toward a solid commitment to change, she or he is ready for a more skills-oriented approach such as CBT that will help implement the change plan.

Substantial evidence exists to support the efficacy of brief motivational interventions for drinking (Bien, Miller, & Tonigan, 1993; WHO Brief Intervention Study Group, 1996), and suggests they can be as powerful as more extended treatments (Project MATCH Research Group, 1997). Recent data also support the efficacy of motivational interventions specifically for gay men with drinking (Morgenstern et al., 2007) and drug use problems (Morgenstern et al., 2009).

Understanding Substance Abuse and HIV Risk Behavior in Gay Men

Substance use and abuse in gay men. There is a long tradition that presumes that gay men are at significantly elevated risk for substance abuse relative to their heterosexual counterparts. However, recent literature suggests that the reality is more nuanced. For example, in a detailed review some years ago I (Bux, 1996) concluded that although gay men are less likely to abstain from alcohol, they are no more likely to experience problems related to drinking or to exhibit symptoms of alcohol abuse or dependence. On the other hand, there is evidence that gay men are more likely both to use and to abuse recreational drugs, especially the so-called "club drugs," methamphetamine, ketamine, MDMA (ecstasy), cocaine, and GHB (King et al., 2008; Stall & Purcell, 2000). There appears to be relatively little information available on the prevalence of marijuana abuse specifically among gay men; one recent study suggested that as much as 40 percent of gay men are at least occasional users of marijuana, although the convenience sample of gay men upon which the finding was based suggests caution in extrapolating the results (Halkitis & Parsons, 2002).

The relationship between substance use and abuse and HIV risk behavior. Drugs and alcohol have long been associated with sexual activity generally, and with HIV risk behavior specifically, both in the research literature and in conventional wisdom. For a variety of reasons, use of various substances is believed to enhance sexual experience, either by reducing sexual inhibitions, enhancing the physical and emotional experience, or facilitating certain sexual acts (Stall & Purcell, 2000).

The association between substance use and sexual behavior has also been shown to extend to sexual risk behavior and HIV transmission among gay men in numerous studies (Halkitis, Green, & Carragher, 2006; Halkitis & Parsons, 2003; Irwin, Morgenstern, Parsons, Wainberg, & Labouvie, 2006; Koblin et al., 2006, 2007; Parsons, Kutnick, Halkitis, Punzalan, & Carbonari, 2005; Purcell, Moss, Remien, Woods, & Parsons, 2005). Although the majority of research has focused on alcohol or so-called "club drug" use, especially methamphetamine use, some research has also demonstrated a relationship between marijuana use specifically and HIV risk behavior (cf. Parsons et al., 2005).

The precise nature of observed associations is far from clear. Some evidence suggests that sexual encounters involving alcohol or drug use are significantly more likely to involve high-risk sexual activities (Irwin et al., 2006; Parsons et al., 2005), and that reducing drug use through treatment is linked to concomitant reductions in sexual risk behavior (Jaffe, Shoptaw, Stein, Reback, & Rotheram-Fuller, 2007). Nevertheless, multiple mechanisms likely account for the relationship between substance use and unprotected sex, including the effects of substances on inhibitions and judgment; mood states such as anxiety, depression, or loneliness that may motivate both behaviors; or underlying traits such as sensation-seeking, impulsivity, or internalized homophobia that may influence both substance use and sexual risk behavior (Cabaj, 2000; Halkitis, Shrem, & Martin, 2005; Stall & Purcell, 2000). Therefore, it would be a mistake to assume that by disconnecting substance use from sexual activity one could reliably eliminate sexual risk behavior in all individuals. Intervention with a gay man such as Scott, who exhibits both substance use and HIV risk behavior, requires a thorough understanding of how these behaviors interact in that particular individual.

Other factors associated with HIV risk behavior. A number of variables not related to substance use have been linked to unprotected anal sex among gay men. Working within a stage-of-change framework, Bauermeister, Carballo-Diéguez, Ventuneac, and Dolezal (2009) examined the decisional balance for gay men regarding unprotected anal sex, and identified coping with various psychological vulnerabilities, and enhancement of pleasure and emotional intimacy with one's partner, as important factors influencing sexual risk-taking. Blais (2006) points to evidence that the large majority of recent cases of HIV transmission take place between regular sex partners (Davidovich et al., 2001; Slavin, Richters, & Kippax, 2004; Xiridou, Geskus, de Wit, Coutinho, & Kretzschmar, 2003), and suggests that, with an actual or potential long-term partner, the desire for enhanced intimacy and trust overrides the desire to protect against HIV. In a related vein, Torres and Gore-Felton (2007) propose that loneliness plays a significant role in the decision to engage in unprotected sex. Finally, Bimbi et al. (2006) reported that individuals who engage in unprotected sex while intoxicated were more likely to endorse strong desires for intimacy and romantic connections.

Other psychological variables, such as general psychological distress (e.g., anxiety and depression) have been identified in numerous studies as predictive of HIV risk behavior (Marks, Bingham, & Duval, 1998; Rosario, Hunter, Maguen, Gwadz, & Smith, 2001; Rosario, Schrimshaw, & Hunter, 2006; Rotheram-Borus, Rosario, Reid, & Koopman, 1995; Strathdee et al., 1998), as has the construct of internalized homophobia (Cabaj, 2000; Rosario et al., 2006). Finally, the personality trait of sensation-seeking has been proposed as a factor underlying drug use, unprotected sex, and the association between the two (Ross, Mattison, & Franklin, 2003). Optimism about the availability and effectiveness of antiretroviral treatments has also been associated with higher frequencies of unprotected sex in some studies (Van de Ven, Prestage, Crawford, Grulich, & Kippax, 2000; Van de Ven, Rawstorne, Nakamura, Crawford, & Kippax, 2002), although not in others (Abelson et al., 2006; Williamson & Hart, 2004).

A comment. Since the advent of the AIDS epidemic, virtually everything that is known about substance abuse in the gay community has been the product of research on substance abuse as a risk factor for HIV transmission. While this body of research has yielded invaluable information on the topic, I believe that it in some ways diminishes the value of gay men always to be viewed through the lens of HIV risk behavior, because there are certainly numerous other factors that influence substance abuse treatment for gay men than their being potential vectors of HIV transmission. Nevertheless, clinical interventions (such as MI) for various health behavior problems do share some important commonalities, and because the intersection of these behaviors poses such a significant public health problem for gay men, it remains imprudent to discuss substance abuse without consideration of risk behaviors for transmission of HIV.

The foregoing review is far from exhaustive, but suffices to demonstrate that a number of psychological variables may influence decision-making concerning HIV risk behavior. Of particular importance for understanding the phenomenon may be the search for intimacy and the ways some gay men may choose to seek and express it.

The Initial Interview with Scott

I generally have two primary goals in the initial session with a client reporting harmful or potentially harmful behaviors, whether they be substance abuse or HIV risk behavior. The first is assessment. My assessment of substance abuse generally will focus on four primary dimensions: frequency, quantity, and pattern of use; history; problems related to use (including whether the client appears to meet diagnostic criteria for a substance use disorder that should be a focus of treatment); and motivation or readiness to change. Although it is not appropriate to draw a direct parallel between substance abuse and HIV risk behaviors, the approach to assessing HIV risk behaviors is essentially similar.

The second primary goal of the initial session is, as noted above, the establishment of a positive and change-facilitating environment in the therapy setting consistent with MI. It is vitally important for the therapist to establish this therapeutic stance from the beginning of treatment in order to maximize her or his effectiveness in facilitating change.

Assessment of substance use and HIV risk behavior. Frequency and quantity of substance use should be evaluated with as much specificity as possible, as this allows the establishment of a baseline for the client from which progress can be measured. Frequency of use is a straightforward question: How many days per week does the client use? Part of the question of frequency of use, however, also concerns the *pattern* of use: When (on what days of the week, at what times of the day, under what circumstances) does the client typically use, and when does he *not* use? Through a thorough understanding of the client's pattern of use, the client's motivations for use will begin to emerge, which will inform the road map to be followed in therapy in facilitating change. For example, Scott reports (P114) that he smokes marijuana to "stop thinking," and that his "mind's always racing" without the drug. Were I interviewing Scott I would inquire further about his experience of racing thoughts and the role of drug use in managing this experience; for example, my line of questioning might include the following:

> **T:** You say your mind is always racing. Are there times of day when you're particularly aware of that, for example, when you're getting home from work and trying to wind down, or trying to get to sleep at night? Is the problem as bad on the weekends as during the week? Have you had periods in your life when it bothered you more or less than others? Are there times when smoking seems more effective than others in helping you manage the thoughts?

Although Scott reports that his drinking is "very controlled" (P107), I would also inquire further into his drinking habits. He states that he drinks "often," meaning at least twice per week, which would not in itself raise any alarms for me. However, his response to Silverstein's question about drinking alone comes across to me as somewhat defensive (P109): "**I don't think there's anything wrong** with having a drink or two by myself before I go out or if I'm going to stay home alone." [Emphasis added.] This would raise a red flag for me in assessment, and I would inquire further about his pattern of drinking and the quantity consumed on these occasions, to ensure that he is not minimizing this behavior, posing the following questions:

1. What time of day do you usually drink? Ever drink in the morning or early in the day? (Early drinking is a common sign of drinking to avoid withdrawal symptoms.)
2. What days during the week do you drink typically?
3. Which days are you more likely to be drinking at home?
4. What days do you usually go out, and where do you go out?
5. When you drink at home, what do you usually drink?
6. How much might you have when you drink at home?
7. What about when you go out? What do you drink then? How much?
8. What's the most you've had to drink, say in the past month?
9. Have you ever had so much to drink that you got sick or passed out, or lost time? (Loss-of-control drinking is a common feature of alcohol dependence.)

Evaluating the *quantity* consumed of alcohol or prescription drugs is a relatively straightforward task, because these substances are readily available in standardized doses that never vary; thus, for example, any quantity of any type of alcohol can easily be converted to ounces of pure ethanol.[2] In contrast, evaluating the quantity used of illicit substances such as marijuana is necessarily less precise, because the amount of tetrahydrocannabinol (THC, the psychoactive substance in marijuana) in a given amount of marijuana can vary considerably depending on the quality of the source. For example, if Scott were to obtain more potent marijuana from a new source he may find he needs fewer puffs to get the desired effect, but objectively he could still be consuming the same amount of THC, if not more. Therefore, to assess quantity consumed of marijuana, I would ask Scott to estimate the number of puffs on a pipe, the number of joints, or the dollar amount consumed per occasion or per day as a rough approximation of the amount of the psychoactive substance consumed. However, when evaluating changes in apparent quantity of use, either historically or during the course of therapy, I would want to inquire as to whether he had acquired a new source for marijuana, and/or whether he noticed any sudden changes in the strength of the drug or in his sensitivity to the drug's effects that might suggest a change in its potency.

Concerning Scott's HIV risk behavior, a similar set of questions would be appropriate: That is, how often, with how many partners, and under what circumstances does he engage in unprotected sex? However, it is important to be clear regarding what specific types of sexual behavior are to be the focus of discussion. Generally, unprotected insertive and especially receptive anal sex are the behaviors of most concern for gay men, as these carry the greatest risk of transmission of HIV. Apart from assessing the frequency with which, and the number of partners with whom Scott has engaged in these behaviors, it would also be valuable to inquire whether he has taken any steps to mitigate his risk from unprotected sex. For example, Scott indicates that he has tried to limit himself to unprotected sex with men whom he is dating. Other gay men will report strategies such as "serosorting" (limiting themselves to unprotected sex with men whose serostatus is concordant with their own), withdrawal prior to ejaculation (to limit exposure to potentially infected semen), or other forms of negotiated safety. Although these strategies may be of imperfect efficacy, they signal that the client is to some degree invested in reducing risk, which provides a foundation upon which to build in treatment.

It is also important to evaluate the circumstances under which Scott engages in unprotected sex. As noted above, substance use before or during sex is associated with increased incidence of risk behaviors; however, in Scott's case there is no evidence that being high is a factor in his pattern of unprotected sex. In fact, what Scott does say about his marijuana use strongly implies that it serves an entirely

---

[2] For example, 12 oz of beer, 5 oz of wine, and 1.5 oz of 80-proof distilled spirits each contains one "standard unit" of absolute ethanol. Other alcoholic beverages, such as malt liquor, fortified wine, cognac, or high-proof brands such as Bacardi 151™ each have unique but standardized concentrations of ethanol from which the number of standard drinks can be calculated.

different function in his life than enhancement of sexual experiences: He smokes in order to shut his mind off, and usually watches television when he is high. Of course, further inquiry should be undertaken to ensure that sexual risk is not linked to marijuana use, but I suspect it will not be a significant factor in Scott's case. Alcohol, on the other hand, may be somewhat of a factor in Scott's sexual behavior, if for no other reason than he is probably more likely to have been drinking if he is out on a date or meets someone in a bar. The degree to which this is the case should be evaluated by discussing Scott's recent experiences of unprotected sex from the standpoint of whether alcohol was involved, and if so, how much.

Quantity and frequency of both substance use and HIV risk behavior can be assessed as part of the clinical interview, or if time permits, using an interview such as the Timeline Follow-Back (TLFB; Sobell & Sobell, 1995). The TLFB is a semi-structured interview that relies on the use of a daily calendar, with special events and dates important to the client filled in as anchor points, to reconstruct a retrospective record of the client's daily use over a fixed period of time. One advantage of the TLFB technique is that it requires a fairly exhaustive and detailed examination of the client's use, providing a "big picture" perspective on use that most clients have never had. By completing such a painstaking, retrospective, daily account of one's substance use and HIV risk, the individual can be struck by the magnitude of the problem; often, after completing the TLFB the client often has an "aha" experience, reacting to the assessment with statements such as, "I never realized how much I use." The TLFB can often also be used to highlight the relationship between sex and substance use, if it becomes apparent that the two behaviors tend to coincide regularly.

As part of the evaluation of problem behaviors, an important goal of the first session with Scott would also be to teach him how to monitor systematically and reliably his behaviors on an ongoing basis during therapy. I would encourage Scott to estimate the amount of marijuana smoked on a given occasion and to write down the amount used *at the time it is consumed*. Likewise I would encourage him to keep a journal of his unprotected sexual encounters in which he might record various details of the event (who the partner was, whether he was high or drunk, what feelings—e.g., excitement, loneliness, anxiety, horniness—he associated with the encounter). This provides an in vivo record of both behaviors that is likely to be more reliable than a retrospective recall collected in the weekly session. It also carries the added benefit of increasing his focus on and awareness of the *acts* of use and of unprotected sex, and of bringing these behaviors forward in his consciousness. Much like the dieter counting calories, if Scott can be trained to monitor his intake of marijuana continuously he will be more likely to think twice before taking a given dose, which is of course one of the objectives of psychotherapy.

Critical to the decision of how to approach these behaviors clinically, I would want to know more about Scott's perception of negative consequences associated with his use of marijuana or his HIV risk behavior. Scott's first mention of marijuana is that he smokes it "way too much." This would beg the question for me, "What makes you say that?" Clearly Scott has some awareness that his level of smoking is excessive; the question to examine is what makes it excessive to Scott by exploring whether Scott has noticed any concrete problems arising from his smoking, such as:

1. Depression,
2. Apathy or lack of motivation,
3. Paranoia or anxiety,
4. Tolerance to the drug,
5. Health problems such as chronic cough or fatigue,
6. Interpersonal problems or conflict about his use,
7. Problems in role functioning such as poor performance at work or missing time at work, and
8. Any sense of dissonance between his behavior and his broader self-concept or personal goals (e.g., "I don't like thinking of myself as some burned-out pot head.").

Likewise, Scott's perception of negative consequences associated with unprotected sex should be explored: He indicates some recognition that unprotected sex is "stupid," but it is important not to regard as self-evident Scott's reasons for expressing this sentiment, and instead to ask, "Why do you say that?" Aside from actual infection with HIV, other possible negative consequences of unprotected sex commonly expressed by gay men include:

1. Other sexually transmitted infections,
2. Anxiety about contracting HIV,
3. HIV "scares"; that is, common illnesses such as fever or flu symptoms being misinterpreted as HIV seroconversion,
4. Dissonance about the behavior itself as being out of character for him (e.g., "I don't like being so irresponsible about my health."), and
5. A partner's assuming that he is HIV-positive based on his willingness to engage in unprotected sex.

In the case both of marijuana use and of unprotected sex, it would be important to encourage Scott to elaborate on his own perceptions of harm associated with his behavior, rather than to assume the harm to be self-evident or to attempt to impose the therapist's own assumptions about these behaviors on Scott. Particularly with sexual risk behavior, serious harm may only be a hypothetical eventuality (contracting HIV) that has little salience for him in his day-to-day decision-making relative to whatever advantages he perceives in the heat of the moment.

It is always valuable to have at least a basic understanding of the client's history with a problem behavior. Scott reports that he has smoked marijuana since age 13, apparently more than half his life. This suggests that any goal to change or eliminate marijuana use will probably represent an enormous change in his lifestyle that may be hard for him to envision: Scott literally has had no experience of life without marijuana for most of his living memory, and it may be a daunting prospect to give up or substantially curtail its use. He reports using cocaine and ecstasy "a lot" through high school and college, and reports moderate alcohol consumption presently, but marijuana clearly remains his drug of choice. I would inquire further into his history of other drug use, and explore his decision to stop using other drugs. I would also examine further his history of marijuana use, including whether the current period represents his heaviest use, and whether he has ever discontinued or moderated his use for any period of time, and if so, when, why, how, and for how long. This information will be useful in evaluating the viability of various change options and providing evidence of his ability to effect change again.

Likewise, I would want to know more about the chronology of unprotected sex: He implies that this is a relatively recent development in his life (P121: "I fucked up a lot, this past year."), and seems to link the change to the end of an extended period of unprotected sex within the context of a monogamous relationship. I would want to get more information about how this shift in his sexual script occurred.

A brief evaluation of Scott's readiness or intention to make real, sustained change in his marijuana use and in his HIV risk behavior would provide the therapist an initial idea of how to tailor interventions to fit Scott's stage of readiness to change. Construction of a *decisional balance*, exploring both the positive and negative aspects of marijuana use and unprotected sex, would provide the therapist with further information on which to determine Scott's readiness to change, as well as establish the open, nonjudgmental atmosphere that is essential to MI.

Based on the limited information presented from this interview, Scott appears to have concerns about both behaviors, but also expresses important positive aspects of both behaviors, suggesting that he experiences significant ambivalence about them. This information alone would suggest that Scott is at the *contemplation* stage of change for both behaviors, indicating that the therapist's task will be primarily to help Scott resolve his ambivalence toward these behaviors and enhance discrepancy surrounding them, with the goal of moving Scott toward greater readiness for and commitment to change.

It is noteworthy that in one exchange Scott somewhat emphatically refers to unsafe sexual behavior in the past tense, in which he implies that he may have made a decision very recently consequent to witnessing his brother's death:

> **P130:** I like sex without a condom. It's better. It is. I enjoy it more. I mean maybe it's partially a physical thing. But, but it's a mental thing too. ... I want that intimacy. And maybe it's just sort of, I'm seeking it—*sought, it's in past tense, especially after this whole drama*. I **sought** it in the wrong guy .... [Emphasis added.]

This statement might appear to suggest that Scott has moved beyond ambivalence toward preparation or action; that is, he has made a firm commitment to eliminating unprotected sex from his repertoire, as a consequence of "this whole drama" (presumably, his brother's death). However, I would not proceed on this assumption without further exploring the degree of his commitment to this change, especially since the statement is immediately preceded by a statement describing (in the *present tense*) his strong preference for unprotected sex. As a therapist working in a motivational framework, I would have picked up on this theme and asked Scott to elaborate further; for example:

> **T:** You really want unprotected sex to be past tense since going through losing your brother that way. [Highlighting client's statements supportive of change]

P: I don't know. ... I know it has to change, but it's hard. I really enjoy it.

T: So although on the one hand you really do enjoy sex without a condom better for all sorts of reasons, David's death has been kind of a wake-up call to you, and you want to make a change. [Double-sided reflection summarizing both sides of ambivalence]

It is important not to accept clients' statements of commitment to change too readily, as they may often be motivated by what they believe the therapist wishes to hear and an expression of a desire to *want* to change, but without a complete understanding of what factors may undermine the *commitment* to change. The purpose of helping the client to elaborate on both sides of his ambivalence is to provide him with a thorough understanding of why he does what he does, as well as why he needs to change what he does *in spite of the positive effects of his current behavior.* In a sense, MI helps the client make a truly informed decision about change that is rooted in a realistic understanding of what he is up against inside himself.

Understanding Marijuana Use and Unprotected Sex in Scott

Why does Scott smoke marijuana? Considering the diversity of themes explored in this initial interview, it is commendable that the therapist successfully elicited a good deal about Scott's motivations for smoking marijuana. When asked for his substance use history, Scott immediately responds by saying, "I'm a pot head. I smoke pot. Way too much. Almost every day" (P107). This strikes me as a fairly strong statement of self-labeling, offered without any sense of irony or self-deprecating humor, that makes me think Scott has at least some concern about his marijuana use. After a brief discussion about drinking and past use of other drugs, Dr. Silverstein explores Scott's marijuana use further:

T114: Why do you think you smoke so much pot?

P114: I don't know. I love it. I mean, I've been doing it since I was 13 years old. And, uh, there's something about it that numbs me, where I get dumb and I'm just able to mellow out, stop thinking, I, I, the thoughts, always have a lot of thoughts running through my head. I find it very, very difficult to quiet myself, to relax, and my mind's always racing. And marijuana is like the one thing that just stops everything.

T115: Well, what thoughts are racing through your mind if you're not smoking pot?

P115: I mean it's work-related, of course. I have a stressful job. Or it's men. ... That fucking loser I've been seeing. What their reactions mean. What does that mean? What does that movement mean? You know. Or it was mostly something about my brother. Or it was the drama with my parents. Money, and as a the whole molestation thing ... thoughts that kind of flood my mind and I smoke weed and then I'll put on the idiot box and watch some television and not, you know, think about it as much.

From this exchange, it is actually quite clear why Scott smokes marijuana, and the reason cited is a quite common motivation for substance use: relief from stress and anxiety. Scott seems plagued by intrusive, ruminative thoughts that fill his mind and that he is unable to shut off. They appear to cause him significant anxiety and distress. It is unclear how aversive the experience of ruminating is to Scott, but he clearly believes that he needs marijuana in order to cope. The range of themes that preoccupy him suggests to me an almost obsessional quality to Scott's thinking, but his account of the experience also suggests to me that Scott may have a low level of distress tolerance, such that he is unable to endure these thoughts and the anxiety they provoke. Both of these are characteristics that would respond very well to behavioral coping strategies such as distraction, meditation, or even physical exercise, as well as to cognitive strategies such as cognitive restructuring. In later sessions I would want to explore further Scott's experience of ruminative thinking and consider offering training in the use of such strategies as potential alternatives to smoking pot.

Silverstein continues:

T116: The drug pushes the thoughts to the back of your mind.

Here Silverstein uses an excellent reflection of the client's statement, without any further comment. Note what happens next:

P116: It can, it can. **Sometimes it has the adverse effect where I'm even worse,** where my thoughts are even more stress. Where I'm lying in bed, stoned, trying to go to bed, and I can't pass out because I'm crazy thoughts, you know, even worse. [Emphasis added.]

Scott responds to Silverstein's reflective statement by qualifying his description of the effects of the drug, and elaborating further that he often has a paradoxical reaction to marijuana, thereby suggesting that in fact the effects of the drug are quite unreliable and unpredictable. (In fact, marijuana can often cause increased anxiety in the user, to the point of paranoia or even panic [Stephens, 1999].) What is striking to me in this exchange is that, given validation of his perceptions of the positive aspects of marijuana, Scott then feels comfortable enough to present evidence that argues *against* its use, almost as though Silverstein's empathic endorsement of Scott's feelings has obligated Scott to give him the *whole* story. This is an excellent demonstration of how the open dialogue fostered by Silverstein in the MI spirit operates to encourage the client to explore for himself both sides of his ambivalence.

Again, as a therapist operating within the MI framework, I might (hypothetically) have followed up on this statement further:

T: So it sounds like although you use pot to zone out and escape from stress, it's actually not always consistent that way, and sometimes you actually end up feeling worse. [Use of double-sided reflection to highlight contradiction in his motivations for using]
P: Yeah, actually that can happen a lot.
T: Sounds like the way you've been trying to cope with stress isn't as reliable as you'd like. [Reflection to highlight need for change]
P: Yeah, I guess I could do better.
T: Got anything in mind?

It would be my expectation that, by providing Scott with the "space" to talk freely but without pressure about the downside to using as he experiences it, a great deal more evidence would emerge that would argue against continued use. This process would afford me the opportunity to simply reflect what I have heard, in Scott's own words, and leave it to him to draw the obvious conclusions. Note in the above hypothetical exchange I would refrain from offering suggestions before probing from him what ideas he has, since this may reveal strategies with which he has had some prior success and upon which the therapy could build. If he had no ideas, it would be entirely consistent with MI to ask him if he would be open to suggestions, and then offer a tentative alternative strategy.

Does Scott have a problem with marijuana? As noted at P107, Scott appears to express at least some concern about his marijuana use; I would want to encourage him to elaborate further on this:

T: What makes you say you smoke way too much?
P: I smoke every day. I know I smoke a lot more than most people. And I guess I just think I need it more than I should.
T: That worries you.

Of course, this hypothetical dialogue could go in any number of directions; I would nevertheless expect Scott to elaborate on worries that he has about his marijuana use, either relating to the impact that it has had on his life and role functioning, or to a dissonance between his behavior and his internal self-concept. In the exchange above I presume that the discrepancy he experiences is primarily of the latter nature: although he perhaps does not experience many obvious, objective consequences of his use, Scott nevertheless worries about it because he doesn't like the *idea* of being psychologically dependent on a substance. It is difficult to overestimate how powerful a conversation such as this can be to a client. Often it will be the first time a client in the contemplation stage has given voice to such concerns, and speaking them aloud can be a very painful emotional experience. This is in fact another aspect of MI that is somewhat unique: It is often the goal of the therapist to guide the client to a place where she or he feels acutely unhappy, in order to help her or him connect with the negative effect surrounding the behavior that will ultimately be a key driving force toward change.

Whether Scott has a problem with marijuana is a question that can ultimately be answered only by Scott. Based on what is presented in this initial session, I would suspect that he does, if for no other reason than the fact that, despite the advantages Scott sees in smoking pot, there is something about the habit that he fundamentally does not like. A skilled MI therapist will elicit this material in a gentle and empathic manner, along with all of the painful affect that accompanies it.

What should be the goal for Scott with regard to marijuana use? This is a controversial subject in the substance abuse field, but increasingly researchers and even frontline clinicians are allowing for more flexibility in goal choice in the treatment process. It is far from clear at this stage whether Scott has a serious problem with marijuana that would require abstinence; however, even if evidence were to emerge indicative of a problem it is unlikely that Scott would readily buy into a goal of complete abstinence. I would instead approach the question as part of the motivational process:

T: You don't like being so dependent on pot.
P: No.
T: What do you think is the answer?
P: I guess if I could just limit it to the weekends, it wouldn't be such a big deal. Have it be more something I do for fun, not something I need.
T: You don't see yourself giving it up altogether, but you'd like to be able to take it or leave it, not feel like you *have* to have it.
P: No, I definitely still want to smoke sometimes; I still really like the feeling of getting stoned.

Importantly, and particularly if I suspected that a moderation goal were unrealistic for Scott, I would encourage him build into his change plan some mechanism for evaluating the results of his efforts, so that, if after some period of time it became clear that he was failing to moderate his use, the goal could be revisited and modified, possibly to an abstinence goal. Among clients still reluctant to endorse a goal of abstinence, I often will propose that they experiment with a "trial run" of abstinence for a fixed period of time, as a way to encourage some success with abstinence without the requirement of what may otherwise seem an unattainable goal.

Why does Scott have unprotected sex? Why do some diabetics fail to adhere to their dietary and medication regimens? Why do some individuals with tuberculosis fail to complete their medication regimens? The question of Scott's occasionally engaging in unsafe sexual practices is an important one to be explored in psychotherapy, but not necessarily because his behavior is so self-evidently harmful as to suggest a complete lack of judgment or self-destructive impulses. For the purposes of MI, the therapist should address this question no differently than she or he might consider a different question: Why do some people persist in eating beef, considering its well-documented relationship to cardiovascular disease? In this context, it becomes clearer how each individual makes a private decision about a multitude of health behaviors on a daily basis, each based on her or his own unique calculus of risk versus reward.

For many, the risk of contracting HIV from even a single, unprotected sexual encounter is far too great to be worth any positive aspect of the experience. But clearly for Scott, there are important elements of an unprotected sexual encounter that make it worth the risk to him, at least in the moment he is making the decision.

Scott appears to acknowledge that he shouldn't be engaging in unprotected sex:

T121: ... Do you have safe sex?
P121: I mean **I'm pretty good, but I fucked up a lot**, this past year.
T122: Meaning?
P122: Meaning I didn't have safe sex
T123: Meaning you let guys fuck you without a condom?
P123: Right.
T124: [pause] **Why would you *do* that?**
P124: [slowly] I don't know. **Stupid. Stupid. There's no explanation for it**.
T125: Can I assume these are just tricks you're talking about?

P125: No, no. 'Cause like I say I'm risky, but I'm not that risky. .... And especially with this most recent guy that, that I was hanging out with. I really liked him and I slept with him on the first night and he stayed for 72 hours, didn't leave. Really liked each other. And I just, I don't know I— **there's no excuses, there's no explanation**. [Emphasis added.]

Here Scott gives a clear indication that he understands unprotected sex is unacceptable. However, it is noteworthy that his expression of shame is prompted by a leading question from Silverstein: "Why would you do that?" This choice of wording and tone, although probably intended to express empathy and concern for Scott, actually violates the spirit of MI, in that it conveys a sense of incredulity or negative judgment that sets up an implicit expectation for what the client should say next, as well as running the risk of shaming the client. Note that following Silverstein's question, Scott disavows the behavior and obediently expresses strong feelings of shame, but any meaningful exploration of his underlying motives for engaging in unprotected sex is effectively shut down for the moment. As an MI therapist, I would be far from convinced that the viewpoint on unprotected sex is Scott's own, rather than the straight "party line" on unprotected sex. I would therefore want to elicit more about Scott's feelings on his sexual history to determine to what extent he actually regards unprotected sex as a problem.

As an alternative, consider the following (hypothetical) exchange:

T123: ... Meaning you let guys fuck you without a condom?
P123: Right.
    T: Tell me more about that. [Open question to elicit more information and encourage continued discussion]
    P: Maybe four guys in the past couple of years I've had sex without a condom.
    T: What made those guys different from the other guys you've been with? [Open question to elicit information about client's motivation to engage in unprotected sex]

Here the MI therapist can make a small inferential leap and ask a question designed to elicit from the client what specific circumstances lead him to make different and seemingly unwise decisions concerning unsafe sex. In fact, Scott does disclose a good deal about his motivation for unsafe sex later in the session:

P130: I tried it. I tried it. I like sex without a condom. It's better. It is. I enjoy it more. I mean maybe it's partially a physical thing. But, but it's a mental thing too. You know. You, I never had unprotected sex until my ex-boyfriend, my most recent boyfriend, and, I loved it, you know **I loved being that close to him and I feel that I'm looking for that again maybe. I want that closeness, I want that intimacy**. And maybe it's just sort of, I'm seeking it—sought, it's the past tense. Especially after all this drama. I sought it in the wrong guy, in being unsafe with guys I, I thought were going to be something more significant than they were. The more I spent time with them, the more I realized you're not a good person. [Emphasis added.]

T: It's really hard to go back to safe sex after you've gotten used to that intimacy you have without condoms. [Paraphrasing; expressing empathy with the implicit dilemma the client is experiencing]

P: Yeah. It's just not the same.

T: You know, you called unprotected sex "fucking up" earlier, but it sounds to me like you actually get a lot out of it. [Rolling with resistance]

P: I do, but it's such a huge risk too. I mean my brother just died of AIDS. It's not like I don't know what can happen.

T: That scares you, what could happen to you. [Reflection of affect]

P: Yeah, a lot. I could never put my parents through that again.

T: So you have a real dilemma here: On the one hand, you really enjoy, you really miss the feeling of intimacy you get when you don't use a condom, but it also scares you that you're risking dying the same way your brother died. [Summary and double-sided reflection]

In this hypothetical exchange, I would attempt to accomplish several things. First, I would want to elicit more information about Scott's risky sexual behavior, and particularly about Scott's concerns regarding his sexual risk. Given that the behavior in question is arguably more stigmatized than drug use, I would choose my words very carefully in order to avoid activating feelings of shame and/or defensiveness and potentially shutting down the discussion. Once Scott has said that he has only had unprotected sex with three to four partners, indicating that unprotected sex is the exception rather than the rule for him, I would inquire as to those factors that led to his decision not to use condoms in those instances, again in as nonjudgmental a manner as possible. I would choose to highlight the theme of intimacy, emphasizing its importance with certain men with whom he feels an emotional connection, and especially its importance to the unique experience of intimacy and closeness he had experienced in his previous relationship. I also would want to validate his difficulties returning to condom use. I would then attempt to shift the discussion back toward an argument for change, by making a paradoxical intervention suggesting that Scott may actually be acting rationally given what he enjoys about condomless sex. This forces Scott into the position of advocating for change, which then can be magnified through simple and double-sided reflections.[3]

Scott makes it clear that he sets limits on his unsafe sexual behavior, demonstrating that he does have the capacity to consider the relative risk of various choices and attempt to moderate his risk in significant ways:

T125: Can I assume these are all just tricks [that you're having unsafe sex with]?

P125: No, no. 'Cause like I say I'm risky, **but I'm not that risky.** I mean, I must say all of them, maybe four guys I slept with in the past year or two I slept

---

[3] It is important to note that when using double-sided reflections, the latter part of the reflection should always be the argument in favor of change. In other words, when using a "on the one hand, on the other hand" type of intervention, the "other hand" argument, the last argument the client hears, should be the "take home message" the therapist wants the client to be left with. In the above case, it is important to validate the client's enjoyment of sex without condoms, but more important for the case of change that he be reminded of the fact that unprotected sex is scary.

with without a condom. One of them was a one night thing, **but in the heat of the moment I caught myself and said okay stop, stop, stop. Put a condom on, and he did**. The other two or three guys **were guys that I had been seeing that I thought were going to move in a proper direction**. [Emphasis added.]

Clearly, Scott has made some effort to limit the degree of risk he is exposed to from unprotected sex, by being selective in the partners with whom he has unprotected sex, and in fact by interrupting unprotected sex when with a novel partner. This is also valuable information in that it represents a foundation of commitment to practicing safer sex that can be built upon:

T125: Can I assume these are all just tricks [that you're having unsafe sex with]?
P125: No, no. 'Cause like I say I'm risky, but I'm not that risky. I mean, I must say all of them, maybe four guys I slept with in the past year or two I slept with without a condom. One of them was a one night thing, but in the heat of the moment I caught myself and said okay stop, stop stop. Put a condom on, and he did. The other two or three guys were guys that I had been seeing that I thought were going to move in a proper direction.
T: You're really trying to be selective about who you have unsafe sex with. [Therapist focuses on client's strengths.]

Here my primary objective would be to affirm the client's current risk-reduction strategies, rather than highlight their dubious effectiveness, and provide space for *Scott* to elaborate on the ways in which he remains unsatisfied with them, thus:

T: You're really trying to be selective about who you have unsafe sex with.
P: Well yeah, but I'm kidding myself if I think I'm staying safe. I'm still doing it with guys I don't know very well.
T: **So you think you need to be *more* selective**. [Use of reflection to highlight potential change strategy]

I always try to build from clients' existing strengths, because they usually provide the best entrée into ongoing change strategies. For example, in the above hypothetical exchange I would frame a change strategy for Scott's HIV risk behavior by establishing a goal of increasing his selectivity in partners, rather than swearing off all unprotected sex. The latter is likely to seem too daunting, because it does not lay out a discernable pathway to change in the same way that "I will be more selective in who I decide to have unprotected sex with" does, elements of which already exist in Scott's repertoire.

What should Scott's goal be concerning condom use? From the perspective of a therapist all too familiar with the risks of unprotected sex and the complications of HIV disease, it is very tempting to give in to the urge to press urgently for the complete elimination of unprotected sex with a client like Scott, as the next encounter could be the one that results in seroconversion. However, as with drug use, it is vital that the therapist allow Scott the space to explore for himself what decision makes the most sense for him. As noted above, Scott clearly experiences discrepancy about his sexual risk behavior. It will be critical to help him identify a goal that will feel achievable and realistic for him, rather than one that necessarily eliminates all risk. I would probably start by exploring with Scott how he came to the decision to stop using condoms in his last relationship, and ask Scott how his current goals are similar or different from his goals at that time. Again, this strategy builds upon a foundation of prior success that will bolster the sense that the goal is within reach.

Summary Impressions of Scott

Scott comes across as quite forthcoming, clearly eager, and in some senses almost bursting to talk about a wide variety of issues that have been troubling him. Given how easily he falls into his role as a client, it is surprising that this is his first foray into intensive psychotherapy, and reinforces my impression that he is "ready" to address a variety of problems and make changes in his life. As a clinician specializing in motivational and cognitive-behavioral interventions for health behavior problems, I find this very encouraging, as it suggests that Scott is already highly motivated to find answers to his problems, and will probably exhibit relatively little defensiveness when exploring the sensitive issues around his drug use and sexual behavior.

I get the sense that Scott's internal experience is often one of turmoil; he seems frequently to feel as though he cannot shut his mind off, and he seldom is able to escape from his own anxious and ruminative thoughts, turning to marijuana as the only thing that provides relief. I also suspect that part of Scott's difficulty is a low threshold of tolerance for unpleasant affect, which makes his drive to escape his inner turmoil all the more compelling. The effective expression of empathy for this experience by the therapist will be critical to getting his buy-in to alternative strategies for coping as a part of the overall change strategy for reducing marijuana use.

Scott strikes me as lonely. In his description of one of the encounters in which he had unprotected sex, he states:

> **P125:** [...] especially with this most recent guy that, that I was hanging out with. **I really liked him** and I slept with him the first night and he stayed for 72 hours, didn't leave. **Really liked each other**. [Emphasis added.]

In this encounter, Scott appears to have mistaken strong sexual chemistry for a true emotional connection, and then made a decision about condom use in order to enhance those feelings. Afterward he seems to quickly realize that what he perceived in these men was fleeting and false, saying, "He's a douche bag" and giving no indication that he saw the man again after this first encounter, and even suggests that, "I [always] knew it. Not a good guy." Scott clearly longs for the emotional and physical closeness of a romantic relationship, to the point where he perceives romantic connections where they don't exist, and then acts prematurely on those feelings.

To the extent that this is the case, it is probably also related to his low tolerance for unpleasant affect generally: His search for intimacy through unprotected sex with inappropriate partners is akin to his search for relief from stressful affect through the use of marijuana. This is also a cause of some concern to me, because although Scott alludes to being motivated to eliminate unsafe sex since his brother's death, the loss of his brother undoubtedly will be linked to profound feelings of loneliness in the months ahead. Scott refers to David as his "best friend in the world" (P18) and his "Number One—he had so much love to give me. It was unconditional" (P23). Particularly because of the closeness he reports with his brother, I would have real concerns that Scott could easily turn to unprotected sex as a way of coping with the loss of such a profoundly intimate relationship.

Scott appears to be searching for an emotional connection like the one he experienced with his last boyfriend, but is doing so with what strikes me as a sense of near-desperation, and is using unprotected sex as an artificial way of recreating that experience. MI and CBT can be of considerable help to Scott in identifying and elaborating on these themes, but a deeper exploration of the themes of loneliness and intimacy, and the dysfunctional ways Scott seems to attempt to deal with them, will be important to Scott's long-term well-being.

Clearly both Scott's marijuana use and unprotected sex are at least potentially if not actually harmful; however, it is important to note that I do not regard Scott's marijuana use or his sexual behavior as self-*destructive*, nor is it helpful from an MI or CBT perspective to invoke such unconscious motives to account for his presentation. On the contrary, from Scott's perspective his behaviors are quite rational in the sense that they bring real, concrete results that he desires in the moment that he chooses to engage in them.

In particular with regard to his sexual behavior, it would be tempting to view his choices in the context of his brother's recent death as indicative of a strong self-destructive impulse or even a death wish; however, as noted above, a closer examination of what Scott actually says about this suggests exactly the opposite:

P130: I like sex without a condom. It's better. It is. I enjoy it more. I mean maybe it's partially a physical thing. But, but it's a mental thing too. ... I want that intimacy. And maybe it's just sort of, I'm seeking it—*sought*, it's past tense. **Especially after this whole drama**. I sought it in the wrong guy .... [Emphasis added.]

In context it seems obvious that "this whole drama" refers to his brother's death, the "drama" that brought Scott to therapy in the first place; thus, the death seems at least for the time to have motivated Scott to stop seeking intimacy in the form of unprotected sex. More broadly, however, unprotected sex as a means to achieving feelings of intimacy provides a far more parsimonious account for his behavior, and a far more helpful conceptualization from the standpoint of treatment planning, than to invoke a concept such as "self-destructive."

Counter-transference in the delivery of MI. A common challenge in the delivery of MI is the client who reports engaging in behaviors that the therapist regards as patently unhealthy, or worse, immoral. Despite our best efforts at maintaining neutrality, we as therapists inevitably encounter clients who challenge our own value systems. As discussed earlier, Silverstein shows evidence of this himself in his comment,

"Why would you *do* that?" (T124), where he reveals his own incredulity that any gay man in Scott's position would engage in unprotected sex. Even more challenging, than seemingly self-destructive clients like Scott, are HIV-positive clients who report unprotected sex, particularly insertive anal sex with partners of unknown or discordant status. It is often tempting to jump to conclusions about such clients, giving in to anger or frustration at their apparent stupidity or callousness, and resort to confrontational techniques where mere empathy seems inadequate if not impossible to achieve; how, after all, can a therapist be empathic toward a sociopath apparently willing to infect unwitting partners with HIV? However, I can attest through personal experience that the power of the MI approach, if adhered to faithfully, is sufficient to address even the most challenging cases. The stance of the MI therapist is always to assume that there is room within the client to build discrepancy about a given behavior. For example, in a clinical trial focused on reducing HIV risk behaviors in HIV-positive and HIV-negative gay men, I found that virtually all HIV-positive men who engaged in unprotected sex experienced considerable concern and guilt over potentially exposing their partners to HIV, but that because of the degree of stigma and negative judgment they anticipated or experienced as a result of their behavior, coupled with the stigma of their HIV status, these men almost universally felt unable to discuss these feelings openly with anyone. Although maintenance of a nonjudgmental and nonconfrontational stance poses a unique challenge with such clients, it also has the potential to elicit intensely emotional and transformative reactions from clients who are able to give voice for the first time to their own painful ambivalence about sex. For example, consider the following exchange, based on an actual client:

> **P:** Look, the way I see it, if a guy is willing to let me fuck him without a
> condom, that's on him. I figure if he does that he's probably HIV anyway.
> **T:** So if you found out you'd given someone HIV, it wouldn't particularly bother
> you?
> **P:** Oh my God, if I found out some guy I'd been with got it from *me*, I'd be
> devastated.
> **T:** Why?
> **P:** I mean, that's life changing. HIV sucks. I wouldn't wish it on anybody. I
> wouldn't want that responsibility.
> **T:** So on the one hand, it's not your responsibility if you fuck without condoms,
> but yet you'd still feel responsible if he got infected as a result?

Here, the therapist using simple MI strategies was able to highlight for the client an inherent paradox in his thinking, namely that he can shift responsibility for sexual decision-making to his partner in the abstract, but that ultimate responsibility for transmitting the virus remains with him should a specific person become infected.

It is also important to remember that clients have various and complex motivations for engaging in particular behaviors, including even the most challenging clients such as those who knowingly expose others to HIV. Feelings of being "diseased" and "outcast" from the gay community often contributes to feelings of intense loneliness, and to a corresponding desire for the feelings of closeness and intimacy associated with condom-free sex, as well as a desire to avoid potential rejection. Moreover, most gay men with HIV understand that the possibility of unprotected sex, if not sex altogether, will be taken off the table with most potential sex partners should their HIV-positive status be disclosed, a fact that can create powerful incentives to withhold that information. Yet it should also be clear that only in a context in which these complex and contradictory motivations (i.e., the desire to have unprotected sex and the guilt associated with it) can be fully articulated will the individual be able to resolve this discrepancy adequately. In short, it is always essential to strive to understand the emotional needs at the root of clients' behavior, because it is this understanding that illuminates the pathway to change.

The role of homophobia in Scott's case. At this point I would like to consider Scott's case in the broader context of the legal and societal status of gay men's and lesbian's relationships. Scott reports that his most significant and intimate relationship ended because the couple accepted jobs in cities separated by over 6000 miles, essentially prioritizing their careers over the relationship. As a clinician and a gay man, I often hear similar histories of same-sex relationships falling victim to career or other choices on the part of one or both partners. At first glance, such a history might suggest that Scott, his boyfriend, or both lacked a serious sense of commitment to the relationship. After all, although divorce is far from uncommon among heterosexuals, it is fairly uncommon for a heterosexual marriage to break up because one spouse takes a job in another country.

This might beg the question, how serious could Scott's relationship really have been? On the other hand, it may be precisely because marriage, with all of its implications and assumptions of commitment and permanence, has always been available to heterosexual couples that career decisions are unlikely to be prioritized over a marital relationship. In contrast, gay men and lesbians grow up with the understanding that same-sex relationships are necessarily less significant than heterosexual marriages in very real, legal, and socially meaningful ways.

It has long been my strong impression that gay men's and lesbians' relationships more often and more quickly become casualties of typical relationship problems, including career considerations, than heterosexual marriages, and that this is due in some measure to three related factors:

1. That same-sex relationships have historically been excluded from legal and societal recognition, a factor that precludes many institutional and legal supports for dual-career couples that help to preserve marriages confronted with a major career change. These include, just to name two examples, relocation and job placement services for spouses of newly hired workers, and automatic citizenship for foreign-born spouses of citizens;
2. That because of this lack of legal and social sanction, there is a subtle but often significant diminution of the relationship, of perceptions of its permanence, and of the priority it is given relative to other life goals, on the part both of the couple and of outside observers. In other words, the lack of legal and societal sanction, for some individuals and couples, undermines the commitment to prioritize the relationship in making important life decisions.
3. That gay men and lesbians internalize these tacit and explicit societal messages about their relationships from an early age, such that, even for someone with relatively little direct experience with homophobia as Scott, a subtle cynicism can emerge about their relationships that leads to an expectation of temporariness, rather than of permanence.

I cannot begin to count the number of times, both in the office and in my personal life, that I have heard from gay men: (1) the belief that "gay relationships don't last," (2) astonishment at encountering a gay male couple who have been together for more than a couple of years, or (3) some variant of the joke, "We've been together 5 years, but that's like 50 in gay years." All of these of course betray an underlying assumption that gay men's relationships are transient, which in turn I believe reveals part of the enduring impact of societal homophobia. I believe that Scott's relationship history, his apparent loneliness, his intimacy needs, and his ineffectual and misdirected efforts to attain intimacy are all related in no small measure to the injury he shares with most if not all gay men and lesbians: that of having internalized the notion that the best he can hope for in a relationship is a pale, watered down, and unstable facsimile of a "real" relationship (i.e., heterosexual marriage).

All this being said, it should also be noted that societal attitudes are in constant flux, and that the growing availability and societal acceptance of marriage for same-sex couples presents the exciting possibility that this reality may be in the process of undergoing radical change for young gays and lesbians, who increasingly will have the opportunity to grow up with the same assumptions about commitment in their relationships that heterosexual youth have had.

Although well outside the narrow purview of MI and CBT for substance abuse or HIV risk behavior, I believe that the issues of intimacy, relationship skills, and relationship expectancies, and how these have been influenced by societal and internalized homophobia, will nevertheless eventually emerge as central themes in Scott's treatment.

References

Abelson, J., Rawstorne, P., Crawford, J., Mao, L, Prestage, G., & Kippax, S. (2006). HIV optimism does not explain increases in high-risk sexual behaviour among gay men of positive or negative HIV status in Sydney, Australia. *AIDS*, 20(8), 1215–1216.

Bauermeister, J. A., Carballo-Diéguez, A., Ventuneac, A., & Dolezal, C. (2009). Assessing motivations to engage in intentional condomless anal intercourse in HIV risk contexts ("bareback sex") among men who have sex with men. *AIDS Education and Prevention*, 21(2), 156–168.

Bien, T. H., Miller, W. R., & Tonigan, J. S. (1993). Brief interventions for alcohol problems: A review. *Addiction*, 88, 315–336.

Bimbi, D. S., Nanin, J. E., Parsons, J. T., Vicioso, K. J., Missildine, W., & Frost, D. M. (2006). Assessing gay and bisexual men's outcome expectancies for sexual risk under the influence of alcohol and drugs. *Substance Use & Misuse*, 41, 643–652.

Blais, M. (2006). Vulnerability to HIV among regular male partners and the social coding of intimacy in modern societies. *Culture, Health & Sexuality*, 8(1), 31–44.

Bux, D. A. (1996). Epidemiology of problem drinking in gay men and lesbians: A critical review. *Clinical Psychology Review*, 16(4), 277–298.

Cabaj, R. P. (2000). Substance abuse, internalized homophobia, and gay men and lesbians: Psychodynamic issues and clinical implications. *Journal of Gay & Lesbian Psychotherapy*, 3(3/4), 5–24.

Davidovich, U., de Wit, J., Albrecht, N., Geskus, R., Stroebe, W., & Coutinho, R. (2001). Increase in the share of steady partners as a source of HIV infection: A 17-year study of seroconversion among gay men. *AIDS, 15*, 1303–1308.

Halkitis, P. N., Green, K. A., & Carragher, D. J. (2006). Methamphetamine use, sexual behavior, and HIV seroconversion. *Journal of Gay & Lesbian Psychotherapy, 10*(3/4), 95–109.

Halkitis, P. N., & Parsons, J. T. (2003). Recreational drug use and HIV-risk sexual behavior among men frequenting gay social venues. *Journal of Gay & Lesbian Social Services, 14*(4), 19–38.

Halkitis, P. N., Shrem, M. T., & Martin, F. W. (2005). Sexual behavior patterns of methamphetamine-using gay and bisexual men. *Substance Use & Misuse, 40*, 703–719.

Irwin, T. W., Morgenstern, J., Parsons, J. T., Wainberg, M., & Labouvie, E. (2006). Alcohol and sexual HIV risk behavior among problem drinking men who have sex with men: An event level analysis of timeline followback data. *AIDS and Behavior, 10*(3), 299–307.

Jaffe, A., Shoptaw, S., Stein, J. A., Reback, C. J., & Rotheram-Fuller, E. (2007). Depression ratings, reported sexual risk behaviors, and methamphetamine use: Latent growth curve models of positive change among gay and bisexual men in an outpatient treatment program. *Experimental and Clinical Psychopharmacology, 15*(3), 301–307.

King, M., Semlyen, J., Tai, S. S., Killaspy, H., Osborn, D., Popelyuk, D., et al. (2008). A systematic review of mental disorder, suicide, and deliberate self harm in lesbian, gay and bisexual people. *BMC Psychiatry, 8*, 70–86.

Koblin, B. A., Husnik, M. J., Colfax, G., Huang, Y., Madisone, M., Mayer, K., et al. (2006). Risk factors for HIV infection among men who have sex with men. *AIDS, 20*, 731–739.

Koblin, B. A., Murrill, C., Camacho, M., Xu, G., Liu, K. -L., Raj-Singh, S., & Torian, L. (2007). Amphetamine use and sexual risk among men who have sex with men: Results from the national HIV behavioral surveillance study—New York City. *Substance Use & Misuse, 42*, 1613–1628.

Marks, G., Bingman, C. R., & Duval, T. S. (1998). Negative affect and unsafe sex in HIV-positive men. *AIDS and Behavior, 2*, 89–99.

Miller, W. R., & Rollnick, S. (2002). *Motivational interviewing: Preparing people for change* (2nd ed.). New York: Guilford Press.

Morgenstern, J., Bux, D. A., Parsons, J., Hagman, B. T., Wainberg, M., & Irwin, T. (2009). Randomized trial to reduce club drug use and HIV risk behaviors among men who have sex with men. *Journal of Consulting and Clinical Psychology, 77*(4), 645–656.

Morgenstern, J., Irwin, T. W., Wainberg, M. L., Parsons, J. T., Muench, F., & Bux, D. A., et al. (2007). A randomized controlled trial of goal choice interventions for alcohol use disorders among men who have sex with men. *Journal of Consulting and Clinical Psychology, 77*(1), 72–84.

Parsons, J. T., Kutnick, A. H., Halkitis, P. N., Punzalan, J. C., & Carbonari, J. C. (2005). Sexual risk behaviors and substance use among alcohol abusing HIV-positive men who have sex with men. *Journal of Psychoactive Drugs, 37*(1), 27–36.

Prochaska, J. O., & DiClemente, C. C. (1986). Toward a comprehensive model of change. In W. R. Miller, & N. Heather (Eds.), *Treating addictive behaviors: Processes of change* (pp. 3–27). New York: Plenum.

Project MATCH Research Group (1997). Matching alcoholism treatments to client heterogeneity: Project MATCH posttreatment drinking outcomes. *Journal of Studies on Alcohol, 58*, 7–29.

Purcell, D. W., Moss, S., Remien, R. H., Woods, W. J., & Parsons, J. T. (2005). Illicit substance use, sexual risk, and HIV-positive gay and bisexual men: Differences by serostatus of casual partners. *AIDS, 19*(Suppl. 1), S37–S47.

Rosario, M., Hunter, J., Maguen, S., Gwadz, M., & Smith, R. (2001). The coming-out process and its adaptational and health-related associations among gay, lesbian, and bisexual youths: Stipulation and exploration of a model. *American Journal of Community Psychology, 29*, 133–160.

Rosario, M., Schrimshaw, E. W., & Hunter, J. (2006). A model of sexual risk behaviors among young gay and bisexual men. *AIDS Education and Prevention, 18*(5), 444–460.

Ross, M. W., Mattison, A. M., & Franklin, D. R. (2003). Club drugs and ex on drugs are associated with different motivations for gay circuit party attendance in men. *Substance Use & Misuse, 38*(8), 1173–1183.

Rotheram-Borus, M. J., Rosario, M., Reid, H., & Koopman, C. (1995). Predicting patterns of sexual acts among homosexual and bisexual youths. *American Journal of Psychiatry, 152*, 588–595.

Slavin, S., Richters, J., & Kippax, S. (2004). Understanding of risk among HIV seroconverters in Sydney. *Health, Risk & Society, 6*, 39–52.

Sobell, L. C., & Sobell, M. B. (1995). *Alcohol timeline followback users' manual*. Toronto, Canada: Addiction Research Foundation.

Stall, R., & Purcell, D. W. (2000). Intertwining epidemics: A review of research on substance use among men who have sex with men and its connection to the AIDS epidemic. *AIDS and Behavior, 4*(2), 181–192.

Stephens, R. S. (1999). Cannabis and hallucinogens. In B. S. McCrady, & E. E. Epstein (Eds.), *Addictions: A comprehensive guidebook* (pp. 121–140). New York: Oxford University Press.

Strathdee, S. A., Hogg, R. S., Martindale, S. L., Cornelisse, P. G. A., Craib, K. J. P, & Montaner, J. S. G., et al. (1998). Determinants of sexual risk taking among young HIV-negative gay and bisexual men. *Journal of Acquired Immune Deficiency Syndromes and Human Retrovirology, 19*, 61–66.

Torres, H. L., & Gore-Felton, C. (2007). Compulsivity, substance use, and loneliness: The loneliness and sexual risk model (LSRM). *Sexual Addiction and Compulsivity, 14*, 63–75.

Van de Ven, P., Prestage, G., Crawford, J., Grulich, A., & Kippax, S. (2000). Sexual risk behaviour increases and is associated with HIV optimism among HIV-negative and HIV-positive gay men in Sydney over the 4 year period to February 2000. *AIDS, 14*(18), 2951–2953.

Van de Ven, P., Rawstorne, P., Nakamura, T., Crawford, J., & Kippax, S. (2002). HIV treatments optimism is associated with unprotected anal intercourse with regular and with casual partners among Australian gay and homosexually active men. *International Journal of STD & AIDS, 13*(3), 181–183.

WHO Brief Intervention Study Group (1996). A cross-national trial of brief interventions with heavy drinkers. *American Journal of Public Health, 86*, 948–955.

Williamson, L. M., & Hart, G. J. (2004). HIV optimism does not explain increases in high-risk sexual behaviour in Scotland. *AIDS, 18*(5), 834–835.

Xiridou, M., Geskus, R., de Wit, J., Coutinho, R., & Kretzschmar, M. (2003). The contribution of steady and casual partnerships to the incidence of HIV infection among homosexual men in Amsterdam. *AIDS, 17*, 1029–1038.

11 Cognitive-Behavioral Therapy

DeMond M. Grant and LaRicka R. Wingate

Department of Psychology, Oklahoma State University,
Stillwater, OK, USA

Cognitive-behavioral therapies (CBT) had their underpinnings in classical learning theories (Pavlov, 1941; Skinner, 1953; Watson, 1970). These theories focused on how conditioning processes elicited changes in specific identified measurable behaviors (Pavlov, 1927). At this early point in the history of psychology, theories were concerned primarily with observable behavior (largely in laboratory animals) and were not focused on the application of these frameworks to the therapeutic process. However, as the popularity and understanding of learning theory grew, these approaches began to be applied to the development of psychopathology. One example is the two-factor theory of avoidance learning, which used classical conditioning to describe how anxiety can be paired with nonemotional stimuli (Mowrer, 1939). Specifically, this theory suggested that when a neutral stimulus is paired with an emotional stimulus resulting in a fear response, over time the neutral stimulus can trigger that fear on its own. In addition, when the conditioned stimulus is avoided, anxiety decreases in the short term, but in the long run the anxious response is sustained, leading to increased symptoms. Over time several classical learning and behavioral theories led to specific predictions regarding the development of psychopathology.

One pioneer within the behavioral tradition was Joseph Wolpe. Wolpe believed that a person could not experience two incongruous feelings (e.g., anxiety and calmness) at once, and the way to make an individual feel less anxious was to associate their feared situation with relaxation (Wolpe, 1982). What was interesting about Wolpe is that he was able to combine scientific empirical research on desensitizing cats to a feared stimulus and make it applicable to the treatment of patients. For example, through working with war veterans that were suffering from posttraumatic stress disorder, he began to think of new ways of treating clients, such as pairing a feared stimulus (e.g., intrusive memories of the trauma) with a neutral stimulus (e.g., relaxation training), thus developing the technique termed *systematic desensitization*.

As behavioral principles were applied to decrease psychopathology, other theorists began expanding on these behavioral learning frameworks by including the influence of thoughts on behaviors (Beck, 1970; Ellis, 1962; Meichenbaum, 1977). Specifically, cognition, or thought activity, can include judgments about a specific

The Initial Psychotherapy Interview. DOI: 10.1016/B978-0-12-385146-8.00011-0

situation, rules, or assumptions about one's behavior, and beliefs about the self, world, or future. Cognition is differentiated from emotions, defined as one's subjective feelings and physiological arousal in response to a given situation. Thus, following a specific event, an individual's cognitions (i.e., judgments) about that event can influence their emotions (e.g., anxiety), in turn influencing their behavior (e.g., avoidance of the feared stimulus). The inclusion of cognitive approaches to traditional behavioral interventions occurred mainly in the late 1960s and early 1970s. This movement developed in part because specific constructs in psychology could not be fully explained by learning models in which a specific stimulus leads to a specific response. For instance, a learning model cannot explain the development of fears based on erroneous beliefs or modeling (Wolpe, 1982).

Thus, advancements within the field were occurring as a result of incorporating cognitive activity into behavioral models, such as the influence of cognition on avoidance behaviors as a result of experiencing anxiety (Lazarus, 1966). Based on these principles, several forms of CBT were developed, including rational emotive therapy (Ellis, 1962), cognitive-behavioral modification (Meichenbaum, 1977), and cognitive therapy (Beck, 1967). Although there is variation in the specific approaches to treatment, such as a focus mainly on cognitive-restructuring (Beck, 1967) versus problem-solving techniques (D'Zurilla & Goldfried, 1971), these approaches share many commonalities. Shared features of these treatments include changing maladaptive cognitions and behaviors, forming a collaborative relationship whereby the client and the clinician work together to increase the client's skills, and working on specific problems. Additional characteristics include a focus on the present, conscious thought, and short-term treatment. A number of cognitive-behavioral approaches have been developed for a variety of psychological disorders (e.g., major depressive disorder, anxiety disorders, personality disorders, substance use disorders, and eating disorders; see Nathan & Gorman 2007).

CBT are the most well-researched psychological treatments, and they have demonstrated efficacy in the treatment of a range of psychological disorders (Chambless & Ollendick, 2001). Within these treatments, researchers outline specific techniques (e.g., relaxation techniques) within a treatment manual developed for a specific disorder (e.g., generalized anxiety disorder, GAD). Once these techniques have been supported as efficacious through research, the manual would provide a general overview of the techniques that should be helpful in treating these disorders, defined as the nomothetic treatment. Nomothetic treatment approaches are general techniques that should apply to a wide range of individuals with similar presenting concerns. For example, having a client engage in relaxation training is one technique used in the cognitive-behavioral treatment of anxiety disorders. In contrast, idiographic approaches focus on understanding the individual, and any specific aspects of their behavior that might influence the course of treatment. Idiographic approaches usually are based on the nomothetic treatment, but would include either adding a technique that could be useful or taking out a treatment that could be harmful. To help clinicians learn how to move from a nomothetic treatment to an idiographic treatment, CBT case conceptualization has been developed by several authors (Beck, 1995; Nezu, Nezu, Friedman, & Haynes, 2007;

Persons & Tomkins, 2007). Although the specific techniques used to treat an individual patient will vary based on the specific case, there are core features to cognitive-behavioral treatments. CBT approaches are based on the assumption that cognitive activity affects behavior, and that behavior change can occur through changing this cognitive activity, and vice versa (Dobson & Dozois, 2001). The focus of these therapies is on changing a patient's dysfunctional thoughts and behaviors in order to help them cope with distressing emotions. Below we will briefly describe both CBT and psychodynamic therapy to help elucidate the core techniques of CBT, and articulate how they differ from psychodynamic therapy.

Differences Between CBT and Psychodynamic Therapy

There are several notable differences between CBT and psychodynamic therapy. First, CBT is typically a time-limited treatment, generally lasting approximately 12–20 weeks. Psychodynamic therapy tends to last for many years, although there are several short-term versions described within the literature (Messer & Warren, 1995). Second, although a therapeutic rapport is important to both treatments, it is a core aspect in psychodynamic therapy, but only a nonspecific component of CBT. That is, in the former this relationship is often a main topic of discussion, whereas in the latter the therapeutic relationship is generally not discussed directly as part of the treatment. Third, CBT tends to consist of highly structured activities and assignments, with much of the work taking place outside of therapy during homework assignments. Thus, CBT sessions tend to be focused on teaching the patient skills that will help in decreasing their symptoms, and these skills are practiced throughout the week by the patient. This is a core aspect of CBT treatment. Psychodynamic therapies typically do not use homework assignments and most of the work occurs during session.

Differences are also evident in the structure of therapy within the session. Psychodynamic therapies typically tend to be less structured within each session, and the topic of the intervention is often set by specific occurrences in the patient's life or past relational patterns that have caused problems for the patient. In CBT, however, each session is relatively structured. The basic premise is one of collaborative empiricism, in which the clinician and the patient work together to decrease the patient's symptomatology. That is, both client and clinician are knowledgeable, can think about situations and symptoms in a scientific and data-driven way, and will use their individual expertise (i.e., the client's problems and the techniques of CBT) to decrease the patient's symptoms. As an example, in any given session, the main goal of the CBT clinician is to teach or hone a patient's skill set regarding a specific situation. Thus, the clinician's goal may be to work on refuting thoughts, whereas the client's goal may be to discuss a stressful situation they had at work. With collaborative empiricism, both goals are met, as the work situation is discussed in session, which provides the clinician with the opportunity to emphasize refuting dysfunctional thoughts.

Perhaps the main difference between CBT and psychodynamic therapies involves the way cases are conceptualized. Psychodynamic case conceptualizations usually focus on early childhood experiences, unconscious desires within current relationships, and defense mechanisms that protect the self from negative thoughts and feelings. Specifically, the main aspects of psychodynamic case formulation include structural features of personality (i.e., the way patients generally relate to others), dynamic features of personality (i.e., the motives associated with the symptomatology or interaction patterns), developmental antecedents, and personal strengths (Messer & Wolitzky, 2007).

CBT case conceptualizations, in contrast, generally focus on a functional analysis of the patients' symptoms, the patient's specific symptomatology (i.e., DSM diagnoses), and other problems, schemas, and origins of the schemas (Persons & Tomkins, 2007). While psychodynamic conceptualizations focus considerably on a patient's unconscious desires and motives, CBT focuses on specifically identifiable thought patterns, dysfunctional behaviors, and how these patterns interact to cause and maintain negative emotions. CBT case conceptualizations will be described in more detail next.

Cognitive-Behavioral Case Conceptualization

One central aspect of developing a case formulation from a CBT perspective involves a functional analysis (Nezu et al., 2007; Persons & Tomkins, 2007). A functional analysis consists of forming hypotheses about the functional relationships of the patient's symptoms and other related problems in order to guide treatment (Haynes & O'Brien, 2000; Haynes & Williams, 2003). The goal of the case formulation is to integrate the patient's symptomatology, other problems, and personal history into a coherent, data-driven framework that will aid in eliciting hypotheses and clinical decisions (Nezu et al., 2007; Person & Tomkins, 2007). The functional analysis therefore is the first step of this process.

During the assessment, several sources can be used to identify problem areas associated with the patient's concerns. The most common resources include the use of a clinical interview and self-report questionnaires. A functional analysis can be accomplished by focusing on the symptoms of the patient (e.g., sleep difficulties) or other problems (e.g., financial difficulties), and assessing for the antecedents and consequences of these issues. This allows the clinician to begin to hypothesize about how certain symptoms are related. Thus, during the initial assessment the CBT clinician is assessing for specific DSM symptoms, other problems, and for factors that are increasing or exacerbating these concerns. A good functional analysis provides hypotheses about the causal or maintaining factors associated with the clients' symptoms, which in turn will lead to hypotheses about where best to intervene (Haynes & O'Brien, 2000; Haynes & Williams, 2003).

The primary complaint of the patient is an obvious important consideration in the case formulation. Some CBT clinicians have advocated for distinguishing between ultimate treatment goals and instrumental outcomes (Mash & Hunsley, 1993; Nezu et al., 2007). Ultimate treatment goals are usually focused on resolving the main reason the patient sought treatment, or the patient's presenting problem. An example of an ultimate treatment goal is to ensure that the patient is remitted from symptoms of depression for six consistent weeks. Instrumental outcomes are derived directly from the functional analysis, and will lead to specific areas of intervention. An example of an instrumental outcome is to ensure that the patient takes her or his antidepressant medications as prescribed. These therapeutic techniques in turn should lead to the ultimate outcome goals being met.

The functional analysis is a core technique in CBT case formulation. The actual case formulation expands on the functional analysis to provide an overall framework for choosing the treatments to be used. Despite the development of several empirically supported treatments within a CBT framework (Chambless & Ollendick, 2001) with documented efficacy for a variety of disorders, case conceptualization skills are highly needed among CBT clinicians. Whereas most treatment manuals are focused on the specific methods used to treat a single disorder (Heimberg & Becker, 2002), comorbidity (i.e., when an individual is experiencing two or more disorders concurrently) often is the norm among clinical populations rather than the exception (Kessler et al., 1994). Therefore, although the techniques do not radically change for different disorders, the approach to treatment, and the specific techniques used, can change based on a variety of factors, comorbid diagnoses, medical conditions, and/or high risk behaviors (e.g., suicidal behaviors). CBT case conceptualization allows one to skillfully apply these techniques to complex cases, and help guide clinicians' treatment choices based on empirical evidence.

In CBT case conceptualization frameworks, the first step of treatment would involve a thorough and detailed assessment of the patient's presenting problem and comorbid disorders. These diagnoses then direct which nomothetic treatment would be most useful to the patient. More explicitly, diagnosis directs treatment. After diagnoses the clinician lists any remaining symptoms and other problems that are not part of the DSM diagnosis under the "problem list." It is important to note that the problem list can include several concerns that the patient is facing, even those that will not be the focus of treatment, such as medical diseases (Persons & Tomkins, 2007). Therefore, these two sections (the DSM diagnoses and the problem list) should be made up of the presenting concerns of the patient.

The core of the case conceptualization involves describing the mechanisms that are hypothesized to be causing the patient's symptoms (Persons & Tomkins, 2007). These can include psychological, biological, and somatic areas, although the psychological mechanisms should be emphasized. The case conceptualization also will describe distal predictors of these problems, or the "origins" of the formulation. Additionally, the CBT case formulation would include the specific stressors that either led to or exacerbated the patient's current symptoms.

Finally, the individual aspects of the case conceptualization are organized into a coherent, logical narrative that outlines the hypotheses about the origins of a patient's symptoms, and the mechanisms that are maintaining them (Persons & Tomkins, 2007). Thus, the finished case conceptualization will lead to direct hypotheses about which empirically supported treatments should be most useful in helping the patient with their concerns. This will allow treatments that are supported by research to be applied flexibly to individual patients (Kendall, Chu, Gifford, Hayes, & Nauta, 1998). Lastly, Persons and Tomkins (2007) focus on the importance of continued assessment throughout the intervention. This will allow the clinician to determine if the initial hypotheses about the patient's instrumental outcomes need to be revised, and do so accordingly.

Scott

Areas of Assessment with the Initial Interview

Although building rapport is an important initial step across all orientations of therapy, the specific areas of the assessment can vary greatly by clinician. The literature suggests that there is considerable variability in the structure of the initial session with a patient. That being said, there are certain areas of the interview with Scott that we might have addressed differently, or at a later stage of treatment. For example, given that in P14 the patient noted that he was coming into treatment as a result of the death of his brother, from a CBT perspective, it would have been useful to have the patient describe how he thinks he is coping with his brother's death earlier in the interview. There was some interesting information gathered from this section of the interview, and it might have helped set up a CBT case conceptualization a little earlier. In addition, although past history and significant relationships in a patient's life would be discussed under a CBT framework, these issues might not have been covered in such great depth in the first interview. One specific reason for this is that Scott did not indicate that his sexuality, sexual history, or romantic relationships seemed to be a significant concern of his. Thus, we likely would have focused less time on the patient's first boyfriend and the client's sexual relations.

Although there are many areas that a clinician can cover in an initial interview, especially considering that the assessment period could take up to three or four sessions, the CBT clinician usually begins focusing on which specific DSM-IV diagnoses the patient is experiencing and other aspects of the problem list. In the initial interview with Scott, several areas stood out as possible targets to address during treatment. Specifically, these areas include grief, anxiety, substance-related difficulties, and suicidal ideations. Each of these areas will be discussed next.

Grief

Scott reported a number of symptoms related to a possible grief reaction. Of course, before considering bereavement as a diagnosis, it is important to assess for a specific loss event. In Scott's case, he indicated in P17 that his brother, David, recently died from complications of AIDS. Scott mentioned that he was close with his brother and that he is taking grieving day by day in P33. Scott later mentioned in the interview that he has some feelings of guilt related to his brother's death.

Specifically, in P134 Scott stated that he thought he would be a "basket case" when his brother died, but actually has good days and bad days. It seems that some of Scott's concern was not only that he was dealing with his brother's death, but whether it is appropriate for him to have good days when his brother recently died. Given that treatment for Scott's concerns related to the loss of his brother may differ depending on his actual DSM diagnosis, it is important to gather sufficient information to either rule out or diagnose bereavement. Specifically, it would be important to assess the length of time since his brother's death as well as the level of impairment it causes him in his daily life. It is quite possible that Scott is going through a normal grief process that would be considered regular and healthy. This is distinguished from a grief process that is beyond what is typical for the average person. This includes grief that significantly interferes with a person's functioning beyond the general time frame of 2 months after the loss.

Given that Scott's brother died within the past 3 weeks, as stated in P12, Scott may be experiencing normal reactions to the death of a loved one, and cannot yet meet the criterion to be diagnosed with major depressive disorder. However, this would be important for the therapist to assess repeatedly over time. It would be expected that with the passage of time, the client would go through the natural grief process and show improvement in functioning and mood. If significant symptoms and impairment persist beyond 2 months, they may be signs of a complicated grief reaction that warrant specific targeted treatment. It also would be pertinent to assess whether the symptoms of sadness, guilt, and thoughts of death occurred before his brother died. If so, the therapist will need to distinguish between preexisting symptoms of depression and rule out preexisting major depressive disorder and/or dysthymic disorder. (See DSM for a differential diagnosis between these disorders.)

Anxiety

Scott identified several indicators that he may be experiencing clinically significant symptoms of anxiety. For example, in P115 Scott noted that he has been anxious lately, and has worried about a number of different topics, including his job, his brother, and stressors with his family. By the patient's self-report, it appears that one diagnosis that may be the focus of his treatment is GAD. Thus, one difference that might have occurred in the intake interview is a greater focus on assessing specific DSM symptomatology of GAD. Given the increased stress Scott was experiencing as a result of the death of his brother, it would be important to determine whether this high level of worry is characteristic of the patient (i.e., was he experiencing this prior to his brother's death), or whether this worry became problematic only since David's death. Based on the cognitive-behavioral case conceptualization discussed above, if the patient met the criteria for this diagnosis, then this would be added to the diagnosis portion of the case conceptualization. This diagnosis, along with other comorbid diagnoses, would be used to choose which CBT techniques would be most useful for Scott's treatment.

Because of high levels of comorbidity across the anxiety disorders, we would also assess for the presence of other anxiety disorders (Kessler et al., 1994). The

National Comorbidity Survey suggested that up to 91.3 percent of GAD patients would meet criteria for another DSM diagnosis within their lifetime (Kessler et al., 1997). The specific techniques may have to be adjusted based on the comorbid symptoms that the patient presents with. For example, if a patient has comorbid depression with suicidal ideation, treatment should start with reducing the suicidal ideation (Leahy, 2004). Other common comorbid disorders include social phobia, other anxiety disorders, and cluster C personality disorders (Kessler et al., 1994).

Finally, there are several symptoms and features of GAD that should be assessed, as they also can help in the treatment planning stage. First, because individuals with GAD, by definition, worry about a number of topics (e.g., relationships, finances, and health concerns), obtaining information about the specific domains of worry that bother these individuals can be useful. Second, there are several features, although not symptoms of GAD, which can inform the use of techniques to be used when treating this disorder. Research by Dugas, Buhr, and Ladouceur (2004) has suggested that one construct that influences the symptoms and coping responses of individuals with GAD is *intolerance of uncertainty*, or the tendency to react to uncertain future events with high levels of distress. Third, due to the nature of their worries, individuals with GAD often engage in excessive procrastination and have difficulty with time management (Brown, O'Leary, & Barlow, 2001). Thus, behavioral techniques aimed at addressing these concerns can also be part of the treatment (Brown et al., 2001; Leahy, 2004). Finally, patients with GAD will experience dysfunctional thinking due to faulty beliefs about the world or themselves. Assessment of these dysfunctional cognitions during the assessment phase can add hypotheses about which treatment techniques can be useful (Brown et al., 2001; Leahy, 2004).

Substance Use

The client also indicated that he had both a history of and current problematic substance issues. Specifically, Scott reported in P107 that he is a "pot head" and also drinks regularly. The first area of assessment regarding these symptoms would be to determine the level of marijuana and alcohol use, the timeline of Scott's use, and whether this use led to significant distress. The specific DSM (APA, 2000) criteria would be assessed regarding both substance abuse and substance dependence.

It is also important to note that there is a substantial amount of comorbidity between substance use disorders and anxiety disorders (Kessler et al., 1997) and several hypotheses have been proposed to explain these high comorbidity levels. The self-medication hypothesis suggests that individuals will use substances in order to help themselves cope with negative symptoms of anxiety and depression (Khantzian, 1985). Specifically, individuals will use substances to decrease their uncomfortable symptoms, leading to a subjective feeling of relief. However, the substance serves both to reinforce their cognitive distortions about not being able to cope with their symptoms, and as an avoidance mechanism for dealing with stress. For example, it has been proposed that people who are socially anxious will use alcohol to decrease their physiological symptoms of anxiety in social situations (Thomas, Randall, & Carrigan, 2003). As a result, they are unable to disconfirm their negative beliefs about their ability to perform in social situations, and the alcohol serves as a way of avoiding their feelings of negative evaluation. Therefore, by self-medicating patients are only maintaining their anxious and depressive symptoms (Khantzian, 1997).

Based on this hypothesis, it would be important to assess the functional purpose of Scott's alcohol and drug use. In the initial interview, there is some evidence of Scott using marijuana to help cope with his anxiety symptoms. Specifically, in P114 he notes that "he finds it very, very difficult to quiet himself and relax" and that his "mind's always racing," and that marijuana is one thing that can stop these thoughts. Thus, it appears that his substance use may relate directly to his anxiety symptoms. In this case, having a functional assessment of the patient's presenting concerns can inform the treatment. That is, the extent that the substance use is problematic, and whether it should be one of the first aspects of treatment is reliant on the functional analysis. Given the information provided on the initial interview, it seems likely that the patient's substance use problems would decrease as his anxiety levels decreased.

Suicidal Concerns

Finally, and arguably most importantly, Scott indicated that he was having some symptoms of suicidal ideation. Specifically, he stated that thoughts of suicide run through his mind in P132. He elaborated that the thoughts of suicide have not been as strong as they currently are since he was a teenager. With the mention of suicidal concerns, it is important to follow up on suicide risk to both prevent the client from self-harm and protect the therapist against liability concerns (Wingate, Joiner, Walker, Rudd, & Jobes, 2004). It is a common myth that asking about suicide will actually increase the likelihood that a client will attempt suicide. The simple act of following up on a client's suicidal ideations and behavior will not make someone become suicidal. When assessing for suicidal ideation, it is important to use a suicide risk assessment framework. This allows a sense of security and direction to therapists who may be concerned about addressing suicidal issues, as well as possible support against concerns of the therapists' liability for the clients' suicidal behavior. Three important risk areas to assess for include the client's multiple attempt status, whether they are resolved on plans and preparations, and elevated on suicidal ideation and desire. (See Joiner, Walker, Rudd, & Jobes, 1999; Wingate et al., 2004.) After the client's risk and dangerousness level are determined, the therapist should then act accordingly and document her or his actions. Depending on the client's risk level, the therapist's response can vary widely. Some examples of possible therapist responses range from providing such clients with a list of emergency numbers and encouraging clients to utilize them if they feel that they cannot control their thoughts of or actions related to suicidal behavior, increasing the frequency that clients attend sessions, finding a guardian to stay with the client, and committing the client to inpatient care. For those clients that are at risk for suicidal behavior, the therapist will need to continue to document their risk status and any resolution regularly beyond the initial interview.

If we had conducted the initial assessment of Scott, significantly more time would have been spent on assessing Scott's level of risk. Whether Scott initiated the discussion (as he did in the interview) or not, we would have, at a minimum, assessed for suicidal ideation, plans or preparations, and a history of previous suicidal behavior. If any of Scott's responses were affirmative, we would have requested more detailed information and addressed his suicidal concerns. At the very least, we would have reminded Scott of the emergency contact information, including 911, and provided a list of emergency resources. Because more information about suicidal ideation was not collected in Scott's initial interviews, we cannot currently provide a risk category for Scott.

Case Conceptualization

Based on the initial interview, the basic case conceptualization would have likely unfolded as follows. The patient is a 30-year-old, Caucasian gay male who recently lost his brother to AIDS. He presented to the clinic with concerns related to grief from his brother's recent death, feelings of excessive anxiety and worry, problematic drug use, and suicidal ideation.

The patient's problem list consists of the recent death of his brother, problematic relationships with parents (especially his father due to a reported history of sexual abuse), excessive and uncontrollable worries about a number of activities and situations, problematic substance use, and current suicidal ideation. In addition to the problem list, specific DSM diagnoses would be assigned. With respect to the anxiety, it appears that the patient would likely have met criteria for GAD. Specifically, the patient noted recent excessive anxiety. He also reported that he frequently worries about a number of topics, including his job, his brother's death, stressors involving his parents, and his past history of molestation. It seemed as if many of these worries have been ongoing for some time, and particularly before his brother's death. No other specific diagnoses stand out from the initial interview. However, as noted above, any specific symptoms associated with his normal grieving process would not be included in the DSM diagnoses due to the recency of his brother's passing. Therefore, it would be important to assess the timeline of the patient's worries (and any depressive symptoms reported) and ensure he met criteria for GAD prior to the brother's death. If these criteria were met, GAD would likely be the patient's anchoring diagnosis as well.

The next aspect of the treatment would be selecting a nomothetic treatment plan based on the patient's anchoring diagnosis (Persons & Tomkins, 2007). Thus, CBT treatments for GAD would be the starting point for treatment (Brown et al., 2001; Leahy, 2004). However, this aspect would likely need to be modified in important ways. As several studies have suggested that grief counseling can be problematic, especially during the early stages of grief (Bonnano & Lilienfeld, 2008; Neimeyer, 2000), we would not intervene into the patient's natural grieving process. Therefore, no specific interventions would be used to work on the patient's worry about his brother's death, as these worries may not be problematic and may be occurring within the normal realm of the grief process at this point in time.

The next part of the case conceptualization involves positing hypotheses about the origins of the patient's mechanisms. There was no clear evidence of Scott experiencing cognitive distortions within this initial interview, thus making discussion of any negative schemas and core beliefs somewhat premature. However, given the evidence of the patient's worries, one could hypothesize about some core beliefs that the patient may be experiencing. One typical schema developed by individuals with GAD is, "Something bad is going to happen, and I won't be able to cope with it." Therefore, this schema lends itself to the core belief of "I'm incapable" or "I'm inadequate." With a complete diagnostic history a therapist would be able to hypothesize about specific events associated with the development of this core belief. Again, in Scott's case, there is some evidence to support the development of these dysfunctional beliefs. The sexual abuse that the patient described could easily have led to the development of negative beliefs about something negative happening in the future. In addition, Scott noted that his mother is also a worrier. Therefore, his symptomatology also may have developed through modeling, where he learned that worrying is one way of coping with stress. It would appear that the main precipitant of Scott's current symptoms is the death of his brother, who was a major support for him. This major life stressor likely increased his negative beliefs about his ability to cope with situations. Finally, because of the ongoing troubles with the patient's parents, and the reported child abuse, there were several enduring stressors that were likely exacerbated as a result of this loss.

Specific CBT Interventions

Based on the case conceptualization, two aspects of CBT treatment stand out as likely areas of intervention. Specifically, the first would involve helping the patient through the difficult and transitory time in his life associated with the death of his brother. Initial discussions would address validating the thoughts and feelings that the client has surrounding David's death. It is important to let him address his feelings in a safe and supportive environment. It would be important to provide psycho-education about the grief process. Included in this would be discussion about how many people handle grief in different ways, and that no way is particularly "correct." We could emphasize that he may be responding differently than others to his brother's death, and that is okay. We would also discuss common reactions to the death of a loved one in attempts to normalize Scott's feelings. It is normal to feel reactions of guilt, anger, sadness, and self- and other-blame. Additionally, it may be important to encourage Scott to engage in behavioral activation that will build relationships with others that serve to fulfill the areas of friendship that his brother once filled. The therapist will need to continue to track and assess Scott's symptoms of bereavement to assess for any changes. If his reaction to his brother's death is normal, we would expect that his symptoms of sadness and guilt would decrease over time. Additionally, we would expect that his feelings related to his brother's death do not significantly interfere with his daily functioning. If his feelings do not remit, or they increase after several months, the therapist should consider a more severe diagnosis and course of treatment focused specifically on grief.

In addition to addressing the patient's feelings of grief, it would be important to implement treatment to help the patient learn skills to cope with his symptoms of anxiety. Based on the initial interview it is likely that the patient met criteria for GAD. Several CBT approaches have been developed for treating GAD (Brown et al., 2001; Leahy, 2004). Overall, the main components of CBT treatment for GAD include providing a rationale for treatment, psycho-education, behavioral techniques to manage anxiety, increasing time management skills, worry reduction skills, and skills to modify core beliefs. Each of these techniques will be discussed in turn.

The basic rationale for CBT is that dysfunctional thoughts influence feelings, which in turn influence behavior. Thus, CBT interventions typically focus on modifying these thoughts and the dysfunctional behaviors that serve to maintain these thoughts and negative emotions. Anxiety-related thoughts often focus on overestimation of the probability of future negative events, and catastrophizing about the consequences of these thoughts. Behaviors driven by anxiety typically include avoiding situations that remind the patient of their negative thoughts and avoidance of situations that might elicit anxiety. By addressing the distorted thoughts and the avoidance behaviors associated with anxiety, patients can learn techniques to reduce symptoms of anxiety and feel more in control of their worry.

Psycho-education is a core feature of CBT, and thus this is often one of the first matters discussed when treating anxiety disorders. Typically, this component of treatment focuses on describing the evolutionary purpose of anxiety and that anxiety serves an adaptive purpose, although excessively high levels of anxiety can be problematic. Patients are told that through CBT they will learn skills to help manage and decrease their anxiety. It is also helpful to educate the patients about the GAD diagnosis. Specifically, patients learn about the specific symptoms of GAD, including excessive worries, physical symptoms, and thoughts that their worries are out of control. In addition, it is discussed with the patient that GAD is a chronic condition that is fairly common in the population. Therapists will also stress that CBT techniques have been proven to decrease the negative symptoms of GAD, thus providing patients with a sense of hope about the outcome of treatment.

Behavioral techniques used in the treatment of GAD usually include some type of relaxation training. Although typical GAD protocols include progressive muscle relaxation (PMR), other relaxation techniques, such as breathing retraining can be useful. PMR involves taking patients through a cycle of tension and relaxation for each of their major muscle groups (Bernstein & Borkovec, 1973). This training allows patients to determine the difference between tension and relaxation and through further practice notice when they are experiencing high levels of tension, and then relax their bodies. PMR usually is first taught in session with the clinician, and then practiced at home several times per week. Once the patient has considerable practice with PMR, the number of muscle groups taken through the tension—relaxation cycle is reduced, until patients are asked to relax each major muscle group by recall. This technique is fairly easy to learn through practice, and can readily be applied in stressful situations.

Patients with GAD often have difficulty managing their time and/or they engage in procrastination, which adds to their levels of stress (Leahy, 2004). Thus, time management techniques are often taught to patients with GAD. Specific aspects include prioritizing the patient's time, scheduling activities, and rewarding the self for maintaining a schedule. In addition, it can be helpful to work with patients in session about the problems or concerns that they may encounter that might lead to procrastination. For example, often GAD patients become overwhelmed when trying to start a new task because they are focused on all that they have to accomplish and the possibility of failing. Thus, helping the patient break down each task into smaller steps can be helpful for the GAD patient. Leahy (2004) recommends teaching the patient questions they can ask themselves, such as "What goal do you want to accomplish? What is the first step you can take in reaching your goal? What are the advantages and disadvantages of taking the first step?" Helping the patient work through these questions, and then practice answering them outside of treatment, can be useful in decreasing procrastination and increasing time management skills.

Several techniques have been described to reduce worrying. Two of the most widely used include scheduling worry time, and worry exposure. When patients are asked to schedule worry time, they designate a time during the day, typically an hour or less, in which they worry intensely about several different topics. When a specific worry occurs to a patient, they are asked to write down that worry, so that they can remember to come to it during their worry time. The rationale behind worry time is that it trains patients to worry only during a given period of the day, providing them with more control over when they worry. Worry exposure consists of having the patient engage in their worries while in a controlled situation, so that they become used to the feared stimulus. The fears stimulus in GAD is typically some unknown future event, and thus the exposure piece focuses on having patients picture these feared images in their minds while worrying, with the final goal of extinguishing their fears.

In addition to the above behavioral techniques, cognitive-restructuring techniques are also useful in decreasing a patient's worries. There are several different cognitive distortions associated with psychopathology, including (1) mindreading (assuming you know what others are thinking), (2) fortune-telling (predicting negative things will occur in the future), (3) overgeneralizing (thinking that several other negative things will happen as a result of one negative thing happening), (4) overestimation (thinking that the likelihood of an event occurring is higher than it actually is), and (5) catastrophizing (thinking that the consequence of a situation that occurring is worse than it actually is).

CBT teaches patients how to identify when they are having dysfunctional thoughts, specify the specific type of negative thought they are experiencing, and refute these thoughts. Importantly, refuting dysfunctional thoughts is not necessarily about thinking positively, but rather about having more balanced thoughts. Although there are specific techniques to challenge most of the cognitive distortions, typically patients are asked to find evidence in support of the thought, evidence against the thought, and come to a more balanced conclusion as a result. For example, when a patient engages in overestimation, she or he may be asked to note how often she or he has actually experienced the feared event, in comparison to how likely it is the patient thinks the event will occur. Though discussing the number of times that patients actually experienced the event, their estimation of the likelihood of the event actually occurring will decrease. In addition, for catastrophizing thoughts, patients may be asked to write down the perceived negative consequences they associated with the negative event. They are then asked to write down the worst situation that could happen, the best situation, and then describe a more balanced outcome.

Finally, in addition to restructuring specific negative thoughts, it also could be useful to work on modifying Scott's negative core beliefs. Typically, dysfunctional thoughts of patients with anxiety and depressive disorders are driven by their negative schemas/core beliefs. As discussed in the case conceptualization, it is possible that Scott is experiencing the core belief that he "is incapable." When addressing core beliefs, the patient is asked to identify his specific core belief, in this case, "I am incapable," and the percentage that they believe the core belief at that time. Next, the patient is asked to come up with a new, balanced core belief, typically something such as "I am a capable person," or "There are many areas in which I am capable." The patient then generates evidence supporting their old core belief and evidence supporting their new core belief. Finally, patients are asked to indicate how much they believe both the old belief and the new belief. Over time, by working on this technique both within session and outside of session, the percentage that patients believe the old belief decreases, while the percentage that they believe the new believe increases.

Based on the initial interview with Scott, it is expected that several if not all of these techniques (behavioral relaxation, time management, exposure to worry, and cognitive restructuring) would be useful in decreasing his symptoms and stress. In particular, based on the case conceptualization, it appears that he is having some trouble regulating his anxiety and other negative emotions. As a result, the behavioral skills would help provide him with techniques to relax when he is feeling stressed. In addition, time management skills would likely be useful during this time that he is grieving for his brother (similar to the behavioral techniques described above). Finally, the techniques to manage and decrease his worry would likely be helpful to Scott's normal response style when dealing with stress. The cognitive techniques could be used to challenge specific worries that the patient is having. Finally, by modifying core beliefs, the amount of time that Scott experiences feelings of uncontrollability should decrease, thus decreasing his psychological symptoms. The specific techniques chosen, and the order that they are discussed in treatment, would depend considerably on the case conceptualization. However, by continually reassessing the case over time with a functional analysis, and modifying the treatment as such, CBT should be able to help Scott reach all of his treatment goals.

Summary

This chapter reflected upon the initial interview with Scott, a 30-year-old gay male, from a CBT perspective. The authors suggested that the initial interview may have been conducted somewhat differently from their CBT orientation. Specifically, the interview would have likely been more structured, and would have focused on gathering information about specific problems and symptoms that would lead to a DSM diagnosis. From the information gathered during the initial interview, it appeared that Scott had four main areas of concern. Specifically, Scott described feelings of grief following the recent death of his brother, persistent symptoms of anxiety across various domains, regular substance use, and suicidal ideation. In an ideal situation, additional information would be gathered about each of Scott's areas of concern. More data, including added self-report information as well as psychological measures would greatly assist in a more thorough case conceptualization. After ensuring no significant suicidal risk, our likely initial therapeutic target would include briefly addressing and normalizing the feelings of grief and guilt associated with his brother's death. Following this, the main target of treatment would be alleviating Scott's symptoms of GAD. With support through the normal course of grief, and treating GAD with the many techniques described in the chapter, it is expected that Scott's quality of life will increase greatly, and likely will result in less substance use and less suicidal ideation.

If You Want to Learn More About CBT

Beck, J. S. (1995). *Cognitive therapy: Basics and beyond*. New York: Guilford Press.
Beck, A. T. (1979). *Cognitive therapy and the emotional disorders*. New York: Penguin.
Burns, D. D. (1999). *The feeling good handbook*. New York: Plume/Penguin Books.
Leahy, R. L., & Holland, S. J. (2000). *Treatment plans and interventions for depression and anxiety disorders*. New York: Guilford Press.
Persons, J. B. (2008). *The case formulation approach to cognitive-behavior therapy*. New York: Guilford Press.

References

American Psychiatric Association (2000). *The diagnostic and statistical manual of mental disorders* (4th ed.). Washington, DC: Author.
Beck, A. T. (1967). *Depression: Causes and treatment*. Philadelphia, PA: University of Pennsylvania Press.
Beck, A. T. (1970). Cognitive therapy: Nature and relation to behavior therapy. *Behavior Therapy, 1*, 184—200.
Beck, J. S. (1995). *Cognitive therapy: Basics and beyond*. New York: Guilford Press.
Bernstein, D. A., & Borkovec, T. D. (1973). *Progressive relaxation training: A manual for the helping profession*. Champaign, IL: Research Press.

Bonnano, G. A., & Lilienfeld, S. O. (2008). Let's be realistic: When grief counseling is effective and when it's not. *Professional Psychology: Research and Practice*, *39*, 377–378.

Brown, T. A., O'Leary, T. A., & Barlow, D. H. (2001). Generalized anxiety disorder. In D. H. Barlow (Ed.), *Clinical handbook of psychological disorders* (pp. 154–208). New York: The Guilford Press.

Chambless, D. L., & Ollendick, T. H. (2001). Empirically supported psychological interventions: Controversies and evidence. *Annual Review of Psychology*, *52*, 685–716.

Dobson, K. S., & Dozois, D. J. A. (2001). Historical and philosophical bases of the cognitive-behavioral therapies. In K. S. Dobson (Ed.), *Handbook of cognitive-behavioural therapies* (pp. 3–39). New York: Guilford Press.

Dugas, M. J., Buhr, K., & Ladouceur, R. (2004). The role of intolerance of uncertainty in etiology and maintenance. In R. G. Heimberg, C. L. Turk, & D. S. Mennin (Eds.), *Generalized anxiety disorder: Advances in research and practice* (pp. 143–163). New York: Guilford Press.

D'Zurilla, T. J., & Nezu, A. (1971). Problem-solving and behavior modification. *Journal of Abnormal Psychology*, *78*, 107–126.

Ellis, A. (1962). *Reason and emotion in psychotherapy*. New York: Stuart.

Haynes, S. N., & O'Brien, W. H. (2000). *Principles and practice of behavioral assessment*. New York: Kluwer Academic/Plenum Press.

Haynes, S. N., & Williams, A. E. (2003). Case formulation and design of behavioral treatment programs: Matching treatment mechanisms to causal variables for behavior problems. *European Journal of Psychological Assessment*, *19*, 164–174.

Heimberg, R. G., & Becker, R. E. (2002). *Cognitive-behavioral group therapy for social phobia: Basic mechanisms and clinical strategies*. New York: Guilford Press.

Joiner, T., Walker, R., Rudd, M. D., & Jobes, D. (1999). Scientizing and routinizing the outpatient assessment of suicidality. *Professional Psychology: Research & Practice*, *30*, 447–453.

Kendall, P. C., Chu, B., Gifford, A., Hayes, C., & Nauta, M. (1998). Breathing life into a manual: Flexibility and creativity with manual-based treatments. *Cognitive and Behavioral Practice*, *5*, 177–198.

Kessler, R. C., Crum, R. M., Warner, L. A., Nelson, C. B., Schulenberg, J., & Anthony, J. C. (1997). Lifetime co-occurrence of DSM-III-R alcohol abuse and dependence with other psychiatric disorders in the National Comorbidity Survey. *Archives of General Psychiatry*, *54*, 313–321.

Kessler, R. C., McGonagle, K. A., Zhao, S., Nelson, C. B., Hughes, M., & Eshleman, S., et al. (1994). Lifetime and 12-month prevalence of DSM-III-R psychiatric disorders in the United States. *Archives of General Psychiatry*, *51*, 8–19.

Khantzian, E. J. (1985). The self-medication hypothesis of addictive disorders. *American Journal of Psychiatry*, *142*, 1259–1264.

Khantzian, E. J. (1997). The self-medication hypothesis of substance use disorders: A reconsideration and recent applications. *Harvard Review of Psychiatry*, *4*, 231–244.

Lazarus, R. S. (1966). *Psychological stress and the coping process*. New York: McGraw-Hill.

Leahy, R. L. (2004). Cognitive-behavioral therapy. In R. G. Heimberg, C. L. Turk, & D. S. Mennin (Eds.), *Generalized anxiety disorder: Advances in research and practice* (pp. 265–292). New York: Guilford Press.

Mash, E. J., & Hunsley, J. (1993). Assessment considerations in the assessment of failing psychotherapy: Bringing the negatives out of the darkroom. *Psychological Assessment*, *5*, 292–301.

Meichenbaum, D. H. (1977). *Cognitive-behavior modification*. New York: Plenum Press.

Messer, S. B., & Warren, C. S. (1995). *Models of brief psychodynamic therapy: A comparative approach*. New York: Guilford Press.

Messer, S. B., & Wolitzky, D. L. (2007). The psychoanalytic approach to case formulation. In T. D. Eells (Ed.), *Handbook of psychotherapy case formulation* (pp. 67–104). New York: Guilford Press.

Mowrer, O. H. (1939). A stimulus–response analysis of anxiety and its role as a reinforcing agent. *Psychological Review, 46*, 553–565.

Nathan, P. E., & Gorman, J. M. (2007). *A guide to treatments that work* (3rd ed.). New York: Oxford University Press.

Neimeyer, R. A. (2000). Searching for the meaning of meaning: Grief therapy and the process of reconstruction. *Death Studies, 24*, 541–558.

Nezu, A. M., Nezu, C. M., Friedman, S. H., & Haynes, S. N. (2007). Case formulation in behavior therapy: Problem-solving and functional analytic strategies. In T. D. Eells (Ed.), *Handbook of psychotherapy case formulation* (pp. 368–401). New York: Guilford Press.

Pavlov, I. P. (1927). *Conditioned reflexes* (G.V. Anrep, Trans.). New York: Liveright.

Pavlov, I. P. (1941). *Conditioned reflexes and psychiatry* (W. H. Gantt, Trans.). New York: International.

Persons, J. B., & Tomkins, M. A. (2007). Cognitive-behavioral case formulation. In T. D. Eells (Ed.), *Handbook of psychotherapy case formulation* (pp. 314–339). New York: Guilford Press.

Skinner, B. F. (1953). *Science and human behavior*. New York: Macmillan.

Thomas, S. E., Randall, C. L., & Carrigan, M. H. (2003). Drinking to cope in socially anxious individuals: A controlled study. *Alcoholism: Clinical and Experimental Research, 27*, 1937–1943.

Watson, J. B. (1970). *Behaviorism*. New York: Putnam.

Wingate, L. R., Joiner, T. E., Walker, R. L., Rudd, M. D., & Jobes, D. A. (2004). Empirically informed approaches to topics in suicide risk assessment. *Behavioral Sciences and the Law, 22*, 651–665.

Wolpe, J. (1982). *The practice of behavior therapy* (3rd Ed.). New York: Pergamon Press.

12 Family Systems (The Relational Contexts of Individual Symptoms)

Corinne Datchi-Phillips

Center for Adolescent and Family Studies, Indiana
University-Bloomington, Bloomington, IN, USA

The family systems approach to psychotherapy is based on the premise that personality is not a static and internal attribute of human beings but the result of complex interactions between individual, interpersonal, and environmental factors (Stanton, 2009). In other words, personality is dynamic and context-dependent, and human behaviors are individuals' responses to specific circumstances rather than the expression of self-contained characteristics. This approach focuses on the familial, cultural, and social systems in which human behaviors are embedded and thereby constitutes a radical departure from psychology's traditional emphasis on the self and its intrapsychic properties such as Freud's structural theory of the id, ego, and superego (Freud, 1989). In addition, its understanding of causality as a process of mutual influence contrasts with the view in cognitive-behavioral and psychodynamic therapies that individuals' dysfunctional thinking, inner life, or past experience is the origin of problems (See Chapters 11 and 13 in this book). From a systemic perspective, it is *what* happens in the context of individuals' interactions with significant others, not the reason *why* it happens, that is the focus of assessment and intervention (Becvar & Becvar, 2006). Psychological, emotional, and behavioral disorders are part of the patterns that characterize clients' relationships with others and that give meaning to their problems. Like cognitive-behavioral therapies, the family systems approach gives emphasis to the here and now; however, it differs in its conceptualization of clients' symptoms as events that both influence and are influenced by others' actions.

This chapter shows how an intake therapist might conduct Scott's initial interview from the perspective of family systems theory. It first gives an overview of the development of family therapy as an established profession, and explains the key theoretical principles that inform the conceptualization of Scott's problem. To write this chapter, I have drawn on my own experience as a multisystemic therapist and on the clinical model that informs my work with couples and families (i.e., Functional Family Therapy, FFT). FFT is an evidence-based intervention originally designed to address the problems of at-risk adolescents. It integrates systemic thinking and constructivist theories with knowledge about family development and

The Initial Psychotherapy Interview. DOI: 10.1016/B978-0-12-385146-8.00012-2

common factors of therapeutic change. My own practice adapts the core principles of FFT to the treatment of various issues, including depression, anxiety, and substance use in adults and their relational context. My description of the family systems approach in this chapter does not represent the variety of family therapy theories that may guide the initial interview and the conceptualization of the client's problem. It is an illustration of my clinical work. Throughout the chapter, I refer to my own practice more or less directly, using the word "I" or the term "family therapist" when I wish to highlight the common characteristics that define the specialty of family psychology. The objectives of this chapter are to highlight what in the initial interview I pay attention to and to what end; to provide specific examples of how I might respond to the client; to compare the style, purpose, and directiveness of my interventions to those of Scott's counselor; and to make explicit the thinking process that underlies my understanding of Scott's difficulties and my clinical decisions.

A Brief History of Family Therapy

The development of the family systems approach into an established profession and specialty of psychotherapy and psychology began in the 1950s with the seminal work of family practitioners and researchers such as Murray Bowen, Nathan Ackerman, Lyman Wynne, Theodore Lidz, John Bell, Carl Whitaker, Virginia Satir, Don Jackson, Gregory Bateson, Jay Haley, and John Weakland (Broderick, 1993; Broderick & Schrader, 1991; Goldenberg & Goldenberg, 2009). These early proponents of the family systems approach studied the relational processes and communication patterns that characterized the familial context of schizophrenia, using the principles of cybernetics and general systems theory. With a few exceptions, these pioneers came from the field of psychiatry, had been analytically trained, and were dissatisfied with the outcomes of one-on-one treatment of psychosis. Influenced by social psychiatry and the work of Eric Fromm and Harry Stack Sullivan, they broke away from the precepts of psychoanalysis and proposed a new view of mental illness that described how familial processes participated in the emergence and maintenance of individual symptoms.

This brief history of family therapy highlights the themes and challenges of the family therapy movement in the periods that follow its emergence, from the 1960s to the present. The 1960s and 1970s were a time of rapid growth with the creation of schools of family therapy, the founding of prominent family therapy journals (e.g., *Family Process* in 1961), the publication of textbooks, the opening of training centers in New York City, Philadelphia, Boston, Palo Alto, Chicago, and Milan, and the formation of the American Family Therapy Association in 1977. The pioneers of the 1950s maintained an instrumental role as they participated in the development of clinical models of family therapy: multigenerational (Murray Bowen), psychodynamic (Nathan Ackerman), experiential (Virginia Satir), structural (Salvador Minuchin), and strategic (Jay Haley, see the section To Learn More About This Approach).

In the 1980s, the family therapy movement continued to expand and to gain national recognition: The number of journals, training institutes, and professional organizations multiplied and in 1984 the Society for Family Psychology of the American Psychological Association was created, an event that symbolized the promotion of the family systems approach as a science (Goldenberg & Goldenberg, 2009). The 1980s were both a period of accomplishments and a time of self-examination prompted by the feminist and postmodern critique of the values and assumptions that underlie family therapy models. This critique challenged the field to consider how the social, cultural, and political contexts influenced the functioning of family systems; it highlighted the differential power of family members in a patriarchal society and called for a better appreciation of human diversity.

In the last two decades, the field of family therapy has turned attention to the challenges of a changing world, in particular globalization and the impact of migration and relocation on families (Kaslow, 2008), and managed care and the pressure for greater accountability and cost containment from health insurance companies in the United States. In response to the requirements of managed care, practitioners and researchers have developed and tested integrative models of family therapy that are grounded in the principles of the family systems approach and supported by empirical evidence of effectiveness (Sexton, Weeks, & Robbins, 2003).

The Family as a Biopsychosocial System

All schools of family therapy share a common epistemology or set of assumptions and rules that define how and what kind of knowledge it is possible to form about reality. The epistemology of family theories and therapies is grounded in a systemic paradigm that frames and connects the fundamental concepts family therapists use to understand human behaviors. This paradigm developed from the integration of two theoretical frameworks, general systems theory (Bertalanffy, 1968) and cybernetics or the science of self-correcting systems (Wiener, 1948). General systems theory and cybernetics originate from the disciplines of mathematics, physics, and engineering, and from the study of the structure and operations of mechanical devices and biological organisms (Broderick, 1993; Guttman, 1991; Nichols, 2006). From a systemic and cybernetic perspective, the family is an open, self-regulating, social system that continuously interacts with the environment and whose individual parts are interrelated. Systems thinking gives emphasis to the dynamic interdependence of individual, interpersonal, and environmental factors that shape behaviors, and offers a view of the family that stresses the complex, reciprocal, and interactive processes and relational patterns in which individual members are embedded (Stanton, 2009). Reciprocity is a central concept of the family systems paradigm together with the notion of wholeness, open systems, self-governance, and morphogenesis or adaptation, which will inform my conceptualization of Scott's difficulties.

From a systemic perspective, the family is a biopsychosocial system of interconnected individuals whose relations to one another are defined by recurring patterns.

To understand the family system, one cannot study individual behaviors as separate units of analysis and then combine the units in order to provide clues into how the family functions. Systemic thinking is guided by the concept of nonsummativity and the idea that the properties of the family as a whole are different from those of its constituent members (Broderick, 1993; Nichols, 2006; Stanton, 2009). It gives emphasis to the interactions of individual family members and to the repetitive patterns that emerge from these interactions. These patterns say something about the structure or organization of the family, that is, the relational processes that govern individual behavior in a rule-like and circular manner. Indeed, systemic thinking requires a conceptual shift from linear causality (i.e., A caused B to do X) to an understanding of individual action as reciprocal and nonsequential. Family members mutually influence each other according to the patterns or rules of the family system's organization.

The family is an open cybernetic or self-regulating system that continuously engages, with its environment and within itself, in a process of reciprocal exchange necessary for its continued existence. This process of reciprocal exchange involves the flow of information and other essential resources across the boundaries of the different systems and subsystems that surround or compose the family (e.g., parent/child, community, workplace, cultural groups, society). The integrity of the family in the context of reciprocal, interactive, and dynamic networks of relationships is a function of both stability and change (Becvar & Becvar, 1982): Families must be able to adapt to variable situations such as the normative and less-normative circumstances of marriage, illness, or unemployment, at the same time as they maintain the organization of the family as a system. Like all systems, the family regulates itself by means of feedback mechanisms. Feedback is information or events that originate from within or outside the family, that constitute deviations from the system's interactive patterns or organization, and that call for the family's corrective response by either restoring the status quo or making adjustments. Cybernetic theory describes two types of feedback mechanism: *Negative feedback* indicates departure from the system's rule-like organization, and calls for the system's return to its original state, whereas *positive feedback* promotes deviations from the ways things are now in the family. From a cybernetic perspective, change occurs at two levels. (1) First-order change corresponds to variations in behaviors; however, the basic rules that govern the family system remain the same. (2) Second-order change is a creative process of adaptation whereby the family system reorganizes itself and moves beyond its existing structure to identify creative solutions to problems. For example, teenage behaviors that defy parental authority (e.g., rejection of directives) call into question the balance between dependence and independence that defines the relationship between parents and younger children. They constitute a deviation from the way things were when children were younger. Parents and adolescents may respond to these behaviors by negotiating the rules of the household and by creating opportunities for the teenager to make decisions. This represents second-order change, that is, change in the relational organization of the family: The family engages in a new set of behaviors (negotiating rather than directing, following, or rebelling) and the adolescent has more power in the family relationships. Family systems therapies are formal processes of second-order change: Therapists intervene to promote families' ability to adapt to various events, normative and nonnormative, by thinking beyond the rules of the system (Becvar & Becvar, 2006; Stanton, 2009).

Last, it is important to note that the family systems approach has integrated systemic and cybernetic principles with constructivist concepts that explain how cognitive and communicative processes participate in family functioning (Nichols, 2006; Stanton, 2009). Constructivism is a theory of knowledge which posits that individuals' perception of reality is a personal construction determined partly by each individual's belief systems, personal experience, emotional states, and information-processing abilities (Carr, 2006). While systemic and cybernetic principles emphasize the family's behaviors and interactions, constructivism calls attention to the family's perceptions and beliefs about their experience; it focuses on the family's interpretation of their problems with a view to constructing new meanings that open the door to new solutions and to new sets of interactions.

The Family Systems Approach to the Initial Interview

In family systems therapy, the initial interview corresponds to the early stage of treatment. Assessment and intervention occur simultaneously as the therapist gathers information about the family's concerns; forms a balanced alliance with the family and between family members; interrupts the enactment of interactional patterns that are associated with blaming communication and negative emotions such as anger; and sets up the stage for change by developing with the family a relational understanding of the presenting concerns that opens new avenues for a solution. The family systems approach involves working with the most relevant relational systems, and thus requires that the therapist determine, if possible, before the onset of treatment, who may participate in the process with the identified patient. The first contact, prior to the initial interview, constitutes an opportunity to create a systemic focus by inquiring about the circumstances of the referral and the identified patient's relations with significant others. For example, my first contact with Scott may be a 15-minute phone conversation during which I would describe my systemic approach to therapy, make explicit my assumption that his struggles have a relational dimension, and explore the following aspects of his current situation:

1. *Scott's referral.* Who first became aware of Scott's struggles? Whose idea was it to seek professional help? Scott himself or somebody else? If somebody else suggested Scott begin therapy, what happened between them that led Scott to make the first contact? What do they think the problem is and to what extent does Scott agree on this definition of the problem? These questions may help to identify which relationships are important to consider as it relates to Scott's experience and perception of the problem. They may also say something about Scott's motivation for change. The act of seeking therapy should not be mistaken for the client's readiness for change. In fact, it most likely

represents his efforts to alleviate psychological and emotional distress or may just be his response to external motivating factors such as a family member's persistent request.

2. *Scott's living situation.* Does Scott live alone? If not, who lives in the same household? Family members, friends, significant others? The family therapist may suggest that influential family members who are most worried about the client's difficulties attend the initial interview. For example, let us imagine that Scott currently lives with his parents and that his mother, concerned about his drug use and emotional upset, encouraged him to initiate counseling. The family therapist may consider including Scott's mother and father in the initial interview to hear all sides of the story and to broaden the focus of the first session to the interpersonal context of the problem. Most adults 25- to 34-years-old (50 percent of men and 57 percent of women) live with a spouse or partner (Fields & Casper, 2001). This relational system is often most relevant to the treatment of adult-focused problems such as depression, anxiety, and substance abuse. However, it is important to be responsive to the client's unique living arrangement in determining who is an important figure in Scott's present life and who may participate in therapy. In my practice of systemic therapy with adult clients, I have adopted a flexible view of the family and, when appropriate and relevant, take steps to engage parents, siblings, other relatives, partners, spouses, and influential others who live in the same household. My decision to include members of the client's relational systems is based on the assumption that individual struggles have an important effect on the relationships of the systems and that these relationships are characterized by interactional patterns that maintain the client's symptoms.

Information about Scott suggests that he is single and sexually active. It does not indicate whether he lives alone or not. It also does not clarify how Scott defines his relationship with "this guy" he met right before his brother's death, and how meaningful this relationship is in the context of Scott's relational systems. Is "this guy" more than a sexual partner? What is the degree and nature of his present involvement in Scott's life? I am asking these questions to highlight information that is missing from the existing initial interview and that would be important to know from the family systems perspective, in order to understand Scott's difficulties and to determine which key players may be invited to participate in the initial interview. Key players are most likely individuals who have frequent and consistent contact with Scott and who have a part in the sequence of behaviors that Scott and others enact around the presenting problem. (See the section A Systemic View of Scott's Difficulties.) For example, if Scott sees Harry, David's partner who "[he] is quite close to now" (P18), as a family member, I will pay attention to what happens between Harry and the client. When Scott stresses over his relationship with his parents, does he confide in Harry? How does Harry respond? And how does his response reinforce the relational patterns in which Scott's problem is embedded? I would not ask these questions directly to the client. In fact, I ask very few questions during the initial interview, unless there is no other way of obtaining information about, for instance, the client's mental health history, suicidal thoughts, or substance use. (In the next section, I explain how I use the skill of reframing to assess and intervene simultaneously, and to engage the client in a conversation about the problem that is intended to instill hope and to build motivation for change.) The aforesaid questions are part of the internal thinking process that guides my clinical decisions.

They illustrate the relational focus I bring to therapy as I assess Harry's role in Scott's relational system, identify what these two men *do* in relation to the client's problem, and whether or not Harry is a key player whose participation in the therapeutic process has the potential to enhance the outcomes of treatment.

Expanding the definition of the family is critical: It enables therapists to be responsive to the particular situation of clients whose relational systems differ from the heteronormative, Euro-American concept of the "traditional" nuclear family. To be responsive, therapists must reflect on their own beliefs and values as they relate to the structure of the family and consider how these beliefs and values define the therapeutic outcomes they are looking to produce. This is an issue I address with the family therapists I train or supervise. I ask them to consider: The kind of family they wish their clients were; the extent to which this kind of family corresponds to their own beliefs and values about what the family is; and how much of their beliefs and values serve to evaluate the success of their work with clients. It is our ethical responsibility to maintain respect for family diversity and human differences. Respect derives from our ability to separate our values from our clinical decisions; from our capacity to appreciate the strengths and challenges of each relational system; and from our capacity to match therapeutic objectives and interventions to the unique organization of the family.

Now let's assume that Scott is a single adult living alone. In this case, it is best to conduct the initial interview individually. However, during the interview, I would aim to identify significant others and evaluate whether it is possible and appropriate to later include them in the therapy process (Hanna, 2007). I would purposefully inquire about Scott's social networks and family life, his living arrangement, his perception of his present relationship with someone he "had sex [with] last weekend" (P95), his brother's ex-boyfriend, and other close friends as well as his relationship with his mother, father, and other key relatives. By doing so, I would call the client's attention to the interpersonal dimension of his experience and use the skill of reframing to construct a relational definition of his struggles. This relational definition is the rationale for including others in treatment; it shows how Scott and significant others share responsibility for resolving the presenting problem.

Interpersonal Versus Intrapersonal

Whether the intake therapist asks questions, repeats the client's words, or points out inconsistencies during Scott's initial interview, he selectively highlights particular aspects of the client's experience. "But what was that experience like for you?" (T23), "So how have you dealt with David's death?" (T33), "What a bold kid you were" (T42), "Well, you must be afraid that he will look down on you in some way" (T55), and "How did you come out sexually?" (T56) are statements that underscore individual factors such as personality characteristics, internal cognitive and emotional processes, and individual development. These factors are important to bear in mind; however, from the family systems perspective, the challenge is to consider how they are part of the client's interactional system. In other words, the task of the therapist is to put individual factors in a relational frame in such a way that it is possible to assign another (interpersonal rather than intrapsychic) meaning to the client's problem. This is accomplished by way of *reframing*, a therapeutic skill I use throughout the course of treatment including the initial interview. In fact, reframing is my primary mode of intervention in the early stage of therapy. It involves: (1) highlighting the client's behavioral response to particular events and acknowledging the underlying beliefs and emotions; (2) linking these behaviors to the interpersonal context in which they occur, that is, redefining the client's struggles as relational difficulties; and (3) pointing out the client's noble intent or what motivates the client's behaviors, and how the client attempts to resolve relational difficulties by means of ill-suited actions that do not produce the desired results.

Reframing occurs in the context of the therapeutic conversation; it is an interactional and collaborative process during which the therapist and the client co-construct another story of the presenting problem. How might this process differ from the interactions of the existing initial interview? The systemic therapist is more active in reconfiguring the client's problem, less concerned about the facts, and more interested in what happens *between* the client and significant others. The initial interview involves (1) formulating hypotheses about the developmental or family-specific themes that describe the client's experience and about the patterning of the client's responses to situations that occur in his relational systems; (2) introducing these hypotheses in the therapeutic conversation and evaluating their fit based on the client's response through the collaborative process of reframing. Let's take an example from the transcript of the initial interview to show how I listen to Scott's story and how I might respond to it. While Scott tells about his brother's death, his father's gambling, and his mother's impassivity, I pay attention to the client's conception of the problem. Scott states that he should but cannot rely on his parents for comfort (P15), that his father is a gambler who has defrauded his children and possibly abused them sexually (P30), and that his mother is seemingly indifferent, conservative, and unsure of herself (P119). Scott suggests that these are the reasons that complicate his grieving process. In other words, he attributes part, if not all, of the problem to the qualities or actions of significant others such as his mother standing by her husband in keeping with her "very traditional 1950s frame of mind." Scott's definition of the problem guides his attempts at resolving difficulties. However, this definition limits his ability to find a satisfying solution and to manage his racing and anxious thoughts. As a result, it breeds hopelessness and other distressing emotions such as anger and resentment.

The task of the therapist is to assist Scott in reframing the problem and, specifically, in developing a relational perspective that will shed light on the family themes or rules that organize the patterns of individual behaviors in the interpersonal context of the family. For example, Scott's statements indicate that protection is an organizing theme of the family interactions. Scott says that his brother, David, was his "protector" and his "angel" (P23); that he has not called the police on his father because "it would have torn my family apart" (P31); and that now his role is to bring his parents comfort (P120). Identifying and developing an organizing theme that speaks to the unique experience of the client is an activity that starts in the initial interview. It guides the therapist's efforts to put the presenting concerns in a different frame, and is related to the process of co-constructing another definition of the problem. I will elaborate on the concept of organizing theme and give an example as I conceptualize Scott's difficulties using the family systems lens in the next section of this chapter. (See A Systemic View of Scott's Difficulties.) For now, I will illustrate the process of reframing and clarify the purpose of my intervention:

Scott (P23):   Dealing with [David's death] or trying to deal with it as best as I can and when I tend to grieve I tend to, I need alone time a lot—but there are times when I want to be with my parents to get that solace, comfort from them and they don't bring it. In fact it's the complete opposite.

Therapist: Your parents and you have come together for David, despite the unfinished business and hurt between you. It is important, yet uneasy, for all of you to be there for each other. And you seem to be the kind of person who deals with pain on his own. That probably makes it even harder to reach out to your parents.

Notice that my response acknowledges Scott's struggle (i.e., dealing with the pain of loss) at the same time as it situates it in the context of family relationships and draws attention to what is happening between Scott and his parents. It also points out how Scott's personal characteristics (i.e., his hypothetical independence) may contribute to the difficulty of getting solace from significant others. The objective of my intervention is to change the locus of blame (i.e., Scott's parents who do not bring comfort) and to build family-shared responsibility for resolving the present concerns. I am testing the hypothesis that being there for one another is an element of the family's organizing theme and that Scott's independence has something to do with the struggle of getting solace. I am doing so respectfully and without making judgments for the purpose of fostering a bond that corresponds to the affective component of the working alliance (Bordin, 1979). I am less concerned about formulating the correct hypothesis than about engaging Scott in a therapeutic conversation that will produce another definition of the problem. I am inviting Scott to work with me and to co-construct a new story that will enable us to see his struggles differently. The process of reframing is related to the two other elements of the working alliance to the extent that the therapist and the client develop a common understanding of the problem, which puts them in a position to agree on the goals and tasks of therapy. Here is another example of reframing with the caveat that the client is an active participant and that his response is equally important yet not represented in the communicative exchange that follows; in other words, the example below provides a truncated picture of the reframing process:

Scott (P30):   [My father] is a gambler. He goes to Gamblers Anonymous is his most recent thing. But um, he'll open up credit cards in my name and sign away, and then I'll find out. . . . And that's happened my

> whole life, as long as I've been aware, as long as I've been able to
> have a credit card, he's had credit cards taken out in my name.
> And, you know, it's the same old process, I get angry, have a huge
> fight. He apologizes, I stay angry for 2 weeks, we get over it. I try
> and move on.

Therapist: Identity theft is a serious thing. And you're in a tough spot, having
to decide what to do to protect yourself, your mother, and your
family at the same time. It sounds like, for all of you, moving on,
forgetting, and maybe forgiving are ways of keeping the family
intact until the next incident. And when it happens again, you are
back in the same difficult position, stuck and angry.

My response acknowledges the gravity of the situation and reframes Scott's conception of the problem (i.e., he has been the victim of his father's gambling) by using the family's organizing theme (i.e., protection and forgiveness). It suggests that all members of the family have a share in the problem without blaming anyone in particular. Creating a sense of shared responsibility helps to reduce blame and negativity, and is all the more important when several family members participate in therapy. Keep in mind that from a constructivist perspective Scott's description of the problem is *his* personal construction of reality. Scott's relatives and friends may have a different perception of the problem that is an equally valid representation of what happens. For example, had Scott's parents attended the initial interview, I imagine they might have disputed his definition of the problem with anger and hurt. They might have said: "We try to help but you won't tell us anything. We can't seem to do right by you." An argument might have ensued escalating into a fight. The success of therapy depends on the therapist's ability to stop the family from enacting the sequence of behaviors that define their interactional patterns and that is associated with hopelessness and the inability to find effective solutions.

The family therapist is active and directive to the extent that she or he interrupts problematic interactions and guides the therapeutic conversation to accomplish the objectives of the initial sessions: (1) To reduce blame and negativity and (2) to develop a relational definition of the problem that connects every family member to the presenting concerns, thus offering a new conception of the problem that underpins the rationale for change, brings hope, and motivates the family to try new behaviors. Being directive is synonymous with being purposeful or focused on the goals described above. These goals require that, in the initial interview, the therapist gather information for the purpose of assessing the nature of the problem at the same time as she or he intervenes to change the sequence of interpersonal events that represent a risk of drop out.

It is impossible to know with certainty, based on the transcript of Scott's interview, why the therapist highlights particular aspects of Scott's experience and what the goals of the existing interview are. However, it is safe to assume that Scott's therapist asks questions (e.g., T35), reflects the client's feelings (e.g., T55) and thoughts (e.g., T46, T52), and points out inconsistencies (T53, T98), in order to convey caring and empathy, build rapport, and gather critical information about the biopsychosocial background of Scott's difficulties. In particular, knowledge about Scott's sexual experience and the circumstances of his coming out to others helps surmise how Scott and his parents have met the developmental challenges peculiar to the families of lesbian and gay youth. The transcript of the initial interview does not show how the therapist uses this knowledge to conceptualize Scott's difficulties. In most instances, the therapist appears to follow the client's lead as regards which topics they address in more or less detail during the conversation (e.g., T30, T31, T34, T35, T51). This differs from the family systems approach I have described: Facts about Scott's biopsychosocial background are important to the extent that they inform the family's organizing theme (see the next section A Systemic View of Scott's Difficulties) and may be used for the purpose of reframing the problem. Consequently, in the initial interview, I may ignore something said or done, and focus on what helps me to accomplish the goals of therapy. I also trust that the client will help me identify what has major significance for the problem, usually by repeating again and again what I have failed to acknowledge. In sum, the initial interview is an opportunity for the client (or the family) and therapist to form a working alliance by participating in a collaborative process in which the therapist contributes to another view of the problem based on her or his assessment and conceptualization of individual and family data.

Process Versus Content

Family processes or interactional sequences are the focus of assessment and intervention in family therapy. The family therapist attends to what happens between family members in relation to the concerns they discuss in session. In general, the character of the events the family describes matters less than the sequence of behaviors they repeatedly enact around these events—for example, how Scott and his parents interact around the issue of molestation, gambling, identity theft, sexuality, death, and grief. *In other words, knowing what happened is less important than discerning how family members consistently respond to it.* With regard to sexual abuse and suicidal ideation, it is the therapist's responsibility to assess the nature and level of risks and to take appropriate actions to protect the safety of the client and others. The family therapist may inquire about the facts, yet maintain a relational focus by placing the information in the context of the family's interactional patterns. For example, in Scott's initial interview, I would pay attention to and discuss how the client and his parents have addressed the allegations of abuse, how they talked about it, and how they responded to each other. Scott briefly mentions how the family handled David's claim of abuse with denial and anger (P27). This is an opportunity to point out the family's organizing theme or the rules that govern their behaviors and that determine how problems get solved. It is also an opportunity to draw attention to the family processes or interactional sequences in which individual actions, thoughts, emotions, and intentions are embedded. Judging from Scott's report, I would guess that the family's interactional sequences involve the following behaviors: In general, Scott's family remains silent about what might possibly hurt their relationships, until an event occurs (e.g., Scott receiving a call about a

Diner's Club Card; coming out; confronting the family about the alleged molestation) that leads to a heated argument between the sons and their father.

The mother intervenes, takes position between her sons and her spouse, thus ending conflict. The sons and the father separate and stop talking with one another. Scott ruminates, worries, uses drugs, and at times thinks about ending his life. Scott's mother gives him a hug (P120). Scott buries his anger and resentment, and stays there, by her side, silent, until the next incident. Before David's death, Scott might have confided in his brother, who probably took upon himself to speak out about the family's problems. In what precedes not only do I connect events (e.g., the allegations of abuse, coming out, identity theft) to the family's interactional patterns, I also put Scott's anxious feelings, worries, drug use, and suicidal ideation in a relational frame with a view to identifying the family processes that seem to underlie individual symptoms. It is these processes that are the target of therapeutic change. The aim is to replace existing relational patterns with new interactional sequences that will decrease the likelihood of adverse mental health outcomes (e.g., drug use, anxiety) and improve functioning at the individual and interpersonal level.

A Systemic View of Scott's Difficulties

From the standpoint of family systems, Scott's struggles are situated in a network of relationships in which individual behaviors are influenced and being influenced by one another. To help Scott resolve his problems, the family systems therapist, myself in this chapter, will pay attention to the personal, interpersonal, and macrosystemic factors that are involved in the client's concerns; to the meanings he gives to his experience; and to the relational patterns in his life. It is by working through the significant relationships that form the interpersonal context of the identified patient that I would address the emotional and behavioral problems of the client. I view these problems as embedded in stable patterns of behaviors or interactional sequences that produce specific relational outcomes, called "relational functions." The target of therapy is the family process or interactions and transactions, not the relational outcomes that individual experience internally and in varying degrees as a sense of relational influence and as a sense of emotional and psychological contact or distance (Sexton & Alexander, 2005). In other words, the goal of therapy is not to make individuals more or less psychologically interconnected. What matters is the family process and the development of new relationship patterns that will increase the family's ability to address normative and nonnormative life events.

In the next paragraphs, I choose to examine Scott's relationship with his parents to develop a systemic understanding of Scott's difficulties. This choice does not signify that Scott's family of origin is the most relevant relational system. At present, I am not able to draw this conclusion for reasons discussed earlier. (See section The Family Systems Approach to the Initial Interview.) However, the client's interview includes many details about his interactions with his parents, which I use to illustrate how symptoms are embedded in relational systems.

Scott is seeking therapy because "a lot of shit happened to [him] this year" (P14), because his brother died and because he has a "screwed up relationship with [his] parents" that makes it impossible to lean on them (P15). In particular, Scott attributes the cause of his difficulties to his father's misdeeds (i.e., gambling, identity theft) and his mother's lack of responsiveness. To some extent, he sees himself as a victim of external circumstances and as a result feels powerless. From a family systems perspective, the objective of the initial interview is to identify relational themes that provide new ways of thinking about the client's problem. In the paragraphs that follow, I will construct a narrative that situates Scott's difficulties in the relational context of his family of origin and that describes the thoughts, emotions, behaviors, and intentions of each individual family member. Early on, in therapy, this narrative is based on the therapist's hypotheses about the family's organizing theme. It then develops from the process of reframing and becomes both the client and the therapist's new definition of the problem. The story I propose to tell is the product of my own theorizing rather than the outcome of the relational process of reframing. It is derived from my understanding of the family's interactional sequences and from information contained in the client's initial interview regarding the noble intent and emotions of family members.

The Family's Organizing Theme

Scott's family is dealing with the premature death of David, an event that brings about a wide range of emotions (anger, sadness, fear, disbelief, guilt, numbness) and that requires them to consider what their ways of life and relationships will be like without their son and brother. Despite past conflict and disagreement, they have come together to be with David until he passed away. They now are struggling to be there for one another as they adjust to the loss of their loved one. Standing by each other has always been of great importance to the family. In many cases, it involves not talking about sensitive subjects (e.g., gambling, sexuality, the circumstances of David's death) that may upset the family and cause strife. The family stays silent to protect their sense of closeness and cohesion. Their challenge is to find new ways of discussing difficult issues while managing feelings of anger, fear, and resentment and maintaining a sense of togetherness. When Scott stops seeing his father for several weeks and smokes pot, he protects the family cohesiveness from the anger and resentment he feels about unfinished family business. He maintains a safe distance and uses drugs to keep a lid on his emotions. When events compel him to confront his parents, Scott is furious, fights with his father, then walks away, and struggles to return to the conversation in order to resolve the problem. He avoids further conflict and thus protects the family relationships from the hurt it may cause. Doing so also enables him to stand by his mother and to be there for her. In the initial interview, Scott suggests that David was the family member who would address sensitive topics such as his sexual orientation (P45). By speaking out about his sexuality, on behalf of his brother and himself, David stood on the line of fire and protected Scott from arguments that might follow (P48). He was Scott's "protector," the one who would lessen the shock of differences within the family, a role that he no longer fulfills since he has passed away. Scott must now consider how he will deal with these differences on his own.

The Family's Relational Functions

To fully understand the family's interactional sequences, it is important to examine their relational functions or outcomes. In my practice of FFT, I focus on two dimensions of the relational functions: (1) relatedness or interdependence and (2) hierarchy or interpersonal influence, which vary in intensity from high to low. High levels of relatedness correspond to a sense of psychological and emotional contact, while low degrees of interdependence denotes feelings of autonomy and distance. Assessing the family's relatedness and hierarchy helps clarify how family processes serve to regulate the relational space between individuals, that is, the amount of closeness and control they experience in their relationships. Relational functions are not a target of change. From the perspective of FFT, it is the family's interpersonal patterns, not the relational outcomes of these patterns, that contribute to the difficulties of individual members. Relational functions are neither good nor bad, but associated with strengths and challenges that the family may tap into or address as they work together to solve the problems of everyday life.

To determine the degree of relatedness and hierarchy between Scott and his parents, I must turn attention to their interactional sequences and use the client's description of his subjective experience. For example, Scott indicates that he senses distance between himself and his parents as a result of their interactions. He also suggests that he feels closer to his mother compared to his father. In other words, the degree of Scott's relatedness to his parents is low; however, the degree of his relatedness to his mother is higher than the degree of his relatedness to his father. Notice that I have only measured Scott's experience of the relational space. This is because the relational functions of the family's interactional sequences may differ for each family member. While Scott senses distance, his mother may experience a high level of psychological contact. If I had the opportunity to work with Scott and his parents, I would be careful to foster new interactional sequences that match the relational functions of the family.

Concluding Comments

I have read the transcript of Scott's interview using a systemic lens that determined what information I paid attention to or ignored. I focused on the processes that characterize the relational systems of the client and formulated hypotheses about Scott's family of origin. I emphasized the stable interactional sequences in which Scott's problem was embedded rather than the content of his struggles—having unprotected sex, smoking pot, anxiety, and suicidal ideation. Doing so allows me to suspend judgment and to appreciate the noble intention that underlies the client's behaviors. It enables me to keep my values at bay and to maintain an attitude of respect toward the client. Acknowledging the client's noble intent does not imply condoning socially undesirable behaviors. For example, hitting, making threats, and yelling are not justified, but may make sense in the context of relationships.

Family systems is neither the right nor the wrong approach to Scott's concerns; it is one of the many therapeutic approaches the intake counselor may use to assess Scott's problems and develop a treatment plan. It provides a unique way of understanding the client's struggles by taking into consideration personal, interpersonal, and environmental factors. The decision to initiate family therapy and to involve significant others depends on the client's expectations and the importance of the client's relationships. During the initial interview, the family therapist will put Scott's concerns in a relational frame, co-construct a relational definition of the problem, and discuss whether to include Scott's parents or significant others in the therapeutic process. The behavioral goals of treatment may be to help Scott's family find healthier ways to be there for one another, to manage conflict, and to address their concerns about gambling or safe sex. The family may learn new communication strategies that would enable them to talk about sensitive topics and to enhance their sense of cohesiveness. Changing the family's interactional sequences may result in the reduction of Scott's symptoms and improve both individual and family functioning.

To Learn More About Family Systems

Ackerman, N. (1966). *Treating the troubled family*. New York: Basic Books.
Bowen, M. (1994). *Family therapy in clinical practice*. Lanham, MD: Jason Aronson.
Haley, J., & Hoffman, L. (1968). *Techniques of family therapy*. New York: Basic Books.
Lebow, J. L. (Ed.), (2005). *Handbook of clinical family therapy* Hoboken, NJ: John Wiley & Sons.
Minuchin, S., & Fishman, H. C. (1981). *Family therapy techniques*. Cambridge, MA: Harvard University Press.
Satir, V. (1964). *Conjoint family therapy*. Palo Alto, CA: Science and Behavior Books.
Walsh, F. (1982). *Normal family processes*. New York: Guilford Press.

References

Becvar, R. J., & Becvar, D. S. (1982). *Systems theory and family therapy: A primer*. New York: University Press of America.
Becvar, D. S., & Becvar, R. J. (2006). *Family therapy: A systemic integration* (6th ed.). Boston, MA: Pearson.
Bertalanffy, L. von (1968). *General systems theory: Foundations, development, applications*. New York: Braziller.
Bordin, E. S. (1979). The generalizability of the psychoanalytic concept of the working alliance. *Psychotherapy: Theory, Research, & Practice, 16*(3), 252–260.

Broderick, C. B. (1993). *Understanding family process: Basics of family systems theory.* Thousand Oaks, CA: Sage.

Broderick, C. B., & Schrader, S. S. (1991). The history of professional marriage and family therapy. In A. S. Gurman, & D. P. Kniskern (Eds.), *Handbook of family therapy* (Vol. II, pp. 3–40). New York: Brunner/Mazel.

Carr, A. (2006). *Family therapy: Concepts, process, and practice* (2nd ed.). Chichester: John Wiley & Sons.

Fields, J., & Casper, L. M. (2001). *America's families and living arrangements.* Washington, DC: US Census Bureau. Retrieved June 15, 2010, from http://www.census.gov/prod/2001pubs/p20-537.pdf.

Freud, S. (1989). *The ego and the id* (J. Riviere, Trans.). New York: Norton.

Goldenberg, H., & Goldenberg, I. (2009). The revolution and evolution of family therapy and family psychology. In J. H. Bray, & M. Stanton (Eds.), *The Wiley-Blackwell handbook of family psychology* (pp. 21–36). Malden, MA: Wiley-Blackwell.

Guttman, H. A. (1991). Systems theory, cybernetics, and epistemology. In A. S. Gurman, & D. P. Kniskern (Eds.), *Handbook of family therapy* (Vol. II, pp. 41–62). New York: Brunner/Mazel.

Hanna, S. M. (2007). *The practice of family therapy: Key elements across models* (4th ed.). Belmont, CA: Thomson & Brooks/Cole.

Kaslow, F. W. (2008). Sameness and diversity in families across five continents. *Journal of Family Psychotherapy, 19*(2), 107–142.

Nichols, M. P. (2006). *Family therapy: Concepts and methods* (7th ed.). Boston, MA: Pearson.

Sexton, T. L., & Alexander, J. F. (2005). Functional family therapy for externalizing disorders in adolescents. In J. L. Lebow (Ed.), *Handbook of clinical family therapy* (pp. 164–191). Hoboken, NJ: John Wiley & Sons.

Sexton, T. L, Weeks, G. R., & Robbins, M. S. (Eds.), (2003). *Handbook of family therapy.* New York: Brunner-Routledge.

Stanton, M. (2009). The systemic epistemology of the specialty of family psychology. In J. H. Bray, & M. Stanton (Eds.), *The Wiley-Blackwell handbook of family psychology* (pp. 5–20). Malden, MA: Wiley-Blackwell.

Wiener, N. (1948). *Cybernetics: On control and communication in the animal and the machine.* Cambridge, MA: Technology Press.

13 Listening as a Psychoanalyst

Ralph Roughton

Psychoanalytic Institute, Emory University, Atlanta, GA, USA

> *A new patient will present a new field of discovery rather than an opportunity for application of acquired knowledge, or a repetition of a crystallized technique.*
>
> **Ella Freeman Sharpe (1947, p. 2)**

The Psychoanalytic Therapies

My exploration of this first session with a new patient is from the psychoanalytic perspective, an important aspect of which is expressed in the quotation above. Psychoanalysis is a process of discovering one's inner life as it unfolds within an intense and profound therapeutic relationship with the analyst. Psychoanalytic technique is simply the means by which we create optimal conditions to allow that discovery to take place.

I acknowledge that psychoanalytic traditionalists in the past often ignored Freeman Sharpe's characterization and approached new patients with theory-derived stereotypes that they looked for—and usually found in the ambiguities of interpreted experiences: for example, oedipus complexes, castration anxiety, and penis envy; or, in the case of gay men, arrested development, negative oedipus complexes, or narcissistic identification.

The classical Freudians were concerned with the vicissitudes of psychic energy and with sexual and aggressive instincts. Their field of interest was what went on within the mind of the patient, conceived as intrapsychic conflicts between impulses and the defenses against those impulses. Transference was seen as a projection onto the analyst of desires and fears from past experiences, while counter-transference was considered a complication to be avoided.

But psychoanalysis has evolved. It is not the ego and the superego that we work with, but whole persons. Instead of instincts, we are more likely to speak of attachments and relationships. Transference in now seen through the lens of the analyst–patient relationship rather than merely as a projection from the past, and counter-transference is not only inevitable but often useful in the analytic process. The analyst has become a real person in a human encounter, as well as a relatively neutral screen upon which the patient can project his transferences.

The Initial Psychotherapy Interview. DOI: 10.1016/B978-0-12-385146-8.00013-4

Rather than presenting psychoanalysis as a theory, I shall discuss the clinical process between the patient and the analyst and point out some ways in which it differs from other treatment methods.

For the purposes of this project, I do not emphasize the differences between psychoanalysis and psychoanalytic psychotherapy. Both are based on the same theory, share the basic technique of exploration, and aim for deeper changes than symptom reduction. They differ primarily in the intensity and depth of the therapeutic process, which becomes apparent only later and thus has little relevance in discussing an initial session. Therefore, when I speak here of psychoanalysis, I mean to include psychoanalytic psychotherapy as well.

However, I do contrast "working analytically" with other forms of therapy. I find it useful to think of the various talk therapies as falling into one of two categories: either the psychoanalytic therapies (PSA) on the one hand or the cognitive, behavioral, and supportive therapies (CBS) on the other. What characterizes this difference is that, in the CBS approaches, the emphasis is on actively working to change symptoms and behaviors, whereas in the PSA the emphasis is on understanding and freeing the patient's inner life.

In the CBS group, the therapist takes a more active role in offering suggestions, clarifications, and supportive comments; she or he often becomes a container for the patient's expression of feelings; she or he may use cognitive and behavioral approaches, giving the patient techniques to better deal with daily life and with troubling thoughts and emotions. The intent is to reduce symptoms and improve functioning without exploring the deeper origins of the problems.

The relationship with the therapist may be an important part of these therapies, but it is not usually the focus of attention, nor is it explored for its transference roots. It is simply allowed to be an unexamined supportive bond and would likely be addressed only if it becomes a negative force that interferes with the treatment.

In contrast, the PSA approach regards symptoms, behavior, and problems in daily living as surface manifestations of the patient's inner life, often reflecting enduring patterns that developed to cope with earlier relationships or traumatic experiences. These patterns persist as unconscious templates, which determine the way the person feels about herself or himself, the way she or he tries to get needs met, and the way she or he responds in interactions with other people. Current life situations trigger these old patterns and result in feelings and actions based as much in the past as in the present.

In the analytic approach, the treatment focus goes beyond the current life events to uncover these unconscious patterns, especially as they are revealed in the developing relationship with the analyst. That relationship itself becomes a fertile field for exploration and analytic work, in effect creating a here-and-now version of the patient's conflicts in the new relationship with the analyst, who changes the dynamics by not responding as others in the patient's life customarily do.

That is not to say that analysts ignore the present reality that the patient must deal with, but an analytic approach will move beyond that to explore the patient's role in her or his current reality as a manifestation of enduring patterns that have developed out of troubled past relationships. This requires the luxury of frequent and unhurried sessions, usually three to five times a week for psychoanalysis and one to two times a week for psychoanalytic psychotherapy. With less-frequent sessions, the emotional engagement and the profound trust necessary for analytic exploration are unlikely to develop fully.

Insight into unconscious conflicts from the past, as well as the experience of recreating and then resolving those conflicts within the analytic relationship, are together what make psychoanalysis effective, often producing deep and lasting changes in a person's life.

I do not mean to imply a value hierarchy between these two categories of therapy. For many patients, one of the CBS approaches may be preferable to embarking on the long and arduous journey of psychoanalysis, either because of the nature of the problems or the goals for treatment, or because the resources available to undertake psychoanalysis are limited.

Neither do I mean to imply that other kinds of therapists never work in this exploratory way or seek similar understanding of meanings in the patterns of behavior. However, if the focus of therapy is consistently on uncovering, discovering, and understanding the patient's inner life and past experiences, as well as on a thorough understanding of the analytic relationship as it develops and is then resolved, then I would call it "working analytically." In this regard I follow Merton Gill, who recommended that "one simply set to work in an analytic way" and do as much analysis as the circumstances allow (1988, p. 271).

What is required for an analytic process to develop? The title for this chapter, "Listening As a Psychoanalyst," implies a particular attitude, in a unique relationship, occurring in a unusual setting.

First of all, it requires in the analyst an *analytic attitude*, by which I mean a stance of nonintrusive curiosity and nonjudgmental acceptance, a desire to discover what is true about another person's emotional life in depth, a respect for the patient's individuality and autonomy (Drescher, 1998), the ability to tolerate ambiguity and not-knowing for a long time, the patience to wait for the unfolding of discovery, and the humility to revise one's conjectures when wrong. A desire to be helpful is necessary, but that help must be understood as a long-range goal rather than as a quick fix.

Second, the analyst must be comfortable enough with herself or himself and free enough from her or his own conflicts to allow the patient to project her or his needs, desires, idealizations, and hate onto the analyst and to be able to work nondefensively with these revelatory expectations. For extended periods of time with some patients, she or he may need to be simply a container for the patient's painful affects, confusion, and hopelessness without succumbing to those feelings herself or himself. The analyst must be receptive to the patient's transference needs and be able to temporarily "wear the attribution" until it can be understood, rather than being quick to "correct the distortions." Being an analyst requires emotional engagement in an intense human relationship, while also maintaining appropriate boundaries, refraining from exploiting the patient's vulnerabilities, and keeping her or his own subjectivities and biases in check so as not to distort the patient's process of self-discovery.

Third, the analytic approach requires an atmosphere of safety, trust, and confidentiality that will allow the patient's inner life to unfold. A completely private setting, with consistency and regularity, is important with regard to appointment time, frequency, and fees. The analytic setting becomes the background of stability against which the patient's inner drama will play out.

All in all, the analytic attitude, the intense and profound relationship between the two partners, and the consistency of the setting all foster the unfolding of an inner life beyond what the patient is consciously aware of, in order to reveal what she or he has spent a lifetime avoiding letting herself or himself know or express. In short, we aim for an atmosphere of safety and nonjudgmental acceptance that allows those "unthought thoughts" to emerge (Bion, 1970; Casement, 1991; Stern, 1997). The analyst is neither a teacher nor a guide but, in Schafer's felicitous phrase, "a seasoned and hardy co-explorer" (1983, p. 26).

Evaluating a New Patient for Psychoanalytic Therapy

An analytic approach is not the treatment of choice for all patients. The old adage that one "must be sick enough to need it, yet well enough to endure it" still bears some truth, although the choice is not simply a matter of diagnostic categories. Many people without significant dysfunction choose it out of a desire for greater self-understanding: for example, writers, leaders in various professions, and especially those who are becoming therapists themselves. Without such an added motivation, it would be impractical to undertake the lengthy treatment in cases of temporary situational or adjustment reactions. Many focal symptoms can be more quickly ameliorated with cognitive-behavioral therapy as an initial approach. However, for those with chronic neurotic or character problems underlying the focal symptoms, an analytic approach may ultimately offer more definitive and lasting change.

At the other end of the spectrum, analytic exploration would not be appropriate for patients with organic mental disorders, and it is not ordinarily used with those in the midst of a psychotic breakdown or an acute major depression. Kernberg, Yeomans, Clarkin, and Levy (2008) have devised a modified form of transference-focused psychoanalytic psychotherapy that is designed specifically for the treatment of borderline patients.

For those for whom psychoanalytic therapy would be appropriate, we assess the patient's motivation and goals for treatment, as well as her or his capacities for introspective and analytic reflection. The patient must be able to see the problems as his or her own and have a desire to understand and change himself or herself, not just to be relieved of symptoms. She or he needs to have sufficient impulse control not to immediately act on disturbing thoughts and feelings as they emerge. The patient needs to be able to tolerate ambiguity and painful affects and to have the patience to wait for improvement. And she or he must have a level of basic trust that allows him or her to form a therapeutic bond and a working relationship with the analyst.

There are no major differences between the way an analyst would conduct an initial interview and Silverstein's interviewing technique with Scott. Both want to get information in order to make a preliminary assessment of the presenting problems, assess the patient's readiness and capacities for treatment, and decide what type of treatment to recommend. As a generalization, I would say that my interview would probably be more open-ended, ask fewer specific questions, and pay more attention to how the patient spontaneously presents his life, how one thought leads to another, and how he puts things together, rather than trying to get a thorough history in one session. Silverstein is obviously more focused on the sexual history, in keeping with his subspecialty as a sexologist, whereas I would be more interested in exploring the quality of Scott's relationships and his feelings about himself. But these are fine points, not major differences, for the initial interview. Those fine points would become more important as therapy progresses in depth and intensity, when it becomes vital that we follow the patient's associations rather than the analyst's agenda. I shall go into this in more detail later, when I discuss the actual process of the interview.

What I hope to accomplish in the initial interview is to get some sense of the presenting problems and of the life history in broad terms, with some understanding of the patient's ways of coping with problems and his capacities for self-reflection. Does he begin to put things together and come up with some new understanding? I look for an opportunity to make a trial interpretation, where I might suggest the possible link between some current behavior and past experience—something like, "I'm struck by the similarity between the way you describe your father and the troubles you're having now with your boss"—and see whether he picks that up and runs with it or, instead, runs away from it. In other words, I am trying out whether he is able to use the exploratory, interpretive approach of analytic therapy. I also have to be alert to the possibility that I might be wrong in such an inference; and, if that turns out to be the case, I would notice whether the patient simply disagrees and explains, or becomes defensive, or acquiesces to my suggestion.

Of equal importance, I want to try out how this particular patient and I will work together. Are we a good match? How anxious or how comfortable he feels is not the crucial measure, because most patients feel some degree of anxiety in an initial session; and, indeed, it would be something to wonder about if there is none. But there needs to be a sense between the two people in the room of a potential mutuality of feeling. The patient needs to feel the beginnings of being understood at a deep level. *The analyst must be able, at the least, to have a sense of empathy for the hurt child in the patient and to want to work with him.*

Because true analytic work will develop only when there is a relationship of emotional engagement for the analyst as well, it is important that he think about how he feels with this patient and ask himself: "Is he the kind of person I tend to be effective with, or does he arouse something in me that interferes with my easy functioning? Will I be able to use self-analysis to clarify and work through whatever that is?"

With those thoughts in mind, I will now consider Silverstein's evaluation of Scott, realizing that some of these questions cannot be answered fully because they would depend on my having actually been the interviewer myself. If that were the case, I would have elicited some different information, and I would have my first-hand emotional reaction, both of which can only be inferred here. Nevertheless, it seems fairly easy to assess the suitability of analytic therapy for Scott based on this transcript. In addition, I have an advantage over the reader in having been able to listen to the recording and to hear Scott's voice, to get a feeling for the pauses, the changes in inflection, and the sense of urgency or calm in what he is saying.

Evaluating Scott for Psychoanalytic Therapy

Scott is a young man who voluntarily sought help on his own, who obviously has the capacity to reflect on his problems and to consider their cause as a combination of the events and relationships in his life, along with his own reactions to those events and relationships. He seems to understand that therapy is a process, not just a service station where he will get a quick repair job and be on his way. He indicates a willingness to explore his life in cooperation with the therapist and to find out how he can be different in some important ways.

His brother's death was a major loss; and his grieving is complicated by the very ambivalent position he is in with his parents, based on his father's gross mistreatment of both sons and on Scott's feeling that he has to tolerate his father's actual criminal behavior in order to spare his mother from further loss.

Scott is somewhat symptomatic, in that he speaks of depression and some suicidal thoughts, but that emerges only at the end of the session when Silverstein asks if there is anything else he needs to know. It did not come up spontaneously in the session, as though it is not really the most important thing to talk about. Or is it that it is too painful and thus avoided? That is not clear. However, there was no indication during the interview itself of a major depressive affect or other defining symptoms of severe depression, such as loss of appetite, insomnia, excessive crying, inability to function in daily life and work situations, and withdrawing from pleasurable activities. In fact, just the prior weekend, he had spent a sex-filled weekend of pleasure with a new guy.

Speaking of depression came only after discussing his use of alcohol and pot to numb his feelings. I assume that there is a significant amount of pain he is masking, but the course of the interview also suggests to me that it is not so much the acute management of his grief feelings as it is the greater sense of being lost in a more existential way. His brother has been an anchor for him, and the sense of loss is acute and painful. But the pattern of numbing his feelings with mind-altering substances did not begin as a way to handle this grief. That has been going on for some time. Why? What about his life or his memories has he had to numb for such a long time? And one wonders whether the unusual closeness of the two brothers developed to compensate for their lack of a secure relationship with the parents during their earlier years.

If we step back and take a broad look at the interview themes that Scott spontaneously brought up, they were mostly about relationships—both good ones and bad ones. He seems to form attachments easily, but there has not been a lot of stability of intimate relationships, except with his brother, whom he has now lost. He does retain relationships—as friends—and those are important to him; but something seems to interfere with his sustaining both intimacy and sex with the same lover over time. That would be a major area to explore, and it will require looking not just at sexual and romantic relationships, but at his history of relationships in general, including that with his parents from the early years.

Scott does show a range of affect: He speaks in glowing terms about the closeness and love he has felt, especially for his brother, but also about the sense of physical intimacy he has felt with some sexual partners. He also has access to his anger, along with the ability to hold it in check, as in his decision not to report his father to the cops in order to maintain family unity. That choice itself would be open to further consideration, but his decision does show that he is able to control his anger and not act precipitously on his feelings.

The most troubling question concerning his affects is how much he seems to need to avoid the painful feelings that lead him to use alcohol and pot to numb himself. I do not get the impression that this is incompatible with an exploratory therapy, as with some patients who cannot tolerate strong affect, but that Scott will need a solid and trusted relationship with a therapist over time to be able to let these feelings surface and experience them. In fact, I think this may be what he is most eager to find: a safe place where he can let it all come out.

One of the ways of evaluating the analytic option for a prospective patient is in the experience of this first interview itself. Scott indicates that he has trouble telling his medical doctor about his life, but he talks very freely with Silverstein, whom he has ascertained in the initial phone call is himself gay. There seemed to be an easy back and forth exchange between them. This was particularly significant, given that Scott's one prior experience with a therapist led him not to return, that he has abundant reasons for not trusting his father, and that he doesn't confide in his medical doctor.

Trying to imagine myself in the therapist's chair, I felt that it would be easy to engage with this young man and that I would like to work with him. One thing I often do near the end of the initial session is to ask, "How has this session been for you?" Or, "Has this felt like something you would like to continue?" This would give him the chance to discuss his level of comfort with me, and it could lead into talking about plans for further therapy.

When they made the arrangements for further sessions, Scott had no hesitancy and, in fact, seemed eager to return. When Silverstein told him of his experience working with gay men with a variety of problems including sexual ones, he said, "Well, I'm in the right place then" (P140). He took the initiative to establish what to call his new therapist and then spoke a rather cheery exit line: "I just unloaded my 30 years of existence on you. ... Thank you. Have a good day." What I think Scott implied in that line was: "I just unloaded on you—and we both survived it, and in fact I feel better for it." That bodes well for an easy initial engagement in therapy.

From this initial interview, I would recommend analytic therapy for Scott. His problems seem to go beyond his acute grief, beyond even the complex nature of his relationships with men. From my perspective, he could benefit from the kind of therapy that will allow him to uncover the deeper pain locked away in past experiences that he has had to numb with alcohol and drugs. His father is clearly an abusive man, and his mother was unable to protect him. To what extent there was actual sexual abuse when he was a child is unclear, but the father has abused the relationship financially and probably in other ways as well.

In addition to exploring his past and how it relates to his present difficulties, Scott very much needs a therapist who will allow him to use the relationship to explore his problems about intimacy and trust of men. He says of the loss of his brother:

> **(P23):** "It was awful—I mean I lost my, my protector—he was my Number One. He wasn't just my brother. You know he was my ego. He was my Number One—he had so much love to give me. It was unconditional. It's been really difficult."

And then he interrupts this line of thought to say he can't share the grief with his parents and can't get the solace he needs from them because of his anger at his father. One of the things he will need in therapy is to form a trusting bond that can withstand his probable need to test it again and again to make sure it is solid, as well as a relationship with a therapist who will neither retaliate, when angry feelings become mobilized and focused on the therapist, nor exploit his erotic feelings that may surface as well. He needs a steady, nonabusive relationship to allow him to feel safe enough to let the pain and the yearning for love come into his consciousness instead of blocking it out.

I want to emphasize that there are two levels of pain that Scott needs help with. The first is the acute grief and his inability to mourn fully. This does not necessarily require the deeper, sustained exploratory work of analytic therapy. I suspect that, given a therapist who can allow him to grieve and who is available as the anchor he needs, he will be able to do that part of the work rather easily.

For some people, however, a pathological grief reaction develops that indicates deeper problems than the acute loss. Three weeks since his brother's death is too early to consider Scott in that category; but if that does occur—measured by his inability to move beyond the mourning and being unduly preoccupied with his brother after many months without any evidence of progress—then a more analytic approach would be indicated for the grief reaction itself.

But behind the acute loss and pain in Scott's case, I postulate that this pattern of numbing the pain and having unavailable parents to help him, antedates the loss of his brother and probably extends back into childhood. The full nature of what that was about will have to await the discovery in therapy, and I do believe that an analytic approach will give him the best chance to bring that into the transference and then finally to resolve it so that he will find a greater sense of "freedom to be."

However, I want to add that it is my impression that Scott could make use of any type of therapy discussed in this book. It is more a question of how far he wants to go in changing his life beyond his acute loss and grief. A supportive approach could help him do much of the grief work. Cognitive-behavioral approaches could help him examine how his feelings about himself may influence and limit the kind of men he chooses to get involved with. Those would all be helpful. I also believe that Scott's problems are rather deep-seated. That does not necessarily imply a severe degree of illness, but rather that the problems started in early relationships in the family and that they have a pervasive effect on his life.

The tone, especially at the ending of the session, suggests to me that Silverstein will be a good fit as a therapist for Scott. So many of the cues I depend on in evaluating a patient are not here for me in trying to assess someone else's interview. I gather much of my sense of how therapy will go with a new patient from nonverbal and visual communication, as well as the subtle context of *my* interaction with him, rather than someone else's interaction. However, given those limitations, I had a good feeling about how they might be able to work together. In a later section, commenting on the interview process itself, I will have some observations about that interaction.

Further Thoughts About Scott As a Patient

As a psychoanalyst I am interested in being able to work together with a patient to make sense of the full arc of his life, and not just in clarifying and changing the current problems. Silverstein's summary at the end of the session (T135) indicates that he is thinking in a similar way. He focuses on the brother's death, Scott's trouble in grieving, his ambivalence about his family, his father's abuses of him, and how he chooses the wrong kind of boyfriends so that he has not been able to settle down.

Those are starting points. What I would want to explore in the coming sessions would be more about his early family life. Has his relationship with his father always been adversarial? Was there a time when he remembers his mother as being able to meet his needs and protect him? Did he form such a close relationship with his brother David because he could not turn to his parents for what he needed? He speaks of being an angry teenager, hating his parents, wanting to be alone (P45), and even had grown distant from David; but then he dismisses this as "normal" teenage angst. We also learn that there was great discord in the family already because of the father's possible molestation of his sons, the mother's siding with him and not believing her sons, and because the parents were not accepting of David's being gay.

How does Scott's early awareness of sexual attraction to males fit into these family dynamics? When he was outed by David to his parents when he was 17, he describes their reaction as, "Fantastic ... supportive ... they've been really great" (P48). And he explains that they perhaps felt bad about the way they reacted to David and were making up for it. But this happened at a time when David was still fighting with them over his own sexual issues. It was in that context that David told them Scott was gay too. How did they abruptly turn to being so accepting of Scott's being gay?

I take this at face value as Scott's conscious memory of it, but it cannot be the whole picture. Long before this experience at 17, ever since age 5, he had known he was different. Perhaps having an admired older brother who had the same feelings made it easier; he was not different from David. But, even in the best of circumstances, children who grow up feeling different in such an elementary way do not experience that early sense of being mirrored in their parents' eyes, based on their expectations of what boys are like and what they desire. A little boy who doesn't say, "I want to marry you, Mommy," but, instead, says, "I want to marry Daddy when I grow up," is unlikely in most families to get those affirming chuckles and smiles.

As a consequence, boys often develop a sense of shame connected with their sexual feelings, because they realize very early that they do not have the "right" kind of feelings. Scott tells us that he and David talked comfortably about their crushes on the camp counselors, but they also knew somehow they must not tell anyone else about this. This is an area that needs to be explored, and it often emerges only later in the course of an analytic treatment. It could be important in understanding Scott's difficulty choosing boyfriends, as would the question of whether Scott was actually molested sexually by his father. At the least, something about the showering made him uncomfortable.

What I am suggesting here is that there are many elements present in this initial interview that suggest a much more complex psychological makeup than an acute grief reaction. Other forms of therapy might be quite helpful, but psychoanalytic therapy would provide the safety and leisure to explore the deeper roots and give Scott the chance to change the future course of his life.

At the end of this first interview, I would be ready to recommend working analytically with Scott. Unless the prospective patient comes already knowing about psychoanalysis and requesting it, I usually start by suggesting that we meet a few times before deciding together on how frequent the sessions should be. This will give him a sense of what analytic therapy can be like. Assuming that the process deepens over a few sessions, I would then tell him that I think he can benefit from either psychoanalysis or psychoanalytic psychotherapy and explain the difference as a matter of degree and depth. The final decision often hinges on his level of interest in investing that much time in himself, as well as his financial resources. Many analysts, myself included, negotiate lower fees when necessary or else refer the patient to a colleague who does or, in cities with a psychoanalytic institute, perhaps to a clinic where analysis might be available at reduced cost.

Listening as a Psychoanalyst to Scott and Silverstein

As a psychoanalyst considering working analytically with a prospective new patient, my priorities are somewhat different from what Silverstein focuses on.
Assuming that there is no immediate crisis requiring intervention, I would want to
take some time to get a sense of who this person is, what his capacities are for
making use of the analytic process, and how well our particular match seems to be
for forming a mutual and collaborative process of discovery.

I am less concerned with getting a complete history in the early sessions, preferring to see how it unfolds in whatever way the patient chooses to tell me his story;
because that in itself, not just the factual information, will tell me what the patient
considers most important, or conversely, what he wants to avoid. I do not find diagnostic categories useful in this assessment, preferring instead to consider whether
the patient can make use of an analytic process. Because of this, I would listen
more and ask fewer questions, be less concerned with getting the facts, and explore
more fully what he brings up about feelings and relationships.

I would also avoid, especially in early sessions, seeming to "take sides" for or
against this or that person in the patient's life, because often those perceptions and
allegiances change over the course of treatment. A mother who was first portrayed
as loving and nurturing turns out to have also had her clutching, manipulative side,
which enrages her superficially adoring son. Perhaps an abusive father, who initially seemed to have no redeeming features, became that only when the patient
was a teenager, masking an earlier warmth and intimate attachment. The analyst
needs to be open to the surprise of such new discoveries, along with his patient, as
well as leaving the patient free to change his story as it evolves, without feeling
that he is then undercutting a shared understanding with the analyst.

I am not suggesting that I would never comment empathically about some great
pleasure or triumph, or some particularly brutal or unfair treatment, as the patient
describes it; but I would most often talk about it as my understanding of what the
experience was like for the patient, rather than passing judgment on the behavior of
others, any more than I would be judgmental of the patient's behavior.

Let us then look at some specific examples of ways in which I might have done
this interview differently. Other than generalizations I have already made, there are
three types of interventions I want to highlight: (1) several times when Silverstein
seemed to abruptly change the subject, (2) an incidence of what seemed to me to
be a misreading of Scott's history, and (3) the general understanding of what Scott
wants in relationships.

At P11 and T12, Scott is telling about the earlier time he went to see a therapist
but didn't return. David was seeing another therapist, and the question came up
about the father having been abusive to David and perhaps to Scott as well. Scott
says, in P11: "the therapist had suggested that maybe it was us coming to terms
with our own sexuality and that we were being put in an environment that made us
feel uncomfortable, when it was actually very normal. But then the older I got
I thought about that, I don't, I don't see that."

I assume what the therapist meant was what Phillips has described as "the over-stimulation of every day life" (2001) in which ordinary experiences like nudity in locker rooms or showers with fathers are, for gay boys, not ordinary at all but highly stimulating. It becomes a situation where they can neither ignore their feelings of attraction nor show the effects of that arousal without terrible shame. The therapist is not wrong about that kind of situation; but, in Scott's perspective, he seemed to be siding with the parents and dismissing the boys' claim of abuse. We don't know what the father was actually doing, but we do know it was disturbing to both boys; and Scott is telling about that.

Silverstein interrupts him to ask, "How much older is your brother?" (T12). I can imagine that he was simply trying to understand the situation, but it seemed to me to put him in the same category as the earlier therapist in dismissing the importance of Scott's feelings. Silverstein then did say that they would get back to this later and went on to ask more about David. But he moved away from Scott and his feelings about the inappropriate, sexually stimulating situation with his father and the possible sexual abuse.

Another example occurs at P31 and T32. Scott is telling about his father's dishonesty in forging credit cards in his name and how he refrained from turning him in to the cops because it would have "torn my family apart." He sounds pretty upset when he says that he didn't speak to his father for months and then David got sick and that forced him to be back involved with his father. Silverstein interrupts this flow of rather strong feelings to ask where the parents live. Again, at P48 and T49, Scott is talking at some length about his parents' reaction to learning he is gay, and Silverstein changes the subject by asking him what his HIV status is.

At P86 and T87, Scott is responding to Silverstein' question about his seeking guys who are unavailable. He is struggling somewhat to explain what he looks for, which prompts Silverstein to ask how long he has been in San Francisco.

And then, finally, at P120 and T121, Scott is talking about the very complicated, ambivalent relationship with his mother. This is his longest continuous speech in the entire session and one of the most emotional, culminating in his saying that he has anger and resentment but also a lot of love for her. Without a pause or acknowledgment, Silverstein refers back to his having mentioned safe sex and asks whether he has safe sex.

I understand that this last example was near the end of the hour, and Silverstein probably felt the need to address that question. But I would suggest the possibility of some counter-transference in these sequences that consistently interrupt the flow of Scott's telling about his life. In each instance, he is expressing a lot of feelings, often about very conflicted aspects of his relationships; and Silverstein changes the subject to ask for facts. Patients very easily discern what interests their therapists and what they want to avoid. The risk here, if this pattern persists later in therapy, is that Scott would assume that Silverstein is uncomfortable when he gets emotional. That could put a significant damper on the freedom to explore and discover the hidden pain he feels compelled to numb.

This is one way in which I would have conducted the interview differently. I would have stayed with these emotional topics, or at least commented, as

Silverstein did in one instance, that we would come back to that later. If one wants to gain a certain amount of factual information in the first interview, it will require more structuring and questioning than my approach; but I would suggest at least some empathic recognition of the emotional situations he is describing before shifting to ask other questions.

Another very interesting interaction took several readings for me to figure out. It seems to me a misreading of Scott's history, but nevertheless it was evocative of some important exploration. Starting at T77, Silverstein asks about experiences with lovers. Scott tells him about his two "serious boyfriends." At T84 Silverstein comments that, in spite of living in San Francisco, "you chose two guys who live in other continents." Scott begins to try to explain about Howard, but then breaks that off and says, "So basically, yea, two different continents, and yea I know the trends. I see the pattern . . . ."

At this point, I was caught up in thinking that Silverstein has misread Scott's history. In fact, the most recent one of these two boyfriends was someone Scott met when he was living in Paris. They lived together there for a year, and then continued a long-distance relationship after Scott returned to the United States. He wanted them to be together and, when the boyfriend did not want to move to the United States, Scott offered to give up his job and move to Paris; but the boyfriend discouraged him and said they should each pursue their careers. Scott started to argue that he was just beginning and had an unimportant job, but then he said he didn't want to push it. I heard that as his saying, "I got the message. His career was more important than our being together. And I wasn't going to beg him."

The other serious relationship was with Howard with whom he was in college in San Francisco. What turned it into "another continent" relationship was that Scott went to school in Italy for a semester, and Howard dropped out of school and returned to New York. This time it was Scott who chose not to continue a long-distance relationship; he had done the same thing with his high school boyfriend when he went away to college. He consciously did not want a long-distance relationship but wanted to be free to be involved with someone there.

So it seems to me that, rather than choosing long-distance relationships, Scott actually tried to arrange to be with the Paris boyfriend and chose not to perpetuate long-distance relationships in other instances. But then here is the interesting thing that happened. At first Scott says he sees the pattern, and I wondered if he was just acquiescing to what seemed like Silverstein pushing his own agenda about choosing men on other continents. But then Scott smoothly shifted the pattern he meant and began talking about realizing that he chooses men who are "emotionally unavailable." Not geographically unavailable, but emotionally unavailable. So Silverstein was correct in picking up on the unavailability, but perhaps he misread the history.

I regard this exchange as a positive indicator of Scott's capacity to make use of an analytic approach. He realized that Silverstein's formulation was not quite right. His initial inclination was to agree, but then he saw the deeper common pattern in his avoiding available men. But what that is about remains to be explored.

This then leads to the question of Scott and relationships in general: what does he want? And what he is avoiding? Clearly, relationships are important to Scott, but he gives somewhat conflicting clues about himself and relationships. He emphasizes over and over again that this or that former boyfriend and he have remained friends. Of one, he says "... he's a good friend of mine now, as well— I love him to death, I love him more now than when I was with him" (P82). And his attachment to his brother was so close that, after he died he got a tattoo of David's name; and he feels lost without him. To Silverstein pushing him about not having a medical doctor he can confide in about HIV questions, he says he isn't comfortable talking with him because, "I don't have a relationship with him."

On the other hand, at P86, he struggles trying to answer Silverstein' question about why he doesn't choose guys who are available. He says, "I don't know" and repeats it twice more. I think he really doesn't know, but he fumbles around talking about how he doesn't want it to be too easy, at least at first. He likes to have to "struggle" to really get to know the other guy; but then you arrive at a common understanding. But if it's too easy, it's boring. And he wants a passionate person, but not just a passionate person, but a good person too.

Clearly he does not know. This is an area that will need much exploration. It seems to me that Scott does have a deep need for an intimate relationship and, at some level, he yearns for it. Take, for example, what he says about having anal sex without a condom (P125): "And there's something about intimacy, I think, I think that's what it is for me, that I feel closer to them by losing that condom." And then again at P130: "I like sex without a condom. ... I mean maybe it's partially a phys-ical thing. But, but it's a mental thing too. ... [with the Paris boyfriend] I loved being that close to him and I feel I'm looking for that again maybe. I want that closeness, I want that intimacy."

Silverstein focuses on why he has unsafe sex. I do not want to condone or mini-mize unsafe sex, and sometimes it is important to confront a patient's denial of risks he is taking with his life. But in this first session, knowing that Scott knows the risks (he has just lost his brother to AIDS), I would have chosen to focus on the wish for intimacy.

I would probably have responded with something like: "I hear your wish for that feeling of intimacy with someone you love; and the fact that you would take the risks that you do with unsafe sex in order to feel that intimacy tells me how very important it must be to you."

Probably not in this initial session, but at some later time I might suggest that he can have that intimacy safely in a monogamous relationship, and it would be important for us to try to understand what keeps him from finding someone to share his life with in that way. I'm suggesting both a different tone and a focus on what he wants, rather than a focus on why he does something risky, which tends to have a punitive ring.

My conjecture is that he does have a deep need for an intimate relationship and that he avoids men who are emotionally available as a protection against letting himself get too attached and then suffering a loss. This certainly would be under-standable with the recent loss of David, his closest attachment ever. But it must precede the loss of David.

He tells us that he first had unprotected anal sex with the Paris boyfriend. When he met him, he says, "I thought he was the one" (P78). I suspect that he was more deeply hurt by this boyfriend's rejection than he has acknowledged. In fact, that was the later of his two "serious boyfriends." Howard came earlier. And he has not been in a relationship since Paris. After that rejection, he settled in San Francisco and has been "having a lot of sex," some of it unprotected. So I would want to explore more about that in order to get to his feelings of loss and yearning for intimacy. A paper by Lynch, "Yearning for love and cruising for sex" (2002) could shed some light on this.

I suggest that he may not be afraid of intimacy and availability; rather, he is afraid of finding it, loving it, and then having it taken away. That is what is so painful to him. To avoid that, he now avoids getting deeply involved, substituting "a lot of sex" for the intimacy he craves. I would go a step further into what might be considered "wild conjecture," based only on this one interview. But it will also illustrate (whether it would prove to be true or not) what can be accomplished in analysis that might not be possible in less-intense therapy.

This goes back to my general comments above about being open to changes in the perception of the people in a patient's life. Isay (1989) first challenged the older psychoanalytic assumption that ascribed the cause of a boy's homosexuality, at least in part, to a distant relationship with an uninvolved or a rejecting father. Isay reinterpreted the often-observed poor relationship as the result, not the cause, of the boy's homosexuality. That is, he postulated that the father was himself uncomfortable with the son's erotic interest in him and withdrew. Most often, men do not remember the early phase before the father got uncomfortable and withdrew.

This is often borne out in analytic experience with gay men, whose initial presentation of their fathers is that they were uninvolved or hostile, that they never felt that their fathers liked them and spent more time with their straight, more sports-minded brothers. Typically they really don't care to spend time with these fathers now and at best have a quiet and distant truce. Often, well into analysis and after erotic feelings have emerged in the transference with the analyst and been partially resolved, the picture of the father begins to change and memories emerge of an early warm and delightful relationship. Unfortunately, as with Isay's formulation, once the boy's homoerotic feelings begin to become apparent, the father often withdraws and the relationship changes. This is a devastating rejection and sometimes has a significant effect, not only on the boy's feelings about his sexual desires but about himself as an unworthy person. Such early experiences may result in sexual desire becoming tainted with shame.

In less-intense therapy, efforts may be taken to help the patient accept himself and his sexuality. But being told by your therapist that, "it's OK to be gay," is not quite as thorough and life-changing as discovering for yourself within an analytic experience the roots of that feeling of not being acceptable or even worthy. My substitute for the gay-affirmative, "it's OK to be gay," is the more analytic, "it's OK to be who you are, and we will try to discover that together."

I suspect that most readers of this case responded negatively, as I did, to Scott's father for his misuse of his sons in his financial swindles, if not also sexual abuse of them as little boys. What we must be open to, however, is the possibility that there may have been an early time when Scott and his father were close, and then he felt rejected by the father's withdrawal. The therapist must understand that both are true in the patient's experience and are not mutually exclusive (Drescher, 1998).

That may not have been the case. He may always have been what he has become. But it would fit the pattern that Scott seems to have developed of yearning for intimacy but afraid to trust it because he expects to be rejected. Clearly, the Paris boyfriend—it's interesting that Scott does not use his name—rejected him in favor of his career and was not even willing for Scott to give up his job to live with him in Paris. David, though not wishing to, has also rejected him by dying. Was this pattern set in early childhood? Only time and analytic exploration would tell.

The one troubling question that all this raises for Scott's prospects as a patient is whether his fear and expectation of being rejected will make it difficult for him to tolerate the intense relationship and prevent him from becoming attached and sticking with the treatment. I am guessing that it will not prove to be intolerable for him, but it would be good to anticipate that possibility and help him when he begins to struggle with it. *The focus should not be on his avoiding commitment but on his fear of becoming committed and then losing that attachment.*

In summary, then, I found Scott to have the qualities and capacities needed to work in an exploratory process of self-discovery in an intense therapeutic relationship. In working with him, I would not conceive of my stance to be one of explaining him to himself but of facilitating his helping me understand him. And, in doing so, he will come to understand himself. As Freeman Sharpe says, "A new patient will present a new field of discovery," if only we will follow Schafer's advice of being that "seasoned and hardy co-explorer."

Suggested Additional Readings

For those who would like to read further about psychoanalytic therapy and issues involving gay men from an analytic viewpoint, I recommend the following sources, in addition to the references cited in the text.

For Psychoanalytic Therapy

Casement, P. (1991). *Learning from the patient.* New York: Guilford Press.

Gabbard, G. (2004). *Long-term psychodynamic psychotherapy: A basic text.* Washington, DC: American Psychiatric Association Press.

McWilliams, N. (2004). *Psychoanalytic psychotherapy: A practitioner's guide.* New York: Guilford Publications.

Renik, O. (2006). *Practical psychoanalysis for therapists and patients.* New York: Other Press.

Schafer, R. (1983). *The analytic attitude.* New York: Basic Books.

For Understanding Psychoanalysis and Gay Men

Annual of Psychoanalysis, 2002. Entire issue devoted to "Rethinking Psychoanalysis and the Homosexualities." *30*.

Blechner, M. (2009). *Sex changes: Transformations in society and psychoanalysis*. New York: Routledge.

Corbett, K. (2009). *Boyhoods: Rethinking masculinities*. New Haven, CT: Yale University Press.

Domenici, T., & Lesser, R. (1995). *Disorienting sexuality: Psychoanalytic reappraisals of sexual identities*. New York: Routledge.

Isay, R. (1989). *Being homosexual: Gay men and their development*. New York: Farrar Straus Giroux.

Isay, R. (1996). *Becoming gay: The journey to self-acceptance*. New York: Pantheon.

Journal of the American Psychoanalytic Association, 2001. Special issue devoted to the topic of psychoanalysis and homosexuality. *49*(4), 1104–1466.

Roughton, R. (2001). Four men in treatment: An evolving perspective on homosexuality and bisexuality, 1965–2000. *Journal of the American Psychoanalytic Association*, *49*, 1187–1217.

Roughton, R. (2002). Rethinking homosexuality: What it teaches us about psychoanalysis. *Journal of the American Psychoanalytic Association*, *50*, 733–763.

Drescher, J. (1998). *Psychoanalytic Therapy and the Gay Man*. Hillsdale, NJ: The Analytic Press.

References

Bion, W. (1970). *Attention and interpretation: A scientific approach to insight in psychoanalysis and groups*. London: Tavistock.

Casement, P. (1991). The analytic space and process. In *Learning from the patient* (pp. 239–256, Chapter 20). New York: Guilford Press.

Drescher, J. (1998). *Psychoanalytic Therapy and the Gay Man*. Hillsdale, NJ: The Analytic Press.

Gill, M. (1988). Converting psychotherapy into psychoanalysis. *Contemporary Psychoanalysis*, *24*, 262–274.

Isay, R. (1989). *Being homosexual: Gay men and their development*. New York: Farrar Straus Giroux.

Kernberg, O., Yeomans, F., Clarkin, J., & Levy, K. (2008). Transference focused psychotherapy: Overview and update. *International Journal of Psychoanalysis*, *89*, 601–620.

Lynch, P. (2002). Yearning for love and cruising for sex: Returning to Freud to understand some gay men. *The Annual of Psychoanalysis*, *30*, 175–189.

Phillips, S. (2001). The overstimulation of everyday life: I. New aspects of male homosexuality. *Journal of the American Psychoanalytic Association*, *49*, 1235–1267.

Schafer, R. (1983). *The analytic attitude*. New York: Basic Books.

Sharpe, E. F. (1947). The psycho-analyst. *International Journal of Psychoanalysis*, *28*, 1–6 (Reprinted in Sharpe, E. F. (1950). M. Brierley (Ed.), *Collected papers on psycho-analysis* (pp. 109–122)).

Stern, D. B. (1997). *Unformulated experience: from dissociation to imagination in psychoanalysis*. Hillsdale, NJ: The Analytic Press.

14 Psychodrama (In Search of Meaning Through Action)

Jacob Gershoni

Psychodrama Training Institute, New York City, NY, USA

Psychodrama is an experiential and expressive method of psychotherapy. It was created in the early 1900s by Jacob Levi Moreno, then a medical student in Vienna, Austria (Blatner, 1973; Marineau, 1989). Observing children at play in a park, Moreno saw their creativity and freedom of expression, and positive effects on those engaged in enacting their fantasies, emotions, and concerns. Fascinated, he would tell these children stories and have them playing various characters in them. This would lead him to experimentation in improvisation techniques involving the children and, at times, their parents. Somewhat later, he established the "Theatre of Spontaneity," open to the public and directing dramas of unscripted and unrehearsed situations from their own lives.

During his training as a psychiatrist, the prevailing school of thought was psychoanalysis, which Moreno viewed as limited and narrow. In a meeting with Freud in 1912, he said: "Well, Dr. Freud, I start where you leave off. You meet people in the artificial setting of your office; I meet them on the street and in their home, in their natural surroundings. You analyze their dreams. I try to give them courage to dream again. ..." (Moreno, 1972, p. 5). Working with people in their context was a radical departure from the hegemony of psychoanalysis.

Moreno continued to develop his ideas in his work with prostitutes in 1913. Appalled by their living conditions, Moreno visited their homes, "not to reform the girls or analyze them, but rather to return them to some dignity." He felt driven to help them, he wrote, "... because the prostitutes had been stigmatized for so long ... they had come to accept this as an unalterable fact" (Moreno, 1989, p. 48). Moreno discovered the healing power of group sharing, noticing that they were feeling less isolated, more identified with each other, and empowered to seek medical treatment when needed. This experience led to more elaborate formulations of what later became known as group psychotherapy and community organization.

Always having viewed patients as a part of a larger relational network, Moreno is considered one of the earliest pioneers of family therapy and systemic thought. His ideas challenged the medical model that was then gaining popularity. He described the goals of group psychotherapy as threefold: achieving a perceptual shift, emotional expression, and behavioral change. Moreno developed many

The Initial Psychotherapy Interview. DOI: 10.1016/B978-0-12-385146-8.00014-6
© 2011 Elsevier Inc. All rights reserved.

techniques, aimed at facilitating spontaneity and creativity, which, in his formulation, were the cornerstones of mental health.

Moreno's work laid the foundations for role theory, theories on creativity and human development. His influence on major figures in psychotherapy was considerable, as some adopted his ideas and integrated them into their own work (Hare & Hare, 1996). Such was the case with Fritz Perls' technique of the "empty chair," Virginia Satir's family sculpting (Duhl & Duhl, 1981; Duhl, Kantor, & Duhl 1973; Nichols, 1984), and family therapy leaders Nathan Ackerman (1945) and Carl Whitaker (Fox, 1987). Other techniques (role play, role reversals, doubling, mirroring) became the mainstay of training and consultation programs. For various reasons, however, Moreno's approach has remained out of the mainstream. Conducting psychodrama sessions is a challenging practice that requires higher levels of creativity, self-disclosure, and resilience than are required for leading more verbal, less action-centered group therapies. Psychodrama with groups requires the director to be spontaneous and active in contrast with the laid back, subdued posture of the analyst. Furthermore, it utilizes action and movement, not just talk, to facilitate expression, insight, and change, elements that are seemingly at odds with the psychoanalytic view of these types of expression as counterproductive and that labels them negatively as "acting out," "histrionic," or interfering with transference or with free association (Blatner, 2000a; Compernolle, 1981; Gershoni, 2009).

Throughout his adult life, Moreno worked with marginalized groups such as refugees, prisoners, juvenile delinquents, and mental patients. During the almost 50 years of his prolific activity in the United States, homophobia was blossoming among psychiatrists and other mental health professionals (Coleman, 1988; Silverstein, 1991). Some claimed to be able to "cure" homosexuality (De Cecco, 1985; Socarides, 1978), while others wrote and taught in ways that were oppressive and outright harmful to people struggling with their sexual identity and society's hostile attitude toward them. Moreno never pathologized same-sex attraction. He would have understood Scott's asking to be seen by a gay therapist. Scott wanted to be treated by someone who would not judge him and who had knowledge of the special problems encountered by gay people.

What is Psychodrama?

In Greek, psychodrama literally means "the soul in action." The major difference between psychodrama and other psychotherapeutic methods is that it uses action, not just words. It is most effective when utilized in groups, but it may also be applied in individual (Stein & Callahan, 1982), couples' (Hayden-Seman, 1998), and family therapy (Farmer, 1996). It can be extremely helpful in resolving interpersonal and intrapsychic issues because it inherently considers the group and the individual's roles in it. Therefore, a patient like Scott, who is dealing with multiple problems with his family (bereavement, enmeshment, separation) and with himself (drug abuse, intimacy) could find it particularly beneficial.

Peter Felix Kellermann (1992, p. 20) defines psychodrama as:

[A] method of psychotherapy in which clients are encouraged to continue and complete their actions through dramatizations, role playing, and dramatic self-presentation. Both verbal and non-verbal communications are utilized. A number of scenes are enacted, depicting, for example, memories of specific happenings in the past, unfinished situations, inner dramas, fantasies, dreams, preparations for future risk-taking situations, or unrehearsed expressions of mental states in the here and now. These scenes either approximate real-life situations or are externalizations of inner mental processes. If required other roles may be taken by group members or by inanimate objects.

Psychodrama involves enactment of internal or external issues and conflicts from the past, present, or the future. Enactments of future scenes are common, involving the imagination and also rehearsing roles not taken before and aimed at reducing anxiety. In my work with the LGBT community, group members who face coming out to their family have a chance to prepare for such an occasion, in action, in ways that build up their confidence before the actual event. It also serves to prepare clients to anticipate anxiety-laden people (e.g., authority figures), events (e.g., going for a job interview), or new roles (e.g., being sober in a party; saying "good-bye" to a drug).

As a group model the process consists of three phases:

1. Warm Up. Group exercises aimed at facilitating safety, openness, and spontaneity.
2. Enactment. Staging of the scene(s).
3. Closure. "De-roling," sharing, and deepening of group support.

In conducting the session, the therapist (often called a director) utilizes group therapy, sociometry, and psychodrama. Revisiting problematic scenes with the help of a skilled director and group members has a powerful healing effect in all three phases that are essential for therapeutic change: cognitive, emotional, and behavioral. The protagonist whose drama is enacted not only benefits from emotional expression and new insights but also has an opportunity to acquire new behaviors relative to problems from the past or in preparation for anticipated difficulties. Group members who play parts in the drama (auxiliaries) as well as other members (audience) also benefit from it directly or indirectly (Dayton, 2005, 1994). During the closure phase, members share their reaction to the enactment and how it touched their own lives, thus eliciting identification—a potent healing factor. The audience is asked not to offer analysis, or advice or to question the protagonist. This further supports the protagonist in a judgment-free setting and paves the way for future work of the protagonist and the group. During this phase group members are instructed not to analyze the protagonist nor to give advice. As they share from their own feelings and experience, the protagonist may also be challenged about her or his own choices, which may be harmful, such as unsafe sex practices or drug use.

Over time, the participation of all group members creates a close and intimate community where people know one another well. Such communal experience could prove especially helpful to Scott, who by his own admission has difficulty forming healthy intimacies.

Through the years of rigorous training required of all psychodramatists, I've learned to listen in certain ways to the narrative of clients and search for clues and metaphors that enable me to transform the narrative and "translate" it into action. Reading the interview, I could envision the many roles that Scott could play in a psychodrama as he does in real life: the grieving brother, the son who is very attached to his mother yet critical of her, the abused son who is enraged at his father, the self-doubting lover, stressed artistic director. These are roles that he can transform and change while in therapy with this method. I agree with Silverstein's statement in Chapter 3 that, as interviewers, we look for meaning in a person's life and that meaning is constructed more by feelings and less by facts. To that extent, more of my effort in interviewing Scott would be devoted to exploring his feelings and seeking ways to deepen emotional expression. It's easy to be a Monday morning quarterback and offer insight in hindsight. Examples of different interventions that I might devise emerged in the following choice points:

> P35: Before moving to a new topic I would ask about his feelings regarding closeness to David, which might lead to more emotional expressions about the depth of the loss.
>
> T49: Again, before the transition to a new albeit very important issue of his HIV status, I would ask some more questions about his parents' feelings—and his own—to his coming out. Taking a clue from his words (P48) I could ask: "What did you see in their eyes?" or "Tell me more about their guilt, what was that like for you?"
>
> T49–T51: While exploring the HIV issue, the interviewer appears to focus more on facts and not much on feelings of anxiety, fear, and doubts.
>
> Similarly to the above, when the interviewer seeks elaborations on the coming out experience and romantic and sexual practices (T56–T78), the questions yield facts and almost no feelings.
>
> T93–T102: A series of factual examinations of Scott's sex life. Oh, Silverstein how could you do that to us? Perpetuating the idea that gay men have sex without feelings! Luckily it may be the case of the patient teaching the therapists when Scott (P103) brings up his anxiety in response to a pause breaker (T102). Long pauses may be the royal road to the emotional world of patients.

Moreno's Role Theory

A major philosophical/theoretical difference between psychodrama and other psychotherapy methods with regard to human development may be summarized in Moreno's statement: "Role playing is prior to the emergence of the self. Roles do not emerge from the self, but the self may emerge from roles," (1972, p. 157). Roles combine behaviors and emotions; they are expressions of one's identity and are inseparable from one's contexts. Moreno's formulation of role theory, starting in 1923, posits that human beings are role players from the moment of birth. The baby relates though her or his body with somatic roles (crier, sleeper, eater, defecator); later, social roles develop, such as son, brother, student, artist, firefighter, and psychological roles including loner, competitor, and joyful. New roles are added to one's repertoire through role playing (e.g., imitation), role taking (adding one's own nuanced version to the role playing), or role creating, the highest degree of learning that requires creating roles that did not exist before.

Connecting to each role cluster, Moreno developed commensurate tools: somatodrama (drama of the body), sociodrama (social roles and general societal issues), and psychodrama (emotional, psychological, and spiritual issues). Role theory represents a rather optimistic view of human development as roles may be developed, changed, retired, and rehearsed throughout the person's life. A basic tenet in psychodrama is that the more unconflicted roles we play over a lifetime, the better off we are. Conflicted roles can be resolved within the psychodrama enactment.

The techniques that Moreno (1972) created parallel his ideas of human development. He believed that the infant needs *doubling* to develop beyond the somatic roles that he plays spontaneously (crying, eating, sleeping), which are essential for his survival. Doubling for others is an expression of empathy, an understanding of their needs, feelings, thoughts, and wishes. When the young person receives enough doubling she can develop a sense of herself reaching the *mirror phase*. This will further develop into role reversal; the ability to "step into someone else's shoes." This is a higher degree of relating, a necessary element in forming close, intimate connections. The ultimate level of relating is the encounter, seeing the other person face-to-face, eye-to-eye and revealing one's truth to the other.

The basic techniques in psychodrama are doubling, mirroring, role reversal, and encounter. The double stands to the side of the protagonist, whose story is enacted, and says what he thinks the protagonist is feeling and thinking but not saying. If the protagonist (patient) agrees with the double, he can say it in his own ways. If he doesn't, he can change it. This technique is akin to a positive double bind, a win—win situation, because either way it helps the protagonist express his true feelings or thoughts. I use doubling to deepen the affect and empower the protagonist and the group to reach as far below the surface as they can in search of meaning, connection, and self-affirmation.

Criteria for Individual or Group Therapy

Following the initial interview a decision should be made about the treatment modality. If I were assigned to work with Scott I would initially see him individually, responding to his request, utilizing traditional psychotherapeutic and psychodramatic techniques. Later on, I would also suggest that he join a group where action methods are employed. Leaders in experiential group psychotherapy such as Yalom (1995) affirm that "there is considerable evidence that group therapy is at least as efficacious as individual therapy." (p. 218). He cites research that indicates "group therapy was more effective in twenty-five percent of the studies. Moreover, there are many therapeutic factors that are helpful to people who struggle with intimacy issues and interpersonal skills to improve by learning to relate, resolve conflicts and improve communication experientially."

Such a sweeping assertion, it seems, would make most people candidates for group therapy. Most group therapists, indeed, mark very few diagnostic categories for exclusion from this treatment method. Yalom's exclusion criteria include persons who are brain damaged, paranoid, addicted to drugs or alcohol, actively psychotic, or sociopathic. In summarizing criteria for inclusion in group therapy, Rutan, Stone, and Shay (2007, p. 118) outlined the following:

- Ability to acknowledge need for others.
- Self-reflective capacity.
- Role flexibility.
- Ability to give and receive feedback.
- Empathic capacity.
- Frustration tolerance.
- No preexisting relationships with other group members.

From these brief summaries it seems that Scott meets the criteria for joining a group and will likely benefit from it. He has the capacity to present his presenting problems and seems motivated to expand his knowledge about himself through the help of others while being available to offer help to them. His initial interview makes it clear that Scott is open to feedback and retains the ability to relate closely, even when challenged (P30, P125, P130).

Scott's individual therapy could be fortified and enriched by participation in group therapy. There are eleven therapeutic factors of group therapy defined and researched by Yalom and Leszcz (2005) for over three decades: (1) instillation of hope, (2) universality, (3) imparting of information, (4) altruism, (5) corrective recapitulation of the primary family group, (6) development of socializing techniques, (7) imitative behavior, (8) interpersonal learning, (9) group cohesiveness, (10) catharsis, and (11) existential factors. In my groups I utilize the triadic system that integrates sociometry, psychodrama, and group psychotherapy. All of the above factors are present and often intensified as the action of the drama speaks louder than just words: It also deepens connections between group members and leaves a lasting memory of the work that's done. More of our senses are engaged in action work as it is done physically and in motion.

The value of group therapy for gay people is especially pronounced as they are still a stigmatized group in a society, lacking the full rights granted to other citizens. Since the process of stigmatization and oppression has been carried out within and by groups, it is this very context of group work that has been very helpful in providing support and has empowered countless persons to come out and lead healthier lives. Peer support has formed the bedrock of an emerging community that dares to counter centuries-old negative attacks and reclaim its pride (Altman, 1971).

As a certified group therapist and psychodramatist, I have worked for many years within the LGBT community in New York City. The elegance of psychodrama and the power of sociometry have been very effective in helping many clients resolve internalized conflicts and find adaptive ways in dealing with external problems (Gershoni, 2003). All my groups are mixed gender, and one of them is for LGBT persons. Given Scott's comfort level with his sexual identity, he may be assigned to a group whose members are gay and nongay. Other variables may be taken into account, such as meeting time and the kind of issues a specific group is dealing with. Another factor in choosing which group to have him join, practical albeit less significant clinically, is Scott's health insurance and its policy. Many health insurance policies limit the number of sessions covered per calendar year. Group therapy is cheaper than individual treatment and thus more affordable. When the client's goals are met, the frequency of the individual sessions may change. All these possibilities are subject to discussion and will need Scott's consent.

Observation

The initial interview with Scott yielded a wealth of information that could lead to developing a detailed treatment plan. Silverstein put the patient at ease by his openness, directness, and highly developed clinical skills—so much so that in the first minute Scott says that as a child he may have been molested by his father (P4). Silverstein's relaxed yet pointed and authoritative approach seems to have helped make Scott comfortable enough to reveal more details on this and other major issues: the hallmarks of building trust and a strong therapeutic alliance with the patient. All this happens while the therapist knows from the introductory telephone conversation that Scott is seeking therapy to help him deal with the death of his gay brother.

In thinking of working psychodramatically with Scott I identified these general areas to elaborate on: mourning the loss of his brother, family-of-origin issues, personal and intimacy problems, molestation, and sexual abuse.

Bereavement: Commemorating Life's End

Dealing with the huge loss of his brother described as an ally, protector, and main source of support is the immediate reason that propelled Scott to seek therapy. Grief work, with its aim toward healing from significant losses, may be facilitated by various psychological approaches. Psychodrama integrates elements of intuition, imagination, emotion, and the power of feeling in action—a kinesthetic sensation that anchors experiences in the body—and thus adds depth of feeling to verbal and cognitive modes of therapy (Blatner, 2000b; Siroka & Scloss, 1968).

It seems to me that grief work could begin early in Scott's therapy. In individual sessions Scott would be encouraged to talk about his connection to his brother, that unique relationship to another gay member of the family, and the special bond that developed between them. Telling his story may lead to expressions of sadness, yearning, and wishes. I may then decide to also move it into action by using sculpting and soliloquy techniques. This could emerge from Scott's words (P23): "It's been really difficult. Dealing with it . . . as best I can and when I tend to grieve I tend to, I need alone time a lot—but there are times when I want to be with my parents to get that solace, comfort from them and they don't bring it. In fact they bring the opposite."

My instruction could be: "Well, Scott, imagine that you are alone grieving. Where will it be? Create that space here. What time of day will it be?" With this question I set the scene to help him get into the feelings as if it were real. I would add, "Without words, sculpt your body in that state of being. Breathe and pay attention to your body posture, your facial expression. What is the soliloquy in your mind? Imagine that there's nobody in this room and give a voice to all the thoughts and feelings that you are having now." This intervention will not only validate his need to grieve and cry but will enable Scott to express feelings, that seem to be stifled by his "stoic" father and his needy and anxious mother.

Another possible intervention is to use the empty chair technique. I would ask Scott to imagine that his brother is seated in the chair across from him and direct him to talk to David. This may facilitate an outpouring of feelings, perhaps crying; just what Scott may need as he seeks relief and release of his pent-up emotions. This may be cathartic—catharsis means cleansing in Greek—but I wouldn't push for it. *It has to occur naturally. I may decide to deepen the affect by doubling for Scott*, helping him to express difficult feeling of regrets, sorrow, and guilt. Doubling will be done by using his lines and talking to David in first person, such as (P23): "You were my Number One," "You were my ego and now that you are gone, I lost part of myself," or "Your love to me was unconditional. Nobody else has given me this love." Consideration of timing will be taken into account. It is important for the director (therapist) to allow enough time for closure before the end of each session and help the client return to the "here and now."

If Scott joins a psychodrama therapy group, the options for grief work multiply. Because bereavement and grief work are not a one-time act, there may be other opportunities to enact Scott's connection to his brother and to help him reach acceptance and resolution of the loss, the residual internal emptiness, and survivor's guilt. After it becomes clear that Scott has formed close and supportive connections within the group, as may be evident by members doubling for him, psychodramatic enactments will take this work to another level by integrating group members in his work.

When Scott expresses the need to deal with the loss of his brother, he will be asked to choose a group member to play David's role. A classical drama may involve scenes from their past and may include other family members at various times. Concretizing such scenes is part of the healing process and is the trance-like feeling that may develop as if the scene is real, not staged ("surplus reality" in psychodrama terms). If the scene is too painful for Scott. I would ask him to choose another member to play him (a "mirror") allowing Scott to observe the action. This, too, may lead to emotional expression and will facilitate a dialogue with himself (the mirror) and expression of feelings of acceptance and compassion for himself. These are possibilities; work in psychodrama is not prescribed and much depends on the narrative of the protagonist, his spontaneity, and the leader's spontaneity, which, with the group, will lead to the co-creation of the drama. The end of such a dramatic enactment usually involves some healing ritual or affirming proclamation made by the protagonist.

Personally I have a special and profound affinity with grief work. Seventeen years after I had immigrated to the United States, my father died suddenly in Jerusalem. On that day I boarded the first flight but arrived after the funeral. For months I would feel bouts of sorrow that I could not be at his bedside to say good-bye to him. The geographical distance and the infrequent physical contact made it difficult for me to accept his passing. Psychodrama was very helpful to me in expressing the sadness over this loss and the missed opportunities for closer connection, as it had been during the last years when he was still living. The earlier work enabled me to open "family secrets" about his childhood as a foundling who never knew his biological parents and was adopted. (What a stigma it was back then!) When I broached this subject in one of my visits, he initially resisted but later was happy to share his childhood stories with me. Recalling these conversations with him are a source of deep inner strength to me, a satisfying sense of completion.

All too often trauma and losses are etched in a person's memory and in her or his body. In this case somatodramas may be both revelatory and healing (Kellermann & Hudgins, 2000; Wiener, 1999). We don't know much about Scott's physical health, but if he tends to somatize, then psychodrama enactments could feature group members playing the roles of body parts where his unexpressed feelings are stored. As he reverses role with each part he will get in touch with these feelings, which will likely transport him into a zone of trance-like reality. Moreno called this "surplus reality." As the drama—usually conflicts between different parts—unfolds, Scott may reach catharsis and another level of physical and emotional corrective healing. A somatodrama may help Scott connect with physical feelings toward David, as these are stored in his body. For example, doubling statements, such as "I'll always carry you in my heart" or "When I close my eyes, I see you as though you are with me," are not uncommon in these dramas. Drawing from Scott's narrative, a double may say (P33): "Your name is engraved on my body."

Family Relationships: Enmeshment, Ambivalence, and Trauma

Scott's problems in grieving the death of his brother were accentuated by his parents' inability to mourn or to help him express his feelings about the loss of David. This issue is like the tip of an iceberg of other problems in his family, which are characterized as simultaneously enmeshed, loving, accepting, manipulative, abusive, angry, and even rageful. Such an intricate web of intense and conflicted roles and emotions is the stuff of classical dramas and may be a case study in multiple potential enactments on the psychodrama stage. Scott's relationship with his mother is described as loving but is also fraught with criticism at her for being dependent on her husband and for siding with him against her children at a time of crisis. His father, a "shady" character, has swindled and abused his children, thus enraging Scott who was unable to resolve these problems with his father and resorted to the only solution he could devise: cutting them off. After 6 months of not talking to his father, Scott forcibly reunited with his parents when David fell ill and died. This "reunion" brought up deep-seated anger toward his father, revived old traumas and old memories of abuse.

Many gay family systems have a built-in conflict: While the major functions of a family are to protect the children and to transmit societal values, in these families living in a society that has remained hostile to LGBT persons, these functions collide. When gay children come out to their parents and then have to "educate" them about the gay experience, the role reversal creates resentment and anger. When such feelings are not expressed, the result may be damaging: physical or emotional problems, strained relationships with the family, and in extreme cases, estrangement and cutoffs.

Group therapy provides a natural setting to help members deal with and resolve family-of-origin issues. Groups are the arena where transference toward the leader(s) and other members form a family-like setting where projections flourish. The projections are fertile ground for explorations, in action, of family-of-origin issues (Farmer, 1996; Farmer & Geller, 2003). Scott's coming out to his parents was not problematic, preceded and made easier by David's revelations that he is gay. David was an ally in this family system, and even though he outed Scott to their parents, Scott has no anger toward David. However, other family issues warrant attention in treatment: his father's abuse of trust and his mother's overly close alliance with Scott. I can imagine that in the group Scott will receive sufficient support that will empower him to get in touch with the feelings of hurt and betrayal and express them on the psychodrama stage, and possibly in real life later. In these enactments, he will also be able to address his mother who was unable to stop her husband and now needs her son's emotional support.

At one point in the interview, when Scott seems to have difficulty understanding his mother and his ambivalence toward her, Silverstein asks a question about action, not words (T120). This leads to detailed revelations about the parents' problems in grieving, as well as his mother's despair and suicidal thoughts following the swindling discovery. (It seems that Scott's reaction to Silverstein's changed line of questioning—action versus words—bodes well for a psychodramatic approach.) Scott's relationship with them is further complicated by the role reversal after David's death, engendering resentment and unspoken grief in the loss of his parents as parents. Now he is their caretaker and not the other way around, and all in the midst of trying to deal with past traumas with his father.

Trauma has been defined as a rupture in an affiliate bond (Herman 1992; Lindemann, 1944) with multilayered impact of the person emotionally, physically, and spiritually. It results in losses in one's connection to the self and others, and the ability to trust and to progress constructively with one's life choices. Many trauma victims exhibit psychosomatic symptoms as their ability to express their feelings in words is damaged and is then expressed by physical dysfunction. Thus, talk therapy may be viewed as insufficient. Patients need help in order to express their emotions in other modes and also to take action to represent their triumph over despair that they have endured and develop different roles to move away from helplessness. Dayton (2000) elaborates on group therapy and psychodrama techniques (e.g., narrative trauma lines and the living genograms) that begin with paper-and-pencil exercises and move into action.

There is no hint that Scott's parents would go to therapy, either with him or as a couple to deal with the complex problems in this family. Instead, such work may be done with Scott in a psychodrama group. The issue of swindling Scott and the betrayal he has felt is potentially explosive and must be handled with care; action work without proper warm-up can be harmful, just because of its power. After assessing Scott's readiness to deal with a problem that in the past led to a cutoff, and after building safety in the session, I would start by directing a dialogue between Scott and his mother. In such a drama, as in others, Scott would choose a group member to play the role of his mother. Helping this member to "become" Scott's mother is done in role training whereby Scott has to role reverse with his mother and show (not tell!) how his mother acts. The person who plays mother then acts as her and Scott can correct and change this role play until the player "gets it right." In this process Scott enters into the surplus reality sphere and the rest of the group (audience) are like the guests who are invited into Scott's world. They can also double for Scott and help him find his words and solutions in action. A drama like this may take Scott, for example, to the time he discovered that his father took out credit cards in Scott's name and his rage and helplessness when he wanted to call the cops but his mother begged him not to. It may go into his expressions of hurt and disappointment that she did not help him, but found ways to cover up for her husband. The psychodramatic role reversals will open doors for deeper understanding of his mother and could lead to solutions that will work for him. The scene will likely end in expressions of emotional closeness and also a need to separate; it cannot be foretold, as such decisions will emerge from the protagonist and only from him.

In psychodrama enactments we move from the periphery to the core. Having worked on his issues with his mother will pave the way for Scott to deal with his father. I would anticipate fierce resistance from both Scott and his father. It is a systemic problem that both have not been able to communicate, express their thoughts and feelings, and remain in touch. I imagine many dramas, enacting scenes of telephone conversation between Scott and an auxiliary playing his father, riddled with objections, avoidance, and denial. What father would want to readily acknowledge his roles as a gambler and a swindler of his own children? There may even be threats of future cutoffs and actual hang-ups of the phone. The goal of such enactments will be primarily to ensure continued communication in spite of the emotional pain that results. The group members who play the roles of the father will give Scott important feedback from their role about the "internal" feelings as they played the father. This, in turn, will give Scott ideas as to how to proceed and expand his role-repertoire, moving him from being stuck to having more options vis-à-vis his father. It will be an encumbered process that may ultimately lead to direct and honest dialogues about the financial and emotional abuse. Such confrontations could start with an auxiliary playing the father, but I think that the deep expressions of anger, betrayal, and hurt might be better made at an empty chair so as to protect the auxiliary. I choose not to subject group members to outbursts of anger that have nothing to do with them, even if the goal is to help the protagonist express her or his feelings and come to terms with what happened, or reach novel decisions about her or his next course of action.

Drug Abuse, Self-Esteem, and Intimacy

Scott's description of himself as a "pot head" and the issues related to his self-image and overall functioning point to another area of work needed in his treatment. He says (P107): "I'm a pot head. I smoke pot. Way too much. Almost every day. Um, I'm a drinker but I'm not an uncontrolled drinker, I don't love alcohol as much as I love marijuana. I drink often, ah, at least twice a week. But it's not, uh, I'm very controlled. I'm never . . ."

In this rambling that appears atypical for this articulate and self-aware man and reflective of his internal conflict, Scott contradicts himself and simultaneously acknowledges a problem with drug use and then tries to minimize it. Are we observing denial here? In response to questions he further elaborates that smoking pot helps him "numb" out when he is anxious, his mind racing and unable to relax. This response may be interpreted as an attempt to self-medicate: When faced with uncomfortable feelings or when trying to deal with problems that he cannot resolve, he uses drugs or alcohol to soothe himself. Continuous reliance on these substances leads to dependence and thus the devised solution becomes another, often bigger, problem. He says that he has been smoking marijuana since the age of 13, and that his brother David was also a drinker who had smoked and used drugs until he became a nurse. We already know that his father is a gambler. And as if to provide material to theoreticians who postulate that underlying addictions there is usually trauma (Brook & Spitz 2002; Dayton, 2000, 1994), Scott, in response to probing questions by Silverstein (T107, T116) offers a range of stressors and traumatic events (P115): work-related problems, dating, intimacy, and the "drama" with his parents regarding the money and molestation. A moment later he acknowledges that his drug abuse is a problem that creates more stress and makes it difficult to sleep (P116). More exploration of the dimension of his drug abuse and dependence would be needed in both individual and group sessions. In these instances, psychodrama could serve as a diagnostic tool that could help assess the damage that his drug use has inflicted on him and how it has affected his professional functioning and self-esteem.

The use of group psychotherapy and self-help groups has been documented as a clinically effective and cost-effective part of patients' treatment in dealing with substance abuse (Brook & Spitz, 2002). Many treatment centers for substance abuse—whether inpatient or outpatient—use group therapy and psychodrama as an integral part of their work with their clients. Hannah Weiner (1967), a noted trainee of Moreno, worked extensively with alcoholics and trained others to use psychodrama in their practice. Among LGBT persons, substance abuse seems to be more prevalent than in the larger community for various reasons (Cabaj, 1995; Finnegan & McNally, 1987; Ziebold & Mongeon, 1982) such as the stress of dealing with homophobia, the centrality of gay bars in the socialization in the gay community, and fear of ostracism, discrimination, or violence. McDowell (2002, p. 263) writes: "To distinguish between substance use, abuse, and dependence, one needs to take into account the social milieu of the particular patient. Substance ingestion may be said to go from use to abuse when it impairs some functioning in the person's life. For many gays and lesbians, the use of recreational drugs is quite common and socially acceptable and is, therefore, in some sense 'normal'."

The goal in working with substance abuse psychodramatically would be to help Scott see his actions, and not just cover them up with denial and rationalization. It will also help him to confront difficult situations and persons in his life and express feelings that he would rather avoid. He would then decide, with help from his group members, whether or not to also join a twelve-step program, and to choose solutions such as abstinence, rehabilitation, or harm reduction.

Scott's image of himself is brought up in connection with his mother, to whom he is very close. Describing his own anxiety, Scott says that his mother is similar to him (P118). He also describes her (P31) as dependent (on her husband) and helpless parent who cannot give comfort to him when he needs it. When Scott says, "she doesn't know her own self-worth" (P119), I wonder what he may think about his own self-esteem. Both Scott and his mother have had suicidal thoughts at a time of crisis (P31, P132). This may impede his efforts to separate emotionally: Much time could be devoted to working on these issues in the group setting.

Group therapy provides a viable setting to address issues of self-esteem (Yalom & Leszcz, 2005) toward self-acceptance and acceptance of others. In group there may be many opportunities for Scott to receive feedback from other group members how they view him and how he views himself. Sociometric exercises will facilitate this process as well as intrapsychic psychodramas to bring his self-image to the fore. This may lead to many revelations and deepening insights. In these dramas, he may look at various roles that are defining who he is: loving brother, failed lover, drug user, angry son, talented artist, and so on. Playing out such roles may propel him to make pivotal decisions and select directions for future self-development work. Which roles to modify? Which roles to retire? Which roles to bolster?

A direct result of self-revelations and action work will increase intimacy in the group as it becomes cohesive. This may be the time to address some of his self-proclaimed problems with nonplatonic intimacy. His romantic relationships do not last long and he seems to choose men who are either physically or emotionally unavailable (P84, P86). Furthermore he equates sex, and especially unprotected sex, with intimacy: a risky proposition, especially since drug use is involved. The multiple causes of difficulties with forming and sustaining intimacy may be related to attachment problems (e.g., the absence of role models or broken bonds with his brother and others). Scott advocated for his mother to leave his father and is critical of their abilities as parents. This is an important area of exploration: Does Scott's view of his parents' relationship inform his idea that he cannot have intimacy? Does he see close connections as invariably hurtful and damaging? To further reinforce Scott's perception about intimacy, his brother, who was closest to him, dies a tragic death. Again, these conflicts could be worked out psychodramatically, helping him to define his own needs and take appropriate action.

Dealing with Sexual Abuse and Confronting His Father

Working with trauma and sexual abuse will probably occur once other issues are dealt with and adequately resolved. This is a very delicate endeavor that requires special care, whatever modality is used. Once there is some transformation of roles and Scott becomes more confident in his ability to deal with conflicts, we can address this very thorny problem that has been shrouded in secrecy for a long time. It is also important to ascertain that this work will heal and not re-traumatize Scott.

There are many reasons to use action methods in dealing with trauma and abuse. Bessel van der Kolk, the Harvard researcher, is known for his advocacy for body-centered experiential methods in treatment of trauma survivors. He wrote:

> Prone to action, and deficient in words, these patients can often express their internal states more articulately in physical movement or in pictures than in words. Utilizing drawings and psychodrama may help them develop a language that is essential for effective communication and for the symbolic transformation that can occur in psychotherapy (van der Kolk, 1996, p. 195).

Kellermann (2000) delineates the process of working with severe trauma into several stages in which the enactments lead to catharsis, working through of unconscious conflicts and replacing isolation with development of meaningful connections to others.

I envision gradual work on this sensitive issue that could begin with a dialogue with Scott's mother, to be played by a group member, focusing specifically on the molestation and her inability to help her children. This would allow Scott to let out the emotions buried from long ago and receive support—an antidote to the shaming silence from her experience in real life. Because of Scott's concern for his mother's fragility, the confrontation may remain only in the group, on the psychodrama stage. He may not be able to tell her everything in his encounters with her, but the healing effect will be helpful.

Later, I can see possibilities of inviting his father "out of the shade" and onto the stage to create a situation that will enable them to open deeply held secrets about the molestation, and about the story that David told Scott about the circle jerk. Staging dialogues with his father may be preceded by another scene of visiting David's grave and asking him both for permission to talk with their father about the sexual abuse and to receive strength and courage to go through this process. Being able to do it in therapy will increase the likelihood that he will be able to talk to his father about this explosive issue in real life. Like previous work with the father, this process is expected to take a long time and to involve progress and regressions. When the father seems ready to ask Scott for forgiveness, there is a potential for deeper enactments in the group and in real life. The search for meaning could take them to explorations about the father's family of origin and his own development. If the father is unwilling to reach this hoped-for resolution, Scott will be helped by the group to find peace and solace by himself and by the support network that he will have developed.

End Notes

While reading the interview transcript and listening to the audio I developed warm feelings toward Scott. The picture grew in my mind of a friendly young man who is very open, insightful, and searching for ways to improve his life. Forming this image was made possible by the knowledgeable and empathetic interviewer, joining the patient in nonjudgmental ways and creating a structure, a frame to that picture. And yes, other persons were included as well, at least metaphysically: Scott's brother, parents, ex-lovers. Indeed, every therapy is group therapy, and it feels good to have been invited in.

This also represents an opportunity to focus on counter-transference issues as they emerge. I would ask myself if my strong liking of Scott reflects an issue that I must deal with outside of the therapy room. As his therapist, I need to be very cautious at the slightest sign that I want to befriend him, lest this lead to crossing of professional boundaries—a serious violation of the code of ethics to which I swore. Further, is there a hint of a rescue fantasy in me? This might be coming from my own needs and therefore should be dealt with separately, because of potential inadvertent harm to the client and to other group members who may sense that I favor him. These are serious questions that I would take to my own supervision group where much of the work is done in action. Working psychodramatically with my peers has enhanced my work and my own personal development—a strong motivating factor, however unconscious, in my choice of profession.

Unique to psychodrama is that the search for meaning is done through not just words, but also action, which facilitates the expression of feelings. Toward the end of the interview Scott confirms (P140) that there is a good alliance created with the therapist. This bodes well for a successful treatment that will help Scott transform by shedding roles that are dysfunctional and adopting others that are healthier after rehearsing them with the support of the group and the therapist. Psychodrama can help Scott become emotionally separate from his parents through dialogues and not a cutoff, come to term with the loss of his brother, and let go of the role of the addict by finding other roles of dealing with emotions, stresses, and the need for intimacy.

If You Want to Learn More About Psychodrama

www.asgpp.org. <http://www.asgpp.org/>
www.GrouPsychodrama.com. <http://www.groupsychodrama.com/>
http://psychodramacertification.org/

References

Ackerman, N. W. (1945). Some theoretical aspects of group psychotherapy. In J. L. Moreno (Ed.), *Group psychotherapy: A symposium* (pp. 117–124). New York: Beacon House.

Altman, D. (1971). *Homosexual oppression and liberation*. New York: Outerbridge & Dierstfrey (Dutton).

Blatner, A. (1973). *Acting in: Practical applications of psychodramatic methods*. New York: Springer Publishing Co.

Blatner, A. (2000a). *Foundation of psychodrama: History, theory and practice* (4th ed.). New York: Springer.

Blatner, A. (2000b). Psychodramatic method for facilitating bereavement. In P. F. K. Kellermann & M. K. Hudgins (Eds.), *Psychodrama with trauma survivors: Acting out your pain*. London: Jessica Kingsley Publishers.

Brook, D. W., & Spitz, H. I. (Eds.), (2002). *The group therapy of substance abuse*. New York: Haworth Medical Press.

Cabaj, R. P., & Stein, T. S. (1996). *Textbook of Homosexuality and Mental Health*. Washington DC: The American Psychiatric Press.

Coleman, E. (Ed.), (1988). *Integrated identity for gay men and lesbians—psychotherapeutic approaches for emotional well-being*. New York: Harrington Park Press.

Compernolle, T. (1981). J. L. Moreno: An unrecognized pioneer of family therapy. *Family Process, 20*, 331–335.

Dayton, T. (1994). *The drama within: Psychodramatic and experiential therapy*. Deerfield Beach, FL: Health Communication.

Dayton, T. (2000). *Trauma and addiction*. Deerfield Beach, FL: Health Communication.

Dayton, T. (2005). *The living stage: A step-by-step guide to psychodrama, sociometry and experiential group therapy*. Deerfield Beach, FL: Health Communications.

De Cecco, J. P. (Ed.), (1985). *Bashers, baiters & bigots: Homophobia in American society*. Binghamton, NY: Harrington Park Press.

Duhl, B. S., & Duhl, F. J. (1981). Integrative family therapy. In A. S. Gurman, & D. P. Kniskern (Eds.), *Handbook of family therapy* (pp. 483–513). New York: Brunner Mazel.

Duhl, F. J., Kantor, D., & Duhl, B. S. (1973). Learning space and action in family therapy: A primer for sculpture. In D. Bloch (Ed.), *Techniques of family therapy* (pp. 47–63). New York: Grune and Straton.

Farmer, C. (1996). *Psychodrama and systemic therapy*. London: Karnac.

Farmer, C., & Geller, M. (2003). Applying psychodrama in the family systems therapy of Bowen. In J. Gershoni (Ed.), *Psychodrama in the 21st century: Clinical and educational applications*. New York: Springer.

Finnegan, D. G., & McNally, E. B. (1987). *Dual Identities: Counseling Chemically Dependent Gay Men and Lesbians*. Hazelden.

Fox, J. (Ed.), (1987). *The essential Moreno: Writings on psychodrama, group method and spontaneity by J. L. Moreno*. New York: Springer.

Gershoni, J. (Ed.), (2003). *Psychodrama in the 21st century: Clinical and educational applications*. New York: Springer Publishing Co.

Gershoni, J. (2009). Bringing Psychodrama to the Main Stage of Group Psychotherapy, Group (the Journal of the Eastern Group Psychotherapy Society), *33*(4).

Hare, P. A., & Hare, J. R. (1996). *J. L. Moreno, Key Figures in Counseling and Psychotherapy*. London: Sage Publication.

Hayden-Seman, J. (1998). *Action modality couples therapy: Using psychodramatic techniques for helping troubled relationships.* Northvale, NJ: Jason Aronson.

Herman, J. L. (1992). *Trauma and recovery.* New York: Basic books.

Kellermann, P. F. (1992). *Focus on Psychodrama: The Therapeutic Aspects of Psychodrama.* London: Jessica Kingsley Publishers.

Kellermann, P. F., & Hudgins, M. K. (Eds.), (2000). *Psychodrama with trauma victims: Acting out your pain.* London: Jessica Kingsley.

Lindemann, E. (1944). Symptomatology and management of acute grief. *American Psychiatrist,* 141−149.

Marineau, R. (1989). *Jacob Levi Moreno.* New York: Routledge.

McDowell, D. M. (2002). Group therapy for substance abuse with gay men and lesbians. In D. W. Brook, & H. I. Spitz (Eds.), *The group therapy of substance abuse.* New York: Haworth Medical Press.

Miller, W. R., & Rollnick, S. (2002). *Motivational interviewing: Preparing people for change (2nd ed.).* New York, NY, US: Guilford Press.

Moreno, J. L. (1972). *Psychodrama, Vol. 1* (4th ed.). New York: Beacon House.

Moreno, J. L (1989). The autobiography of J. L. Moreno, MD. *Journal of Group Psychotherapy, Psychodrama and Sociometry, 42*(1), Spring.

Nichols, M. (1984). *Family Therapy Concepts and Methods.* London & New York: Gardner Press.

Rutan, J. S., Stone, W. N., & Shay, J. J. (Eds.), (2007). *Psychodynamic group psychotherapy* (4th ed.). New York: Guilford Press.

Silverstein, C. (Ed.), (1991). *Gays, lesbians and their therapists: Studies in psychotherapy.* New York: W. W. Norton.

Siroka, R. W., & Scloss, G. A. (1968). The death scene in psychodrama. *Psychotherapy: Theory, research & practice, 5,* 355−361.

Socarides, C. W. (1978). *Homosexuality.* New York: Jason Aronson.

Stein, M. B., & Callahan, M. L. (1982). The use of psychodrama in individual psychotherapy. *Journal of Group Psychotherapy, Psychodrama & Sociometry, 35,* 118−129.

van der Kolk, B. A. (1996). The body keeps the score: Approaches to the psychobiology of posttraumatic stress disorder. In B. A. van der Kolk, A. C. McFarlane, & L. Weisaeth (Eds.), *Traumatic stress: The effects of overwhelming experience on mind, body and society.* New York: Guilford Press.

Weiner, D. J. (Ed.), (1999). *Beyond Talk Therapy: Using Movement and Expressive Techniques in Clinical Practice.* Washington, DC: American Psychological Association.

Weiner, H. B (1967). Psychodramatic treatment for the alcoholic. In R. Fox (Ed.), *Alcoholism: Behavioral research therapeutic approaches.* New York: Springer Publishing Co.

Yalom, I. D. (1995). *The theory and practice of group psychotherapy* (4th ed.). New York: Basic Books.

Yalom, I. D., & Leszcz, M. (2005). *The theory and practice of group psychotherapy* (5th ed.). New York: Basic Books.

Ziebold, T., & Mongeon, J. (1982). *Alcoholism and homosexuality.* New York: Haworth Press.

15 Gay-Affirmative Psychotherapy in Real Time (A First Interview)

Armand R. Cerbone

Private Practice, Chicago, and Board of Directors, The American
Psychological Association

My Career as a Gay-Affirmative Psychotherapist

There have been many steps in my development from traditional psychology
toward embracing a gay-affirmative point of view. My interest has its roots in my
development as a psychologist and the years during which I came to terms with my
homosexuality. From 1963 to 1969, while in my 20s, I entered psychotherapy with
the goal of changing my sexual orientation. The only treatment for homosexuality
at the time was sexual orientation change. (See Silverstein, Chapter 1.) There were
no other options. I longed to be heterosexual, to be called "normal," and believed
that my "homosexual tendencies" were impediments to my masculinity, and a
crucible to test my spiritual mettle. I was unaware that there were psychologists
conducting studies during that decade that would lead to the declassification of
homosexuality as an illness and who challenged their profession's treatment of gay
people (Davison, 1974; Halleck, 1977; Hooker, 1957, 1971). I was not even aware
of Kinsey's (1948) massive study that demonstrated how common homosexual
behavior was in our society. Like others from my generation, I swam in the waters
of sexual orientation change (Duberman, 1991).

After reporting my first sexual intercourse with a woman, my psychiatrist rose
from his chair, crossed the room, and shook my hand. He said that he considered
me one of his successes. He said that because in our society sex with a woman is
socially sanctioned. This was not gay-affirmative psychotherapy! The real success
of that first sexual experience was in breaching the moral and psychological
barriers to being sexually intimate at all; it made possible my exploring the experience of human sexuality and, finally, the intimacy of gay relationships.

The amelioration of religious[1] and psychological impediments led to my coming
out to myself. It meant losing my membership in the heterosexual club and with it
the heterosexual privilege that accompanied it. On the positive side it also meant
regaining hope for an integrated sexual identity. Yet it took five more years of
confronting fears of reprisals before I came out publicly.

---

[1] I was a graduate of St. John's Catholic Seminary in Boston.

The Initial Psychotherapy Interview. DOI: 10.1016/B978-0-12-385146-8.00015-8

It is important to mention that in several subsequent psychotherapies, I have never worked with a gay psychotherapist. The reason is simple. My visibility in both gay and straight professional circles was high, as it is for many gay activist psychologists around the country. The probability of finding a conveniently located gay psychotherapist with whom I was not professionally connected or likely to become so was limited. It was easier to find a psychotherapist who was outside this circle of gay colleagues. Unfortunately, there were times that my expertise on gay issues exceeded that of my heterosexual therapist with the consequence that in at least two cases, good judgment required me to terminate the psychotherapy.

This raises an important question: Should gay men seek treatment with only gay therapists? Certainly the gay men who sought my help in the early years of my practice preferred me rather than running the risk of being shamed or demeaned for their homosexuality by an unempathic or unenlightened straight therapist. They wanted someone who understood what it means to be gay in a heterosexual world, who understood the diversity of gay sexual expression, and finally, who supported gay love relationships (Haldeman, 2010). In many cases my clients were men who transferred to me from straight therapists. In the 1970s and 1980s, there was little expertise about sexual orientation and few openly gay counselors, even in large cities. There were a few gay-operated clinics such as those in Boston, New York, Philadelphia, Chicago, and Los Angeles, but because they were poorly funded, most gay people either knew little about them or were afraid of being so open about their sexual orientation (Silverstein, 1997). Seeing a gay therapist offered significant advantages for a gay man, particularly for those who were just coming out or were dealing with residual heterosexism (Herek, 1984).

The options for gay men have improved considerably since the years of my youth. There are now many competent psychotherapists trained in the needs of gay people, and more accurate information is now available to therapists who find themselves confronted with a gay client (Ross, 1988; Stein & Cohen, 1986). Metropolitan areas lead in this diversity, but the message has gotten out to some (but not all) rural areas, so that gay people have more choices today than ever before for seeking gay-affirmative therapy. I might add that there are several heterosexual therapists who practice from a gay-affirmative framework to whom I refer gay men. I sometimes need to make these referrals because of economic, geographic, or insurance reasons.

In 1973 I attended my first American Psychological Association (APA) convention. With my newly minted graduate degree, I went looking for a job. I was also beginning to talk more openly about my sexuality. While at the convention, I attended a presentation on the use of aversive conditioning of homosexual men with electric shock as the preferred treatment to change their sexual orientation from gay to straight. (See Bancroft, 1974, and Feldman & MacCullough, 1971, for a review of aversion therapy.) While listening to the presenter, I was stunned by his idea of using torture in order to cure the homosexuality of his patient. Then, as from nowhere, I saw several gay psychologists storm the stage, guerrilla-like, to commandeer microphones, effectively disrupting the entire program. I had never seen anything like that before—fellow professionals who felt oppressed and demanding to be heard. I was both frightened by their unprofessional behavior and excited by seeing homosexual psychologists demonstrating at a professional conference. I followed them as they adjourned to a hotel room upstairs, checking often to be sure that no one saw me. In a packed hotel room I stood in the shadows by the door and watched as they formed the Association of Gay Psychologists (which later morphed to become the Association of Lesbian and Gay Psychologists, and most recently called the Association of Lesbian, Gay, Bisexual and Transgender Psychologists). Fourteen years later I was elected president of that organization, and also have served as a member of the Board of Directors of the APA.

The History of Gay-Affirmative Psychotherapy

Gay-affirmative psychotherapy developed over a period of many years following the declassification of homosexuality by the American Psychiatric Association in 1973 (Bayer, 1981). The declassification was made possible by the accumulation of critical research that undermined prevailing paradigms of homosexuality as pathological, and confirmed it as a normal expression of human sexuality (Bell & Weinberg, 1978; Paul, Weinrich, Gonsiorek, & Hotvedt, 1982). This shift also owes a considerable debt to the activism of gay and allied professionals who confronted mental health professionals with the harmful consequences of pejorative diagnoses and treatment (Silverstein, 2007; Suppe, 1984).

Malyon (1985) was the first to describe gay-affirmative psychotherapy as "a special range of psychological knowledge that challenges the traditional view that homosexual desire and fixed homosexual orientations are pathological" (p. 69). Affirmative therapy values a gay sexual orientation as mentally healthy and a positive trait of one's personality, rather than the traditional pathology model that resulted from antigay theories that tortured gay people, such as the lecture I attended at APA in 1973 (Socarides, 1968). It aims to correct the noxious effects of historical, cultural, and professional bias against nonheterosexual orientations that afflict the lives and relationships of gay persons. Medical and psychological discrimination against gay people have led to many forms of harmful treatments meant to extinguish homosexual desire, from electric shock therapy (Bancroft, 1974; Coleman, 1982b), to religious-based programs to convert homosexuals to heterosexuality (Besen, 2003).[2] While declassification has purged the more egregious forms of reparative therapies, some psychotherapists and organizations, such as North American Reparative Therapy for Homosexuals (NARTH), still recommends sexual orientation change. More recently a claim by Spitzer (2003) to document a successful religious-based treatment program has been strongly challenged by a large number of experts in the field (Drescher & Zucker, 2006). These religious-based groups seldom cite the difficulties that gay people present as the effects of stigma, only as caused by their homosexuality. In an exhaustive review

---

[2] See Silverstein (1991, 1996), for a review of this history.

of the literature, the American Psychological Association (2009) found that reparative therapies were unlikely to succeed in changing sexual orientation. Furthermore, the report cautioned that deleterious effects, such as depression, suicidal ideation and attempts, and anxiety often result from these therapies.

Gay-affirmative therapy is a set of principles that guide a psychotherapist's assessment and treatment of gay clients. While Cochran (2001) has expressed concern that research has not yet been conducted to corroborate the effectiveness of gay-affirmative psychotherapy per se, there is wide professional consensus that confirms the relevance and value of gay-affirmative psychotherapy. In many ways, gay-affirmative therapy is a corrective lens through which a psychotherapist may view and assess the problems a gay client presents for treatment. A gay-affirmative psychotherapist will apply expert knowledge about the effects of antigay stigma and accurate knowledge about gay subcultures to support gay lives. Further, an affirmative psychotherapist will strive to recognize how antigay stigma contributes to and causes individual psychopathology.

In contrast to a psychotherapist who may not be sensitive to the differences in psychosocial development of gay persons, an affirmative therapist might explore the coming out process and its impact on the person's family and career. That is the process of "coming out." The expression "coming out" is a contraction of "coming out of the closet," meaning that the gay man or woman no longer hides her or his homosexuality both from herself or himself or from others.

Coming out has been conceptualized as a process of progressing through developmental stages (Cass, 1979; Coleman, 1982a) during which gay persons recognize the nature and meaning of their sexual desires and shift from negative to positive attitudes toward their homosexuality (Hanley-Hackenbruck, 1988). This usually progresses to disclosing one's homosexuality to others and increased involvement with other gays, and may extend to gay activism (Cass, 1979). These stages are not necessarily strictly sequential but may overlap. Nor does one need to become an activist as an end point. However, much of the positive social change we have witnessed is the result of people, gays and straight allies, who have been willing to be counted in the struggle for our civil rights.

The expert therapist might explore how far advanced the client may be in the coming out process. A primary role for the therapist is to help the client assess the risks in going through these coming out stages and comparing them to the disadvantages of remaining in the "closet," and continuing a hidden or partially hidden life. For example, a gay-affirmative therapist might assess the client's management of risk factors if she or he is married with children, making coming out more complicated and challenging than if single. In such a case, the therapist must check for personal bias that might prematurely encourage the client either to remain in "the closet" so as to protect the partner and children or come out in order to integrate sexual identity with other aspects of her or his life. In the first session, a culturally competent therapist would avoid influencing or pressuring the client, even if she or he appears committed to coming out. Together they can identify social supports such as friends or counselors who may help discover a range of viable options not previously considered. In doing so, the affirmative therapist is more likely to learn which patterns of behavior are idiopathic and those that are more likely to represent adjustments to antigay stigma.

The internalization of stigma has been one of the primary problems for gay people for many years. Goffman (1963) wrote of its devastating effects. In my judgment, the effects of stigma on the lives of gay persons have been significantly underestimated, primarily, because their pervasiveness makes it a constant in the lives of gay persons. Because antigay stigma is imposed as early as childhood, it has a toxic effect like polluted water to fish, and often, particularly in older generations, accepted as natural.[3] As a result, gay men and women can become so inured to the effects of stigma that they minimize whatever cultural toxicity exists in their lives. A psychotherapist well versed in the adaptations of gay persons to stigma will listen carefully to discern such effects in the client's presenting problems and in failed attempts to work them through. Silverstein's exploration of Scott's coming out history early in the first session is such an example.

In a survey of over 2000 psychologists, Garnets, Hancock, Cochran, Goodchild, and Peplau (1991) found that many of them still continued to pathologize the lives and relationships of lesbian and gay clients. This was almost 20 years after homosexuality was declassified as a mental illness. This prejudice persisted despite the finding in the study that 99 percent of responding psychologists reported having seen at least one gay man or lesbian in their careers. Other studies (Nystrom, 1997; Pope, Tabachnik, & Keith-Spiegel, 1987) noted similar reports of bias in the treatment of gay people by psychotherapists. Still other studies (Bell & Weinberg, 1978; Bieschke, McClanahan, Tozer, Grzorek, & Park, 2000; Jones & Gabriel, 1999) noted that gay men and lesbians seek psychotherapy more often and remain longer than their heterosexual counterparts. Notably, therapist familiarity with gay life has also been found to correlate positively with client satisfaction (Liddle, 1996). Gay clients often prefer a gay therapist because they sense that they will find more empathy, and hence it will be easier for them to establish a therapeutic alliance. Those who came from traditional therapists also felt protected from the heterosexism of the previous therapist.

Homophobia and Heterosexism

Weinberg (1972) was the first person to coin the term "homophobia," meaning a morbid fear of gay people; hence, a person with this fear would be called homophobic. He perceived this trait as an individual pathology within the homophobic person as a counter to those who viewed a homosexual as suffering from pathology.

Malyon (1982, 1985, 1993) took the next step by stating that a gay person could himself carry within him these negative opinions about homosexuality, and he called that "internalized homophobia." A gay person suffering from internalized

---

[3] It has been encouraging to see many younger gay people who have grown up never questioning their homosexuality, nor understanding the pain that previous generations experienced in society.

homophobia is one who identifies with the negative stereotypes about gay people, including, but not limited to, the inability to form stable love relationships.

Herek (1984, 1996) objected to the term homophobia because it "implicitly conveys the assumption that antigay prejudice is an individual, clinical entity rather than a social phenomenon rooted in cultural ideologies and intergroup relations" (1996, pp. 101–102). He suggested that antigay sentiment in society paralleled other forms of prejudice such as sexism, racism, and anti-Semitism. He also found that one foundation of heterosexist attitudes in our society is its rigid definition of masculinity (Herek, 1986). Herek's definition of heterosexism attributes responsibility for discrimination against gay people to society, rather than to individual pathology. As this seems a more accurate nomenclature, I will use that term throughout this paper.

A primary goal of gay-affirmative psychotherapy is to reverse the process of heterosexism. Gay-affirmative therapy encourages clients to recognize the extent to which a heterosexist culture pressures a gay person to regard his homosexuality as the cause of his psychological troubles. Gay-affirmative therapy allows a client to shift the responsibility more appropriately to discrimination in society. The shift has the healing effect of normalizing one's gay feelings and desires. A second goal of gay-affirmative psychotherapy is to mitigate the damages of cultural oppression by enhancing the psychotherapists' ability to make diagnostic distinctions between individual psychopathology, maladaptive adjustments to stigma, and the interaction between the two. Third, it helps gay clients understand that while they are not responsible for the effects of stigma, they nevertheless bear a responsibility, however unfair, to resolve those conflicts.

Affirmative Guidelines for Psychotherapy with Gay Clients

Malyon (1993) said that gay-affirmative psychotherapy is a "developmental process that aims at facilitating both conflict-resolution and self-actualization" (p. 82). He noted three foundations for treatment:

1. Homosexuality is not pathological.
2. Sexual and affectual capacities are valued and facilitated.
3. Corrective experiences should be provided in order to ameliorate the consequences of discrimination.

Malyon was writing only about sexual orientation, whether one was homosexual or heterosexual. Today we also include gender identity in all of its varieties to the list of people who must come to terms with heterosexism in society.

Recognizing its charge to oppose heterosexism, and to inform psychologists with accurate and clinically helpful information, the American Psychological Association adopted *Guidelines for Psychotherapy with Lesbian, Gay, and Bisexual Clients* (APA, 2000). The *Guidelines*, which are aspirational only and not enforceable standards, identify unique issues that are likely to affect the lives and loves of lesbian, gay, bisexual, and transgender (LGBT) clients and offer recommendations to psychotherapists that can lead to positive outcomes in practice. Their strong foundation in empirical evidence and professional consensus increases their value and relevance to practice. As such, the *Guidelines* become an operational definition of gay-affirmative psychotherapy. They also constitute a good reference for consumers who may want reliable criteria in their search for a knowledgeable and affirming psychotherapist.

Self-examination by a psychologist about one's own prejudice is very important. This includes antigay prejudice by homosexual as well as heterosexual counselors. Unconscious bias may lurk in the best of us, the result of growing up in a prejudiced society. Heterosexist values may infiltrate the work among those of us who think of ourselves as accepting variant sexual orientations and gender identities. All psychotherapists, despite training, are equally vulnerable to unconscious prejudice. Unconscious bias is not always negative but can take the form of a halo effect, such as the predisposition to view gay clients positively or as sympathetic victims. For example, I have learned to be mindful of my own vulnerability to counter-transference. On occasion I have been guilty of negative transference to clients who are critical of other gays or whose politics allow them to support antigay candidates or policies (Cerbone, 1991). I have been equally vulnerable to a positive transference toward attractive men, women, and straight allies who advocate for gay rights. The former instance of counter-transference has resulted in my over-pathologizing, the latter to under-pathologizing. Both gay-affirmative psychotherapy and the *Guidelines* do more than alert psychotherapists to the pitfalls of unconscious bias. They also advise and inform psychotherapists of the realities of living in a heterosexist society and invite them to develop the necessary personal competence to treat gay men and women appropriately.

Theoretical Orientation and Guiding Principles

So much of the damage done over the years to LGBT people has been justified by misinterpreting the findings of research to pathologize homosexuality or promoting results of studies with flawed methodologies, such as the Spitzer (2003) study referred to earlier. Even when conceding that homosexuality is not an illness, some researchers have cherry-picked data to reinforce the superiority of heterosexuality or to argue the appropriateness of change therapies for those gay individuals who wish to change without reference to the influence of stigma (Glassgold, Fitzgerald, & Haldeman, 2002; Yarhouse & Throckmorton, 2002).

Such positions and practices reveal the extent to which human sexuality has been understood exclusively through a heterosexual paradigm of sexuality. The emergence of homosexuality, bisexuality, and transgender sexuality from their closets has threatened the hegemony of heterosexuality. The result has been to mobilize resistance against acceptance of homosexuality as normal and healthy, and to reinforce the domination and authority of heterosexuality as the only legally acceptable form of relationships. By contrast, the model of sexuality implied in gay-affirmative psychotherapy does not denigrate heterosexuality, but assumes that sexuality is more fluid and variable than exclusive heterosexuality allows. While sexual orientation (whether one is gay, straight, bisexual, or transgender) may be relatively fixed, sexual identity (whether one calls oneself gay, straight, bisexual, transgender, or not) and sexual behavior are more variable.

Homosexuality was deleted from the *Diagnostic and Statistical Manual* in 1973. That year marked both an end and a beginning (Bayer, 1981). It marked the official end to the American Psychiatric Association's pathologizing of homosexuality, and the recognition to understand gay people as they were, not by the standard of heterosexual behavior. With the founding of the Association of Gay Psychologists in 1973, there emerged a cadre of gay and lesbian psychologists who undertook the critical research that today informs treatment and assessment and who would lobby their colleagues with that research to change forever the psychology of sexual orientation. The body of specialized knowledge that they developed and its application to treatment became what is recognized today as gay-affirmative psychotherapy.

Stigma and Gay-Affirmative Psychotherapy

The core of antigay stigma is sexual behavior between persons of the same gender. Cultural and religious repugnance to sex between two men or two women accounts for the etiology, maintenance, and virulence that have complicated the psychosexual development of any individual who varied from heterosexual norms. I have come to regard it as the central factor shaping the lives and problems of gay men and women.

Meyer (1995) and Greenan and Tunnell (2003) have argued that the psychological functioning of gay men must be understood and evaluated in the context of negative social attitudes. Meyer identifies several issues that gay-affirmative psychotherapists will be sensitive to and likely to explore. Among them is heterosexism that can take subtle forms such as personal discomfort with public displays of same-sex affection. Meyer also lists norms for sexual expression and relationships that are discordant with traditional heterosexual norms. Both of these are pertinent to Scott's interview (e.g., P51ff., T76ff.). Also, gay men may experience or witness antigay violence or discrimination; for many even the fear of such experiences will negatively shape identity development, integration of sexuality, expectations for relationships, and career choice (Meyer & Dean, 1998).

The power of antigay stigma is so pervasive that its effects have been attributed to gay people themselves. Bieber (1962), for example, saw the failure of homosexuals to adapt to heterosexual norms of development, such as establishing long-term intimate relationship with a woman, as a sign of mental illness and immaturity, instead of recognizing that sexual stigma and oppression prevented gay men from forming intimate relationships. What makes this effect so toxic is that some gay men also believed it. Even among gay clients who have sought psychotherapy explicitly to integrate their homosexuality, I have been impressed with and troubled by the extent to which they seem inured to the effects of stigma and heterosexism in their lives and often regard their career and relationship problems as exclusively the result of their personality deficiencies. "Scott," the subject of this book, reports his history of failed or ambivalent romantic relationships with no consideration for the negative influences of societal bias in forming and maintaining them (P76–P86). This is worthy of later exploration in psychotherapy. When Scott offered his reason for ending a high school relationship as not wanting to take it with him into college (P76), I might have asked if he was open about this relationship and whether family or friends accepted it. In my clinical work I explore the positive and negative adaptations to stigma that informs clients' development and presenting problems. I believe it a crucial aspect of our therapeutic work together.

At the time Malyon (1985) first described gay-affirmative psychotherapy, sodomy was a felony or misdemeanor in more than twenty states. A challenge to the sodomy law in Georgia reached the Supreme Court. The question before the court was the constitutional right to privacy. The court found that privacy was not constitutionally protected even though the Georgia sodomy law applied only to homosexuals and that heterosexuals were exempt from prosecution (Bowers v Hardwick, 1986).

But in 2003, the Supreme Court reversed itself by ruling that private sexual behavior was protected by the Constitution (Lawrence v Texas, 2003). It is worth noting the lag of 30 years between the elimination of homosexuality from the *Diagnostic and Statistical Manual* and the court's ruling gay sex in private as constitutionally protected.

Decriminalization removed a major impediment to advancing gay rights and cleared the way for the passage of laws *protecting* sexual minorities. Yet, there remains significant discrimination, particularly in rural areas where supports for gays are few or nonexistent, in regions where politically and sexually conservative standards are the norm, and among extremist fundamentalist groups. In these geographical areas, entrenched antigay attitudes continue to threaten the lives of nonheterosexual people. Finding appropriate mental and physical health services is difficult, if not impossible in these areas. Often gay men and women seeking care will travel many miles or migrate to urban gay Meccas rather than risk inappropriate care or exposure in their home communities. Consequently, a gay-affirmative psychotherapist will often inquire about a client's background in order to assess the effects of regional heterosexism on the client's psychosexual development, relationships, and careers. The differences between growing up in an accepting environment and an oppressive one have significant implications for the treatment plan of a gay client. It makes sense, then, that Silverstein asks not only when and how Scott came out but where he did (T35ff.).

Another byproduct of shifting attitudes about one's homosexuality has been to compound age cohort effects. Where younger gay men now have access to information about other gay people, older gay men did not. The proliferation of gay images, particularly those that are compassionate and supportive, in today's visual, print, and online media, can be contrasted with their absence 40 or 50 years ago. What images existed then were unqualifiedly negative and dire. For example, when Hollywood dealt with same-sex passion, a gay character always met with catastrophe, oftentimes death, as in *The Children's Hour* or *Suddenly Last Summer*. Less tragically, they portrayed men of questionable sexual orientation as exceedingly fey and always devalued, the gay equivalent of the racist Stepin Fetchit. Contrast that with the sympathetic rendering of gay male love in the film *Brokeback Mountain*. (But even in that gay-positive film, their affair ends disastrously.)

The differing effects on self-image and self-acceptance between seniors and youth are startling. I once had an anxious mother send her openly gay son to me for counseling. She reported he had grown up in a progressive environment that accepted her son's sexuality. Now that he was going off to college in another country, she feared his naivety about antigay bias made him vulnerable to unsuspected harm. Indeed, her son verified that he had no experience of antigay prejudice and viewed his mother's concern as unwarranted. By contrast, my work with adult gay men 20 and 30 years ago would invariably include significant work to reverse the damage of both internalized and externally derived antigay stigma.

Objectives and Format

The first interview of a gay man that Silverstein presents offers an opportunity to examine gay-affirmative psychotherapy in practice. It also affords an occasion to reflect on its relevance to the treatment of gay clients[4] and its development since it was first conceptualized by Malyon (1985). Further, it provides an opportunity to explore several issues that often emerge in the treatment of gay men and that distinguish gay-affirmative psychotherapy from psychotherapy with heterosexual men. Among those issues that arise in Scott's first interview are childhood sexual abuse (P4 passim), other forms of abuse (P30), coming out (beginning with P11), ambivalent or negative relationships with parents (P24, P28, P30–P31, P44–P48), HIV/AIDS anxieties (P49ff.), grief following HIV-related losses (passim), conflicts in the development and maintenance of intimate relationships (P76ff.), gay adaptations in sexual expression (P43–P44), substance use (P107ff.), and depression and anxiety (P102ff.).

Each of these issues is influenced by stigma and discrimination against nonheterosexual orientations. All emerge in the first session and all receive attention (to some extent) from Silverstein. In this chapter I discuss several of these to illustrate how gay-affirmative psychotherapy can contribute to the treatment of LGBT persons. I do not treat these presenting problems as pathology but recognize them as exemplars of the issues that arise or inform psychotherapy with gay persons and

---

[4] While I refer almost exclusively to *gay* clients and persons in this chapter, I ask the reader to understand that in most instances *gay* is meant to include lesbian, bisexual, and transgender persons, except where it is obvious that I am referencing only gay men, e.g., references to Scott, the client in this interview.

that benefit from gay-affirmative psychotherapy. My intent is to begin to distinguish stigma-induced conflicts from those that may be pathological adaptations regardless of sexual orientation and to normalize for the client those conflicts that may be unduly influenced by antigay stigma. It has been my experience that doing so relieves the client of a responsibility for conflicts that are externally derived and improves the client's buy-in to psychotherapy.

Because of progress in cultural attitudes toward gays, antigay stigma does not always arise explicitly in a first interview, as it did as few as 10 or 15 years ago. Its effects, however, remain *the* issue that informs whatever problems a gay client presents. The welcome attenuation of the virulent forms of antigay stigma in some quarters may have altered how these effects manifest themselves in the problems gays may present in psychotherapy. Yet, antigay bias may endure in more subtle and insidious form.

Scott's request for a gay psychotherapist from his insurance company is an indication of how far the medical profession and our culture have traveled since the days of greatest discrimination. It also reveals how far gays have moved in asserting their right to informed care. Years ago an insurance company was not likely to have a referral bank of gay-affirmative psychotherapists. It may be a measure of the effectiveness of gay-affirmative psychotherapy and, of course, its consequent economy that an insurance company would *recommend* a gay-affirmative psychotherapist. Other reasons gays, like Scott, will seek a gay psychotherapist is the assurance that their homosexuality will not become the focus of their treatment.

Years ago it was not unusual for gay clients to prohibit my disclosure of their sexual identity in any report to an insurance company in the belief that having a medical record that identified them as gay could permanently damage their future care, their careers, or future applications for health insurance. As a gay-affirmative psychotherapist who understood the risks of possible "outing," when pressed for sensitive information by an insurance company, I had to find creative resolutions between a client's right to privacy and his insurance company's right to know about treatment. In a few cases a client's refusal to disclose resulted in a denial of benefits. How many others avoid the treatment they needed because of such threats? In this case Scott implies that his concerns for appropriate and informed care had delayed his seeking psychotherapy until his symptoms jeopardized functioning (P4, P11).

Exploring the effects of heterosexism early in psychotherapy is important. Silverstein doesn't explicitly address the effects of stigma. I would have asked why Scott sought a gay therapist as one of my first questions, since this is often instructive in developing a treatment plan. From the outset Silverstein addresses an apparent discrepancy between Scott's reporting that he had never previously been in therapy during the exploratory phone contact, and his reporting in this first interview that he consulted with a psychotherapist 12 or 13 years earlier (P1–P3). The exchange is significant not only because it reveals clinically important material but also because it uncovers an unhappy experience seeking mental health care. This cries out for further investigation, if not in the first, then in subsequent sessions. Although the prior therapy was admittedly brief, it was nonetheless enough to undermine his trust in the health care system for some time. It makes Silverstein's openness about his homosexuality an intuitive step toward reversing Scott's distrust. This is very consistent with the stance of a gay-affirmative psychotherapist.

Coming Out and the Gay-Affirmative Psychotherapist

Silverstein comes out to the client before the first interview. For contemporary gay psychotherapists, coming out to clients is much less a controversy than it was in the 1970s or earlier. The arguments against it varied depending on one's theoretical affiliation, but had in common the criticism that coming out would compromise the integrity of the psychotherapeutic relationship by inappropriately injecting the therapist's value system into the psychotherapy. Psychologists today recognize the influences of antigay prejudice that gave the debate professional credibility. Advances in understanding the effects of antigay stigma on the profession have markedly purged the debate of that credibility. Much as Silverstein and others before me, I resolved the question by being so public that anyone who sought my services knew in advance that I am gay. It is not only positive changes in attitudes toward homosexuality but advances in the credibility of LGBT studies as a distinct specialization that make it safer and more respectable for gay psychologists to disclose their orientation to clients. It is consistent with gay-affirmative psychotherapy for a psychotherapist, regardless of sexual orientation, to discuss sexual orientation; however, the decision to do so rests with the clinical judgment of the therapist.

Scott's requesting a referral to a gay psychotherapist represents both the extent to which gay clients can assert this request and the extent to which gay psychotherapists are available. Furthermore, Scott verifies that the referral is accurate by asking during his phone call if Silverstein is gay. Silverstein readily confirms that he is. It is important to recognize that choice among knowledgeable psychotherapists may still be an urban phenomenon; the situation for both gay clients and gay psychotherapists in rural and more conservative regions is considerably more limited. Antigay bias may make disclosure in these areas risky for clients and psychotherapists alike.

Coming out is the central developmental task for LGBT people. By this I mean discovering and integrating one's nonheterosexual sexuality into one's sexual identity, and adjusting to lifelong challenges of antigay bias (Cerbone, 1990). In fact, coming out is a direct result of antigay stigma; if sexual stigma did not exist, there would be no need to come out. Gay-affirmative psychotherapists grasp the significance of coming out and incorporate it into any early exploration of presenting problems (T35, 45). In my own practice I tend to make the role of stigma explicit with gay clients, especially when exploring a client's coming out history. I find that discussing it provides a normalizing universality that often mitigates negative self-percepts, counteracts a sense of defeatism, and substitutes hopefulness in its place. I find it also helps clients distinguish between whatever aspects of stigma have been internalized, such as antigay attitudes, and those that are imposed externally, such as legally approved antigay discrimination.

For example, in a population study of gay persons, Mays and Cochran (2001) noted the effects of perceived discrimination on the mental health of gay persons, particularly the vulnerability to anxiety and depression, problems that often bring gay persons into psychotherapy. Several other studies have shown that gay men and women seek psychotherapy and remain in it longer than their heterosexual men and women (Jones & Gabriel, 1999; Nystrom, 1997). Psychotherapists who may be consciously or unconsciously biased may attribute depression and anxiety as symptoms of a pathological lifestyle, while a gay-affirmative psychotherapist would recognize these as the result of minority stress. A gay-affirmative psychotherapist will assess psychopathology through the lens of minority stress, while a less-knowledgeable psychotherapist may develop a treatment plan that would regard a person's sexual orientation a contributing factor if not a per se focus of psychotherapy. In this way, a biased psychotherapist would regard coming out as a maladaptive adjustment to the stress of an aberrant lifestyle, while a gay-affirmative psychotherapist would assess coming out as a step toward resolving minority stress. The differences could not be more striking or more likely to compromise or aid the outcomes of treatment.

Sexuality, Counter-Transference, and Gay-Affirmative Psychotherapists

In the opening exchanges (P4ff.), Scott reveals his previous therapy experience to help with his struggles relating to his sexuality. He soon reveals confusion about his father's sexual behavior. While he calls it molestation (P4), he seems very uncertain how to characterize these experiences, but his discomfort is clear. The issue is startling because it is unexpected, given Scott's stated purpose of needing to resolve his grief. Silverstein responds to investigate the report of abuse and returns to explore Scott's grief (T13). His probing reveals many things: a probable reason for seeking a gay psychotherapist (P3, P11), a highly conflicted relationship with his father (P4), longstanding conflicts with his parents (P15), and information that may be pertinent to illuminating the grief over his brother's death. Even though the abuse is not a stated purpose for seeking psychotherapy and because other forms of abuse by his father are reported (P28ff.), the extent to which his relationship with his father is disturbed warrants making this a major focus of treatment. Where Silverstein proceeds to explore the abuse, I might have assessed Scott's reactions to discussing it and have made a more explicit attempt to elicit Scott's agreement in selecting it as a significant focus of his future therapy. Because I will usually negotiate a treatment plan with my patients, I believe it would have been particularly prudent to do so in this first session with Scott. I would also have listed the issues he presented, validating them with him, and discussed the advantages of exploring each in later sessions.

Sex is a sensitive subject to broach in any psychotherapy. While I have found that gay men, in general, are very willing to talk about intimate details of their sex lives, I have been cautious to explain my motives before asking for sexual information. Usually this includes reminding a client of the confidentiality of our exchanges, how I expect this to be relevant to treatment, and a brief statement about the sexual boundaries of a professional relationship. I have learned that this is helpful in building trust and mutual respect, and helps ensure appropriate boundaries, which, in turn, foster greater openness. This is quite different from how Silverstein (Chapters 2 and 3) introduces sexual questions; he just asks and backs off only if he senses his client's discomfort. While stylistic differences exist among psychotherapists as well as theoretical orientations and professional training and experience, they can often lead to different directions in treatment.

My approach has also had unanticipated personal and professional benefits. As a psychologist often seen in the gay community, I am likely to encounter clients in venues and at events where my clients may be socializing. This vulnerability is shared by both gay and heterosexual psychotherapists who live and work in small communities. Negotiating early in therapy privacy boundaries outside the office has proved helpful and wise.

Silverstein explores Scott's coming out experiences (T40ff.). Such explorations are common and necessary with gay male clients. First, given the prevalence of HIV among gay men, and young gay men in particular, is the need to assess HIV status, awareness of and adherence to safe sex practices, and HIV/AIDS-related anxieties and adjustments (T49ff.). Also, because of sexual stigma, gay men are unlikely to proceed through psychosexual developmental stages in the same way heterosexual men do. It is difficult to establish a homosexual identity, explore sexual and intimate relationships, or form long-term attachments with a same-sex partner until one comes out, which, in this context means defying the threat of heterosexist discrimination. The developmental trajectory following coming out is different if achieved in middle age as compared to one's teens. It is important to recognize the considerable achievement made in completing important psychosexual milestones, even if they seem chronologically delayed or take a form different from heterosexual norms. These adaptations may vary widely, depending on factors such as age cohort, coming out, and regional, cultural, and religious influences.

The sensitivity and complexity of sexual questioning requires considerable skill on the part of the psychotherapist. Anxieties about disclosure vary among clients and the wiser course is to make no assumptions. Because of their expert knowledge of stigma and the sexual adaptations of gay men, gay-affirmative psychotherapists intuitively grasp the need to communicate respect for the client's experience and seek permission to explore sexuality. Telling a client that he does not have to answer any question that makes him feel uncomfortable or reaffirming the client's rights to privacy will often increase trust and clarify the client's controls in discussing sensitive issues.

At the same time, a gay-affirmative psychotherapist will recognize the importance of the potential for transference when discussing sexual behavior. In my practice, I have learned to monitor any curiosity about the sexual behavior of clients, particularly with men toward whom I may have erotic fantasies. To reassure clients of my respect for their privacy and to maintain trust, I will invite the client to ask any questions he may have regarding the relevance of my questions about his experience or behavior. In my own psychotherapy with a straight psychologist I was keenly aware of my vulnerability to shame and the ambivalence I experienced when answering questions about my sexual behavior: Was he attracted to me? Was he ignorant about gay men? From this I learned to anticipate how a client might experience my question before asking it. Silverstein is more direct with Scott than I would be in a first session. His directness with Scott, however, is consistent across subject matter and may convey a comfort with and confidence that Scott may find reassuring. Scott gives no suggestion that he is uncomfortable with Silverstein's frankness, so there is no evidence of an empathic break in the growing relationship. I might theorize that this is because both of them share common values; they are both white, Jewish, from the East Coast, publicly gay, and comfortable discussing intimate sexual behavior. It may be that similarity in values inspires trust and confidence in a therapist.

HIV and Gay-Affirmative Psychotherapy

One critical issue affecting the gay community is HIV/AIDS. Noting its early association with the gay community and its insidious character, Susan Sontag (1988) has compared HIV/AIDS to other great plagues in history. More importantly, she has cogently argued that the sexual nature of the disease and its emergence at a time when gay men were asserting their right to be sexual is responsible for the virulence of the HIV-related stigma that has befallen gay men, whether infected or not (Herek & Glunt, 1988). Rates of infection continue to remain high among gay men. Scott's reporting that his brother died of an HIV infection that had been undetected (P20) reminds us that, despite medical advances in detection and treatment, HIV remains a sinister infection, devastating one's immune system surreptitiously while furtively infecting others. This is a terror gay men continue to live with.

HIV/AIDS affects age cohorts of gay men differently, an awareness that gay-affirmative psychotherapists incorporate into their assessment of gay men. Men in their 20s have never known a time when HIV was not a factor in their sexual coming of age; their adjustments are complex, reflected sometimes in frustrations with the cautions they must take to practice safe sex, and sometimes in the envious pining they express for an idealized time of uninhibited sexual adventures that older gay men recount. Men in their 60s are facing declining years without the circle of supportive friends they anticipated; as they face the inevitability of their own death and the deaths of remaining friends from natural causes, they often experience a second wave of grief for those they nursed and lost 20 or 30 years ago.

Gay-affirmative psychotherapists, versed in the history of HIV/AIDS, understand its complicated impact on the psychosexual development of gay men, whether infected or not. Many older gay men were activists who stormed the medical and political establishments for better treatment, much as they had advocated earlier for diagnostic declassification or for other gay rights. Researchers have noted that some gay men will engage in risky sexual behavior, such as "barebacking" or "raw" (anal intercourse without using a condom), and have acknowledged the complex set of variables that may contribute to having unsafe sex, such as the use of party drugs as disinhibitors leading to unsafe sex. (See Theodore, Chapter 9.) Interestingly, researchers and psychotherapists have noted one possible factor, AIDS-fatigue, that is, the tendency to grow lax in practicing safe sex from battle fatigue. Gay-affirmative psychotherapists will investigate each client's experience with HIV without assumptions but respectfully exploring individual adjustment to HIV/AIDS, the effects of HIV and antigay stigma, and their current management of guidelines for safe sex.

Scott reports his concern about HIV infection (P50). How intensely he experienced this before learning of David's infection, rapid decline, and death can only be inferred from the information provided in this interview, but it is reasonable to surmise that it has only intensified. How this complicates his grief, influences his sexual behavior, and affects his pattern of intimate relationships would be important topics for treatment. In this regard, Silverstein inquires about Scott's safe sex practices. Scott admits that he has not always played safely. The thoroughness of Silverstein's exploration also reveals an important attitude of gay-affirmative psychotherapy: Make no assumptions about the forms of expression of a gay client's sexuality.

Silverstein's asking Scott (T51) if his doctor is aware of David's HIV-related death highlights the importance of developing a relationship with a primary care physician who has expertise in treating HIV and gay men. Scott reports that he is not out to his physician and that his reason is that he does not trust him because he is straight (P50). The *New York Times* (Sewell, 2008) reported that in a recent study of gay men, 39 percent of them did not inform their physicians of their sexuality; the percentages were higher among men of color. A psychotherapist with less awareness of HIV/AIDS and the gay subculture might have ended his examination with determining Scott's HIV-negative status and focused solely on the effects of his brother's death to HIV/AIDS.

Relationships, Attachments, and Gay-Affirmative Psychotherapy

Gay couples face the same challenges in establishing and maintaining intimate relationships that heterosexual couples face; they also derive the same satisfactions and rewards that heterosexuals report (Greenan & Tunnell, 2003, and Chapter 7). However, same-sex couples face hurdles and obstacles that heterosexuals do not by virtue of the stigma against such relationships, and the fact that gay marriage is still illegal in most of the United States.[5] As a result, close to one-third of gay male couples seek psychotherapy (Green, 2000). Gay-affirmative psychotherapists recognize that the effects of stigma are frequently a contributing factor that brings a couple to seek psychotherapy. Further, they recognize that gay couples have adapted to these hurdles by developing strategies and practices that often do not conform to traditional norms for intimate couples. For instance, many gay couples are not monogamous. Affirmative psychotherapists will not assume that a couple is or is not monogamous. Nor will an affirmative psychotherapist assume that both men in a gay relationship share the same value regarding monogamy. Hence, Silverstein's exploring Scott's romantic and sexual relationships gives no evidence of surprise or negative judgment about Scott's behavior. Rather, he notes, assesses, and remarks on the patterns of Scott's romantic attachments.

Like Silverstein, I would have asked Scott how he understands his pattern of relationships (P84–P86), although I may have been less interpretive. This is a difference between us in directiveness in psychotherapy. Instead, I would have asked Scott if troubled relationships is an issue he wishes to resolve in psychotherapy, especially since his stated purpose is to resolve his grief. I may also have asked if this pattern of attachment has changed in any way since his brother David's death. One purpose in my investigation would be to begin an assessment of Scott's success and disappointments in establishing and maintaining levels of intimacy and attachment that are rewarding for him.

Heterosexual norms continue to impose social, legal, and religious barriers to gay relationships. None of the justifications offered as a basis for legal and social discrimination are supported by science (APA, 2004) or by the evidence of increasing numbers of healthy gay families or the rush of same-sex couples to marry in American jurisdictions. Gay-affirmative psychotherapy engages the psychotherapist in an examination of the criteria employed to assess and treat gay individuals and couples. Evaluating gay relationships for the effectiveness of their adaptations is more clinically productive than measuring how well a couple approximates socially derived norms for long-term attachments. Further, in assessing the relative duration of attachments, I have learned to consider an individual's or couple's definition of *long term*. It is not uncommon for gay couples to have had a number of long-term relationships in their lives.

Summary

In summary, gay-affirmative psychotherapy acknowledges the influences of antigay cultural bias, both conscious and unconscious, in psychotherapy and seeks to reduce their interference in order to realize positive psychotherapeutic outcomes. It regards the basis for the stigma and distortions that continues to frustrate the psychosexual and psychosocial development of gay men and women in heterosexual norms for human sexuality in heterosexual repugnance and anxieties regarding

[5] Gay marriage is currently (2010) legal in Connecticut, the District of Columbia, Iowa, New Hampshire, and Vermont. The following countries have legalized gay marriage: Argentina, Belgium, Canada, Iceland, the Netherlands, Norway, Portugal, Spain, and Sweden. Israel recognizes marriage from other countries.

homosexual behavior. Its value and success as a psychotherapeutic strategy lies in its adherence to empirical data on sexual orientation, that is, homosexuality per se is not an illness but a normal variation of human sexuality; in expert knowledge of sexual stigma and its effects; and in extensive knowledge of gay subcultures. In this sense, gay-affirmative psychotherapy represents a corrective lens through which a psychotherapist views and assesses the problems a gay client presents and formulates a gay-affirmative treatment plan. Because it is a strategy for psychotherapeutic practice based on specific knowledge and is not a theory or model of psychotherapy, gay-affirmative psychotherapy may be usefully employed by a psychotherapist of any theoretical orientation. As also discussed, gay-affirmative psychotherapy understands this discrimination as a contemporary manifestation of an ongoing cultural and scientific revolution regarding human sexuality.

For Further Information on Gay-Affirmative Psychotherapy

American Psychological Association (2005). Policy statement on evidence-based practice in psychology. Policy adopted by APA council of representatives, August, 2005. Retrieved December 28, 2008 from http://www.apa.org/practice/ebreport.pdf.

American Psychological Association has many relevant policies that affirm LGBT lives and relationships. They can be retrieved at http://www.apa.org/pi/lgbt/index.aspx.

Bieschke, K. J., Perez, R. M., & DeBord, K. A. (Eds.), (2007). *Handbook of counseling and psychotherapy with lesbian, gay, bisexual, and transgender clients* (2nd ed.). Washington, DC: American Psychological Association.

Garnets, L. D., & Kimmel, D. C. (Eds.), (2003). *Psychological perspectives on lesbian, gay, and bisexual experiences.* (2nd ed.). New York: Columbia University Press.

Ritter, K. Y., & Terndrup, A. I. (Eds.), (2002). *Affirmative psychotherapy with lesbians and gay men.* New York: Guilford Press.

References

American Psychological Association (2000). Guidelines for psychotherapy with lesbian, gay, and bisexual clients. *American Psychologist, 55*(12), 1440–1451.

American Psychological Association (2009). Resolution on appropriate affirmative responses to sexual orientation distress and change efforts. Policy adopted by the APA council or representatives, August, 2009.

American Psychological Association/Working Group on Same-Sex Families and Relationships (2004). Resolution on sexual orientation and marriage. Policy adopted by APA council of representatives, July 28 & 30, 2004. Retrieved December 28, 2008 from http://www.apa.org/lgbc/policy/marriage.html.

Bancroft, J. (1974). *Deviant sexual behavior.* Oxford: Claredon Press.

Bayer, R. (1981). *Homosexuality: The politics of diagnosis.* New York: Basic Books.

Bell, A., & Weinberg, M. (1978). *Homosexualities: A study of diversity among men and women.* New York: Simon & Schuster.

Besen, W. (2003). *Anything but straight: Unmasking the scandals and lies behind the ex-gay myth.* New York: Harrington Park Press.

Bieber, I. (1962). *Homosexuality: A psychoanalytical study.* New York: Vantage Books.

Bieschke, N., McClanahan, M., Tozer, E., Grzorek, J. L., & Park, J. (2000). Programatic research on the treatment of lesbian, gay, and bisexual clients: The past, the present, and the course of the future. In R. M. Perez, K. A. DeBord, & K. J. Bieschke (Eds.), *Handbook of counseling and psychotherapy with lesbian, gay, and bisexual clients* (pp. 207−223). Washington, DC: American Psychological Association.

Bowers v Hardwick, 478 US 186, 1986.

Cass, V. C. (1979). Homosexual identity formation: A theoretical model. *Journal of Homosexuality, 4*(3), 219−235.

Cerbone, A. R. (1990). Coming out as a lifelong developmental task: Erik Erikson rethought. Poster session presented at the Association Psychological Association Annual Convention. Boston, MA, 1990.

Cerbone, A. R. (1991). The effects of political activism on psychotherapy: A case study. In C. Silverstein (Ed.), *Gays, lesbians, and their therapists: Studies in psychotherapy* (pp. 40−51). New York: W. W. Norton.

Cochran, S. D. (2001). Emerging issues in research on lesbians' and gay men's mental health: Does sexual orientation really matter. *American Psychologist, 56*(11), 931−947.

Coleman, E. (1982a). Developmental stages of the coming out process. *Journal of Homosexuality, 7*(1), 31−43.

Coleman, E. (1982b). Changing approaches to the treatment of homosexuality: A review. 81−88. In W. Paul, J. D. Weinrich, J. C. Gonsiorek, & M. E. Hotvedt (Eds.), *Homosexuality: Social, psychological and biological issues* (pp. 81−88). Beverly Hills, CA: Sage Publications.

Davison, G. (1974). *Presidential Address to the Eighth Annual Convention of theAssociation for the Advancement of Behavior Therapy.* Chicago, IL. November 2.

Drescher, J., & Zucker, K. J. (Eds.), (2006). *Ex-gay research: Analyzing the Spitzer study and its relation to science, religion, politics, and culture.* New York: Harrington Park Press.

Duberman, M. (1991). *Cures.* New York: Dutton.

Feldman, M. P., & MacCullough, M. J. (1971). *Homosexual behavior: Therapy and assessment.* New York: Pergamon Press.

Garnets, L., Hancock, K., Cochran, S., Goodchild, J., & Peplau, L. (1991). Issues in psychotherapy with lesbians and gay men: A survey of psychologists. *American Psychologist, 46*(9), 964−972.

Goffman, E. (1963). *Stigma: Notes on the management of spoiled identity.* Englewood Cliffs, NJ: Prentice-Hall.

Green, R. J. (2000). Lesbians, gays, and family psychology: Resources for teaching and practice. In B. Greene, & C. G. Groom (Eds.), *Education, research, and practice in lesbian, gay, bisexual and transgendered psychology: A resource manual* (pp. 203−225). Thousand Oaks, CA: Sage.

Greenan, D. E., & Tunnell, G. (2003). *Couple therapy with gay men.* New York: The Guilford Press.

Haldeman, D. C. (2010). Reflections of a gay male psychotherapist. *Psychotherapy: Theory, Research, Practice, Training, 47*(2), 177−185.

Halleck, S. L. (1971). *The politics of therapy.* New York: Science House Inc.

Hanley-Hacjenbruck, P. (1988). "Coming out" and psychotherapy. *Psychiatric Annals, 18,* 29−32.

Herek, G. M. (1984). Beyond "homophobia": A social psychological perspective on attitudes toward lesbians and gay men. *Journal of Homosexuality, 10*(1/2), 1–21.

Herek, G. M. (1986). On heterosexual masculinity: Some psychical consequences of the social construction of gender and sexuality. *American Behavioral Scientist, 29*(5), 563–577.

Herek, G. M. (1996). Heterosexism and homophobia. In R. P. Cabaj, & T. S. Stein (Eds.), *Textbook of homosexuality and mental health* (pp. 101–113). Washington, DC: American Psychiatric Association.

Herek, G. M., & Glunt, E. K. (1988). An epidemic of stigma: Public reactions to AIDS. *American Psychologist, 43*(11), 886–891.

Hooker, E. (1957). The adjustment of the overt male homosexual. *Journal of Projective Techniques, 21,* 17–31.

Hooker, E. (1971). Homosexuality. In *U. S. Task force on homosexuality: Final report and background papers.* Rockville, MD: National Institute of Mental Health.

Jones, M. A., & Gabriel, M. A. (1999). Utilization of psychotherapy by lesbians, gay men, and bisexuals: Findings from a nationwide survey. *Journal of Orthopsychiatry, 69,* 209–219.

Kinsey, A. C., Pomeroy, W. B., Martin, C. E., & Gebhard, P. H. (1948). *Sexual behavior in the human male.* Philadelphia, PA: W.B. Saunders.

Lawrence v Texas. 539 US 558, 2003.

Liddle, B. J. (1996). Therapist sexual orientation, gender, and counseling practices as they relate to ratings of helpfulness by gay and lesbian clients. *Journal of Counseling Psychology, 43,* 394–401.

Malyon, A. K. (1982). Psychotherapeutic implications of internalized homophobia in gay men. *Journal of Homosexuality, 7*(2/3), 59–69.

Malyon, A. K. (1985). Psychotherapeutic implications of internalized homophobia in gay men. In J. Gonsiorek (Ed.), *A guide to psychotherapy with gay and lesbian clients* (pp. 59–69). New York: Harrington Park Press.

Malyon, A. K. (1993). Psychotherapeutic implications of internalized homophobia in gay men. In C. Cornett (Ed.), *Affirmative dynamic psychotherapy with gay men.* Northvale, NJ: Jason Aronson.

Mays, V., & Cochran, S. D. (2001). Mental health correlates of perceived discrimination among lesbian, gay, and bisexual adults in the United States. *American Journal of Public Health, 91*(11), 1869–1876.

Meyer, I. H. (1995). Minority stress and mental health in gay men. *Journal of Health and Social Behavior, 36,* 38–56.

Meyer, I. H., & Dean, L. (1998). Internalized homophobia, intimacy, and sexual behavior among gay and bisexual men. In G. M. Herek (Ed.), *Stigma and sexual orientation: Understanding prejudice against lesbians, gay men, and bisexuals. psychological perspectives on lesbian and gay issues* (Vol. 4). Thousand Oaks, CA: Sage Publications.

Nystrom, N. (1997). *Oppression by mental health providers: A report by gay men and lesbians about their treatment.* Unpublished doctoral dissertation, University of Washington, Seattle, Washington.

Paul, W., Weinrich, J. D., Gonsiorek, J. C., & Hotvedt, M. E. (1982). *Homosexuality: Social, psychological, and biological issues.* Beverly Hills, CA: Sage Publications.

Pope, K., Tabachnik, B., & Keith-Spiegel, P. (1987). Ethics of practice: The beliefs and behaviors of psychologists as therapists. *American Psychologist, 42*(11), 993–1006.

Ross, M. W. (Ed.), (1988). *The treatment of homosexuals with mental health disorders*. New York: Harrington Park Press.

Sewell, C. (2008, July 24). Many gays don't tell their doctors their sexuality, study finds. The New York Times. Retrieved July 29, 2008 from http://cityroom.blogs.nytimes.com/2008/07/23/many-gays-dont-tell-doctors-their-sexuality-study-finds/index.html?scp=3&sq=gay&st=cse.

Silverstein, C. (1991). Psychotherapy and medical treatment of homosexuality. In J. Gonsiorek, & J. A. Weinrich (Eds.), *Homosexuality: Research implications for public policy*. Newbury Park, CA: Sage Publications.

Silverstein, C. (1996). The medical treatment of homosexuality. In R. Cabaj, & T. Stein (Eds.), *Textbook on homosexuality*. Washington, DC: American Psychiatric Association.

Silverstein, C. (1997). The origin of the gay psychotherapy movement. In M. Duberman (Ed.), *A queer world*. New York: New York University Press.

Silverstein, C. (2007). Wearing two hats: The psychologist as activist and professional. In J. Glassgold, & J. Dreascher (Eds.), *Journal of Gay and Lesbian Psychotherapy* (11, pp. 1–35). Haworth Press.

Socarides, C. W. (1968). *The overt homosexual*. New York: Grune and Stratton.

Sontag, S. (1988). *AIDS and its metaphors*. New York: Farrar, Strauss, and Giroux.

Spitzer, R. L. (2003). Can some gay men and lesbians change their sexual orientation? 200 participants reporting change from homosexual to heterosexual orientation. *Archives of Sexual Behavior, 32*(5), 403–417.

Stein, T. S., & Cohen, C. J. (1986). *Contemporary perspectives on psychotherapy with lesbian and gay men*. New York: Plenum Medical Book Company.

Suppe, F. (1984). Classifying sexual disorders: The diagnostic and statistical manual of the American Psychiatric Association. *Journal of Homosexuality, 9*(4), 9–28.

Weinberg, M. S. (1972). *Society and the healthy homosexual*. New York: St. Martin's.

LaVergne, TN USA
19 February 2011
217083LV00003B/107/P